MW01593485

Diana Hacker

Nancy Sommers
Harvard University

A
Writer's
Reference

TENTH EDITION

2021 MLA Update

bedford/st.martin's
Macmillan Learning

Boston | New York

Vice President, Humanities: Leasa Burton
Program Director, English: Stacey Purviance
Director of Content Development: Jane Knetzger
Senior Executive Editor: Michelle M. Clark
Associate Editor: Melissa Rostek
Assistant Editor: Aislyn Fredsall
Director of Media Editorial: Adam Whitehurst
Senior Media Editor: Barbara G. Flanagan
Marketing Manager: Vivian Garcia
Director, Content Management Enhancement: Tracey Kuehn
Senior Managing Editor: Michael Granger
Executive Content Project Manager: Gregory Erb
Senior Workflow Project Manager: Jennifer L. Wetzel
Production Supervisor: Brianna Lester
Director of Design, Content Management: Diana Blume
Interior Design: Claire Seng-Niemoeller
Cover Design: William Boardman
Text Permissions Editor: Hilary Newman
Text Permissions Researcher: Elaine Kosta, Lumina Datamatics, Inc.
Photo Permissions Editor: Angela Boehler
Photo Researcher: Krystyna Borgen, Lumina Datamatics, Inc.
Director of Digital Production: Keri deManigold
Senior Media Project Manager: Allison Hart
Editorial Services: Lumina Datamatics, Inc.
Composition: Lumina Datamatics, Inc.
Printing and Binding: LSC Communications

Library of Congress Control Numbers: 2020933031, 2020933120 (Writing about Literature)

ISBN 978-1-319-16940-4 (Comb binding)
ISBN 978-1-319-33293-8 (Paperback)
ISBN 978-1-319-33288-4 (Loose-leaf)
ISBN 978-1-319-19190-0 (Writing about Literature Edition)
ISBN 978-1-319-33287-7 (Instructor's Edition)

Printed in the U.S.A.

1   2   3   4   5   6   7   26   25   24   23   22

Acknowledgments

Text acknowledgments appear at the back of the book on page 512, which constitutes an extension of the copyright page. Art acknowledgments and copyrights appear on the same page as the art selections they cover.

For information, write: Bedford/St. Martin's, 75 Arlington Street, Boston, MA 02116

Preface for Instructors

Dear Colleagues,

Welcome to the tenth edition of *A Writer's Reference*. For this edition, we've gone big and bold, creating a digital product that promises to transform the way we teach and the way students learn. We did what we tell our students to do: Push boundaries, think outside the box, and ask "What if . . ." questions. We wanted to imagine the power and possibilities of digital writing tools to create individualized learning pathways for students. With this tenth edition of *A Writer's Reference*, you have both an e-book and a print handbook, and you have **Achieve**, Macmillan's new digital course experience, easy and intuitive to use so that you can design individualized instruction for each student's success as a college writer. As a fellow teacher of writing, I couldn't be happier with this innovation.

To say that the tenth edition transforms the way we teach and the way students learn is an exciting announcement. How did we arrive at this moment? For every edition of *A Writer's Reference*, we have partnered with teachers to develop innovative instruction to answer students' questions and support their writing development. This is our tradition; this is how we innovate. Bedford/St. Martin's, my editors, and I love working with instructors to help us solve teaching challenges and create learning solutions. I very much enjoyed working closely with a faculty advisory board (see p. xvii) to strengthen the handbook and investigate possibilities for the digital product.

Over the past two years, instructors asked questions such as these:

- What if we had a digital product that could help us understand how students revise and use feedback?
- What if we had more visibility into students' writing habits and decision making to see what happens between drafts?
- What if we had instruction when students need it, tied to assignment goals?

We listened to these questions and said *Yes, we can do this; we can solve these problems.* With the help of 600 instructors and 1,000 students, we co-designed Achieve, an integrated suite of writing tools and learning solutions to engage students in their own writing processes and to help instructors design assignments, comment on students' drafts, and measure students' writing progress.

Here's what Achieve makes achievable. For the first time, we have deeper visibility into students' writing processes so that we can individualize instruction and feedback to help students develop their writing skills across drafts and assignments. With Achieve, we have an integrated suite of writing tools to help us customize assignments, put revision at the center of our courses, and make peer review easier to manage and more effective for learning. In Achieve, students write drafts, reflect on their work, make action plans, revise, and submit. The tools link feedback to e-book instruction, providing students with point-of-need guidance and direction and measuring each student's progress through an assignment and through the semester.

And for the first time, we will gain an understanding of why our students choose to use some comments and disregard others, and of how to help them build rhetorical awareness around their writing and revising choices. Built into Achieve are a set of reflection tools to guide students as they articulate their writing choices, move from assignment to draft, and decide why and how to use feedback. Achieve's suite of reflection tools promotes the transfer of writing skills as students reflect on their choices, learn who they are as writers, and use their learning to develop and deepen their writing skills. Achieve makes transfer achievable.

The Hacker tradition is one of innovation. With the tenth edition, we have imagined something new, something wonderful to make college success more achievable for all students. Colleagues who have field-tested our interconnected suite of digital writing tools enthusiastically report that their students are more engaged as writers. Ask your Macmillan representative to show you Achieve so you can see what it will do for your students' learning. Achieve is exciting; it is bold. This is our moment — and our students' moment — to achieve.

Welcome to the Tenth Edition

Achieve with *A Writer's Reference*

Achieve is an exciting, new, and comprehensive set of interconnected teaching and assessment tools. It integrates the most effective elements from Bedford/St. Martin's market leading digital solutions you may be familiar with — including LaunchPad and LearningCurve — in a single powerful, easy-to-use platform.

Values we share. We are proud to present **Achieve with *A Writer's Reference*,** which rests on three core values:

- **Engaging students for better outcomes.** Pre-built assignments include a variety of activities — from skill-building exercises to multi-draft writing assignments — to engage students both in and out of class.
- **Supporting students of all levels.** Achieve was designed for all students, whether they are high achievers or need extra support.

- **Partnering with teachers and learners.** Bedford/St. Martin's is dedicated to unparalleled customer experience. We depended on extensive learning research and rigorous testing, and we co-designed Achieve with instructors and students over several years and in hundreds of courses.

Superior content you trust.   We know that you have long depended on Bedford/St. Martin's to provide content from respected authors whose work is based on expert teaching, vetted scholarship, and bright-eyed innovation. The best, most effective, most thoroughly-tested course materials — developed in the Bedford tradition — live in Achieve and provide a foundation for your course.

- **An interactive e-book for *A Writer's Reference*** brings together the resources students need to prepare for your class. Students can download the e-book to read offline or to have read aloud to them.

- **LearningCurve adaptive quizzing** offers personalized question sets and feedback for each student based on correct and incorrect responses. Questions are conveniently tied back to the e-book to encourage students to access help when they need it.

- **Videos, writing prompts, and other activities** have been developed to support the Hacker/Sommers approach, designed to deliver a coherent learning experience, and will make prep, practice, and review both easy and engaging.

Innovative writing videos build students' confidence as they write analysis and argument essays and annotated bibliographies.

> **❝**One of my teaching philosophies has always been that students get out of a class what they put into it. Students can achieve their own writing growth and their own writing success with the right tool. Achieve is that tool."
>
> — Jennifer Duncan, *Georgia State University, Perimeter College*

Writing tools that keep writing and revision at the center of your course. Based on leading scholars' work on writer development, Achieve for *A Writer's Reference* gives teachers deeper visibility into students' writing processes so they can target instruction and feedback to help writers grow and develop across drafts, across assignments, and across courses. Students do the work of the course in a contained and active writing space that includes a suite of powerful writing tools.

- **Revision** The Revision Plan helps writers turn feedback into concrete strategies and take ownership of their revision planning. For students, the Revision Plan creates accountability; for teachers, it provides insights about how well students understand the feedback they receive.

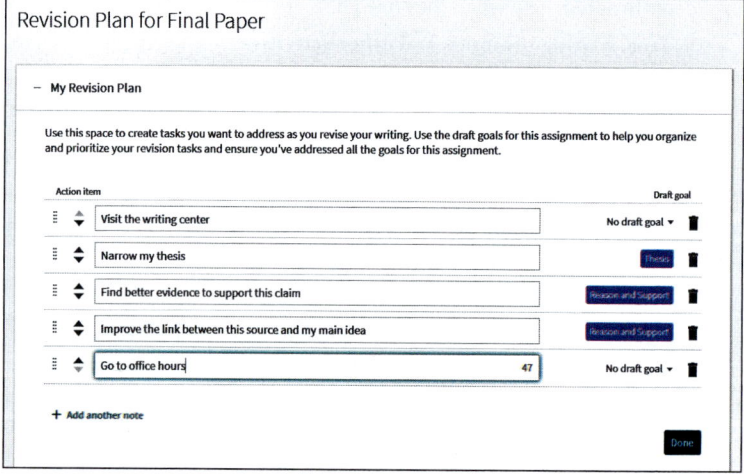

- **Reflection** The writing tools increase students' rhetorical awareness and promote the transfer of skills and habits from draft to draft. How? By prompting students to articulate the choices they make as writers and to communicate their confidence in the drafts they write. You can choose and customize reflection prompts to fit your course and assignment goals.
- **Instructor feedback tools** Powerful and customizable commenting tools allow you to focus your feedback on success criteria — Draft Goals that you set — and efficiently mark patterns of error. Feedback links to

e-book content to give students point-of-need support in the context of their own writing.

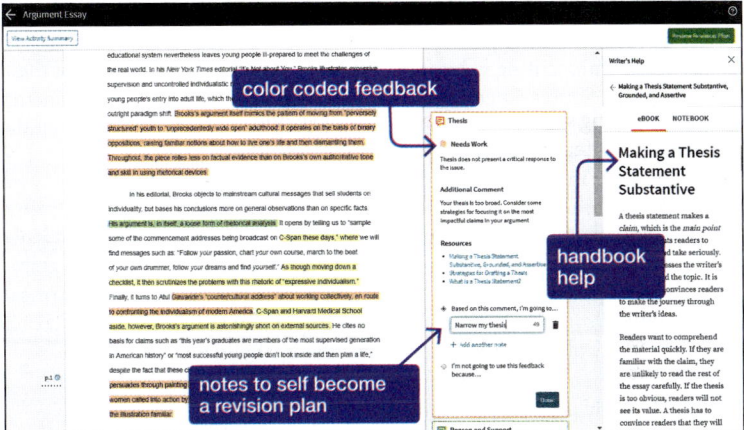

- **Peer review tools** When you empower students to seek feedback from and offer feedback to one another, you invite them to become *writers*, not just students of writing. Achieve's tools scaffold and support students' development as peer reviewers — and allow you to easily facilitate and monitor the process.

"Achieve presents a new way for students not only to receive feedback but to *act on it*."
— Joel Wilson, *Keiser University and Community College of Allegheny County*

Pre-built assignments and units that make your life easier.   A flexible assignment building tool allows you to assign ready-made writing prompts — all fully customizable — or create your own. For *A Writer's Reference*, Achieve includes the following assignments, all with rubrics and Draft Goals that you can use as is or tailor to your needs:

- Introductory assignment: Your strengths as a writer
- Annotated bibliography
- Argument essay
- Narrative essay
- Researched argument
- Rhetorical analysis

Achieve for *A Writer's Reference* also comes as a curated course option that you can adapt to fit your needs; add, hide, and rearrange resources and assignments — conveniently available in a searchable library — until the course works for you.

Source Check plagiarism prevention that teaches. The Source Check feature integrated into Achieve offers students opportunities to become more responsible and ethical researchers and writers. By enabling Source Check during assignment creation, you can allow students to scan their papers for potential plagiarism *before* they submit them for review, allowing students to learn academic writing habits and citation practices in the context of their own writing. A Source Check report flags matches and then connects students to instruction that helps them determine where their writing may contain originality issues and how to edit to avoid plagiarism.

Diagnostics and study plans that give students ownership. Diagnostics help establish a baseline for student performance — a mark from which students can make progress throughout the course. You can assign diagnostics for grammar, style, and punctuation, for reading comprehension strategies, or for critical reading skills. Promoting personalized learning, Achieve helps students create actionable study plans to strengthen their skills and build their confidence.

❝With the study plans, my students were able to get individualized instruction, based on *their* strengths and *their* weaknesses, during the first two weeks of class.❞

— Jennifer Duncan, *Georgia State University, Perimeter College*

Reporting and insights that inform your teaching. Achieve does the heavy lifting for you with powerful analytics that highlight student engagement, provide opportunities for intervention, and allow you to visualize trends in student progress across assignments. You can easily track what students do with instructor and peer feedback. What's more, you can use reflection data to understand students' thinking about their work in the course.

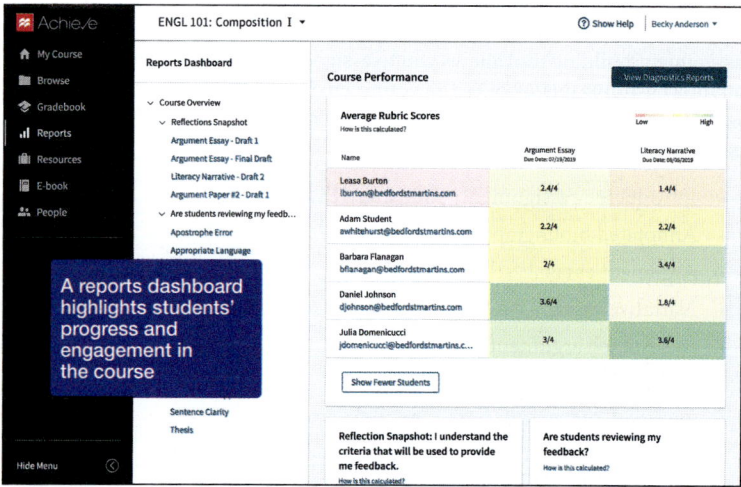

What's new in the book?

- **Reorganized for academic writers.** To make using *A Writer's Reference* easier than ever, we've clustered all of the material critical to the composition course and essential for the most common assignments up front: coverage of the writing process, critical reading, argument and analysis — and now research and documentation. The first half of the book becomes a robust how-to guide, and the second half of the book functions as a quick reference for style, grammar, and punctuation topics designed for writers with a wide variety of experience with English.

- **More help for working with sources: Paraphrasing and fact-checking.** We responded to users' feedback — as we have done for three decades — and added stronger material on paraphrasing sources. A new how-to guide (see MLA-3a) gives students a writing process for paraphrasing original material, along with a concrete example to follow. We also developed new help for students who may be lost at sea in the (mis) information age; new advice for detecting false and misleading sources encourages students to ask critical questions about the news, data, and other information they encounter as part of an academic or everyday writing task.

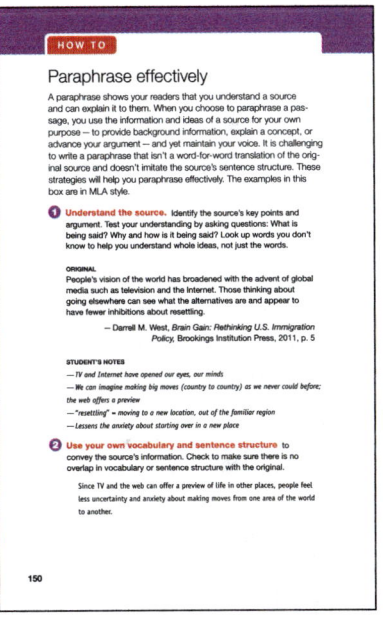

- **A new "Note to self" feature that encourages good writers' habits.** Aligned with the pedagogy of Achieve — the pedagogy that stems from the scholarship of Nancy Sommers — the handbook helps students with reflection and revision planning. A new boxed feature models the kind of thinking and planning that successful writers do as they move from assignment to draft or from one draft to another. The digital platform includes reflection and revision planning as part of the assignment building tool. Both

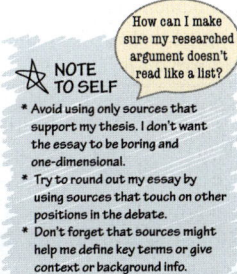

Achieve and the handbook foster the active and personalized learning that research shows leads to greater success rates for a wide variety of students.

- **A more engaging visual approach.** For students who respond to information presented visually, we offer a more visual approach. New visuals complement the written instruction in coverage of working with sources, testing assumptions, writing conclusions, and understanding the rhetorical situation.

- **A new case study to help with a common college assignment.** Teachers of introductory composition courses have told us that their staple assignment requires students to analyze a text in order to take and support a position about that text — essentially, students write an argument about an argument. A new case study (see A4-d) maps out a step-by-step approach for students and models the kind of interaction with and inquiry about a text that forms the basis of successful analysis.

- **Up-to-date MLA (2021) and APA (2020) formatting and documentation guidelines.** The advice and models in the tenth edition of *A Writer's Reference* align with MLA's 2021 guidelines for students writing in the humanities and with APA's 2020 guidelines for students writing in social science, education, business, or nursing courses.

- **New affordable options.** To allow you to meet the price point that you and your students are comfortable with, Bedford/St. Martin's offers *A Writer's Reference* in a number of options, all with our signature quality: classic comb-bound with tabs, traditional paperbound with no tabs, loose-leaf and hole-punched, stand-alone e-book, and Achieve with e-book.

A new resource for corequisite composition

Writers develop over time — and some writers need more time and more practice to develop the skills and habits that help them meet the challenges of the first-year writing course. For those students enrolled in paired, corequisite, or ALP sections of composition, *A Student's Companion to Hacker Handbooks* offers practical support that will help them get up to speed and perform on-level.

The first half of the workbook offers instruction, opportunities for reflection, and graphic organizers for many kinds of writing. It also includes important college success strategies, including time management and planning. The second half offers more than 60 exercises that students can complete right in the workbook; these exercises cover a wide range of topics, from thesis statements, unity, plagiarism, and paraphrasing to fragments, run-ons, commas, and verb tenses. Substantial coverage of reading strategies — along with a variety of reading activities — helps reinforce the link between reading and writing performance at the college level.

A Student's Companion to Hacker Handbooks is available as a print workbook, as a convenient e-book, or as a module through Achieve. Even better, the print companion is available packaged with the handbook at no additional cost to students.

What hasn't changed?

The handbook **covers a lot of ground**. Neither Google nor an OWL can give students the confidence that comes with a coherent reference that covers all the topics they need in a writing course. *A Writer's Reference* supports students as they compose for different purposes and audiences and in a variety of genres and as they collaborate, revise deeply, conduct research, document sources, format their writing, and edit for clarity.

- It's **easy to use and easy to understand**. The handbook's explanations are brief, accessible, and illustrated by examples, most by student writers. The book's many boxes, charts, checklists, and menus are designed to help users find what they need quickly. Our digital products, too, are designed for users' convenience as an accessible homework or classroom tool.

- It provides **authoritative, trustworthy instruction**. With the tenth edition of *A Writer's Reference*, students have content that has been class-tested by hundreds of thousands of students and instructors. Users who loved the **writing guides** and **how-to boxes** in the ninth edition will be pleased to know they are still here in the tenth — as are the engaging **writing videos** that help with argument, analysis, and annotated bibliography.

- It comes with the **service and support** you have come to expect from Bedford/St. Martin's. We have been in the field of composition with you for more than thirty-five years. We provide professional resources, professional development workshops, training for digital tools, and quick, personal service when you need it.

You get more with Bedford/St. Martin's

- **Join our English Community.** At Bedford/St. Martin's, providing support to teachers and their students who use our books and digital tools is our top priority. The dynamic Bedford/St. Martin's English Community is our home for professional resources, including *Bedford Bits*, our popular blog with new ideas for the composition classroom, and *Teaching with Hacker Handbooks*, our popular and practical instructor's manual. To connect with our authors and your colleagues, join us at **community .macmillan.com**, where you can download titles from our professional resource series, browse teaching ideas, or sign up for webinars and demos.

- **Your course, your way: Tailoring resources to meet your needs.** Talk with our Curriculum Solutions team or your publisher's rep to determine what kind of custom product might fit your needs and could possibly deliver a royalty to your department. Our popular MAP program lets you choose to include excerpts from trade titles, and our ForeWords for English program offers brief chapters on time management, writing a proposal, using sentence guides (templates) for academic writing, strengthening English skills, and more. Including your own original material and assignments is also an option.

Ordering information

DIGITAL

Achieve with *A Writer's Reference* (six-month access)	ISBN 978-1-319-33305-8
Stand-alone e-book for *A Writer's Reference* (Classic), Tenth Edition	ISBN 978-1-319-45448-7
Stand-alone e-book for *A Writer's Reference with Exercises*, Tenth Edition	ISBN 978-1-319-45511-8
Stand-alone e-book for *A Writer's Reference with Writing about Literature*, Tenth Edition	ISBN 978-1-319-45513-2
Stand-alone e-book for *A Student's Companion to Hacker Handbooks*, Second Edition	ISBN 978-1-319-45565-1

PRINT

A Writer's Reference (Classic), Tenth Edition

Comb-bound with tabs	ISBN 978-1-319-16940-4
Paperback	ISBN 978-1-319-33293-8
Loose-leaf	ISBN 978-1-319-33288-4

A Writer's Reference with Exercises, Tenth Edition

Comb-bound with tabs	ISBN 978-1-319-19188-7
Loose-leaf	ISBN 978-1-319-33290-7

A Writer's Reference with Writing about Literature, Tenth Edition

Comb-bound with tabs	ISBN 978-1-319-19190-0

A Student's Companion to Hacker Handbooks, Second Edition

	ISBN 978-1-319-24421-7

Contact your Bedford/St. Martin's sales representative for additional pricing and packaging information.

Acknowledgments

I am grateful for the expertise, enthusiasm, and classroom experience that so many individuals brought to the tenth edition.

Meet our Faculty Advisory Board

The following fellow teachers of writing worked with us to strengthen the coverage of research and academic writing and to imagine digital possibilities for the new edition of the handbook. Students across the country will benefit from their expertise and their passion for fostering writers' skills and habits.

Elizabeth Acosta, *El Paso Community College* | "I really, *really* like the emphasis on revision planning," Liz told us. She embraced the idea that a revision plan, covered in the book and offered in Achieve, allows students ownership of their writing and their writing processes.

Katie Adams, *Appalachian State University* | We learned so much from Katie, who is an experienced user of digital tools; she models for us how to get students engaged and active and social. She confirmed that our increased visual representation of handbook concepts in this edition will be "more engaging and inviting" for students.

N. Rochelle Bradley, *Blinn College* | Rochelle was very positive about using sentence starters as a strategy for new college writers, who often struggle to develop an academic voice and to position their own ideas among those of peers and sources. We added sentence starters to the handbook's coverage of integrating sources — and we use them as reflection prompts in Achieve.

Ashley Eakes-Henderson, *Troy University* | Ashley chooses technology that has some element of "student-specific," personalized help; she told us how much she enjoys adaptive quizzes for grammar and style topics. We made sure to maintain our superior coverage of more than 50 sentence-level topics in the book — and to offer diagnostic tests with personalized study plans and adaptive activities.

L. Adam Mekler, *Morgan State University* | Adam gave us good ideas about peer review and reminded us that beginning college writers need to develop confidence as critical reviewers, noting that "being nice is often not the same as being helpful." The peer review tools in Achieve guide students as they read their own work and the work of classmates. Maybe Achieve also helps students to be nice? We'll see.

C. Cole Osborne, *Guilford Technical Community College* | When we proposed reorganizing the book to move research forward, this was Cole's unambiguous reply: "*YESSSSS!!!!*" He also helped us think through our approach to and placement of critical advice on paraphrasing, summarizing, and quoting sources.

Christina Tarabicos, *Delaware Technical Community College* | Imagining help and advice delivered at point-of-need was important to Christina; she pressed us to ensure that the tools in Achieve anticipate students' challenges and offer go-to solutions, readings, and activities.

Bridgette Weir, *Nashville State Community College* | "Honestly, what my students struggle most with," according to Bridgette, "is their thinking." This statement stuck with us and led us to do more to model inquiry in the book and develop an active learning environment within Achieve.

Tammy Winner, *University of North Alabama* | Tammy emphasized the need for Achieve to be a space in which "students feel comfortable making mistakes" and reflecting on those mistakes as part of their development as writers. Tammy also encouraged us to develop activities for a mobile environment.

Reviewers

T. Parish Akin, Southwest Tennessee Community College; Joann Furlow Allen, Oral Roberts University; Paul Beehler, University of California, Riverside; Charlotte Brammer, Samford University; Bryonie A. Carter, St. Charles Community College; Kirk Curnutt, Troy University; Sharifa Djurabaeva, University of Massachusetts Lowell; Michael Duffy, Moorpark College; Anna Marie Erwert, Portland Community College; Lauren Garcia-DuPlain, University of Akron; Christine A. Geyer, Cazenovia College; Michael Gos, Lee College; Maura K. Grady, Ashland University; Milena Gueorguieva, University of Massachusetts Lowell; Laurie Camp Hatch, Vanguard University; Jenee' Higgins, Howard College; Jennifer Hippensteel, Southwestern Community College; Okechukwu Igboeli, University of Waterloo; Donna Kessler-Eng, Bronx Community College; Laura S. Krohn, Oral Roberts University; Henry K. McClintock, Cape Cod Community College; Ashley Meyer, Metropolitan Community College–Penn Valley; Tracy Michaels, University of Massachusetts Lowell; Luke Niiler, University of Alabama; Lisa Oldaker Palmer, Quinsigamond Community College; Abbey Payeur, Bethel University; Kevin Petersen, University of Massachusetts Lowell; Paula Rash, Caldwell Community College and Technical Institute; Kristin L. Redfield, Forsyth Technical Community College; Danielle Reites, Lake-Sumter State College; Cheryl Renee, Eastern Florida State College; Ramone C. Smith, Southwest Tennessee Community College; Roxana Spano, Cazenovia College; Nathaniel Wallace, South Carolina State University; Carrie Wilson, Appalachian State University; Kathryn Winograd, Arapahoe Community College.

Focus Group Participants

Shannon Butts, University of Florida; Joshua Chase, Michigan Technological University; Nina Feng, University of Utah; Misty Fuller, Louisiana State University; Leah Beth Johnston, University of Arkansas; Caitlin Martin, Miami University (Ohio); Marissa McKinley, Quinnipiac University; Salena Parker, Texas Women's University; Karen Tellez-Trujillo, New Mexico State University.

Contributors

I thank the following fellow writing teachers for important content and smart revisions. Our exciting new resource for corequisite composition, *A Student's Companion to Hacker Handbooks*, was made possible with the help of Sylvia Basile (Midlands Technical College), who wrote material on integrating sources; Sandra Chumchal (Blinn College), who wrote advice and activities for two chapters on active reading; Sarah Gottschall (Prince George's Community College), who contributed content to help students avoid plagiarism and write stronger thesis statements; and Paul Madachy (Prince George's Community College), who wrote an important chapter on audience awareness. I am also grateful to colleagues who have contributed to the previous editions; their important work informs the tenth edition: Margaret Price (The Ohio State University) helped us to think about gender and pronouns and inclusivity; Robert Koch (Merrimack College) wrote "Writer's Choice" boxes that help students think about grammar rhetorically; Kimberli Huster (Robert Morris University and Duquesne University) updated advice for multilingual writers; and Sara McCurry laid the groundwork for the current version of *Teaching with Hacker Handbooks*.

Student Contributors

Including sample student writing in each edition of the handbook and its media makes these resources more useful for you and your students. I would like to thank these students for letting us adapt their work as models: Ned Bishop, Sophie Harba, Sam Jacobs, Michelle Nguyen, Emilia Sanchez, April Bo Wang, Matt Watson, and Ren Yoshida.

Bedford/St. Martin's

Developing handbooks, e-books, and digital writing tools is highly collaborative business, and it is my pleasure to acknowledge the enormously talented Bedford/St. Martin's media and editorial teams, whose focus on students informs each new feature of *A Writer's Reference* and *Achieve for A Writer's Reference*. Leasa Burton, vice president, Macmillan Learning Humanities, generously offers her deep knowledge of the field of composition and the ways in which it continues to transform. Stacey Purviance, program director for English, and Adam Whitehurst, director of media editorial for Humanities, led an extraordinary effort to develop and test the writing tools in Achieve, and I thank them for their creative energy and their dedication to engaging instructors and students in our process. Both are enormously talented. Many thanks to Bedford marketing colleagues Joy Fisher Williams and Vivian Garcia — who, like me, spend many hours on the road and in faculty offices — for their treasured advice and feedback. Doug Silver, product manager, helps us to reimagine writers' and teachers' opportunities with digital tools.

Michelle Clark, senior executive editor, is the editor every author dreams of having. She manages to be exacting and endearing all at once — a treasured friend and colleague and an endless source of creativity. Michelle combines imagination with practicality and hard work with good cheer. She led the effort to make the tenth edition a more visually engaging resource; and, a composition instructor herself, she wrote an early draft of the instructor materials for Achieve. Melissa Rostek, associate editor, brings fresh ideas, bold questions, and excellent editorial instincts to our collaboration. I am grateful for her work on *A Student's Companion to Hacker Handbooks* and the research workbook. I am fortunate to work with such a talented editor. Barbara Flanagan, senior media editor, sets the bar high for all of us, and we benefit from her tremendous talent. Barbara manages content development for Achieve with *A Writer's Reference*, ensures that the e-book is accessible, navigable, and robust, and contributes in important ways on matters of documentation and student writing. Thanks also to Aislyn Fredsall, assistant editor, for overseeing the review and permissions processes and for developing ancillary materials. Jane Carter, executive editor; Melissa Rostek, associate editor; and Aislyn Fredsall worked hard to understand the changes in the latest edition of APA's *Publication Manual* (2020) and shape the advice and models in the book and media accordingly. I am enormously grateful to them for their efforts.

Many thanks to the media production team, especially Allison Hart, senior media project manager, for delivering engaging and accessible handbook tools, including new e-books, for students composing in the digital age. Thanks also to Gregory Erb, executive content project manager, for his experience with our handbooks and for his careful eye and smart management of the content production process; to Arthur Johnson, copy editor, for his thoroughness and attention to detail; to Claire Seng-Niemoeller, who kept our design clean, simple, and elegant — as always; and to Billy Boardman, senior design manager, who has created a bold, striking new cover for this milestone tenth edition.

Last, but never least, I offer thanks to my own students who, over many years, have shaped my teaching and helped me understand their challenges. Thanks to my friends and colleagues Jenny Doggett, Joan Feinberg, Suzanne Lane, Maxine Rodburg, Laura Saltz, and Kerry Walk for sustaining conversations about the teaching of writing. And thanks to my family: to Joshua Alper, an attentive reader of life and literature, for his steadfastness across the drafts; to my parents, Walter and Louise Sommers, who encouraged me to write and set me forth on a career of writing and teaching; to my extended family, Ron, Charles, Mary, Alexander, Demian, Devin, Liz, Kate, Sam, Terry, Steve, and Yuval, for their good humor and good cheer; and to Rachel and Curran, Alexandra and Brian, world-class listeners, witty and wise beyond measure, always generous with their instruction and inspiration in all things that matter. They share my thrill when they hold this handbook in their hands. And to my grandchildren, Lailah and Oren, thanks for the joy and sweetness you bring to life.

Nancy Sommers

A
Writer's
Reference

C

Composing and Revising

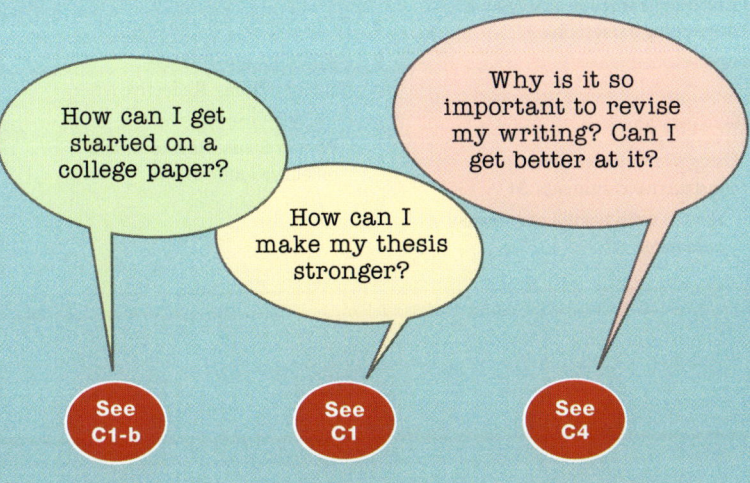

How can I get started on a college paper?

See C1-b

How can I make my thesis stronger?

See C1

Why is it so important to revise my writing? Can I get better at it?

See C4

C Composing and Revising

Welcome to *A Writer's Reference* — your guide to college writing. One of the pleasures of college writing is exploring ideas and discovering what you think about a subject. You may find that the writing process leads you in unexpected directions. The more you learn, the more questions you form. It's in the process of writing and thinking about ideas that you discover what's interesting in a subject and why you care about it.

C1 Planning

- Checklist for assessing your writing situation **5**
- How to solve five common problems with thesis statements **10**
- Sample formal outline **12**

C1-a Assess your writing situation.

Before writing a first draft, spend time asking questions about your writing situation. Each situation presents you with choices to make about your subject, purpose, audience, and genre. (See the checklist at the end of this section.)

Subject	**Purpose**
What you write about	Your reason for writing

YOUR WRITING SITUATION

Audience	**Genre**
Your readers	The type of document you write

Subject

Often your subject, or what you will be writing about, will be assigned to you.
When you are free to choose what to write about, select subjects that interest or puzzle you. Start with your curiosity: What problems or issues intrigue you? What subject needs to be explored? Writing is much more interesting when you explore questions you don't have answers to.

Keep in mind that a broad subject such as advertising can be a good starting point, but choosing one aspect of that subject — in other words, narrowing to a smaller topic — will make the writing more manageable. For example, you might narrow the subject of advertising to *the use of pop songs in advertising* or to *the influence of ads on body image.*

Purpose

In many writing situations, part of your challenge will be determining your purpose, or reason for writing. If you are given an assignment, look closely at its wording to see whether it might suggest its purpose. If no guidelines are given, you may need to ask yourself, "What do I want to accomplish?" and "What do I want to communicate to my audience?" Identify which one or more of the following aims you hope to accomplish.

COMMON PURPOSES FOR WRITING

to inform	to analyze
to explain	to synthesize
to summarize	to propose
to persuade/argue	to call readers to action
to evaluate	to reflect

Audience

You are always writing to readers, so take time to consider their interests and expectations. Ask questions such as these: Who are your readers? What kind of information will they need to understand your ideas? What is your relationship to them? What kind of response do you want?

For some writing situations, you will be able to analyze the interests of your readers, but for other situations, such as social media posts, you might never know your readers. The more your post travels and your words stay in motion, the larger your online audience grows. Whatever you write, whether for digital or print delivery, consider the words you choose and the tone you take so that you accomplish your purpose for communicating.

Writing for an audience: Email messages

Keep your audience in mind when writing an email message:
- Use a concise, specific subject line.
- State your main point at the beginning of the message.
- Keep paragraphs brief and focused.
- Avoid writing anything that you wouldn't say directly to your reader(s).
- If you include someone else's words, let your reader(s) know the source.
- Proofread for typos and errors.

Genre

Pay attention to the genre, or type of writing, assigned. Each genre is a category of writing meant for a specific purpose and audience and with its own set of agreed-upon expectations and conventions for style, structure, and format. Genres include essays, lab reports, business memos, research proposals, letters, position papers, and so on. Often the genre is assigned, but sometimes the genre is yours to choose. If you're choosing your genre, consider how and why a specific genre helps you achieve your purpose and reach your audience.

> How can I make sure I understand a writing assignment?

NOTE TO SELF

* Read the assignment carefully.
* Look for words like <u>explain</u>, <u>analyze</u>, <u>persuade</u>, or <u>synthesize</u> to help me understand what I've been asked to do.
* Look for expectations about style and format. Do I need to use MLA style? What is the length requirement?

Checklist for assessing your writing situation

Subject

- Has the subject been assigned, or are you free to choose your own?
- Why is your subject worth writing about?
- What questions would you like to explore?
- Do you need to narrow your subject to a more specific topic?

Purpose

- Why are you writing: To inform readers? To persuade them? To call them to action? For some combination of purposes?
- What is your message?

Audience

- Who are your readers? How well informed are they about the subject? What are their interests and motivations?
- What information do readers need to understand your ideas?
- Will your readers resist any of your ideas? What objections will you need to anticipate and counter?

Checklist for assessing your writing situation, *continued*

Genre

- What genre or type of writing is required: Essay? Report? Analysis? Argument? Something else?
- What are the expectations for your genre? For example, what type of evidence is typically used?
- Does the genre require a specific organization or set of design features?

Length and format

- Are there length requirements? Format requirements?
- What documentation style is required: MLA, APA, CMS, or something else?
- Do you have guidelines or examples to consult?

Deadlines

- Do you know the rough draft due date? The final due date?
- How should you submit your writing — by printing, posting, emailing, or sharing?

C1-b Explore your subject.

Academic writing is a process of figuring out what you think about a subject — and exploring questions to which you don't have answers. You might find it useful to explore your subject with sentence starters; in the examples below, "X" is the subject you're interested in:

Here's something I would like to understand about X: _____.

What doesn't make sense about X is _____.

What if we looked at X this way: _____?

Why hasn't anyone asked this question about X: _____?

Experiment with the following strategies to help you generate ideas for your writing.

Asking questions

Questions are the engines of writing. They propel you forward, one question leading to another, sparking ideas and possibilities. Asking questions and answering them focuses your attention and helps you discover and generate ideas. Start with your curiosity, posing questions about what puzzles you or doesn't make sense about a subject you are exploring or a text you are reading. Try asking *why* and *how* questions that are not easily answered and that push you beyond simple yes or no answers. And use questions to test your assumptions and gather multiple perspectives to deepen your understanding of an issue.

Talking and listening

Talking about your ideas will help you develop your thoughts and discover what your listeners find interesting, what they are curious about, and where they disagree with you. If you are writing an argument, you can try it out on listeners with other points of view to hear their ideas.

Reading and annotating texts

Reading is an important way to deepen your understanding of a topic, learn from the insights and research of others, and expand your perspective. Annotating (making notes) on a text encourages you to read actively — to highlight key concepts, to note possible contradictions in an argument, or to raise questions for further research and investigation.

Brainstorming and freewriting

Brainstorming and freewriting are good ways to figure out what you know and what questions you have. Write quickly and freely, without pausing to think about word choice, to discover what questions are on your mind and what directions you might pursue.

Keeping a journal

A journal is a collection of informal or exploratory writing. You might pose questions, comment on an interesting idea from one of your classes, or keep a list of observations that occur to you while reading. You might imagine a conversation between yourself and your readers or stage a debate to understand opposing positions.

Blogging

Although a blog is a type of journal, it is a public rather than a private writing space. In a blog, you can explore an idea for a paper by writing posts from different angles. Since most blogs allow commenting, you can start a conversation by inviting readers to give you feedback in the form of questions, counterarguments, or links to other sources on a topic.

C1-c Draft and revise a working thesis statement.

For many types of writing, you will be able to assert your central idea in a sentence or two. Such a statement, which ordinarily appears at the end of your introduction, is called a *thesis statement* or, sometimes, simply a *thesis*.

Understanding what makes an effective thesis statement

An effective thesis statement is a central idea that conveys your purpose, or reason for writing, and that requires support. It is often an answer to a question you have asked or a solution to a problem you have identified.

Drafting a working thesis

As you explore your topic, you will begin to see possible ways to focus your material. You might try stating your topic as a question and then turning your question into a position. You'll find that the process of answering a question or taking a position on a debatable topic will focus your thinking and lead you to develop a working thesis.

An effective thesis

States a debatable position that needs to be explained and supported

Uses concrete language

Passes the "So what?" test (p. 9)

Is the right scope and appropriate for the length requirement of the assignment (not too broad or too narrow)

Here, for example, are one student's efforts to pose a question and draft a working thesis for an essay in his ethics course.

QUESTION

Should athletes who enhance their performance through biotechnology be banned from athletic competition?

WORKING THESIS

Athletes who boost their performance through biotechnology should be banned from athletic competition.

This working thesis offers a useful place to start writing, a way to limit the topic and focus a first draft, but it doesn't respond to readers who will wonder why this topic matters or why these athletes should be banned.

Debatable position   ✔
Concrete language   ✔
Right scope   ✔
"So what?" test   ✗

To fully answer his own question, the student might push his thinking with the word *because.*

STRONGER WORKING THESIS

Athletes who boost their performance through biotechnology should be banned from competition because biotechnology gives athletes an unfair advantage and disrupts the sense of fair play.

Revising a working thesis

As you move toward a clearer and more specific position you want to take, you'll start to see ways to revise your working thesis. As your ideas develop, your working thesis will change, too. You may find that the evidence you have collected supports a different thesis, or that your position has changed as you have learned more about your topic. Or you may find that your position isn't clear and needs to become more specific.

How can I revise my working thesis?

NOTE TO SELF

* Ask a question and then turn my question into a statement of my position.
* Imagine a conversation with a friend.
  FRIEND: What's your position? Why does it matter?
  ME: My position is _____ , and it matters because _____ .

Putting your working thesis to the "So what?" test

Use the following questions to help you revise your working thesis statement.

- Why would readers want to read an essay with this thesis?
- How would you respond to a reader who hears your thesis and asks "So what?" or "Why does it matter?"
- Is your thesis debatable? Can you anticipate counterarguments (objections) to your thesis?
- How will you establish common ground with readers who may not agree with your argument?

Solve five common problems with thesis statements

Revising a working thesis is easier if you have a method or an approach. The following problem/solution approach can help you recognize and solve common thesis problems.

1 Common problem: The thesis is a statement of fact.

Solution: Enter a debate by posing a question about your topic that has more than one possible answer. For example: Should the polygraph be used by private employers? Your thesis should be your answer to the question.

Working thesis: *The first polygraph was developed by Dr. John Larson in 1921.*

Revised: *Because the polygraph has not been proved reliable, even under controlled conditions, its use by private employers should be banned.*

2 Common problem: The thesis is a question.

Solution: Take a position on your topic by answering the question you have posed. Your thesis statement should be your answer to the question.

Working thesis: *Would President John F. Kennedy have continued to escalate the war in Vietnam if he had lived?*

Revised: *Although President John F. Kennedy sent the first American troops to Vietnam before he died, an analysis of his foreign policy suggests that he would not have escalated the war if he had lived.*

3 Common problem: The thesis is too broad.

Solution: Focus on a subtopic of your original topic. Once you have chosen a subtopic, take a position in an ongoing debate and pose a question that has more than one answer. For example: Should people be tested for genetic diseases? Your thesis should be your answer to the question.

Working thesis: *Mapping the human genome has many implications for health and science.*

Revised: *Now that scientists can detect genetic predisposition for specific diseases, policymakers should establish clear guidelines about whom to test and under what circumstances.*

Common problem: The thesis is too narrow.

Solution: Identify challenging questions that readers might ask about your topic. Then pose a question that has more than one answer. For example: Do the risks of genetic testing outweigh its usefulness? Your thesis should be your answer to the question.

Working thesis: *A person who carries a genetic mutation linked to diabetes might develop diabetes.*

Revised: *Avoiding genetic testing is a smart course of action because of both its emotional risks and its medical limitations.*

 Common problem: The thesis is vague.

Solution: Focus your thesis with concrete language and clues about where the essay is headed. Pose a question about the topic that has more than one answer. For example: How does the physical structure of the Vietnam Veterans Memorial shape the experience of the visitors? Your thesis, which is your answer to the question, should use specific language.

Working thesis: *The Vietnam Veterans Memorial is an interesting structure.*

Revised: *By inviting visitors to see their own reflections in the wall, the Vietnam Veterans Memorial creates a link between the present and the past.*

C1-d Draft a plan.

To help you develop your thesis and focus your thinking, try listing and organizing supporting ideas, whether informally or formally, to group and order your ideas.

When to use an informal outline

An informal outline can be drafted and revised quickly to help you figure out a tentative structure. Informal outlines can take many forms. Perhaps the most common is simply the thesis followed by a list of major ideas.

Here is one student's informal outline.

INFORMAL OUTLINE

Working thesis: Animal testing should be banned because it is bad science and doesn't contribute to biomedical advances.

- Most animals don't serve as good models for the human body.
- Drug therapies can have vastly different effects on different species— ninety-two percent of all drugs shown to be effective in animal tests fail in human trials.
- Some of the largest biomedical discoveries were made without the use of animal testing.
- The most effective biomedical research methods—tissue engineering and computer modeling—don't use animals.
- Animal studies are not scientifically necessary.

When to use a formal outline

Early in the writing process, rough outlines have certain advantages: They can be produced quickly, and they can be revised easily. However, a formal outline may be useful later in the writing process, after you have written a rough draft, to see whether the parts of your essay work together and whether your essay's structure is logical.

The following formal outline is the basis for the research paper that appears in MLA-5b. The student's thesis is an important part of the outline. Everything else in the outline supports the thesis, directly or indirectly.

FORMAL OUTLINE

Thesis: In the name of public health and safety, state governments have the responsibility to shape health policies and to regulate healthy eating choices, especially since doing so offers a potentially large social benefit for a relatively small cost.

I. Debates surrounding food regulation have a long history in the United States.

    A. The 1906 Pure Food and Drug Act guarantees inspection of meat and dairy products.

B. Such regulations are considered reasonable because consumers are protected from harm with little cost.

C. Consumers consider reasonable regulations to be an important government function to stop harmful items from entering the marketplace.

II. Even though most foods meet safety standards, there is a need for further regulation.

A. The typical American diet—processed sugars, fats, and refined flours—is damaging over time.

B. Related health risks are diabetes, cancer, and heart problems.

C. Passing chronic-disease-related legislation is our single most important public health challenge.

III. Food legislation is not a popular solution for most Americans.

A. A proposed New York City regulation banning the sale of soft drinks greater than twelve ounces failed in 2012, and in California a proposed soda tax failed in 2011.

B. Many consumers find such laws to be unreasonable restrictions on freedom of choice.

C. Opposition to food and beverage regulation is similar to the opposition to early tobacco legislation; the public views the issue as one of personal responsibility.

D. Counterpoint: Freedom of "choice" is a myth; our choices are heavily influenced by marketing.

IV. The United States has a history of regulations to discourage unhealthy behaviors.

A. Tobacco-related restrictions faced opposition.

B. Seat belt laws are a useful analogy.

C. The public seems to support laws that have a good cost-benefit ratio; the cost of food/beverage regulations is low, and most people agree that the benefits would be high.

V. Americans believe that personal choice is lost when regulations such as taxes and bans are instituted.

A. Regulations open up the door to excessive control and interfere with cultural and religious traditions.

B. Counterpoint: Burdens on individual liberty are a reasonable price to pay for large social health benefits.

VI. Public opposition continues to stand in the way of food regulation to promote healthier eating. We must consider whether to allow the costly trend of rising chronic disease to continue in the name of personal choice, or whether we are willing to support the legal changes and public health policies that will reverse that trend.

C2 Drafting

C2-a Draft an introduction.

Introductions are often called *hooks* because their purpose is to capture the attention of readers and give them a reason to say "Yes, I want to read your essay." Your introduction will usually be a paragraph of 50 to 150 words (in a longer paper, it may be more than one paragraph) and will include your thesis statement. Perhaps the most common strategy is to open with sentences that engage readers, establish your purpose for writing, and lead readers to your thesis statement.

As you draft your introduction, try to avoid broad, sweeping opening statements such as "Since the beginning of mankind . . ." or "In today's society . . ."; such broad statements don't hook readers or show them why your essay is worth reading. Also avoid dictionary definitions or a restatement of the assignment. (See also C1-c.)

An effective way to hook readers is with an engaging question. In the following introduction, a student reaches out to her readers with this question: Should the government enact laws to regulate healthy eating choices? By showing the debate around the question, she establishes common ground with her readers. The thesis statement answers the question and takes a

Strategies for drafting an introduction

- Offer a surprising statistic or an unusual fact
- Ask a question
- Introduce a quotation
- Introduce a debate
- Establish common ground with readers
- Provide historical background
- Define a key term or concept
- Point out a problem, contradiction, or dilemma that needs resolution
- Use a vivid example or image

For Multilingual Writers If you come from a culture that prefers an indirect approach in writing, you may feel that asserting a thesis in your introduction sounds impolite, or even rude. In the United States, however, readers appreciate a direct approach and expect to see in your introduction a clear thesis stating your position on the topic.

position. Notice how all the sentences in the introduction move clearly and logically to prepare readers for the student's thesis.

Opening question engages readers.

Should the government enact laws to regulate healthy eating choices? Many Americans would emphatically answer "No," arguing that what and how much we eat should be left to individual choice rather than to unreasonable laws. Others might argue that it would be unreasonable for the government not to enact legislation, given the rise of chronic diseases that result from harmful diets. In this debate, both the definition of reasonable regulations and the role of government to legislate food choices are at stake. In the name of public health and safety, state governments have the responsibility to shape health policies and to regulate healthy eating choices, especially since doing so offers a potentially large social benefit for a relatively small cost.

Shows two sides of the debate to establish common ground.

All the sentences lead readers to the thesis.

Thesis answers question and offers writer's position.

— Sophie Harba, student

NOTE: For more examples of effective introductions, see the model essays on pages 65, 92, and 200.

C2-b Draft the body.

As you draft the body of your essay, you might naturally ask: What should I say? How will I write an entire essay on my topic? You will find the process easier if you have a working thesis to guide the drafting process. If your thesis suggests a plan (see C1-d) or if you have sketched a preliminary outline, try to organize your paragraphs accordingly. Draft the body of your essay by writing at least one paragraph about each supporting point you listed in the planning stage.

Asking questions as you draft

As you draft, keep asking questions like the ones on the following page. Continue to try to anticipate what your readers may want to know or need to know to follow your train of thought or your trail of evidence.

QUESTIONS TO ASK AS YOU DRAFT

Who are my readers?

What is my purpose?

What does my thesis promise readers?

What is my position on the topic?

How will I support my position?

What information do my readers need to understand my ideas?

Remember that first drafts aren't finished drafts. They are just *first*, a place to begin. Find your momentum and keep writing.

For more detailed help with drafting and developing paragraphs, see C3.

Using sources responsibly   As you draft, keep notes about sources you read and consult. (See R2-c.) If you quote, paraphrase, or summarize a source, include a citation, even in your draft. You will save time and avoid plagiarism if you do so.

Adding visuals as you draft

As you draft, you may decide that support for your thesis could come from one or more visuals. Visuals can convey information concisely and powerfully. Graphs and tables, for example, can simplify complex numerical information. Images — including photographs and diagrams — often express ideas vividly. Keep in mind that if you download a visual or use published information to create your own visual, you must credit your source. Also be sure to choose visuals to supplement your writing, not to substitute for it.

The chart on pages 17–18 describes eight types of visuals and their purposes.

Using sources responsibly   If you create a chart, timeline, or other visual using information from your research, cite the source of the information even though the visual is your own. If you download a photograph from the web, credit the person or organization that created it.

Choosing visuals to suit your purpose

Pie chart

Pie charts compare a part or parts to the whole. Segments of the pie represent percentages of the whole (and always total 100 percent).

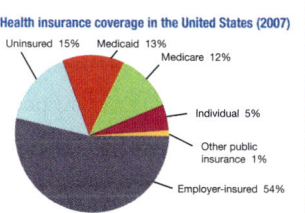

Health insurance coverage in the United States (2007)

Uninsured 15% Medicaid 13%
Medicare 12%
Individual 5%
Other public insurance 1%
Employer-insured 54%

Bar graph (or line graph)

Bar graphs highlight trends over a period of time or compare numerical data. Line graphs display the same data as bar graphs; the data are graphed as points, and the points are connected with lines.

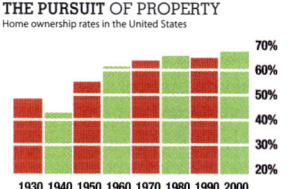

THE PURSUIT OF PROPERTY
Home ownership rates in the United States

1930 1940 1950 1960 1970 1980 1990 2000

Infographic

An infographic presents data in a visually engaging form. The data are usually numerical, as in bar graphs or line graphs, but they are represented by a graphic element rather than bars or lines.

Just 8% of kids growing up in low-income communities graduate from college by age 24.

Table

Tables display numbers and words in columns and rows. They can be used to organize complicated numerical information into an easily understood format.

Prices of daily doses of AIDS drugs (SUS)

Drug	Brazil	Uganda	Côte d'Ivoire	US
3TC (Lamuvidine)	1.66	3.28	2.95	8.70
ddC (Zalcitabine)	0.24	4.17	3.75	8.80
Didanosine	2.04	5.26	3.48	7.25
Efavirenz	6.96	n/a	6.41	13.13
Indinavir	10.32	12.79	9.07	14.93
Nelfinavir	4.14	4.45	4.39	6.47
Nevirapine	5.04	n/a	n/a	8.48
Saquinavir	6.24	7.37	5.52	6.60
Stavudine	0.56	6.19	4.10	9.07
ZDV/3TC	1.44	7.34	n/a	18.78
Zidovudine	1.08	4.34	2.43	10.12

Source: UNAIDS, 2000

Choosing visuals to suit your purpose, *continued*

Photograph

Photographs vividly depict people, scenes, or objects discussed in a text.

Library of Congress, Prints & Photographs Division [LC-DIG-highsm-04024]

Diagram

Diagrams, useful in scientific and technical writing, concisely illustrate processes, structures, or interactions.

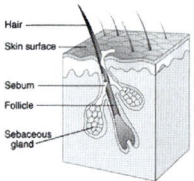

National Institute of Health

Flowchart

Flowcharts show structures (the hierarchy of employees at a company, for example) or steps in a process and their relation to one another. (See also p. 316 for another example.)

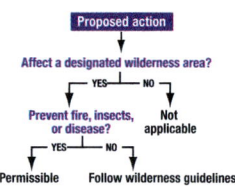

Map

Maps illustrate distances, historical information, or demographics and often use symbols for geographic features and points of interest.

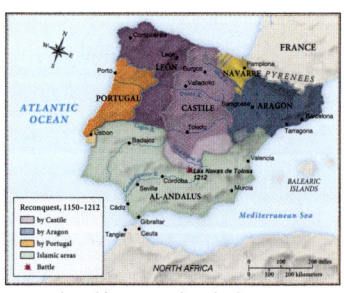

From *Making of the West: Peoples and Cultures*, 6e, by Lynn Hunt, et al. Copyright 2019 by Bedford/St. Martin's. All rights reserved. Used by permission of the publisher Macmillan Learning.

C2-c Draft a conclusion.

A conclusion completes an essay, reminding readers of the essay's main idea without repeating it. By the end of the essay, readers should already understand your main position, so the concluding paragraph is often relatively short. An effective conclusion rounds out an essay by giving readers a sense of completion or by issuing a call for action.

Always end your essay on a strong, positive note. You don't need to use phrases such as *In conclusion* or *In summary* because your readers should understand that your essay is concluding. The conclusion is your chance to have the last word on the subject and remind readers why your essay was worth reading.

To make your conclusion memorable and to give a sense of completion, you might bring readers full circle by linking your last paragraph to your first one, returning to the thesis or including a detail from the introduction. To conclude his argument essay about the shift from print to online news, student writer Sam Jacobs returns to the hook from his introduction, the phrase *fit to print*, and echoes his thesis to show the broader importance of his argument.

"Full circle" strategy

Fit to print = newsworthy

Ordinary citizens now have a voice in what's fit to print

Media professionals have always delivered news

Online news lets consumers be producers

Online news opens a conversation about what's newsworthy

Here are the introduction and conclusion from Jacobs's essay. See the full essay in section A4-h.

SAMPLE INTRODUCTION

"All the news that's fit to print," the motto of *The New York Times* since 1896, plays with the word *fit*, asserting that a news story must be newsworthy and must not exceed the limits of the printed page. The increase in online news consumption, however, challenges both meanings of the word *fit*, allowing producers and consumers alike to rethink who decides which topics are worth covering and how extensive that coverage should be. Any cultural shift usually means that something is lost, but in this case there are clear gains. The shift from print to online news provides unprecedented opportunities for readers to become more engaged with the news, to hold journalists accountable, and to participate as producers, not simply as consumers.

Strategies for drafting a conclusion

In addition to echoing your main idea, a conclusion might do any of the following:

- Briefly summarize your essay's key points
- Return to the hook used in the introduction
- Propose a course of action
- Offer a recommendation
- Suggest the topic's wider significance or implications
- Pose a question for future study

SAMPLE CONCLUSION

The Internet has enabled consumers to participate in a new way in reading, questioning, interpreting, and reporting the news. Decisions about appropriate content and coverage are no longer exclusively in the hands of news editors. Ordinary citizens now have a meaningful voice in the conversation—a hand in deciding what's "fit to print." Some skeptics worry about the apparent free-for-all and loss of tradition. But the expanding definition of news provides opportunities for consumers to be more engaged with events in their communities, their nations, and the world.

NOTE: For more examples of effective conclusions, see the model essays on pages 66 and 204.

C3   Writing paragraphs

- Writing focused and unified paragraphs **22**
- Common transitions **26**

A paragraph is a group of sentences that focuses on one main point or example. Except for special-purpose paragraphs, such as introductions and conclusions (see C2-a and C2-c), paragraphs are units of organization that develop and support an essay's main point, or thesis. Aim for paragraphs that are well developed, organized, coherent, and neither too long nor too short for easy reading.

C3-a Focus on a main point.

An effective paragraph is unified around a main point. The point should be clear to readers, and all sentences in the paragraph should relate to it.

Stating the main point in a topic sentence

A clear topic sentence, a one-sentence summary of the paragraph's main point, acts as a signpost pointing in two directions: backward toward the thesis of the essay and forward toward the body of the paragraph.

Usually the topic sentence comes first in the paragraph.

> All living creatures manage some form of communication. The dance patterns of bees in their hive help to point the way to distant flower fields or announce successful foraging. Male stickleback fish regularly swim upsidedown to indicate outrage in a courtship contest. Male deer and lemurs mark territorial ownership by rubbing their own body secretions on boundary stones or trees. Everyone has seen a frightened dog put his tail between his legs and run in panic. We, too, use gestures, expressions, postures, and movement to give our words point.
>
> — Olivia Vlahos, *Human Beginnings*

In college writing, topic sentences are often necessary for advancing or clarifying lines of an argument and introducing evidence from a source. In the following paragraph on the effects of the 2010 oil spill in the Gulf of Mexico, the writer uses a topic sentence to state that the extent of the threat is unknown, before quoting three sources that illustrate her point.

> To date, the full ramifications [of the oil spill] remain a question mark. An August report from the National Oceanic and Atmospheric Administration estimated that 75 percent of the oil had "either evaporated or been burned, skimmed, recovered from the wellhead, or dispersed." However, Woods Hole Oceanographic Institution researchers reported that a 1.2-mile-wide, 650-foot-high plume caused by the spill "had and will persist for some time." And University of Georgia scientists concluded that almost 80 percent of the released oil hadn't been recovered and "remains a threat to the ecosystem."
>
> — Michele Berger, "Volunteer Army"

Sticking to the point

Sentences that do not support the topic sentence destroy the unity of a paragraph. In the following paragraph describing the inadequate facilities in a high school, the information about the chemistry instructor is clearly off the point.

> As the result of tax cuts, the educational facilities of Lincoln High School have reached an all-time low. Some of the books date back to 1990 and have long since shed their covers. The few computers in working order must share one printer. The lack of lab equipment makes it necessary for four or five students to work at one table, with most watching rather than performing experiments. Also, the chemistry instructor left to have a baby at the beginning of the semester, and most of the students don't like the substitute. As for the furniture, many of the upright chairs have become recliners, and the desk legs are so unbalanced that they play seesaw on the floor.

Writing focused and unified paragraphs

A strong paragraph supports a thesis, opens with a topic sentence, focuses on and develops a main point, and holds together as a unit. As you build and revise your paragraphs, ask these questions:

- Does each paragraph support the thesis?
- Does each paragraph open with a clear topic sentence?
- Does each paragraph focus on a main point and develop the point?
- Is each paragraph organized and coherent?
- Is each paragraph the right length for its topic?
- Does each paragraph contain transitions to help readers move from sentence to sentence and between paragraphs?

C3-b   Develop the main point.

Though an occasional short paragraph is fine, particularly if it functions as a transition or emphasizes a point, a series of brief paragraphs suggests inadequate development. How much development is enough? That varies, depending on the writer's purpose and audience.

For example, when health columnist Jane Brody wrote a paragraph attempting to convince readers that it is impossible to lose fat quickly, she knew that she would have to present a great deal of evidence because many dieters want to believe the opposite. She did *not* write only the following.

UNDERDEVELOPED PARAGRAPH

When you think about it, it's impossible to lose — as many diets suggest — 10 pounds of *fat* in ten days, even on a total fast. Even a moderately active person cannot lose so much weight so fast. A less active person hasn't a prayer.

This three-sentence paragraph is too skimpy to be convincing. But the paragraph that Brody did write contains enough evidence to convince even skeptical readers.

WELL-DEVELOPED PARAGRAPH

When you think about it, it's impossible to lose — as many . . . diets suggest — 10 pounds of *fat* in ten days, even on a total fast. A pound of body fat represents 3,500 calories. To lose 1 pound of fat, you must expend 3,500 more calories than you consume. Let's say you weigh 170 pounds and, as a moderately active person, you burn 2,500 calories a day. If your diet contains only 1,500 calories, you'd have an energy deficit of 1,000 calories a day. In a week's time that would add up to a 7,000-calorie deficit, or 2 pounds of real fat. In ten days, the accumulated deficit would represent nearly 3 pounds of lost body fat. Even if you ate nothing at all for ten days and maintained your usual level of activity, your caloric deficit would add up to 25,000 calories. . . . At 3,500 calories per pound of fat, that's still only 7 pounds of lost fat.

— Jane Brody, *Jane Brody's Nutrition Book*

C3-c Make paragraphs coherent.

When sentences and paragraphs flow from one to another without noticeable bumps, gaps, or shifts, they are said to be coherent. Coherence can be improved by strengthening the ties between old information and new. A number of techniques for strengthening those ties are detailed in this section.

Linking ideas clearly

Readers expect to learn a paragraph's main point in a topic sentence early in the paragraph. Then, as they move into the body of the paragraph, they expect to encounter specific details, facts, or examples that support the topic sentence — either directly or indirectly.

If a sentence does not support the topic sentence directly, readers expect it to support another sentence in the paragraph and therefore to support the topic sentence indirectly. The following paragraph begins with a topic sentence. The highlighted sentences are direct supports, and the rest of the sentences are indirect supports.

Topic sentence provides a preview of the paragraph.

Though the open-space classroom works for many children, it is not practical for my son, David. First, David is hyperactive. When he was placed in an open-space classroom, he became distracted and confused. He was tempted to watch the movement going on around him instead of concentrating on his own work. Second, David has a tendency to transpose letters and numbers, a tendency that can be overcome only by individual attention from the instructor. In the open classroom, he was moved from teacher to teacher, with each one responsible for a different subject. No single teacher worked with David long enough to diagnose the problem, let alone help him with it. Finally, David is not a highly motivated learner. In the open classroom, he was graded "at his own level," not by criteria for a certain grade. He could receive a B in reading and still be a grade level behind, because he was doing satisfactory work "at his own level."

Highlighted sentences answer the question "Why is the classroom not practical?"

— Margaret Smith, student

Repeating key words

Repetition of key words is an important technique for gaining coherence. To prevent repetitions from becoming dull, you can use variations of a key word (*hike, hiker, hiking*), pronouns referring to the word (*gamblers . . . they*), and synonyms (*run, spring, race, dash*). In the following paragraph describing plots among indentured servants, historian Richard Hofstadter binds sentences together by repeating the key word *plots* and echoing it with a variety of synonyms.

> Plots hatched by several servants to run away together occurred mostly in the plantation colonies, and the few recorded servant uprisings were entirely limited to those colonies. Virginia had been forced from its very earliest years to take stringent steps against mutinous plots, and severe punishments for such behavior were recorded. Most servant plots occurred in the seventeenth century: a contemplated uprising was nipped in the bud in York County in 1661; apparently led by some left-wing offshoots of the Great Rebellion, servants plotted an insurrection in Gloucester County in 1663, and four leaders were condemned and executed; some discontented servants apparently joined Bacon's Rebellion in the 1670's.
>
> — Richard Hofstadter, *America at 1750*

Using parallel structures

Parallel structures are frequently used within sentences to underscore the similarity of ideas (see S1). They may also be used to bind together a series of sentences expressing similar information. In the following passage describing folk beliefs, anthropologist Margaret Mead presents similar information in parallel grammatical form.

> Actually, almost every day, even in the most sophisticated home, something is likely to happen that evokes the memory of some old folk belief. The salt spills. A knife falls to the floor. Your nose tickles. Then perhaps, with a slightly embarrassed smile, the person who spilled the salt tosses a pinch over his left shoulder. Or someone recites the old rhyme, "Knife falls, gentleman calls." Or as you rub your nose you think, That means a letter. I wonder who's writing?
>
> — Margaret Mead, "New Superstitions for Old"

Providing transitions

Transitions are bridges between what has been read and what is about to be read. They help readers move from sentence to sentence and from paragraph to paragraph.

Sentence-level transitions Certain words and phrases signal connections between (or within) sentences. Frequently used transitions are included in the chart on page 26.

In the following paragraph, taken from an article about how Amazon has changed consumer habits, Joshua Rothman uses transitions to guide readers from one idea to the next.

> It hasn't always been obvious that Amazon would transform the feeling of everyday life. At first, the company looked like a bookstore; next, it became a mass retailer; later, for somewhat obscure reasons, it transformed into a television and movie studio. It seemed to be growing horizontally, by learning to sell new kinds of products. But Amazon wasn't just getting wider; it was getting deeper, too. It wasn't just selling products but inventing a new method of selling; behind the scenes, it was using technology to vertically integrate nearly the entire process of consumption.
>
> — Joshua Rothman, "What Amazon's Purchase of Whole Foods Really Means"

Paragraph-level transitions Paragraph-level transitions usually link the *first* sentence of a new paragraph with the *first* sentence of the previous paragraph. In other words, the topic sentences signal global connections.

Look for opportunities to echo the subject of a previous paragraph (as summed up in its topic sentence) in the topic sentence of the next one. In his essay "Little Green Lies," Jonathan H. Adler uses this paragraph-level transition strategy to link topic sentences.

> Consider aseptic packaging, the synthetic packaging for the "juice boxes" so many children bring to school with their lunch. One criticism of aseptic packaging is that it is nearly impossible to recycle, yet on almost every other count, aseptic packaging is environmentally preferable to the packaging alternatives. Not only do aseptic containers not require refrigeration to keep their contents from spoiling, but their manufacture requires less than one-10th the energy of making glass bottles. What is true for juice boxes is also true for other forms of synthetic packaging. The use of polystyrene, which is commonly (and mistakenly) referred to as "Styrofoam," can reduce food waste dramatically due to its insulating properties. (Thanks to these properties, polystyrene cups are much preferred over paper for that morning cup of coffee.) Polystyrene also requires significantly fewer resources to produce than its paper counterpart.

Common transitions

TO SHOW ADDITION	also, and, besides, further, furthermore, in addition, moreover, next, too, first, second
TO GIVE EXAMPLES	for example, for instance, in fact, specifically, to illustrate
TO COMPARE	also, likewise, similarly
TO CONTRAST	although, but, even though, however, in contrast, nevertheless, on the contrary, on the other hand, still, though, yet
TO SUMMARIZE OR CONCLUDE	in conclusion, in other words, in short, therefore, to summarize
TO SHOW TIME	after, as, before, during, finally, immediately, later, meanwhile, next, since, then, when, while
TO CREATE A CONNECTION	as a result, because, consequently, for this reason, if, since, so, therefore, thus

C3-d If necessary, adjust paragraph length.

Most readers feel comfortable reading paragraphs that range between one hundred and two hundred words. Shorter paragraphs can require too much starting and stopping, and longer ones can strain the reader's attention span. There are exceptions to this guideline, however. Paragraphs longer than two hundred words frequently appear in scholarly writing, where writers explore complex ideas. Paragraphs shorter than one hundred words occur in business writing and on websites, where readers routinely skim for main ideas; in newspapers because of narrow columns; and in informal essays to quicken the pace.

In an essay, the first and last paragraphs will ordinarily be the introduction and the conclusion. These special-purpose paragraphs are likely to be shorter than paragraphs in the body of the essay. Typically, the body paragraphs will follow the essay's outline: one paragraph per point in short essays, several paragraphs per point in longer ones. Some ideas require more development than others, however, so it is best to be flexible. If an idea stretches to a length unreasonable for a paragraph, you should divide the paragraph, even if you have presented comparable points in the essay in single paragraphs.

Paragraph breaks are not always made for strictly logical reasons. Writers use them for all of the following reasons.

REASONS FOR BEGINNING A NEW PARAGRAPH

- to mark off the introduction and the conclusion
- to signal a shift to a new idea
- to indicate an important shift in time or place
- to emphasize a point (by placing it at the beginning or the end, not in the middle, of a paragraph)
- to highlight a contrast
- to signal a change of speakers (in dialogue)
- to provide readers with a needed pause
- to break up text that looks too dense

Beware, however, of using too many short, choppy paragraphs that read like a list. Readers want to see how your ideas connect, and they become irritated when you break their momentum by forcing them to pause every few sentences. Here are some reasons you might have for combining some of the paragraphs in a rough draft.

REASONS FOR COMBINING PARAGRAPHS

- to clarify the essay's organization
- to connect closely related ideas
- to bind together text that looks too choppy

C3-e Choose a suitable strategy for developing paragraphs.

Although paragraphs and essays may be developed in any number of ways, certain methods of organization occur frequently, either alone or in combination:

illustrations (p. 27)   analogy (p. 30)
narration (p. 28)   cause and effect (p. 30)
description (p. 28)   classification (p. 30)
process (p. 29)   definition (p. 31)
comparison and contrast (p. 29)

These strategies for developing paragraphs have different uses, depending on the writer's subject and purpose.

Illustrations

Illustrations are extended examples and can be a vivid and effective means of developing a point. The writer of the following paragraph uses illustrations to support his point that Harriet Tubman was a genius at eluding her pursuers.

Part of [Harriet Tubman's] strategy of conducting was, as in all battle-field operations, the knowledge of how and when to retreat. Numerous allusions have been made to her moves when she suspected that she was in danger. When she feared the party was closely pursued, she would take it for a time on a train southward bound. No one seeing Negroes going in this direction would for an instant suppose them to be fugitives. Once on her return she was at a railroad station. She saw some men reading a poster and she heard one of them reading it aloud. It was a description of her, offering a reward for her capture. She took a southbound train to avert suspicion. At another time when Harriet heard men talking about her, she pretended to read a book which she carried. One man remarked, "This can't be the woman. The one we want can't read or write." Harriet devoutly hoped the book was right side up.

— Earl Conrad, *Harriet Tubman*

Narration

A paragraph of narration tells a story or part of a story. Narrative paragraphs are usually arranged in chronological order, but they may also contain flashbacks, interpretations that take the story back to an earlier time. The following paragraph recounts an author's experiences in the African wild.

One evening when I was wading in the shallows of the lake to pass a rocky outcrop, I suddenly stopped dead as I saw the sinuous black body of a snake in the water. It was all of six feet long, and from the slight hood and the dark stripes at the back of the neck I knew it to be a Storm's water cobra — a deadly reptile for the bite of which there was, at that time, no serum. As I stared at it an incoming wave gently deposited part of its body on one of my feet. I remained motionless, not even breathing, until the wave rolled back into the lake, drawing the snake with it. Then I leaped out of the water as fast as I could, my heart hammering.

— Jane Goodall, *In the Shadow of Man*

Description

A descriptive paragraph sketches a portrait of a person, place, or thing by using concrete and specific details that appeal to one or more of the senses — sight, sound, smell, taste, and touch. Consider, for example, the following description of the grasshopper invasions that devastated the midwestern landscape in the late 1860s.

They came like dive bombers out of the west. They came by the millions with the rustle of their wings roaring overhead. They came in waves, like the rolls of the sea, descending with a terrifying speed, breaking now and again like a mighty surf. They came with the force of a williwaw and they formed a huge, ominous, dark brown cloud that eclipsed the sun. They dipped and touched earth, hitting objects and people like hailstones. But they were not hail. These were *live* demons. They popped, snapped, crackled, and roared. They were dark brown, an inch or longer in length, plump in the middle and tapered at the ends. They had transparent wings, slender legs, and two black eyes that flashed with a fierce intelligence.

— Eugene Boe, "Pioneers to Eternity"

Process

A process paragraph is structured in chronological order. A writer may choose this pattern either to describe how something is made or done or to explain to readers, step by step, how to do something. Here is a paragraph explaining how to perform a "roll cast," a popular fly-fishing technique.

Begin by taking up a suitable stance, with one foot slightly in front of the other and the rod pointing down the line. Then begin a smooth, steady draw, raising your rod hand to just above shoulder height and lifting the rod to the 10:30 or 11:00 position. This steady draw allows a loop of line to form between the rod top and the water. While the line is still moving, raise the rod slightly, then punch it rapidly forward and down. The rod is now flexed and under maximum compression, and the line follows its path, bellying out slightly behind you and coming off the water close to your feet. As you power the rod down through the 3:00 position, the belly of line will roll forward. Follow through smoothly so that the line unfolds and straightens above the water.

— *The Dorling Kindersley Encyclopedia of Fishing*

Comparison and contrast

To compare two subjects is to draw attention to their similarities, although the word *compare* also has a broader meaning that includes a consideration of differences. To contrast is to focus only on differences.

Whether a paragraph stresses similarities or differences, it may be patterned in one of two ways. The two subjects may be presented one at a time, as in the following paragraph of contrast.

So Grant and Lee were in complete contrast, representing two diametrically opposed elements in American life. Grant was the modern man emerging; beyond him, ready to come on the stage, was the great age of steel and machinery, of crowded cities and a restless, burgeoning vitality. Lee might have ridden down from the old age of chivalry, lance in hand, silken banner fluttering over his head. Each man was the perfect champion of his cause, drawing both his strengths and his weaknesses from the people he led.

— Bruce Catton, "Grant and Lee: A Study in Contrasts"

Alternatively, a paragraph may proceed point by point, treating the two subjects together, one aspect at a time. The following paragraph uses the point-by-point method to contrast speeches given by Abraham Lincoln in 1860 and Barack Obama in 2008.

Two men, two speeches. The men, both lawyers, both from Illinois, were seeking the presidency, despite what seemed their crippling connection with extremists. Each was young by modern standards for a president. Abraham Lincoln had turned fifty-one just five days before delivering his speech. Barack Obama was forty-six when he gave his. Their political experience was mainly provincial, in the Illinois legislature for both of them, and they had received little exposure at the national level — two years in the House of Representatives for Lincoln, four years in the Senate for Obama. Yet each was seeking his party's nomination against a New York senator of longer standing and greater prior reputation — Lincoln against Senator William Seward, Obama against Senator Hillary Clinton.

— Garry Wills, "Two Speeches on Race"

Analogy

Analogies draw comparisons between items that appear to have little in common. Writers use analogies to make something abstract or unfamiliar easier to grasp or to provoke fresh thoughts about a common subject. In the following paragraph, physician Lewis Thomas draws an analogy between the behavior of ants and that of humans.

> Ants are so much like human beings as to be an embarrassment. They farm fungi, raise aphids as livestock, launch armies into wars, use chemical sprays to alarm and confuse enemies, capture slaves. The families of weaver ants engage in child labor, holding their larvae like shuttles to spin out the thread that sews the leaves together for their fungus gardens. They exchange information ceaselessly. They do everything but watch television.

— Lewis Thomas, "On Societies as Organisms"

Cause and effect

A paragraph may move from cause to effects or from an effect to its causes. The topic sentence in the following paragraph mentions an effect; the rest of the paragraph lists several causes.

> The fantastic water clarity of the Mount Gambier sinkholes results from several factors. The holes are fed from aquifers holding rainwater that fell decades — even centuries — ago, and that has been filtered through miles of limestone. The high level of calcium that limestone adds causes the silty detritus from dead plants and animals to cling together and settle quickly to the bottom. Abundant bottom vegetation in the shallow sinkholes also helps bind the silt. And the rapid turnover of water prohibits stagnation.

— Hillary Hauser, "Exploring a Sunken Realm in Australia"

Classification

Classification is the grouping of items into categories according to some consistent principle. The principle of classification that a writer chooses ultimately depends on the writer's purpose. The following paragraph classifies species of electric fish.

> Scientists sort electric fishes into three categories. The first comprises the strongly electric species like the marine electric rays or the freshwater African electric catfish and South American electric eel. Known since the dawn of history, these deliver a punch strong enough to stun a human. In recent years, biologists have focused on a second category: weakly electric fish in the South American and African rivers that use tiny voltages

for communication and navigation. The third group contains sharks, nonelectric rays, and catfish, which do not emit a field but possess sensors that enable them to detect the minute amounts of electricity that leak out of other organisms.

> — Anne and Jack Rudloe, "Electric Warfare:
> The Fish That Kill with Thunderbolts"

Definition

A definition puts a word or concept into a general class and then provides enough details to distinguish it from others in the same class. In the following paragraph, the writer defines *crowdsourcing* as a savvy business practice.

> Despite the jargony name, *crowdsourcing* is a very real and important business idea. Definitions and terms vary, but the basic idea is to tap into the collective intelligence of the public at large to complete business-related tasks that a company would normally either perform itself or outsource to a third-party provider. Yet free labor is only a narrow part of crowdsourcing's appeal. More importantly, it enables managers to expand the size of their talent pool while also gaining deeper insight into what customers really want.

> — Jennifer Alsever, "What Is Crowdsourcing?"

C4 Reviewing, revising, and editing

To revise is to *re-see*, and the comments you receive from reviewers — instructors, peers, and writing center tutors — will help you re-see your draft through readers' eyes. Asking your readers simple questions such as "Do you understand my main idea?" and "Is my draft organized?" will help you learn how to revise your draft to clarify and organize your ideas. Writing multiple drafts allows you to write in stages, seek feedback, and strengthen your work through revising and editing.

C4-a Use peer review: Give constructive comments.

Peer review offers you an opportunity to read the work of your classmates, pose questions and suggestions, and help them see their drafts through your eyes. As you offer advice about how to strengthen a thesis, for example, or how to use a visual to convey information, you are learning, too, about the purpose of a thesis or about the role of visuals.

Write helpful peer review comments

1 **View yourself as a colleague, not a judge.** Think of yourself as asking questions and proposing possibilities, not dictating solutions. Help your peer identify the strengths of a draft and build on those strengths. Try phrasing comments this way: "Have you thought about . . . ?" or "How can you help a reader understand this point?"

2 **Pay attention to global issues first.** Focus on the big picture — purpose, thesis, organization, and evidence — before sentence structure, word choice, and grammar. You might, for instance, want to play devil's advocate and offer counterarguments to a peer's thesis, or you might suggest places where additional evidence will make an argument more persuasive. Use the checklist for global revision on page 38 to help you focus on global issues.

3 **Restate the writer's main idea.** As a reader, you can help your peer see whether points are expressed clearly. Can you follow the writer's train of thought? Restate the writer's thesis and main ideas to check your understanding.

4 **Be specific.** Point to specific places in a draft and show your classmate how, why, and where a draft is effective or confusing. Instead of saying "I like your introduction," say exactly what you like: "You use a surprising statistic in your introduction, and it really hooks me as a reader." And end your peer review session with specific recommendations for revising.

C4-b Learn from peer review: Revise with comments.

Peer review gives you an opportunity to learn what's working and not working in your draft and can help you meet the goals of a particular draft.

The following guidelines will help you learn from your reviewers' comments and revise successfully.

Be active Guide reviewers to understand your purpose and goals for writing, including why you chose your topic and what you hope to accomplish in your draft. Tell reviewers your specific concerns so they can focus their feedback. Ask reviewers to show you what puzzles them about your draft and what is unclear. And always ask questions to make sure you understand your reviewers' comments.

Have an open mind After you've worked hard on a draft, you might be surprised to hear reviewers tell you it still needs more development. Responding to readers' objections — instead of dismissing them — will strengthen your ideas and make your essay more persuasive.

Weigh feedback carefully Your reviewers will offer more suggestions than you can use, so be strategic. Sort through all the comments you receive with your original goals in mind, and focus on global concerns first — otherwise, you'll be facing the impossible task of trying to incorporate everyone's advice.

Keep a revision and editing log To help you become a stronger writer, make a list of the global and sentence-level concerns that keep coming up in your reviewers' comments. For more on improving your writing with editing logs, see page 40.

Revise with comments: What does "be specific" mean?

Often the comments you'll receive are written as shorthand commands, such as "Be specific!" Such comments don't show you *how* to revise, but they do identify where you want to focus your attention. When reviewers say that you need to "be specific," for example, the comment often signals that you could strengthen your writing by including additional evidence or by analyzing the evidence.

Strategies for revising

- **Reread your topic sentence** to understand the focus of the paragraph. (See C3-a.)
- **Ask questions.** Does the paragraph contain claims that need support? Have you provided evidence — specific examples, vivid details and illustrations, statistics and facts — to help readers understand your ideas and find them persuasive? (See A4-f.)
- **Analyze your evidence.** Remember that details and examples don't speak for themselves. You will need to show readers how evidence supports your claims. (See A1-d.)

Excerpt from an online peer review session

Juan (peer reviewer): Rachel, your essay makes a great point that credit card companies often hook students on a cycle of spending. But it sounds as if you're blaming students for their spending habits and credit card companies for their deceptive actions. Is this what you want to say?

Peer reviewer restates writer's main point and asks a question to help her clarify her ideas.

Rachel (writer): No, I want to keep the focus on the credit card companies. I didn't realize I was blaming students. What could I change?

Writer takes comment seriously and asks reviewer for specific suggestion.

Juan (reviewer): In paragraphs three and four, you group all students together as if all students have the same bad spending habits. If students are your audience, you'll be insulting them. What reader is motivated to read something that's alienating? What is your purpose for writing this draft?

Peer reviewer points to specific places in the draft and asks questions to help writer focus on audience and purpose.

Rachel (writer): Well . . . It's true that students don't always have good spending habits, but I don't want to blame students. My purpose is to call students to action about the dangers of credit card debt. Any suggestions for narrowing the focus?

Writer is actively engaged with peer reviewer's comments and doesn't take criticism personally.

Juan (reviewer): Most students know about the dangers of credit card debt, but they might not know about specific deceptive practices companies use to lure them. Maybe ask yourself what would surprise your audience about these practices.

Peer reviewer responds as a reader and acts as a coach to suggest possible solutions.

Rachel (writer): Juan, that's a good idea. I'll try it.

Writer thanks reviewer for his help and leaves session with a specific revision strategy.

POST COMMENT

C4-c Reflect on comments: Develop a revision plan.

After receiving comments from your instructor, peers, or writing center tutor, you might wonder where to put your attention and how to prioritize your revisions. Take time to reflect on the feedback you've received and ask questions:

- What do you learn from the comments?
- How will you use your reviewers' suggestions and comments to meet the goals of the assignment?

- Are there suggestions you will choose not to take, and if so, why?
- What do you want to accomplish in your next draft?

After answering these questions, write a brief revision plan to guide your work from one draft to the next. For an example of a revision plan, see the list Michelle Nguyen developed after receiving feedback from her peers (p. 37).

C4-d One student's peer review process

Student writer Michelle Nguyen's assignment, a literacy narrative, asked her to explore this question: *How have your experiences with writing shaped you as a writer?*

Here is Nguyen's draft, along with the questions she gave her peer reviewers before they read her draft.

QUESTIONS FROM NGUYEN TO PEER REVIEWERS

Alex, Brian, and Sameera: Thanks for reading my draft. Here are three questions I have about my draft: Is my focus clear? Is there anything that confuses you? What specifically should I cut or add to strengthen my draft?

ROUGH DRAFT WITH PEER COMMENTS

My family used to live in the heart of Hanoi, Vietnam. The neighborhood was small but swamped with crime. Drug addicts scoured the alleys and stole the most mundane things—old clothes, worn slippers, even license plates of motorbikes. Like anyone else in Vietnam in the 1990s, we struggled with poverty. There was no entertainment device in our house aside from an eleven-inch black-and-white television. Even then, electricity went off for hours on a weekly basis.

I was particularly close to a Vietnam War veteran. My parents were away a lot, so the older man became like a grandfather to me. He taught me how to ride a bicycle, how to read, how to take care of small pets. He worked sporadically from home, fixing bicycle tires and broken pedals. He was a wrinkly man who didn't talk much. His vocal cords were damaged during the war, and it caused him pain to speak. In a neighborhood full of screaming babies and angry shop owners and slimy

> **Alex F:** You might want to add a title to focus readers.

> **Sameera K:** I really like your introduction. It's so vivid. Think about adding a photo so readers can relate. What does Hanoi look like?

> **Brian S:** You have great details here to set the scene in Hanoi, but why does it matter that you didn't have an "entertainment device"? Maybe choose the most interesting among all these details.

criminals, his home was my quiet haven. I could read and write and think and bond with someone whose worldliness came from his wordlessness.

> **Brian S:** Worldliness came from wordlessness— great phrase! Is this part of your main idea? What is your main idea?

The tiny house he lived in stood at the far end of our neighborhood. It always smelled of old clothes and forgotten memories. He was a slight man, but his piercing black eyes retained their intensity even after all these years. He must have made one fierce soldier.

> **Sameera K:** You do a good job of showing us why this Vietnam veteran was important to you, but it seems like this draft is more a story about the man and not about you. What do you want readers to understand about you?

"I almost died once," he said, dusting a picture frame. It was one of those rare instances he ever mentioned his life during the war. As he talked, I perched myself on the side of an armchair, rested my head on my tiny hands, and listened intently. I didn't understand much. I just liked hearing his low, humming voice. The concept of war for me was strictly confined to the classroom, and even then, the details of combat were always murky. The teachers just needed us to know that the communist troops enjoyed a glorious victory.

"I was the only survivor of my unit. Twenty guys. All dead within a year. Then they let me go," he said. His voice cracked a little and his eyes misted over as he stared at pictures from his combatant past. "We didn't even live long enough to understand what we were fighting for."

He finished the sentence with a drawn-out sigh, a small set of wrinkles gathering at the end of his eyes. Years later, as I thought about his stories, I started to wonder why he referred to his deceased comrades by the collective pronoun "we." It was as if a little bit of him died on the battlefield with them too.

Three years after my family left the neighborhood, I learned that the old man became stricken with cancer. When I came home the next summer, I visited his house and sat by his sickbed. His shoulder-length mop of salt and pepper hair now dwarfed his rail-thin figure. We barely exchanged a word. He just held my hands tightly until my mother called for me to leave, his skeletal fingers leaving a mark on my pale palms. Perhaps he was trying to transmit to me some of his

> **Sameera K:** I'm curious to hear more about you and why this man was so important to you. What did he teach you about writing? What did he see in you?

worldliness and his wisdom. Perhaps he was telling me to go out into the world and live the free life he never had.

Some people say that writers are selfish and _____ vain. The truth is, I learned to write because it gave me peace in the much too noisy world of my Vietnamese childhood. In the quiet of the old man's house, I gazed out the window, listened to my thoughts, and wrote them down. It all started with a story about a wrinkly Vietnam War veteran who didn't talk much.

> **Alex F:** This sentence is confusing. Your draft doesn't seem to be about the selfishness or vanity of writers.

> **Brian S:** What does "it" refer to? I think you're trying to say something important about silence and noise and literacy, but I'm not sure what it is.

After rereading her draft and considering the feedback from her classmates, Nguyen realized that she had chosen a good direction but hadn't focused her draft to meet the expectations of the assignment. Her classmates offered her valuable suggestions about adding a photograph of her Hanoi neighborhood and clarifying her main idea. With her classmates' specific questions and suggestions in mind and their encouragement to see the undeveloped possibilities in her draft, Nguyen developed some goals for revising.

MICHELLE NGUYEN'S REVISION GOALS

- Add a title.
- Revise introduction to set the scene more dramatically. Use Sameera's idea to include a photo of my neighborhood.
- Make the story my story, not the man's story. Answer Sameera's question: What did the man see in me and I in him? Delete extra material about the old man.
- Answer Brian's question: What is my main idea?
- Follow Brian's suggestion about the connection between wordlessness and worldliness. Make the contrasts sharper between the neighborhood and the man's house.
- Figure out what main idea I'm trying to communicate. See if there is a possible idea in the various contrasts. The surprise was finding writing in silence, not in the noisy exchange of voices in my neighborhood.

See pages 42–43 for Nguyen's revised draft.

C4-e Approach global revision in cycles.

Revision is more effective when you approach it in cycles, rather than attempting to change everything all at once. Focus on the big-picture global elements — engaging your audience, sharpening your focus, improving organization, and strengthening content — before revising and editing your sentences.

Checklist for global revision

Purpose and audience

- Does the draft address a question, a problem, or an issue that readers care about?
- Is the draft appropriate for its audience? Does it address the audience's knowledge of and attitudes toward the subject?
- Does the introduction hook readers and give them a reason to read the essay?

Focus

- Is the thesis clear? Is it prominently placed?
- Does the thesis answer a reader's "So what?" question? (See p. 9.)
- If the draft has no thesis, do you have a good reason for omitting one?

Organization and paragraphing

- Is each paragraph unified around a main point?
- Does each paragraph support and develop the thesis with evidence?
- Have you stated the main point of each paragraph in a topic sentence?
- Have you presented ideas in a logical order?
- Does each paragraph flow from one to another without gaps or bumps?

Content

- Is the supporting material relevant and persuasive?
- Which ideas need further development? Have you left your readers with any unanswered questions?
- Do major ideas receive enough attention?
- Where might you delete redundant or irrelevant information?

Point of view

- Is the dominant point of view — first person (*I* or *we*), second person (*you*), or third person (*he, she, it, one,* or *they*) — appropriate for your purpose and audience? (See S4-a.)

C4-f Revise globally by making a reverse outline.

Outlines are useful before you write a first draft to help you focus and structure your ideas. They are useful, too, *after* you have written a draft to reveal the organization of your draft. Some writers revise globally by making a **reverse outline**. A reverse outline allows you to examine the logical flow of ideas and to evaluate each paragraph to see how it supports your thesis. By going through your draft paragraph by paragraph, you can see how the parts work together and determine whether each paragraph has a clear focus. Sometimes a reverse outline reveals that your draft has taken a different direction than you planned and thus you need to revise your thesis. Sometimes it reveals gaps in support or paragraphs that need topic sentences. A reverse outline gives you a chance to rethink your thesis and support to see how they work together.

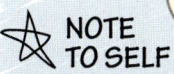

How can I use a reverse outline to plan my revision?

★ NOTE TO SELF

* Reread my draft. Write my main point in the margin.
* Number each paragraph or each part of my draft. Make notes in the margin about each paragraph. What is the topic sentence? What is the main idea of the paragraph?
* Review my notes. Did I leave anything out?
* Make a revision plan based on my answers to these questions.

C4-g Revise and edit sentences.

When you *revise* sentences, you focus on clarity and effectiveness; when you *edit*, you check for correctness. Sentences that are wordy, vague, or rambling may distract readers and make it hard for readers to focus on your purpose or grasp your ideas. Read each sentence slowly to determine whether it communicates your meaning clearly and specifically. You might find it helpful to read your work aloud and trust your ears to detect awkwardness, wordiness, or a jarring repetition.

Below is an excerpt from a student draft that included both errors that needed editing (blue comments) and ineffective or unclear sentences that needed revising (black comment). References to relevant handbook sections appear in parentheses. See the edited passage on page 41.

DRAFT PASSAGE

Wordy sentence (W2) — Although some cities have found creative ways to improve access to public transportation for passengers with physical

Unnecessary comma (P2-a) — disabilities, and to fund other programs, there have been problems in our city due to the need to address budget

Vague pronoun (G3-b) — constraints and competing problems. This has led citizens to question how funds are distributed? **Wrong punctuation for a statement (P6-a)**

Improve your writing with an editing log

An important aspect of becoming a college writer is learning how to identify the grammar, punctuation, and spelling errors that you make frequently. You can use an editing log to keep a list of your common errors, anticipate error patterns, and learn the rules needed to correct the errors.

1 When your instructor or tutor returns a draft, review any errors he or she has identified.

2 Note which errors you commonly make. For example, have you seen "run-on sentence" or "need a transition" marked in other drafts?

3 Identify the advice in the handbook that will help you correct the errors.

4 Make an entry in your editing log. A suggested format appears below.

SAMPLE EDITING LOG PAGE

Original Sentence

Athletes who use any type of biotechnology give themselves an unfair advantage they should be banned from competition.

Edited Sentence

Athletes who use any type of biotechnology give themselves an unfair advantage , and they should be banned from competition.

Rule or Pattern Applied

To edit a run-on sentence, use a comma and a coordinating conjunction (*and, but, or*).

A Writer's Reference, section G6-a

REVISED AND EDITED PASSAGE

Although some cities have found creative ways to improve access to public transportation for passengers with physical disabilities, our city has struggled with budget constraints and competing priorities. The budget crunch has led citizens to question how funds are distributed.

The revised and edited passage is clearer, easier to read, and correct.

C4-h Proofread and format your work.

Proofreading is a special kind of reading: a slow and methodical search for misspellings, typos, and omitted words or word endings.

PROOFREADING TIPS

- Remove distractions and allow yourself ten to fifteen minutes of pure concentration — without your cell phone.
- Proofread out loud, articulating each word as it is actually written.
- Proofread your sentences in reverse order.
- Don't rely heavily on spell checkers and grammar checkers. Before accepting changes, consider the accuracy of the suggestions.
- Ask a volunteer (a friend, roommate, or co-worker) to proofread after you. A second reader may catch something you didn't.

Use the format recommended by your instructor or for your discipline — MLA (Modern Language Association), APA (American Psychological Association), or CMS (*The Chicago Manual of Style*). For student papers in MLA style, see C4-i and MLA-5b. For a paper that shows APA formatting, see APA-5b; for CMS formatting, see CMS-5b.

C4-i Sample student revision: Literacy narrative

In C4-d you'll find Michelle Nguyen's first draft, along with highlights of her peer review process. Comments from reviewers helped Nguyen develop a revision plan (see p. 37). One reviewer asked: "What is your main idea?" Another asked: "What do you want readers to understand about you?" As she revised, Nguyen made global revisions and sentence-level revisions to clarify her main idea and to delete material that might distract readers from her story. Nguyen's final draft, "A Place to Begin," starts on page 42.

Michelle Nguyen

Professor Wilson

English 101

24 September 2019

A Place to Begin

Nguyen formats her final draft using MLA guidelines.

Nguyen revises her introduction to engage readers with vivid details.

I grew up in the heart of Hanoi, Vietnam—Nhà Dầu—a small but busy neighborhood swamped with crime. Houses, wedged in among cafés and other local businesses (see fig. 1), measured uniformly about two-hundred square feet, and the walls were so thin that we could hear every heated debate and impassioned disagreement. Drug addicts scoured the vicinity and stole the most mundane things—old clothes, worn slippers, even license plates of motorbikes. It was a neighborhood where dogs howled and kids ran amok and where the earth was always moist and marked with stains. It was the 1990s Vietnam in miniature, with all the turmoil and growing pains of a newly reborn nation.

Sentences are revised for clarity and specificity.

Nguyen focuses on one key story in response to reviewers' questions.

Nguyen's revisions clarify her main idea.

In a city perpetually inundated with screaming children and slimy criminals, I found my place in the home of a Vietnam War veteran. My parents were away a lot, so the older man became like a grandfather to me. He was a slight man who didn't talk much. His vocal cords had been damaged during the war, and it caused him pain to speak. In his quiet home, I could read and write in the presence of someone whose worldliness grew from his wordlessness.

His tiny house stood at the far end of our neighborhood and always smelled of old clothes and forgotten memories. His wall was plastered with pictures from his combatant past, pictures that told his life story when his own voice couldn't. "I almost died once," he said, dusting a picture frame. It was one of those rare instances he ever mentioned his life during the war.

I perched myself on the side of the armchair, rested my head on my tiny hands, and listened intently. I didn't understand much. I just liked hearing his low, raspy voice.

Nguyen develops her narrative with dialogue.

"I was the only survivor of my unit. Twenty guys. All dead within a year. Then they let me go."

He finished the sentence with a drawn-out sigh, a small set of wrinkles gathering at the corner of his eye.

I wanted to hear the details of that story yet was too afraid to ask. But the bits and pieces I did hear, I wrote down in a notebook. I wanted to

Marginal annotations indicate MLA-style formatting and effective writing.

Nguyen 2

Fig. 1. Photo of the Nhà Dầu neighborhood in Hanoi. By the author, 6 June 2010.

make sure that there were not only photos but also written words to bear witness to the veteran's existence.

Once, I caught him looking at the jumbled mess of sentences I'd written. I ran to the table and snatched my notebook, my cheeks warmed with a bright tinge of pink. I was embarrassed. But mostly, I was terrified that he'd hate me for stealing his life story and turning it into a collection of words and characters and ambivalent feelings.

"I'm sorry," I muttered, my gaze drilling a hole into the tiled floor.

Quietly, he peeled the notebook from my fingers and placed it back on the table.

In his muted way, with his mouth barely twisted in a smile, he seemed to be granting me permission and encouraging me to keep writing. Maybe he saw a storyteller and a writer in me, a little girl with a pencil and too much free time.

The last time I visited Nhà D`âu was for the veteran's funeral two years ago. It was a cold November afternoon, but the weather didn't dampen the usual tumultuous spirit of the neighborhood. I could hear the jumble of shouting voices and howling dogs, yet it didn't bother me. For a minute I closed my eyes, remembering myself as a little girl with a big pencil, gazing out a window and scribbling words in my first notebook.

Many people think that words emerge from words and from the exchange of voices. Perhaps this is true. But the surprising paradox of writing for me is that I started to write in the presence of silence. It was only in the utter stillness of a Vietnam War veteran's house that I could hear my thoughts for the first time, appreciate language, and find the confidence to put words on a page. With one notebook and a pencil, and with the encouragement of a wordless man to tell his story, I began to write. Sometimes that's all a writer needs, a quiet place to begin.

As her peer reviewers suggested, Nguyen adds a photograph to help readers visualize Hanoi.

Nguyen revises to keep the focus on her story and not the old man's, as her peer reviewers suggested.

Nguyen circles back to the scene from the introduction, giving the narrative coherence.

Nguyen revises the final paragraph to show readers the significance of her narrative.

Following a peer reviewer's advice, Nguyen chooses words from her final sentence for her title.

How to write a literacy narrative

A **literacy narrative** allows you to reflect on key reading or writing experiences and to ask: How have my experiences shaped who I am as a reader or writer? A sample literacy narrative begins on page 42.

Key features

- **A well-told narrative** shows readers what happened. Lively details present the sights, sounds, and smells of the world in which the story takes place. Dialogue and action add interest and energy.

- **A main idea or insight** about reading or writing gives a literacy narrative its significance and transforms it from a personal story to one with larger, universal interest.

- **A well-organized narrative,** like all essays, has a beginning, a middle, and an ending and is focused around a thesis or main idea. Narratives can be written in chronological order, in reverse chronological order, or with a series of flashbacks.

- **First-person point of view (*I*)** gives a narrative immediacy and authenticity. Your voice may be serious or humorous, but it should be appropriate for your main idea.

Thinking ahead: Presenting or publishing

You may have some flexibility in how you present or publish your literacy narrative. If you have the opportunity to submit it as a podcast, a video, or another genre, leave time in your schedule for recording or filming. Also, in seeking feedback, ask reviewers to comment on your plans for using sounds or images.

Writing your literacy narrative

1 Explore

What story will you tell? You can't write about every reading or writing experience or every influential person. Find one interesting experience to focus your narrative. Generate ideas with questions such as these:

- What challenges have you confronted as a reader or a writer?
- Who were the people who nurtured (or delayed) your reading or writing development?
- What are your childhood memories of reading or writing?
- What images do you associate with learning to read or write?
- What is significant about the story you want to tell? What larger point do you want readers to take away from your narrative?

❷ Draft

Figure out the best way to tell your story. A narrative isn't a list of "this happened" and then "that happened." It is a focused story with its own logic and order. You don't need to start chronologically. Experiment: What happens if you start in the middle of the story or work in reverse? Try to come up with a tentative organization, and then start to draft.

❸ Revise

Ask reviewers for specific feedback. Here are some questions to guide their comments:

- What main idea do readers take away from your story? Ask them to summarize this idea in one sentence.

- Is the narrative focused around the main idea?

- Are the details vivid? Sufficient? Where might you convey your story more clearly? Would it help to add dialogue? Would visuals deepen the impact of your story?

- Does your introduction bring readers into the world of your story?

- Does your conclusion provide a sense of the story's importance?

C5 Reflecting on your writing; preparing a portfolio

C5-a Reflect on your writing.

Reflection — the process of stepping back periodically to examine your decisions, preferences, strengths, and challenges as a writer — helps you recognize your progress as a writer. Thinking about who you are as a writer and what you've learned about writing makes it possible for you to transfer your learning from one writing assignment to the next. When you complete a piece of writing, reflect on questions such as the following:

- What have you learned about yourself as a writer?
- What parts of the writing process are easy for you? What parts are challenging?

- What do you want to do differently the next time you write?
- Can you identify two or three decisions you made that were successful?
- Can you identify two or three pieces of feedback that helped you revise? What did you learn from the feedback?
- What lessons have you learned about writing? How will you transfer these lessons to your next writing assignment?

C5-b Prepare a portfolio.

At the end of the semester, your instructor may ask you to submit a portfolio, or collection, of your writing. A writing portfolio often consists of drafts, revisions, and reflections that demonstrate your thinking and learning processes or that showcase your best work. Assembling a portfolio gives you an opportunity to reflect, looking back at the writing you've done in the course to identify your favorite sentences and ideas, examining the feedback you've received, and evaluating your writing progress. And it gives you an opportunity to look forward, reflecting on how you will transfer your writing skills to other academic classes.

C5-c Student writing: Reflective letter for a portfolio

You may be asked to write a reflective letter, a focused opening statement, to introduce your portfolio. In your letter you might want to analyze your writing process, describe your composing strategies and techniques, and reflect on your development as a writer.

Here is an excerpt from one student's reflective letter for her portfolio. For a guide to writing a reflective letter, see pages 47–48.

EXCERPT FROM A REFLECTIVE LETTER

The peer review sessions that our class held in October helped me with my analytical response paper. My group and I chose to write about "Jíbara," by Esmeralda Santiago, for the Identity unit. My first and second drafts were unfocused. I spent my first draft basically retelling the events of the essay. I think I got stuck doing that because the details of Santiago's essay are so interesting — the biting termites, the burning metal, and the *jíbara* songs on the radio — and because I didn't understand the differences between summary and analysis. My real progress came when I decided to focus the essay on one image — the mirror hanging in Santiago's small house, a mirror that was hung too high for her to look into. Finding a focus helped me move from listing the events of the essay to interpreting those events. I thought my peers would love my first draft, but they found it confusing. Some of their comments were hard to take, but their feedback (and all the peer feedback I received this semester) helped me see my words through a reader's eyes.

— Lucy Bonilla, student

How to write a reflective letter

A **reflective letter** gives you an opportunity to introduce yourself as a writer, to show your progress and key decisions, and to introduce the contents of a portfolio. A sample excerpt from a student's reflective letter begins on page 46.

Key features

- **First-person perspective (*I*)** gives a reflective statement its individuality and authenticity. You are the writer; you are introducing your work and explaining your choices.

- **A thoughtful tone** shows you examining and learning from your experiences and evaluating your strengths and limitations as a writer. Your honest assessment of your work shows that you are a trustworthy and sincere interpreter of your progress.

- **A focused opening statement** provides readers with specific details to understand the contents and organization of your portfolio.

- **Acknowledgment** of the assistance you received shows that you are responsible to readers and reviewers.

Thinking ahead: Presenting or publishing

You may have some flexibility in how you present or publish a reflective piece for your portfolio. Some instructors require a formal essay; others may ask for a letter. Still others may invite you to submit an audio file. If you are submitting an e-portfolio, chances are that your instructor will require your reflective statement in digital form. If you're publishing for the web, you may want to insert headings for easier navigation.

Writing your reflective letter

① Explore

Generate ideas by brainstorming responses to questions such as these:

- Which piece of writing is your best entry? What does it illustrate about you as a writer, student, or researcher?

- How do the selections in your portfolio illustrate your strengths or challenges?

- What do you learn about your development when you compare your early drafts with your final drafts?

47

- What do your drafts reveal about your revision process? Examine in detail the revisions you made to one key piece and the changes you want readers to notice.

- How will you use the skills and experiences from your writing course in future courses?

❷ Draft

Follow the guidelines given for the form of your reflection — an essay, a cover letter, a memo — and focus your reflections to avoid a list-like structure. Experiment with headings and various chronological or thematic groupings. Ask: What have I learned — and how?

❸ Revise

Ask reviewers for specific feedback. Here are some questions to guide their comments:

- What major idea do readers take away from your reflective statement? Can they summarize this idea in one sentence?

- Where in your piece do readers want more reflection and more detailed explanations?

- Is your reflective statement focused and organized?

- Have you used specific passages from drafts, feedback, or other documents from your portfolio to illustrate your reflections?

- Have you explained how you will apply what you learned to future writing assignments?

- What added details might give readers a fuller perspective of your development and your accomplishments as a writer?

A

Academic Reading, Writing, and Speaking

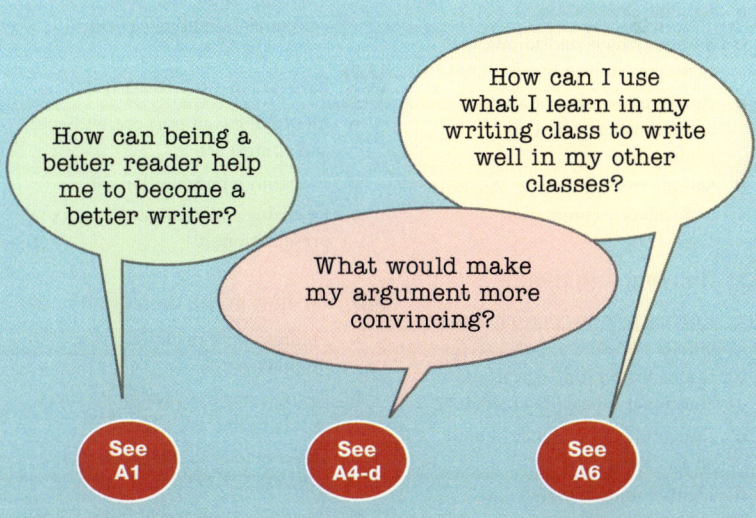

How can being a better reader help me to become a better writer?

See A1

What would make my argument more convincing?

See A4-d

How can I use what I learn in my writing class to write well in my other classes?

See A6

A Academic Reading, Writing, and Speaking

A1 **Reading and writing critically**

- Guidelines for active reading **55**
- How to read like a writer **57**
- How to draft an analytical thesis statement **64**
- How to write an analytical essay **67**

One of the best ways to become a strong college writer is to become a critical reader. When you read critically, you read with an open, curious mind, trying to understand not only what is said but also why and how it's said. And when you write analytically, you respond to a text and its author with your observations and insights. The more you take from your reading, the more you have to give as a writer.

Critical reading involves understanding

WHAT is being said	WHY it's being said	HOW it's being said

A1-a Read actively.

Reading, like writing, is an active process that happens in steps. Most texts, such as the ones assigned in college, don't yield their meaning with one quick reading. Rather, they require you to read and reread to comprehend their ideas and the evidence used to support their claims. When you read actively, you ask questions about a text and pay attention to details you would miss if you just skimmed the text. Active readers preview a text, annotate it, and then converse with it.

Previewing a text

Start by previewing a text to help you understand its basic features and structure. A text's title, for example, may reveal an author's purpose; a text's style and format, either print or digital, may reveal what kind of text it is — a book, a report, a scholarly article, a memo, or something else. The more you know about a text before you read it, the easier it will be to dig deeper into it.

Annotating a text

Annotating a text helps you read, actively and deeply, to understand what the text says and why it was written. Think of annotating as an exchange you have with an author and a text. Your role in the exchange is to respond as a reader, inserting and adding your observations and questions, your responses and reactions. As you read, you note the strengths and limitations of the text, comment on what's clear and what's confusing, and answer the basic question "What is this text about?"

To annotate, you might circle, underline, or bracket the text's thesis, key words, and major pieces of evidence to help you distinguish the main ideas from the supporting ideas. You might use the text's margins to ask questions about the author's purpose and argument, and you might note what surprises or puzzles you about the text or where you agree or disagree with it. Some writers like to use symbols such as asterisks (*), exclamation points (!), and question marks (?) in the margins to help visualize their responses. The more you annotate a text with your words, symbols, and responses, the more you make the text your own — and the easier it is for you to start writing about it.

The following example shows how one student, Emilia Sanchez, annotated an article from *CQ Researcher*, a newsletter about social and political issues.

ANNOTATED ARTICLE

Big Box Stores Are ⟨Bad⟩ for Main Street

BETSY TAYLOR

Title gives away Taylor's position.

There is plenty of reason to be concerned about the proliferation of Wal-Marts and other so-called "big box" stores. The question, however, is not whether or not these types of stores create jobs (although several studies claim they produce a net job loss in local communities) or whether they ultimately save consumers money. The real *con- cern about having a 25-acre slab of concrete with a 100,000 square foot box of stuff land on a town is whether it's good for a community's soul.

Assumes readers are concerned.

*Main point of article. But what does she mean by "community's soul"?

The worst thing about "big boxes" is that they have a tendency to produce Ross Perot's famous "big sucking sound" — sucking the life out of cities and small towns across the country. On the other hand, small businesses are great for a community. They offer more personal service; they won't threaten to pack up and leave town if they don't get tax breaks, free roads and other blandishments; and small-business owners are much more respon- sive to a customer's needs. (Ever try to complain about bad service or poor quality products to the president of Home Depot?)

Lumps all big boxes together.

"Either/or" argument — Main Street is good, big boxes are bad.

Assumes all small businesses are attentive.

Yet, if big boxes are so bad, why are they so successful? One glaring reason is that

True? (we've become a nation of hyper-consumers,) and the big-box boys know this. Downtown shopping districts comprised of small businesses take some of the efficiency out of overconsumption. There's all that hassle of having to travel from store to store, and having to pull out your credit card so many times. Occasionally, we even find ourselves chatting

Word choice makes author seem sentimental. with the shopkeeper, wandering into a coffee shop to visit with a friend or otherwise wasting precious time that could be spent on acquiring more stuff.

But let's face it — bustling, thriving city centers are fun. They breathe life into a community. They allow cities and towns to stand out from each other. They provide an atmosphere for people to

*Shopping at Target to save money — is that bad? interact with each other that *just cannot be found at Target, or Wal-Mart or Home Depot.

Is it anti-American to be against having a retail giant set up shop in one's community? Some people would say so. On the other hand, if you board up Main Street, what's left of America?

Author's argument seems one-sided and makes assumptions about consumers.

Ends with emotional appeal. Seems too simplistic!

Experiment with print and digital annotation methods

The purpose of annotating — to better understand what you are reading — stays the same across print and digital texts. What changes are the available tools. In both print and digital texts, you can highlight or underline key passages, write notes in the margins of the text, and insert your reactions and questions. Highlighting works best when it is accompanied by your own observations about the text and your responses to the words and sentences you have highlighted. Adobe Acrobat, for example, offers annotation tools for PDFs, such as sticky notes, a highlighter, and other commenting features. Mobile phones have built-in annotation tools for text and images. Try experimenting with different annotation methods to find which ones work for you. The guidelines for active reading (pp. 55–56) provide useful entry points for annotating both print and digital texts.

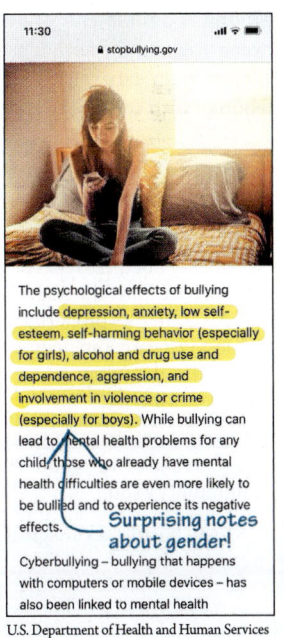

11:30   🔒 stopbullying.gov

The psychological effects of bullying include depression, anxiety, low self-esteem, self-harming behavior (especially for girls), alcohol and drug use and dependence, aggression, and involvement in violence or crime (especially for boys). While bullying can lead to mental health problems for any child, those who already have mental health difficulties are even more likely to be bullied and to experience its negative effects. **Surprising notes about gender!**

Cyberbullying – bullying that happens with computers or mobile devices – has also been linked to mental health

U.S. Department of Health and Human Services

Conversing with a text

Conversing with a text — that is, responding to a text and its author — helps you move beyond your initial notes to draw conclusions about what you've read. Perhaps you ask additional questions, examine the author's assumptions, point out something that doesn't make sense, or explain how the author's ideas suggest wider implications. As you talk back to a text, you look more closely and skeptically at how the author works through a topic, and you analyze the author's evidence and conclusions to question their effectiveness.

Conversing takes your annotations to the next level. You might begin your conversation with a text and its author using sentence starters such as these:

But what about _____?

Have you considered _____?

Here's why I find this text so important: _____.

What's missing here is _____.

Couldn't we also see it this way: _____?

What if we conclude _____ instead of _____?

Many writers use a **double-entry notebook** to converse with a text and its author and to generate ideas. To create one, draw a line down the center of a notebook page or create a two-column table in a Word or Google document. On the left side, record what the author says; include quotations, sentences, and key terms from the text. On the right side, record your observations and questions. A double-entry notebook allows you to visualize the conversation between you and the author as it develops.

Here is an excerpt from student writer Emilia Sanchez's double-entry notebook (with sentence starters highlighted).

IDEAS FROM THE TEXT	MY RESPONSES
"The question, however, is not whether or not these types of stores create jobs (although several studies claim they produce a net job loss in local communities) or whether they ultimately save consumers money."	Why are big-box stores bad if they create jobs or save people money? Taylor dismisses these possibilities without acknowledging their importance. But what about my family? We need to save money and we need jobs more than "chatting with the shopkeeper."
"The real concern . . . is whether [big-box stores are] good for a community's soul." "[S]mall businesses are great for a community."	Taylor is missing something here. Are all big-box stores bad? Are all small businesses great? Has Taylor considered that getting rid of big-box stores won't necessarily save the "soul" of America? Taylor assumes that small businesses are always better for consumers. But couldn't we conclude that some big-box stores are better for consumers because they save them time and money?

....

Using sources responsibly

To avoid plagiarizing, put quotation marks around words you copy from the text, and keep an accurate record of page numbers for quotations.

....

Asking the "So what?" question

As you read and annotate a text, make sure you understand its thesis, or central idea. Ask yourself: "What is the author's thesis?" Then put the author's thesis to the "So what?" test: "Why does this thesis matter? Why does it need to be argued? What's at stake?"

Perhaps you'll conclude that the thesis is too obvious and doesn't matter at all — or that it matters so much that you feel the author stopped short and overlooked key details or asked the wrong questions. Or perhaps you'll see many strengths in the author's argument but feel that a reasonable person might draw different conclusions about the issue.

Guidelines for active reading

Preview a written text.

- Who is the author? What are the author's credentials?
- What is the author's purpose: To inform? To persuade? To call to action?
- Who is the expected audience?
- When was the text written? Where was it published or posted?
- What kind of text is it: A report? A scholarly article? An online news report? A public service video?

Annotate a written text.

- What surprises, puzzles, or intrigues you about the text?
- What words or terms do you need to look up?
- What question does the text attempt to answer, or what problem does it attempt to solve?
- What is the author's thesis, or main idea? What does the author want you to believe or do?
- What type of evidence does the author provide to support the thesis?
- How persuasive is this evidence?
- If the text includes sound or images, what purpose do they serve?
- What do you notice about design details?

Guidelines for active reading, *continued*

Converse with a written text.

- What are the strengths and limitations of the text?
- If it is a multimodal text, has the author chosen the best combination of modes for the message?
- Has the author drawn conclusions that you question?
- Do you have a different interpretation of the evidence?
- Does the text raise questions that it does not answer?
- Does the author consider opposing viewpoints? Does the author treat sources fairly?

Ask the "So what?" question.

- Why does the author's thesis need to be argued, explained, or explored? What's at stake?
- What has the author overlooked or failed to consider in presenting this thesis or message? What's missing?
- Is the thesis debatable? Could a reasonable person draw different conclusions?

Read like a writer

Reading like a writer helps you identify the techniques writers use so that you can use them too. To read like a writer is to pay attention to *how* a text is written and *how* it creates an effect on you.

1 **Review any notes you've made on a text.** What passages do you find effective? What words or sentences did you underline? If you think the text is powerful or well written, figure out *why* and *how* the text works.

2 **Ask *what*, *why*, and *how* questions about the techniques writers use.** *What* techniques do writers use in their introductions, for instance, to hook readers? *How* does a writer's use of a surprising statistic or a provocative question capture your attention? Or *how* does a writer establish common ground to show fairness and lead readers to the thesis? Identify the specific techniques you appreciate as a reader — and name them — so they may become part of your repertoire as a writer.

3 **Observe how writers use specific academic writing techniques you want to learn.** For example, if you're interested in learning how writers introduce and respond to counterarguments or how they quote and paraphrase sources, pay attention to these academic writing techniques when you read.

4 **Use your experiences as a reader to plan the effect you want to create for your readers.** As you draft and revise, make deliberate choices to create this effect.

A1-b Outline a text to identify main ideas.

You are probably familiar with using an outline as a planning tool to help you organize your ideas. An outline is a useful tool for reading, too. Outlining a text — identifying its main idea and major parts — can be an important step in your reading process and can help you prepare to write about a text.

As you outline, look closely for a text's thesis statement (main idea) and topic sentences because they serve as important signposts for readers. Put the author's thesis and key points in your own words to show that you understand the text. Here, for example, are the points Emilia Sanchez identified as she prepared to write her analysis of the text printed on pages 52–53. Notice that Sanchez does not simply trace the author's ideas paragraph by paragraph; instead, she sums up the article's central points.

OUTLINE OF "BIG BOX STORES ARE BAD FOR MAIN STREET"

Thesis: Whether or not they take jobs away from a community or offer low prices to consumers, we should be worried about "big-box" stores like Wal-Mart, Target, and Home Depot because they harm communities by taking the life out of downtown shopping districts.

I. Small businesses are better for cities and towns than big-box stores are.
   A. Small businesses offer personal service; big-box stores do not.
   B. Small businesses don't make demands on community resources as big-box stores do.
   C. Small businesses respond to customer concerns; big-box stores do not.

II. Big-box stores are successful because they cater to consumption at the expense of benefits to the community.
   A. Buying everything in one place is convenient.
   B. Shopping at small businesses may be inefficient, but it provides opportunities for socializing.
   C. Downtown shopping districts give each city or town a special identity.

Conclusion: Although some people say that it's anti-American to oppose big-box stores, actually these stores threaten the communities that make up America by encouraging buying at the expense of the traditional interactions of Main Street.

Reading online

For most assignments, you will be asked to read online sources. It is tempting to skim online texts rather than read them carefully. When you skim a text, though, you are less likely to remember what you have read and less inclined to reread to grasp layers of meaning.

The following strategies will help you read critically online.

Read slowly. Instead of sweeping your eyes across the screen, slow down the pace of your reading to focus on each sentence.

Avoid multitasking. Close other applications, especially messaging and social media. If you follow a link for background or the definition of a term, return to the text immediately.

Annotate. Use annotation tools and commenting features to record your thoughts as you read online texts.

Print the text. If you prefer to read and annotate printed texts, print a copy. Record information about the source so that you can find it again, if needed, and cite it properly.

A1-c Summarize to deepen your understanding.

When you summarize, you test your understanding of a text by putting the main ideas in your own words — concisely, objectively, and accurately — and distinguishing between the text's major and minor points.

Here is Emilia Sanchez's summary of the article that is printed on pages 52–53.

Presents Taylor's ideas with signal phrases and in the third person, present tense.

Summarizes Taylor's article directly and concisely.

Represents Taylor's article accurately and fairly.

Puts Taylor's words in quotation marks and provides a page number in parentheses.

In her essay "Big Box Stores Are Bad for Main Street," Betsy Taylor argues that chain stores harm communities by taking the life out of downtown shopping districts. Explaining that a community's "soul" is more important than low prices or consumer convenience, she argues that small businesses are better than stores like Home Depot and Target because they emphasize personal interactions and don't place demands on a community's resources. Taylor asserts that big-box stores are successful because "we've become a nation of hyper-consumers," although the convenience of shopping in these stores comes at the expense of benefits to the community. She concludes by suggesting that it's not "anti-American" to oppose big-box stores because the damage they inflict on downtown shopping districts extends to America itself.
— Emilia Sanchez, student

Write a summary

1 In the first sentence, mention the **title of the text**, the **name of the author**, and the **author's thesis**.

2 Maintain a **neutral tone**; be objective.

3 Keep your **focus on the text**. Don't state the author's ideas as if they are your own.

4 As you present the author's ideas, use the **third-person point of view and the present tense**: *Taylor argues . . .* , *Taylor explains . . .* (If you are writing in APA style, see APA-3c.) Because the ideas are the author's, avoid writing sentences that begin with *The article says . . .*

5 Put all or most of your **summary in your own words**; if you borrow a phrase or a sentence from the text, put it in quotation marks and give the page number in parentheses. Use a **signal phrase** to introduce any borrowed language: *According to Singh, immigration data "reflect a slow move away from . . ."*

6 Limit yourself to presenting the text's **key points**, not every detail.

A1-d Analyze to demonstrate your critical thinking.

Whereas a summary most often answers the question of *what* a text says, an analysis looks closely at the parts of a text to examine *how* the text conveys its main idea. Looking at the parts — an author's thesis, evidence, arguments, assumptions, biases, and so on — allows you to offer your insights about how the parts and the whole text work together.

Start with questions and observations you have about the text:

- What puzzles you or doesn't make sense about the text?
- What are the strengths of the text?
- What part of the text stands out and needs close scrutiny?
- Is there a contradiction or a misguided assumption in the text?
- Do you have questions about the author's thesis or use of evidence?
- What insights might you offer your readers to help them see the text through your perspective?

Balancing summary with analysis

Summary and analysis need each other in an analytical essay; you can't have one without the other. Your readers may not be familiar with the text you are analyzing, so you should summarize the text briefly to orient readers and to help them understand the basis of your analysis.

What follows is an example of how student writer Emilia Sanchez balances **summary** with **analysis** in her essay about Betsy Taylor's article (see A1-a). Notice that the stu-dent begins her summary sentences by mentioning the title of the text and the name of the author. Before stating her thesis, Sanchez summarizes the author's purpose and central idea for readers who may or may not be familiar with Taylor's article.

> How can I go beyond just summarizing a text?

NOTE TO SELF

* Keep asking <u>how</u> and <u>why</u> questions about the text.
* Include my own ideas and judgments about the text. That's what will keep readers interested.
* Think about how to use summary sentences to introduce my analysis.
* Highlight summary sentences in one color and analysis sentences in a second color to make sure I have a balance.

SAMPLE PARAGRAPH BALANCING SUMMARY AND ANALYSIS

In her essay "Big Box Stores Are Bad for Main Street," Betsy Taylor focuses not on the economic effects of large chain stores but on the effects these stores have on the "soul" of America. She argues that stores like Home Depot, Target, and Wal-Mart are bad for America because they draw people out of downtown shopping districts and cause them to focus on consumption. In contrast, she believes that small businesses are good for America because they provide personal attention, encourage community interaction, and make each city and town unique. But Taylor's argument is unconvincing because it is based on sentimentality — on idealized images of a quaint Main Street — rather than on the roles that businesses play in consumers' lives and communities.

Summary

Analysis

Revise with comments: What does "too much summary, not enough analysis" mean?

If a reviewer tells you that your draft contains "too much summary, not enough analysis," you might wonder how to revise.

- "Too much summary" means that you are describing and restating what a text says without adding your own thoughts or insights. In summarizing, you might write sentences such as *X argues that _____* or *Y explains her research study _____*.

- In analyzing, you go beyond description and summary to offer your judgment of X's argument and Y's research with sentences such as *X's argument is convincing but could also include _____* or *We could draw a different conclusion from Y's research study _____*.

To help you revise, examine your thesis to see whether it communicates a *position* and doesn't just describe a *fact* of the text. Remember that your thesis isn't a restatement of the text's thesis. Also try to examine the structure of your essay to make sure it doesn't follow the organization of the original text from beginning to end.

Drafting an analytical thesis statement

An effective thesis statement for analytical writing responds to a question about a text or tries to resolve a problem in the text. Remember that your thesis isn't the same as the author's thesis or main idea. Your thesis presents your judgment of the author's argument.

If student writer Emilia Sanchez had started her analysis of "Big Box Stores Are Bad for Main Street" (A1-a) with the following draft thesis statement, she merely would have repeated the main idea of the article.

DRAFT THESIS STATEMENT (REPEATS THE TEXT'S ARGUMENT)

Big-box stores such as Wal-Mart and Home Depot promote consumerism by offering endless goods at low prices, but they do nothing to promote community.

Instead, Sanchez wrote this analytical thesis statement, which offers her judgment of Taylor's argument.

REVISED THESIS STATEMENT (OFFERS JUDGMENT OF TEXT'S ARGUMENT)

By ignoring the complex economic relationship between large chain stores and their communities, Taylor incorrectly assumes that simply getting rid of big-box stores would have a positive effect on America's communities.

Writing for an audience

A good strategy for academic writing is to keep your audience in mind as you develop an analysis. Remember that readers are eager to hear what you take from a text; they want to hear your observations, questions, and ideas. Some readers won't necessarily interpret a text as you do, nor will they necessarily draw the same conclusions. Through your careful reading of a text, you show your audience something they might not have seen or understood about it.

When you ask an interesting question about a text, you hook your readers and give them a reason to read your essay. A *how* or *why* question is one that taps into a real debate about a text or shows readers that something in the text is open to debate.

Draft an analytical thesis statement

Analysis begins with asking questions about a text. As you draft your thesis, your questions will help you form a judgment of the text. Let these steps guide you as you develop an analytical thesis statement.

1 **Review your notes to remind yourself of the author's main idea,** supporting evidence, and, if possible, the author's purpose (reason for writing) and audience (intended reader).

2 **Ask *what, why,* or *how* questions to show readers what in the text needs to be explored and is open to debate.** How do the author's perspective and thesis clarify or complicate your understanding of the subject? Why might a reasonable person agree or disagree with the author? What has the author overlooked or failed to consider? Look for patterns among your questions and annotations to help you discover what interests you about the text.

3 **Write your thesis as an answer to the questions** you have posed or as the resolution of a problem you have identified in the text. Remember that your thesis isn't the same as the text's thesis. Your thesis is your position and presents your judgment of the text's thesis.

4 **Test your thesis.** An analytical thesis is arguable, one with which readers might disagree, and not a summary of the text's thesis. Ask: Is your position clear? Is your position debatable? Does your thesis offer a clear judgment of the text? The answer to each question should be yes. Examine your thesis to make sure you state your position specifically and clearly.

5 **Revise your thesis.** Why does your position matter? Put your working thesis to the "So what?" test (see p. 55). Consider adding a *because* clause to your thesis to answer a reader's "So what?" question.

A1-e Sample student essay: Analysis of an article

Following is Emilia Sanchez's analysis of the article by Betsy Taylor (see A1-a). Sanchez used MLA (Modern Language Association) style to format her paper and cite the source.

Sanchez 1

Emilia Sanchez

Professor Goodwin

English 10

22 October 2018

Rethinking Big-Box Stores

In her essay "Big Box Stores Are Bad for Main Street," Betsy Taylor focuses not on the economic effects of large chain stores but on the effects these stores have on the "soul" of America. She argues that stores like Home Depot, Target, and Wal-Mart are bad for America because they draw people out of downtown shopping districts and cause them to focus on consumption. In contrast, she believes that small businesses are good for America because they provide personal attention, encourage community interaction, and make each city and town unique. But Taylor's argument is unconvincing because it is based on sentimentality—on idealized images of a quaint Main Street—rather than on the roles that businesses play in consumers' lives and communities. By ignoring the complex economic relationship between large chain stores and their communities, Taylor incorrectly assumes that simply getting rid of big-box stores would have a positive effect on America's communities.

Taylor's use of colorful language reveals that she has a sentimental view of American society and does not understand economic realities. In her first paragraph, Taylor refers to a big-box store as a "25-acre slab of concrete with a 100,000 square foot box of stuff " that "land[s] on a town," evoking images of a powerful monster crushing the American way of life. But she oversimplifies a complex issue. Taylor does not consider that many downtown business districts failed long before chain stores moved in, when factories and mills closed and workers lost their jobs. In cities with struggling economies, big-box stores can actually provide much-needed jobs. Similarly, while Taylor blames big-box stores for harming local economies by asking for tax breaks, free roads, and other perks, she doesn't acknowledge that these stores also enter into economic partnerships with the surrounding communities by offering financial benefits to schools and hospitals.

Summary of the article's thesis orients readers and prepares them for analysis.

Sanchez begins to analyze Taylor's argument.

Thesis expresses Sanchez's judgment of Taylor's article.

Signal phrase introduces quotations from the source; Sanchez uses an MLA in-text citation.

Sanchez identifies and challenges Taylor's assumptions.

Marginal annotations indicate MLA-style formatting and effective writing.

Sanchez 2

Clear topic sentence announces a shift to a new topic.

Taylor's assumption that shopping in small businesses is always better for the customer also seems driven by nostalgia for an old-fashioned Main Street rather than by the facts. While she may be right that many small businesses offer personal service and are responsive to customer complaints, she does not consider that many customers appreciate the service at big-box stores. Just as customer service is better at some small businesses than at others, it is impossible to generalize about service at all big-box stores. For example, customers depend on the lenient return policies and the wide variety of products at stores like Target and Home Depot.

Sanchez refutes Taylor's claim.

In MLA style, no page number is needed in an in-text citation for a one-page source.

Taylor blames big-box stores for encouraging American "hyper-consumerism," but she oversimplifies by equating big-box stores with bad values and small businesses with good values. Like her other points, this claim ignores the economic and social realities of American society today. Big-box stores do not force Americans to buy more. By offering lower prices in a convenient setting, however, they allow consumers to save time and purchase goods they might not be able to afford from small businesses. The existence of more small businesses would not change what most Americans can afford, nor would it reduce their desire to buy affordable merchandise.

Sanchez treats the author fairly.

Conclusion returns to the thesis and shows the wider significance of Sanchez's analysis.

Taylor may be right that some big-box stores have a negative impact on communities and that small businesses offer certain advantages. But she ignores the economic conditions that support big-box stores as well as the fact that Main Street was in decline before the big-box store arrived. Getting rid of big-box stores will not bring back a simpler America populated by thriving, unique Main Streets; in reality, Main Street will not survive if consumers cannot afford to shop there.

Sanchez 3

Work cited page is in MLA style.

Work Cited

Taylor, Betsy. "Big Box Stores Are Bad for Main Street." *CQ Researcher,* vol. 9, no. 44, 1999, p. 1011.

How to write an analytical essay

An **analysis** of a text allows you to examine the parts of a text to understand *what* the text means and *how* it makes its meaning. Your goal is to offer your judgment of the text and to persuade readers to see it through your analytical perspective. You say to your readers: "Here are my observations and insights about this text. This is what I have discovered about what the text means and why it matters." Sample analytical essays appear in sections A1-e and A2-d.

Key features

- **A careful and critical reading** of a text reveals what the text says, how it works, and what it means. In an analytical essay, you pay attention to the details of the text, especially its thesis and evidence, and — in the case of a multimodal text — its visual or audio presentation.

- **A thesis that offers a clear judgment** of the text anchors your analysis. Your thesis might be the answer to a question you have posed about the text or the resolution of a problem you have identified in the text.

- **Support for the thesis** comes from evidence in the text. You summarize, paraphrase, and quote passages that support the claims you make about the text.

- **A balance of summary and analysis** helps readers who are not familiar with the text you are analyzing. Summary answers the question of *what* a text says; an analysis looks at *how* a text makes its point.

Thinking ahead: Presenting and publishing

You may have the opportunity to present or publish your analysis in the form of a multimodal text such as a slide show or a video. Consider how adding images or sound might strengthen your analysis or help you to better reach your audience. (See section A2.)

Writing your analytical essay

 **Explore**

Generate ideas for your analysis by responding to questions such as the following:

- What is the text about?
- What do you find interesting, surprising, or puzzling about this text?

67

- What do you see as the strengths of the text? How does the text clarify or add to your understanding of the subject?

- What is the author's purpose, thesis, or central idea? Put the author's thesis to the "So what?" test.

- What do your annotations of the text reveal about your response to it?

❷ Draft

- Draft a working thesis to focus your analysis. Remember that your thesis is not the same as the author's thesis or message. Your thesis presents *your* judgment of the text.

- Draft a plan to organize your paragraphs. Your introductory paragraph will briefly summarize the text and offer your thesis. Your body paragraphs will support your thesis with evidence from the text. Your conclusion will pull together the major points and show the significance of your analysis.

- Identify specific words, phrases, and sentences from the text as evidence to support your thesis.

❸ Revise

Ask your reviewers to give you specific comments. You can use the following questions to guide their feedback.

- Is the introduction effective and engaging?

- Is summary balanced with analysis?

- Does the thesis offer a clear judgment of the text?

- What objections might other writers pose to your analysis?

- Is the analysis well organized? Are there clear topic sentences and transitions?

- Have you provided sufficient evidence? Have you analyzed the evidence?

- Have you cited words, phrases, or sentences that are summarized or quoted?

A2 Reading and writing about multimodal texts

In many of your college classes, you'll have the opportunity to read and write about multimodal texts, such as advertisements, podcasts, videos, or websites. Multimodal texts combine two or more of the following modes: words, static images, moving images, and sound. Like a print text, a multimodal text can be read carefully to understand *what* it says and *how* it communicates its purpose and reaches its audience.

Writing about a multimodal text differs from writing about written texts, but there are also similarities. You can use a similar reading process for both — a process that starts with active, critical reading.

A2-a Read actively.

When you read a multimodal text, you are reading more than words; you might also be reading a text's design and composition, and perhaps even its pace and volume. Your work as a reader involves understanding the modes — words, images, and sound — separately and then analyzing how the modes work together.

Use the guidelines for active reading in A1-a to help you preview, annotate, and converse with a multimodal text.

One student, Ren Yoshida, annotated an advertisement for fairly traded coffee. In his annotations (view the annotated ad in this section), you'll see how Yoshida jotted down his observations of the ad's design features and questioned some of the ad's language. He used his annotations to help him converse with the text, questioning what seemed puzzling and contradictory, as he worked to understand the advertisement's message and his response to it. Yoshida's active reading notes provided a basis for the analysis that appears in A2-d.

Annotated advertisement

When you choose Equal Exchange fairly traded coffee, tea or chocolate, you join a network that empowers farmers in Latin America, Africa, and Asia to:

- Stay on their land
- Care for the environment
- Farm organically
- Support their family
- Plan for the future

www.equalexchange.coop

Photo: Jesus Choqueheranca de Quevero,
Coffee farmer & CEPICAFE Cooperative member, Peru

What is being exchanged?

Why is "fairly traded" so hard to read?

"Empowering" — why in an elegant font? Who is empowering farmers?

"Farmers" in all capital letters — shows strength?

Straightforward design and not much text.

Outstretched hands. Is she giving a gift? Inviting partnership?

Hands: heart-shaped, foregrounded.

Raw coffee beans are red: earthy, natural, warm.

Positive verbs: consumers choose, join, empower; farmers stay, care, farm, support, plan.

How do consumers know their money helps farmers stay on their land?

A2-b Summarize a multimodal text to deepen your understanding.

Your goal in summarizing a multimodal text is to state the work's central idea and key points objectively and accurately, in your own words, and usually in paragraph form. Since a summary must be fairly short, you must decide what is most important. Here is the summary Ren Yoshida drafted as he prepared to write an analysis of the advertisement in section A2-a.

> The Equal Exchange advertisement is selling the message that together farmers and consumers hold the future of the planet in their hands. At the center of the ad is a farmer whose outstretched hands, full of raw coffee, offer the fruit of her labor and a partnership with consumers. The ad suggests that in a global world producers and consumers are bound together. A cup of coffee is more than just a morning ritual. A cup of coffee is part of an equal exchange that empowers farmers to stay on their land and empowers consumers to do the right thing.
>
> —Ren Yoshida, student

A2-c Analyze a multimodal text to demonstrate your critical reading.

When you analyze a multimodal text, you say to readers, "Here's my reading of this text. This is what the text means and why it matters." Analysis begins with asking questions about how the text conveys its main idea or message.

Guidelines for analyzing a multimodal text

The following questions will help you examine and interpret a multimodal text.

- What is your first impression of the text? What details in the text create this response?
- When and why was the text created? Where did the text appear?
- What clues suggest the text's intended audience? What assumptions are being made about the audience?
- What is the thesis, central idea, or message of the text?
- Does this text tell a story? How would you sum up the story?
- What modes are used, and why? How do the modes work together?
- How does the arrangement of sounds or design details help convey the text's meaning or serve its purpose?

Balancing summary with analysis

Summary and analysis need each other in an analytical essay; aim to strike a balance. Your readers may not be familiar with the text you are analyzing, so orienting them with a brief summary will help them understand the basis of your analysis. Remember that readers are interested in your ideas about a text, and you can move from summary to analysis by posing *how* and *why* questions that lead to your interpretation of the text.

Drafting an analytical thesis statement about a multimodal text

An effective thesis statement responds to a question about the text or tries to resolve a problem in the text. Remember that your thesis isn't the same as the text's thesis or main idea. Your thesis presents *your judgment* of the multimodal text's message or argument. The draft thesis in this section summarizes the ad printed in A2-a; it doesn't present an analysis. Student writer Ren Yoshida revised his thesis statement by questioning a single detail.

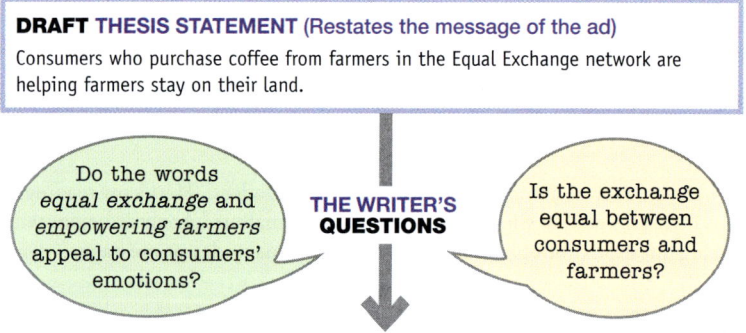

DRAFT THESIS STATEMENT (Restates the message of the ad)
Consumers who purchase coffee from farmers in the Equal Exchange network are helping farmers stay on their land.

THE WRITER'S QUESTIONS

Do the words *equal exchange* and *empowering farmers* appeal to consumers' emotions?

Is the exchange equal between consumers and farmers?

REVISED THESIS STATEMENT (Presents the writer's judgment of the text)
Although the ad works on an emotional level, it is less successful on a logical level because of its promise for an equal exchange between consumers and farmers.

As you draft and revise your thesis, make sure your thesis is arguable, one with which readers might disagree, and not a summary of the text's message or thesis. Ask questions such as these: Is your position clear? Debatable? Does your thesis offer a clear judgment of the text? Consult the advice on how to draft an analytical thesis statement (p. 64) as you draft and revise your thesis about a multimodal text.

A2-d Sample student writing: Analysis of an advertisement

In analyzing the Equal Exchange advertisement, Ren Yoshida asked questions about the ad's design details and its emotional and logical appeals, and he focused his thesis by questioning a single detail in the ad. Here is Yoshida's analysis of the Equal Exchange advertisement that appears in A2-a.

Yoshida 1

Ren Yoshida

Professor Marcotte

English 101

4 November 2019

Sometimes a Cup of Coffee Is Just a Cup of Coffee

A farmer, her hardworking hands full of coffee beans, reaches out
from an Equal Exchange Advertisement. The hands, in the shape of a heart,
offer to consumers the fruit of the farmer's labor. The ad's message is
straightforward: in choosing Equal Exchange, consumers become global
citizens, partnering with farmers to help save the planet. Suddenly, a cup
of coffee is more than just a morning ritual; a cup of coffee is a moral
choice that empowers both consumers and farmers. This simple exchange
appeals to a consumer's desire to be a good person — to protect the
environment and do the right thing. Yet the ad is more complicated than
it first seems, and its design raises some logical questions about such
an exchange. Although the ad works on an emotional level, it is less
successful on a logical level because of its promise for an equal exchange
between consumers and farmers.

The focus of the ad is a farmer, Jesus Choqueheranca de Quevero,
and, more specifically, her outstretched, cupped hands. Her hands are full
of red, raw coffee, her life's work. The ad successfully appeals to consumers'
emotions, assuming they will find the farmer's welcoming face and hands,
caked with dirt, more appealing than startling statistics about the state of
the environment or the number of farmers who lose their land each year.
It seems almost rude not to accept the farmer's generous offering since
we know her name and, as the ad implies, have the choice to "empower"
her. In fact, how can a consumer resist helping the farmer "[c]are for the
environment" and "[p]lan for the future," when it is a simple matter of
choosing the right coffee? The ad sends the message that our future is a
global future in which producers and consumers are bound together.

First impressions play a major role in the success of an advertisement.
Consumers are pulled toward a product, or pushed away, by an ad's initial
visual and emotional appeal. Here, the intended audience is busy people,
so the ad tries to catch viewers' attention and make a strong impression
immediately. Yet with a second or third viewing, consumers might start to

Source is cited in
the text. No
page number is
available for the
online source.

Yoshida
summarizes the
content of the ad.

Thesis expresses
Yoshida's analysis
of the ad.

Details show how
the ad appeals
to consumers'
emotions.

Yoshida interprets
details such as the
farmer's hands.

Marginal annotations indicate MLA-style formatting and effective writing.

Yoshida 2

Yoshida begins to challenge the logic of the ad.

ask some logical questions about Equal Exchange before buying their morning coffee. Although the farmer extends her heart-shaped hands to consumers, they are not actually buying a cup of coffee or the raw coffee directly from her. In reality, consumers are buying from Equal Exchange, even if the ad substitutes the more positive word *choose* for *buy*. Furthermore, consumers

Words from the ad serve as evidence.

aren't actually empowering the farmer; they are joining "a network that empowers farmers." The idea of a network makes a simple transaction more complicated. How do consumers know their money helps farmers "[s]tay on their land" and "[p]lan for the future" as the ad promises? They don't.

Clear topic sentence announces a shift.

The ad's design elements raise questions about the use of the key terms *equal exchange* and *empowering farmers*. The Equal Exchange logo suggests symmetry and equality, with two red arrows facing each other, but the words of the logo appear almost like an eye exam poster, with each line decreasing in font size and clarity. The words *fairly traded*

Summary of the ad's key features serves Yoshida's analysis.

are tiny. Below the logo, the words *empowering farmers* are presented in contradictory fonts. *Empowering* is written in a flowing, cursive font, almost the opposite of what might be considered empowering, whereas *farmers* is written in a plain, sturdy font. The ad's varying fonts communicate differently and make it hard to know exactly what is being exchanged and who is becoming empowered.

What is being exchanged? The logic of the ad suggests that consumers will improve the future by choosing Equal Exchange. The first exchange is economic: consumers give one thing—dollars—and receive something in return—a cup of coffee—and the farmer stays on her land. The second exchange is more complicated because it involves a moral exchange. The ad suggests that if consumers don't choose "fairly traded" products, farmers will be forced off their land and the environment destroyed. This exchange, when put into motion by consumers choosing to purchase products not "fairly traded," has negative consequences for both consumers and farmers. The message of the ad is that the actual exchange taking place is not economic but moral; after all, nothing is being bought, only chosen. Yet the logic of this exchange quickly falls apart. Consumers aren't empowered to become global

Yoshida shows why his thesis matters.

citizens simply by choosing Equal Exchange, and farmers aren't empowered to plan for the future by consumers' choices. And even if all this empowerment magically happened, there is nothing equal about such an exchange.

Advertisements are themselves about empowerment—encouraging viewers to believe they can become someone or do something by

Yoshida 3

identifying, emotionally or logically, with a product. In the Equal Exchange
ad, consumers are emotionally persuaded to identify with a farmer whose
face is not easily forgotten and whose heart-shaped hands hold a collective
future. On a logical level, though, the ad raises questions because
empowerment, although a good concept to choose, is not easily or equally
exchanged. Sometimes a cup of coffee is just a cup of coffee.

Conclusion
includes a
detail from the
introduction.

Conclusion
returns to Yoshida's
thesis.

Yoshida 4

Work Cited

Advertisement for Equal Exchange. *Equal Exchange*, equalexchange.coop.
Accessed 14 Oct. 2019.

A3 Reading arguments

- Recognizing logical fallacies **76**
- Evaluating ethical, logical, and emotional appeals as a reader **77–78**
- Testing inductive reasoning **79**

Many of your college assignments will ask you to read and respond to arguments about debatable issues. The questions being debated might be matters of public policy (*Should corporations be allowed to advertise on public school property?*), or they might be scholarly issues (*What role do genes play in determining behavior?*). On such questions, reasonable people may disagree. You'll find the critical reading strategies introduced in section A1 to be useful as you read an argument and ask questions about its logic, evidence, and use of appeals.

A3-a Read with an open mind and a critical eye.

As you read arguments across the disciplines and enter into academic or public policy debates, keep an open mind about opposing viewpoints. Be curious about the wide range of positions in the arguments you are reading. Examine an author's assumptions (ideas the author accepts as true), assess the

Recognizing logical fallacies

When you evaluate an argument, look closely at the reasoning behind it. Some arguments use unreasonable argumentative tactics known as *logical fallacies*.

A **hasty generalization** is a conclusion based on insufficient or unrepresentative evidence.

> *In a single year, scores on standardized tests in California's public schools rose by ten points. Therefore, more children than ever are succeeding in America's public school systems.*

Stereotypes are hasty generalizations about a group.

> *All politicians are corrupt.*
>
> *Children are always curious.*

A **false analogy** is a comparison that points out a similarity between two things that are unrelated.

> *If we can send a spacecraft to Mars, we should be able to find a cure for the common cold.*

***Post hoc* fallacy** assumes that because one event follows another, the first is the cause of the second.

> *Since Governor Cho took office, unemployment of minorities in the state has decreased by seven percent. Governor Cho should be applauded for reducing unemployment among minorities.*

Either/or fallacy oversimplifies an argument by suggesting that there are only two alternatives when in fact there are more.

> *Our current war against drugs has not worked. Either we should legalize drugs or we should turn the drug war over to our armed forces and let them fight it.*

Non sequitur is Latin for "It does not follow." When a statement or conclusion is an assertion that does not logically follow what came before it, we call it a non sequitur.

> *People should be allowed to drink at age 18 because they can vote at age 18.*

evidence, and weigh the conclusions. The following strategies will help you read with an open mind and a critical eye:

- **Read carefully.** Read to understand an author's argument and point of view. Ask questions: What is the author's thesis? What evidence does the author use to support the thesis? How does the author's argument contribute to your understanding of the subject?

- **Read skeptically.** Read to test the strengths and weaknesses of an author's argument. Ask questions: Are any of the author's assumptions or conclusions problematic? Is the author's evidence persuasive and sufficient? How does the author handle opposing views?

- **Read evaluatively.** Read to evaluate the usefulness and significance of an author's argument. Put the argument to the "So what?" test. Why does the thesis matter? Why does it need to be argued?

A3-b Evaluate ethical, logical, and emotional appeals as a reader.

Ancient Greek rhetoricians distinguished among three kinds of appeals used to influence readers — ethical, logical, and emotional. As you evaluate arguments, identify these appeals and question their effectiveness. Are they appropriate for the audience and the argument? Are they balanced and legitimate or lopsided and misleading?

Evaluating ethical, logical, and emotional appeals as a reader

Ethical appeals (*ethos*)

Ethical arguments, also known as *credibility arguments,* call upon a writer's character, knowledge, and authority. Ask questions such as the following when you evaluate the ethical appeal of an argument.

- Is the writer informed and trustworthy? How does the writer establish authority?
- Is the writer fair-minded and unbiased? How does the writer establish reasonableness?
- Does the writer use sources knowledgeably and responsibly?
- How does the writer describe the views of others and deal with opposing views?

Evaluating ethical, logical, and emotional appeals as a reader, *continued*

Logical appeals (*logos*)

Reasonable arguments appeal to readers' sense of logic, rely on evidence, and use inductive and deductive reasoning. Ask questions such as the following to evaluate the logical appeal of an argument.

- Is the evidence sufficient, representative, and relevant?
- Is the reasoning sound?
- Does the argument contain any logical fallacies or unwarranted assumptions?
- Are there any missing or mistaken premises?

Emotional appeals (*pathos*)

Emotional arguments appeal to readers' beliefs and values. Ask questions such as the following to evaluate the emotional appeal of an argument.

- What values or beliefs does the writer address, either directly or indirectly?
- Are the emotional appeals legitimate and fair?
- Does the writer oversimplify or dramatize an issue?
- Do the emotional arguments highlight or shift attention away from the evidence?

Advertising makes use of ethical, logical, and emotional appeals to persuade consumers to buy a product or embrace a brand. This Patagonia ad uses *ethos*; it makes an ethical appeal with its copy that invites customers to rethink their purchasing practices.

A3-c Evaluate the evidence behind an argument.

Writers draw on facts, statistics, examples, expert opinion, and appeals to support their arguments. As you read an argument, look closely at the evidence behind the argument. Ask the following questions:

- Is the evidence **accurate** and **unbiased**?
- Is the evidence **sufficient**?
- Is the evidence **representative**?
- Is the evidence **relevant**?

Testing inductive reasoning

Though inductive reasoning leads to probable and not absolute truth, you can access a conclusion's likely probability by asking three questions. This chart shows how to apply those questions to a sample conclusion based on a survey.

CONCLUSION   The majority of students on our campus would volunteer at least five hours a week in a community organization if the school provided a placement service for volunteers.

EVIDENCE   In a recent survey, 723 of 1,215 students said they would volunteer at least five hours a week in a community organization if the school provided a placement service for volunteers.

1. Is the evidence sufficient?

   That depends. On a small campus (say, 3,000 students), the pool of students surveyed would be sufficient for market research, but on a large campus (say, 30,000 students), 1,215 students are only 4 percent of the population. If those 4 percent were known to be truly representative of the other 96 percent, however, even such a small sample would be sufficient (see question 2).

2. Is the evidence representative?

   The evidence is representative if those responding to the survey reflect the characteristics of the entire student population: age, gender, race, field of study, overall number of extracurricular commitments, and so on. If most of those surveyed are majors in a field like social work, the researchers should question the survey's conclusion.

3. Is the evidence relevant?

   Yes. The results of the survey are directly linked to the conclusion. A survey about the number of hours students work for pay, by contrast, would not be relevant because it would not be about *choosing to volunteer*.

As you read, take time to reflect on the global elements of the argument — purpose, thesis, evidence, counterargument — to make sure you understand what the author is arguing and why.

Pose counterarguments to the author's argument to test the argument's strengths and limitations and to consider alternative interpretations. Try using these sentence starters:

X argues _____, but what she hasn't taken into consideration is _____.

X's argument rests on this faulty assumption: _____.

Couldn't it also be argued that _____ ?

A3-d Identify underlying assumptions.

An assumption is a claim that is taken to be true without need of proof. As you read and evaluate an argument, identify the underlying assumptions on which the argument is based and look closely at these assumptions to determine whether they need to be stated and supported rather than asserted as true.

Writers often assume that they share values and beliefs with readers and don't make their assumptions explicit. For example, if you read an argument about limiting population growth in developing countries and the writer assumes that readers agree with this goal, you might want to question the assumption by asking, "What evidence shows that population growth is always desirable?" Or if a writer argues that everyone agrees that violent crime is increasing because the death penalty isn't widely used, you might want to question the writer's assumptions by asking, "What evidence shows that the death penalty deters violent criminals and that it is a fair punishment?" Perhaps the unstated assumptions are ones that the writer needs to state as claims and support with evidence.

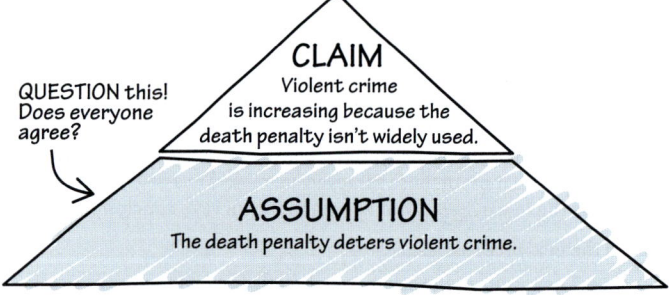

As you read arguments, test the assumptions or ideas on which the arguments are based and the values and beliefs writers assume they share with their readers.

A3-e Evaluate how fairly a writer handles opposing views.

The way in which a writer deals with opposing views is telling. Some writers address the arguments of the opposition fairly, conceding points when necessary and countering others, all in a civil spirit. Other writers will do almost anything to win an argument: either ignoring opposing views altogether or misrepresenting such views and attacking their proponents.

Writers build credibility — *ethos* — by addressing opposing arguments fairly. As you read arguments, evaluate how writers deal with views that don't line up with their own. Trustworthy writers deal with opposing arguments by

- respectfully acknowledging alternative positions
- incorporating elements of the opposition into their arguments
- using precise language to describe opposing views
- quoting opposing views accurately and fairly
- not misrepresenting a source by taking it out of context
- finding common ground among differing positions

Checklist for reading and evaluating arguments

- What is the writer's purpose and thesis?
- Are there any gaps in reasoning?
- On what assumptions does the argument rest? Are any of the assumptions unstated?
- What appeals — ethical, logical, or emotional — does the writer make? Are these appeals effective?
- What evidence does the writer use? Could there be alternative interpretations of the evidence?
- How does the writer handle opposing views?
- If you are not persuaded by the writer's argument, what counterarguments would you make to the writer?

A4 Writing arguments

Writing an argument gives you the opportunity to take a position on a debatable issue and contribute to the ongoing conversation around the issue. You say to your readers, "Here is my position in the debate, here is the evidence that supports that position, and here is my response to other positions on the issue."

A4-a Identify your purpose and context.

As you consider possible topics, start by informing yourself about the debate or conversation around a subject, sometimes called its *context.* Read sources that will help you understand the issues and arguments, approaches and research methods — the ongoing conversation — about a topic. If you are planning to write about the subject of offshore drilling, for example, you might want to read sources that shed light on the social context (the concerns of consumers, the ideas of lawmakers, the proposals of environmentalists) and sources that may inform you about the intellectual context (scientific or theoretical responses by geologists, oceanographers, or economists) in which the debate is played out.

A4-b View your audience as a panel of jurors.

As you build your argument, think about how you will appeal to your audience. It is useful to envision your audience as skeptical readers who, like a panel of jurors, will make up their minds after listening to all sides of the argument. To construct a convincing argument, you need to establish your credibility (*ethos*) and appeal to your readers' sense of logic and reason (*logos*) as well as to their values and beliefs (*pathos*).

For Multilingual Writers Academic audiences in the United States will expect your writing to be assertive and confident — neither aggressive nor passive. You can create an assertive tone by acknowledging different positions and supporting your ideas with specific evidence.

TOO AGGRESSIVE	Of course only registered organ donors should be eligible for organ transplants. It's selfish and shortsighted to think otherwise.
TOO PASSIVE	I might be wrong, but I think that maybe people should have to register as organ donors if they want to be considered for a transplant.
ASSERTIVE	If only registered organ donors are eligible for transplants, more people will register as donors.

Using ethical, logical, and emotional appeals as a writer

Ethical appeals (*ethos*)

To accept your argument, a reader must see you as trustworthy, fair, and reasonable. When you acknowledge alternative positions, you build common ground with readers and gain their trust by showing that you are knowledgeable. And when you use sources responsibly and respectfully, you inspire readers' confidence in your judgment.

> However, not everyone agrees. Critics point out, rightly so, that eliminating grades in academic environments would require massive system-wide rethinking.

Logical appeals (*logos*)

To persuade readers, you need to appeal to their sense of logic and reasoning. When you provide evidence, you offer readers logical support for your argument. And when you clarify assumptions and avoid logical fallacies, you appeal to readers' desire for reason.

> A recent study showed that an overemphasis on grades—and not learning—had led eighty-seven percent of the study participants to cheat on or consider cheating on an exam.

Emotional appeals (*pathos*)

To establish common ground with readers, you need to appeal to their beliefs and values as well as to their minds. When you offer vivid examples, surprising statistics, or compelling visuals, you engage readers in your argument. And when you balance emotional appeals with logical appeals, you highlight the human dimension of an issue to show readers why they should care about your argument.

> Why continue to promote a culture of fear and intimidation with *report-card Fridays*, days when American students are concerned less with what they've learned than they are with how they've scored?

A4-c Build common ground with your audience.

As you construct your argument and counter opposing arguments, try to establish common ground with your readers by finding one or two assumptions you might share with them. If you can show that you share their concerns, your audience will be more likely to accept your argument. By establishing common ground, you show readers, both those who do not initially agree with your views and those who already agree with you, that you are well-informed and reasonable, not one-sided or biased. For example, to convince parents that school uniforms will have a positive effect on academic achievement, a school board would want to create common ground with parents by emphasizing shared values about learning. Having established these values in common, the board might convince parents that school uniforms will reduce distractions, save money, and focus students' attention on learning rather than on clothes.

> **How can I establish ethos as a writer?**
>
> ⭐ **NOTE TO SELF**
> * Take a reasonable position in my thesis statement.
> * Show my knowledge of the debate, what's at stake, and why the debate matters to readers.
> * Seek out trustworthy sources to support my position. Acknowledge positions and points of view different from my own.
> * Cite my sources accurately.

A4-d In your introduction, establish credibility and state your position.

When you construct an argument, make sure your introduction includes a thesis statement, a signpost that lets readers know your position on the issue you have chosen to debate and gives some sense of your reasoning.

In the sentences leading up to the thesis, establish your credibility (*ethos*) with readers by showing that you are fair-minded and knowledgeable about the various positions in a debate. By building common ground with readers who may not at first agree with your views, you show them why they should consider your thesis.

In the following introduction, student writer Kevin Smith introduces both sides of a debate, builds common ground with readers, and presents himself as a fair-minded writer, someone worth listening to.

Smith shows familiarity with the legal issues surrounding school prayer.

    Although the Supreme Court has ruled against prayer in public schools on First Amendment grounds, many people still feel that prayer should be allowed. Such people value prayer as a practice central to their faith and believe that prayer is a way for schools to reinforce moral principles. They also compellingly point out a paradox in the First Amendment itself: at what point does the separation of church and state restrict the freedom of those who wish to practice their religion? What proponents of school prayer fail to realize, however, is that the Supreme Court's decision, although it was made on legal grounds, makes sense on religious grounds as well. Prayer is too important to be trusted to our public schools.

Smith is fair-minded, presenting the views of both sides.

Thesis builds common ground.

— Kevin Smith, student

Draft a thesis statement for an argument

1 **Identify the various positions in the debate you're writing about.** At the heart of a good argument are debate and disagreement. An argumentative thesis takes a clear position on a debatable issue and is supported by a balanced examination of the evidence. Identify the points in the debate on which there is agreement and those on which there is disagreement. Consider your own questions and thoughts about the topic.

2 **Determine where you stand on the issue.** Consider how the sources you have read provide support for your position. Also consider how the sources make you question your position.

3 **Pose a question that doesn't have an easy yes or no answer.** An open-ended question that doesn't have just one correct answer will lead you to developing a stronger thesis. If your question can be answered with a yes or no response, add *why* or *how* to the question to provide an argumentative edge.

4 **Write your thesis as an answer to your question.** Your thesis should be arguable, one with which readers might disagree. Ask: Is your position debatable? Does your thesis state your position specifically and clearly? Will readers understand why your thesis matters?

5 **Test your thesis with a counterargument.** View your argument through the eyes of readers who disagree with you. Try to imagine a reader's counterargument to your argument. Also, ask peers to present alternate perspectives.

6 **Revise your thesis.** Why does your position matter? Put your working thesis to the "So what?" test (see A1-a). Consider adding *because* or *although* to your thesis to show readers the importance of your position or to set it in the context of an opposing view.

Responding to an argument

Many college assignments ask you to write an argument in response to an argument. You will build your argument around a thesis statement that answers your questions about the argument, takes a position, and shows readers what to expect when they read your essay. The following strategies show the process of drafting a thesis statement about a multimodal text, such as this World Wildlife Fund ad. Use the strategies offered here when you respond to a written argument or to a visual argument such as this public service ad.

1 Annotate the text with questions and observations.

Be an active reader by recording your questions and observations about the text.

Graffiti? Usually on urban bridges, not polar bears, not wildlife

wwf.org

Social or political message here?

Tone seems accusatory.

Who's "we"?

What will it take before we respect the planet?

2 Ask *what, why, who,* or *how* questions to explore your thinking and to help you determine what position you want to take.

- **How** do the words and images work together?
- **Why** is there graffiti on the polar bears?
- **How** does the single line *What will it take before we respect the planet?* play on viewers' emotions?

- **Who** is the "we" being addressed in the ad?
- **How** does the ad accomplish its purposes of speaking out on behalf of vulnerable animals and sparking action?

3 **Test possible working thesis statements.**

The World Wildlife Fund advertisement presents a picture of animals and nature defaced.	This sentence is descriptive and factual. There's no position here.
How does the ad encourage action and advocacy on the part of the viewers?	This is a question. There's no position here.
This is a great ad that makes us all aware of endangered polar bears.	This is an opinion, not a position that suggests why the thesis matters.

4 **Pose a *why* or *how* question that is open to debate.**

How does the combination of the image of the defaced polar bears and the words *What will it take before we respect the planet?* play on viewers' emotions? How is emotion related to action?

5 **Draft a thesis that takes a position and imagines a counterargument.**

If the purpose of the World Wildlife Fund ad is to startle, the ad is successful, but if the purpose of the ad is to urge action, it is unsuccessful.

6 **Try adding a *because* clause to suggest why this thesis matters.**

If the purpose of the World Wildlife Fund ad is to startle, the ad is successful, but if the purpose of the ad is to urge action, it is unsuccessful because it will take more than an emotional appeal to motivate humans to act on behalf of endangered species.

A4-e Back up your thesis with persuasive lines of argument.

Arguments of any complexity contain lines of argument that, when taken together, might reasonably persuade readers that the thesis has merit. You can think of lines of argument as your *reasons*. Below, for example, are the main lines of argument that student writer Sam Jacobs uses in a paper about the shift from print to online news (see A4-h).

CENTRAL CLAIM
Thesis: The shift from print to online news provides unprecedented opportunities for readers to become more engaged with the news, to hold journalists accountable, and to participate as producers, not simply as consumers.

SUPPORTING CLAIMS
- Print news has traditionally had a one-sided relationship with its readers, delivering information for passive consumption.
- Online news invites readers to participate in a collaborative process—to question and even contribute to the content.
- Links within news stories provide transparency, allowing readers to move easily from the main story to original sources, related articles, or background materials.
- Technology has made it possible for readers to become news producers—posting text, audio, images, and video of news events.
- Citizen journalists can provide valuable information, sometimes more quickly than traditional journalists can.

A4-f Support your thesis with specific evidence.

You will support your thesis with evidence: facts and statistics, examples and illustrations, visuals, expert opinion, and so on.

Using facts and statistics

A fact is something that is known with certainty because it has been objectively verified: Carbon has an atomic weight of 12. John F. Kennedy was assassinated on November 22, 1963. Statistics are based on data and might or might not be factual, depending on the source of the data. If you choose to use statistics — alcohol impairment is a factor in nearly 31 percent of traffic fatalities, for example, or more than four in ten businesses in the United States are owned by women — look closely at the source of the statistics. Ask questions: Where do the statistics come from? Can they be verified? Facts can't be manipulated, but statistics can easily be manipulated so that they are unreliable and unrepresentative.

Most arguments are supported, at least to some extent, by facts and statistics. For example, in the following passage the writer uses statistics — and cites their source — to show that college students' credit card debt is declining.

> A recent study revealed that undergraduates are relying less on credit cards and are carrying lower debt than they did five years ago. The study credits the change to wider availability of grant and scholarship money. The average credit card debt per college undergraduate dropped more than seventy percent from $3,173 in 2008 to $925 in 2013 (Papadimitriou).

Writers often use statistics in selective ways to bolster their own positions. If you suspect that a writer's handling of statistics is not fair, track down the original sources for those statistics or read authors with opposing views, as they may give you a fuller understanding of the numbers.

Using examples

Examples rarely prove a point by themselves, but when used in combination with other forms of evidence, they add detail to an argument and bring it to life. Because examples are often concrete and sometimes vivid, they can reach readers in ways that statistics and abstract ideas cannot.

In a paper arguing that online news provides opportunities for readers that print does not, Sam Jacobs describes how regular citizens using only cell phones and laptops helped save lives during Hurricane Katrina by sending important updates to the rest of the world.

> Citizen reporting made a difference in the wake of Hurricane Katrina in 2005. Armed with cell phones and laptops, regular citizens relayed critical news updates in a rapidly developing crisis, often before traditional journalists were even on the scene.

Using visuals

Visuals can support your argument by providing vivid and detailed evidence and by capturing your readers' attention. Bar or line graphs, for instance, can describe and organize complex statistical data; photographs can convey abstract ideas; maps can illustrate geography. As you consider using visual evidence, ask whether the evidence will appeal to readers logically, ethically, or emotionally. For examples of eight types of visuals to support your argument, see C2-b.

The following graph could appeal to *logos* (home ownership rates have risen steadily since the 1950s) or to *pathos* (the American dream is coming true for more Americans).

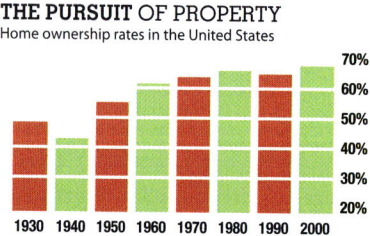

THE PURSUIT OF PROPERTY
Home ownership rates in the United States

Citing expert opinion

Although they are no substitute for careful reasoning of your own, the views of an expert can contribute to the force of your argument. To help readers recognize the expert, provide credentials showing why your source is worth listening to, perhaps listing the person's position or title alongside his or her name. For example, to help make the case that print journalism has a one-sided relationship with its readers, student writer Sam Jacobs cites an expert, Dan Gillmor, and provides the source's credentials.

> With the rise of the Internet, however, this model has been criticized by journalists such as Dan Gillmor, founder of the Center for Citizen Media, who argues that traditional print journalism treats "news as a lecture," whereas online news is "more of a conversation" (xxiv).

A4-g Anticipate objections; counter opposing arguments.

No argument is complete without anticipating, acknowledging, and countering opposing arguments. It might seem at first that drawing attention to an opposing point of view or contradictory evidence would weaken your argument. But if you don't acknowledge counterarguments, your readers will say "How could that be the only answer?" or "Have you thought about this other perspective?" By acknowledging that not everyone draws the same conclusions or holds the same point of view, you show your *ethos* as a reasonable, fair, and well-informed writer who has a thorough understanding of the issue.

There is no best place in an essay to deal with opposing views. Often it is useful to summarize the opposing position early in your essay. After stating your thesis but before developing your own arguments, you might include a paragraph that takes up the most important counterargument. Or you can anticipate objections paragraph by paragraph as you build your case. Wherever you decide to address opposing arguments, you will enhance your credibility if you explain the views of others accurately and fairly.

Anticipating and countering opposing arguments

As you build your argument, focus on the strengths of your position and the reasons a reader might object to your argument. To **anticipate a possible objection**, consider the following questions.

- Could a reasonable person draw a different conclusion from your facts or examples?
- Might a reader question any of your assumptions or offer an alternative explanation?
- Is there any evidence that might weaken your position?

The following questions may help you **respond to a potential objection**.

- Can you concede the point to the opposition but challenge the point's importance or usefulness?
- Can you explain why readers should consider a new perspective or question a piece of evidence?
- Should you explain how your position responds to contradictory evidence?
- Can you suggest a different interpretation of the evidence?

Use sentence starters to signal to readers that you're about to **present an objection**.

Critics of this view argue that _____.

Some readers might point out that _____.

Researchers challenge these claims by _____ .

This conclusion is not one that everyone accepts, however, because _____.

A4-h Sample student writing: Argument

In the following paper, student writer Sam Jacobs argues that the shift from print to online news benefits readers by providing them with opportunities to produce news and to think more critically as consumers of news. Notice how he appeals to his readers by presenting opposing views fairly before providing his own arguments.

When Jacobs quotes, summarizes, or paraphrases information from a source, he cites the source with an in-text citation formatted in MLA style. Citations in the paper refer readers to the list of works cited at the end of the paper. (For more details about citing sources, see MLA-2.)

A guide to writing an argument essay follows the student essay.

Sam Jacobs

Professor Alperini

English 101

16 October 2018

From Lecture to Conversation: Redefining What's "Fit to Print"

In his opening sentences, Jacobs provides background for his thesis.

"All the news that's fit to print," the motto of *The New York* Times since 1896, plays with the word *fit*, asserting that a news story must be newsworthy and must not exceed the limits of the printed page. The increase in online news consumption, however, challenges both meanings of the word *fit*, allowing producers and consumers alike to rethink who decides which topics are worth covering and how extensive that coverage should be. Any cultural shift usually means that something is lost, but in this case there are clear gains. The shift from print to online news provides unprecedented opportunities for readers to become more engaged with the news, to hold journalists accountable, and to participate as producers, not simply as consumers.

Thesis states the main point.

Jacobs does not need a citation for common knowledge.

Guided by journalism's code of ethics — accuracy, objectivity, and fairness — print news reporters have gathered and delivered stories according to what editors decide is fit for their readers. Except for op-ed pages and letters to the editor, print news has traditionally had a one-sided relationship with its readers. The print news media's reputation for objective reporting has been held up as "a stop sign" for readers, sending a clear message that no further inquiry is necessary (Weinberger). With the rise of the Internet, however, this model has been criticized by journalists such as Dan Gillmor, founder of the Center for Citizen Media, who argues that traditional print journalism treats "news as a lecture," whereas online news is "more of a conversation" (xxiv). Print news arrives on the doorstep every morning as a fully formed lecture, a product created without participation from its readership. By contrast, online news invites readers to participate in a collaborative process — to question and even help produce the content.

Source is cited in MLA style.

Transition moves from Jacobs's main argument to specific examples.

One of the most important advantages online news offers over print news is the presence of built-in hyperlinks, which carry readers from one electronic document to another. If readers are curious about the definition of a term, the roots of a story, or other perspectives on a topic, links provide a path. Links help readers become more critical consumers of information by engaging them in a totally new way. For instance, the link

Marginal annotations indicate MLA-style formatting and effective writing.

Jacobs 2

embedded in the story "Credit-Shy: Younger Generation Is More Likely to
Stick to a Cash-Only Policy" (Sapin) allows readers to find out more about
the financial trends of young adults and provides statistics that confirm
the article's accuracy (see fig. 1). Other links in the article widen the
conversation. These kinds of links give readers the opportunity to conduct
their own evaluation of the evidence and verify the journalist's claims.

> Jacobs clarifies key terms (*transparency* and *accountability*).

Links provide a kind of transparency impossible in print because they
allow readers to see through online news to the "sources, disagreements,
and the personal assumptions and values" that may have influenced a
news story (Weinberger). The International Center for Media and the
Public Agenda underscores the importance of news organizations letting
"consumers in on the often tightly held little secrets of journalism." To
do so, they suggest, will lead to accountability, and "accountability leads
to credibility" ("Openness"). These tools alone don't guarantee that news
producers will be responsible and trustworthy, but they encourage an open
and transparent environment that benefits news consumers.

> Jacobs develops the thesis.

Not only has technology allowed readers to become more critical news
consumers, but it also has helped some to become news producers. The
Web gives ordinary people the power to report on the day's events. Anyone
with an Internet connection can publish on blogs and websites, engage in
online discussion forums, and contribute video and audio recordings. Citizen
journalists with laptops, cell phones, and digital camcorders have become
news producers alongside large news organizations.

> Opposing views are presented fairly.

Not everyone embraces the spread of unregulated news reporting
online. Critics point out that citizen journalists are not necessarily
trained to be fair or ethical, for example, nor are they subject to editorial
oversight. Acknowledging that citizen reporting is more immediate
and experimental, critics also question its accuracy and accountability:
"While it has its place . . . it really isn't journalism at all, and it opens
up information flow to the strong probability of fraud and abuse. . . .
Information without journalistic standards is called gossip," writes David
Hazinski in *The Atlanta Journal-Constitution*. In his book *Losing the News*,
media specialist Alex S. Jones argues that what passes for news today is
in fact "pseudo news" and is "far less reliable" than traditional print news
(27). Even a supporter like Gillmor is willing to agree that citizen journalists are "nonexperts," but he argues that they are "using technology to
make a profound contribution, and a real difference" (140).

> Jacobs counters opposing arguments.

Jacobs 3

A vivid example helps Jacobs make his point.

Citizen reporting made a difference in the wake of Hurricane Katrina in 2005. Armed with cell phones and laptops, regular citizens relayed critical news updates in a rapidly developing crisis, often before traditional journalists were even on the scene. In 2006, the enormous contributions of citizen journalists were recognized when the New Orleans *Times-Picayune* received the Pulitzer Prize in public service for its online coverage — largely citizen-generated — of Hurricane Katrina. In recognizing the paper's "meritorious public service," the Pulitzer Prize board credited the newspaper's

Jacobs uses specific evidence for support.

blog for "heroic, multi-faceted coverage of [the storm] and its aftermath" ("2006 Pulitzer Prize"). Writing for the *Online Journalism Review*, Mark

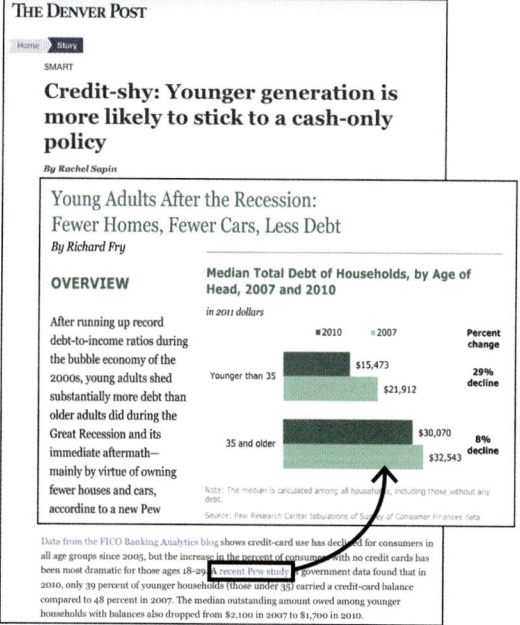

Because source information is provided in the caption and the source is not cited elsewhere in the essay, no entry for the source is needed in the works cited list.

Fig. 1. Links embedded in online news articles allow readers to move from the main story to original sources, related articles, or background materials. Rachel Sapin, "Credit-Shy: Younger Generation Is More Likely to Stick to a Cash-Only Policy," *The Denver Post*, 26 Aug. 2013.

Jacobs 4

Glaser emphasizes the role that blog updates played in saving storm victims' lives. Further, he calls *The Times-Picayune*'s partnership with citizen journalists a "watershed for online journalism."

The Internet has enabled consumers to participate in a new way in reading, questioning, interpreting, and reporting the news. Decisions about appropriate content and coverage are no longer exclusively in the hands of news editors. Ordinary citizens now have a meaningful voice in the conversation—a hand in deciding what's "fit to print." Some skeptics worry about the apparent free-for-all and loss of tradition. But the expanding definition of news provides opportunities for consumers to be more engaged with events in their communities, their nations, and the world.

Conclusion echoes the thesis without dully repeating it.

96

A4-h   Writing arguments

Jacobs 5

Works cited page
uses MLA style.

List is alphabetized
by authors' last
names (or by title
when a work has
no author).

Access date is
used for a web
source that has
no update date.

Works Cited

Gillmor, Dan. *We the Media: Grassroots Journalism by the People, for the People.* O'Reilly Media, 2006.

Glaser, Mark. "NOLA.com Blogs and Forums Help Save Lives after Katrina." *OJR: The Online Journalism Review,* Knight Digital Media Center, 13 Sept. 2005, www.ojr.org/050913glaser.

Hazinski, David. "Unfettered 'Citizen Journalism' Too Risky." *The Atlanta Journal-Constitution,* 13 Dec. 2007, p. 23A. *General OneFile.* go. galegroup.com/ps.

Jones, Alex S. *Losing the News: The Future of the News That Feeds Democracy.* Oxford UP, 2009.

"Openness and Accountability: A Study of Transparency in Global Media Outlets." *ICMPA: International Center for Media and the Public Agenda,* 2006, www.icmpa.umd.edu/pages/studies/transparency/ main.html.

Sapin, Rachel. "Credit-Shy: Younger Generation Is More Likely to Stick to a Cash-Only Policy." *The Denver Post,* 26 Aug. 2013, www.denverpost.com/ci_23929523/ credit-shy-younger-generation-stick-cash-only-policy.

"The 2006 Pulitzer Prize Winners: Public Service." *The Pulitzer Prizes.* Columbia U, www.pulitzer.org/prize-winners-by-year/2006. Accessed 4 Oct. 2018.

Weinberger, David. "Transparency Is the New Objectivity." *Joho the Blog,* 19 July 2009, www.hyperorg.com/blogger/2009/07/19/ transparency-is-the-new-objectivity.

How to write an argument essay

When you compose an **argument**, you propose a reasonable solution to a debatable issue. You state your position, provide evidence to support it, and respond to other views on the issue. A sample argument essay begins on page 92.

Key features

- **A thesis, stated as a clear position on a debatable issue,** frames an argument essay. The issue is debatable because reasonable people disagree about it.

- **An examination of the issue's context** indicates why the issue is important, why readers should care about it, or how your position fits into the debates surrounding the topic.

- **Sufficient, representative, and relevant evidence** supports the argument's claims. Evidence needs to be specific and persuasive; quoted, summarized, or paraphrased fairly and accurately; and cited correctly.

- **Opposing positions are summarized and countered.** By anticipating and countering objections to your position, you establish common ground with readers and show yourself as a reasonable and well-informed writer.

Thinking ahead: Presenting or publishing

You may have some flexibility in how you present or publish your argument. If you submit your argument as an audio or video essay, make sure you understand the genre's conventions and think through how your voice or a combination of sounds and images can help you establish your *ethos*. If you are taking a position on a local issue, consider publishing your argument in the form of a newspaper op-ed or letter to the editor. The benefit? A real-world audience.

Writing your argument

 **Explore**

Generate ideas by responding to questions such as the following.

- What is the debate around your issue? What sources will help you learn more about your issue?

- What position will you take? Why does your position need to be argued?

- How will you establish common ground with your readers?

- What evidence supports your position? What evidence makes you question your position?

- What types of appeals — *ethos, logos, pathos* — might you use to persuade readers? How will you build common ground with your readers?

2 Draft

Try to figure out the best way to structure your argument. A typical approach might include the following steps: Capture readers' attention; state your position; give background information; support your major claims with specific evidence; recognize and respond to opposing points of view; and end by reinforcing your thesis and why it matters.

As you draft, think about the best order for your claims. You could organize by strength, building to your strongest argument (instead of starting with your strongest), or by concerns your audience might have.

3 Revise

Ask your reviewers for specific feedback. Here are some questions to guide their comments.

- Is the thesis clear? Is the issue debatable?

- Is the evidence persuasive? Is more needed?

- Is your argument organized logically?

- Are there any flaws in your reasoning or assumptions that weaken the argument?

- Have you presented yourself as a knowledgeable, trustworthy writer?

- Does the conclusion pull together your entire argument? How might the conclusion be more effective?

A5 Speaking confidently

Effective speakers, like effective writers, identify their purpose, audience, and context. They project themselves as informed and reasonable, establish common ground with listeners, and use specific language and persuasive techniques to capture their audience's attention.

In many college classes, you'll be assigned to give an oral presentation. The more comfortable you become speaking in different settings, the easier it will be when you give a formal presentation. You can practice your speaking skills as well by contributing to class discussions, responding to the comments of fellow students, and playing an active role in team-based learning.

A5-a Identify your purpose, audience, and context.

As you plan your presentation, strategize a bit: Identify your purpose (reason) for speaking, your audience (listeners), and the context (situation) in which you will speak.

PURPOSE	Begin by asking, "Why am I speaking? What is my goal?" Your goal might be to inform, to persuade, to evaluate, to recommend, or to call to action.
AUDIENCE	Effective speakers identify the needs and expectations of their audience and shape their material and their language to meet those needs and expectations. Assess what your audience may already know and believe, what objections you might need to anticipate, and how you might engage your listeners.
CONTEXT	Ask yourself, "What is the situation for my speech? Is it an assignment for a course? The presentation of a group project? A community meeting? And how much time do I have to speak?" The answers to these questions will help you shape your presentation for your particular speaking situation.

A5-b Prepare a presentation.

Knowing your subject

You need to know your subject well in order to talk about it confidently. Although you should not pack too much material into a short speech, you need to speak knowledgeably to engage your audience. In preparing your speech, do some research to know what evidence will support your points, whether statistics, visuals, expert testimony, or something else. The more you know about your subject, the more comfortable you'll be in speaking about it.

Developing a clear structure

A good presentation is easy to follow because it has a clear beginning, middle, and end. In your introduction, preview the purpose and structure of your presentation and the question or problem you are addressing so that your audience can anticipate where you are going. Start with an opening hook: a surprising fact, a brief but vivid story, or an engaging question. For an informative speech, organize the body in a way that helps your audience remember key points of information. For a persuasive speech, organize so that you build enthusiasm for your position. And conclude your presentation by giving listeners a sense of completion. Restate the key points, and borrow phrasing or an image from your opening to make the speech come full circle.

Using signposts and repetition

As you speak, use signposts to remind the audience of your purpose and key points. Signposts, like transitions in writing, guide listeners ("The shift to online news has three important benefits for consumers") and help them to understand the transition from one point to the next ("The second benefit is . . ."). By repeating phrases, you emphasize the importance of key points and help listeners remember them. For more on transitions and repetition, see C3-c.

Writing for the ear, not the eye

Use an engaging, lively style so that the audience will enjoy listening to you. Be sure to use straightforward language that's easy on the ear, not too complicated or too abstract. Occasionally remind listeners of your main point, and keep your sentences short and direct so that listeners can easily follow your presentation. In the following example, the writer adapts a single essay sentence for a speech by breaking it into smaller chunks, engaging the audience with a question, and using plainer language.

SENTENCE FROM AN ARGUMENT ESSAY

In 2006, the enormous contributions of citizen journalists were recognized when the New Orleans *Times-Picayune* received the Pulitzer Prize in public service for its online coverage — largely citizen-generated — of Hurricane Katrina.

ESSAY MATERIAL ADAPTED FOR A SPEECH

The New Orleans *Times-Picayune* newspaper won the 2006 Pulitzer Prize in public service. Why? For its online news about Hurricane Katrina — news generated by ordinary people.

Integrating sources with signal phrases

As you speak, be sure to acknowledge your sources with signal phrases ("According to *New York Times* columnist David Brooks . . ."). If you have slides, you can include signal phrases or citations on the slides. For more on integrating and citing sources, see MLA-3 and MLA-4, APA-3 and APA-4, or CMS-3 and CMS-4, depending on the required style.

Using visuals and multimedia purposefully

Well-chosen visuals, video clips, or audio clips can enhance your presentation and add variety. For example, a photograph can highlight an environmental problem, a line graph can quickly show a trend over time, and a brief video clip can capture listeners' attention.

Visuals and multimedia convey information powerfully, but you need to consider how they support your purpose and how your audience will respond. Too many visuals can be distracting, especially when they are difficult to read or don't convey a clear message, so be sure each visual serves a specific purpose. Multimedia can overwhelm a presentation and leave you without sufficient time to achieve your goals. As in most aspects of life, balance is essential.

A5-c Remix a written essay for an oral presentation.

You may be asked to revise an essay into a spoken presentation. Compare the first paragraph of Sam Jacobs's essay (A4-h) with the opening lines for his presentation below. Notice the important adjustments he made in preparing a speaking script from his argument essay.

Good afternoon, everyone. I'm Sam Jacobs.

> Friendly opening establishes a relationship with the audience.

Jacobs starts with his key question and engages the audience immediately.

Today I want to explore this question: How do consumers benefit from reading news online? But first let me have a quick show of hands: How many of you read news online? If you answered yes, you are part of the 71% of young Americans, ages 18 to 29, who read their news online, according to the Pew Research Center. We've grown up in a digital generation, consuming news on every possible mobile device, especially our cell phones. Most of us don't miss the newspaper arriving on the doorstep every morning. And because we expect to read news online, we take it for granted. But if we take it for granted, we might miss the benefits of participating as producers of news, not simply as consumers. The three benefits I want to explore are . . .

Jacobs uses a source responsibly and integrates it well.

> Establishes common ground with the audience.

> Jacobs repeats words and phrases for emphasis and uses signposts to make it easier for his listeners to follow his ideas.

A6 Writing in the disciplines

- Evidence typically used in various disciplines **103**

College courses introduce you to the thinking of scholars in many disciplines, such as the humanities (literature, music, art), the social sciences (psychology, anthropology, sociology), and the sciences (biology, physics, chemistry). No matter what you study, you will be asked to write for a variety of audiences in a variety of formats and to practice the methods used by the discipline's scholars and practitioners. In a criminal justice course, for example, you may be asked to write a policy memo or a legal brief; in a nursing course, you may be asked to write a treatment plan or a case study. To write in these courses is to think like a criminologist or a nurse and to engage in the debates of the discipline.

A6-a Find commonalities across disciplines.

Good writing in any field needs to communicate the writer's purpose to an audience and to explore an engaging question about a subject. Effective writers make an argument and support their claims with evidence. Writers in most fields show readers the thesis they're developing (or, in the sciences, the hypothesis they're testing) and counter the objections of other writers. All disciplines require writers to document where they found their evidence and from whom they borrowed ideas.

A6-b Recognize the questions writers in a discipline ask.

Disciplines are characterized by the kinds of questions their scholars and practitioners attempt to answer. For example, social scientists, who analyze human behavior, might ask about the factors that cause people to act in certain ways. Historians, who seek an understanding of the past, often ask about the causes and effects of events and about the connections between current and past events.

Whenever you write for a college course, try to determine the kinds of questions scholars in the field might ask about a topic. You can find clues in assigned readings, lecture topics, discussion groups, and the paper assignment itself.

A6-c Understand the kinds of evidence writers in a discipline use.

Regardless of the discipline in which you're writing, you must support any claims with evidence — facts, data, examples, and expert opinion.

The kinds of evidence used in different disciplines commonly overlap. Students of geography, media studies, and political science, for example, might use census data to explore different topics. The evidence that one discipline values, however, might not be sufficient to support an interpretation or a conclusion in another field. You might use interviews in an anthropology paper, for example, but such evidence would be irrelevant in a biology lab report. The box in this section lists the kinds of evidence used in various disciplines.

What counts as evidence in various disciplines?

Humanities: literature, art, film, music, philosophy

- Passages of text or lines of a poem
- Passages of a musical composition
- Details from an image or a work of art
- Critical essays that analyze original works

Humanities: history

- Primary sources such as photographs, letters, maps, and government documents
- Scholarly books and articles that interpret evidence

Social sciences: psychology, sociology, political science, anthropology

- Data from original experiments
- Results of field research such as interviews or surveys
- Statistics from government agencies
- Scholarly books and articles that interpret findings from other researchers' studies
- Primary sources such as maps, objects, artifacts, or government documents

Sciences: biology, chemistry, physics

- Data from original experiments
- Models, diagrams, or animations
- Notes from lab or clinical work
- Scholarly articles that report findings from experiments

A6-d Become familiar with a discipline's language conventions.

Every discipline has a specialized vocabulary. As you read the articles and books in a field, you'll notice certain words and phrases that come up repeatedly. Sociologists, for example, use terms such as *independent variables* and *dyads* to describe social phenomena; computer scientists might refer to *algorithm design* and *loop invariants* to describe programming methods. Practitioners in health fields such as nursing use terms like *treatment plan* and *systemic assessment* to describe patient care. Use discipline-specific terms only when you are certain that you and your readers understand their meaning.

A6-e Use a discipline's preferred citation style.

In any discipline, you must give credit to those whose ideas or words you have borrowed. It is your responsibility to avoid plagiarism by citing sources honestly and accurately.

While all disciplines emphasize careful documentation, each follows a particular system of citation that its members have agreed on. Writers in the humanities usually use the system established by the Modern Language Association (MLA). Scholars in some social sciences, such as psychology and anthropology, follow the style guidelines of the American Psychological Association (APA). Scholars in history and in some humanities typically follow *The Chicago Manual of Style*. For guidance on using the MLA, APA, or CMS (*Chicago*) format, see the appropriate tabbed sections in this book.

Researched Writing

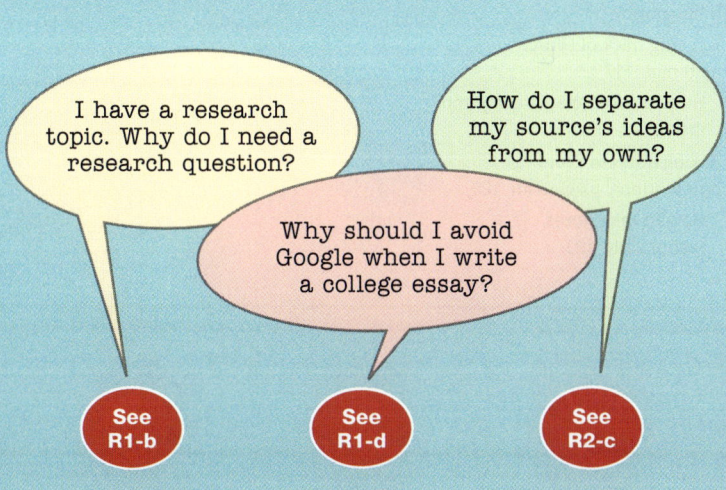

I have a research topic. Why do I need a research question?

See R1-b

Why should I avoid Google when I write a college essay?

See R1-d

How do I separate my source's ideas from my own?

See R2-c

R Researched Writing

A college research assignment asks you to pose questions worth exploring, read widely in search of possible answers, interpret what you read, draw reasoned conclusions, and support those conclusions with evidence. In short, it asks you to enter a research conversation by being *in* conversation with other writers and thinkers who have explored and studied your topic. As you listen to and learn from the voices already in the conversation, you'll find entry points where you can add your own insights and ideas.

R1 Thinking like a researcher; gathering sources

- How to enter a research conversation **110**
- Testing your research question **111**
- How to go beyond a Google search **116**

Keep an open mind throughout the research process, and enjoy the detective work of finding answers to questions that matter to you. Take time to discover what has been written about your topic and to uncover what's missing and needs to be questioned and researched.

R1-a Manage the project.

When you begin a research project, you will need to understand the assignment, choose a direction, and ask questions about your topic. The following tips will help you manage the beginning phase of research.

Managing time

When you receive your assignment, set a realistic schedule of deadlines. Think about how much time you might need for each step of your project. One student created a calendar to map out her tasks for a paper, keeping in mind that some tasks might overlap or need to be repeated.

Sample calendar for a research assignment

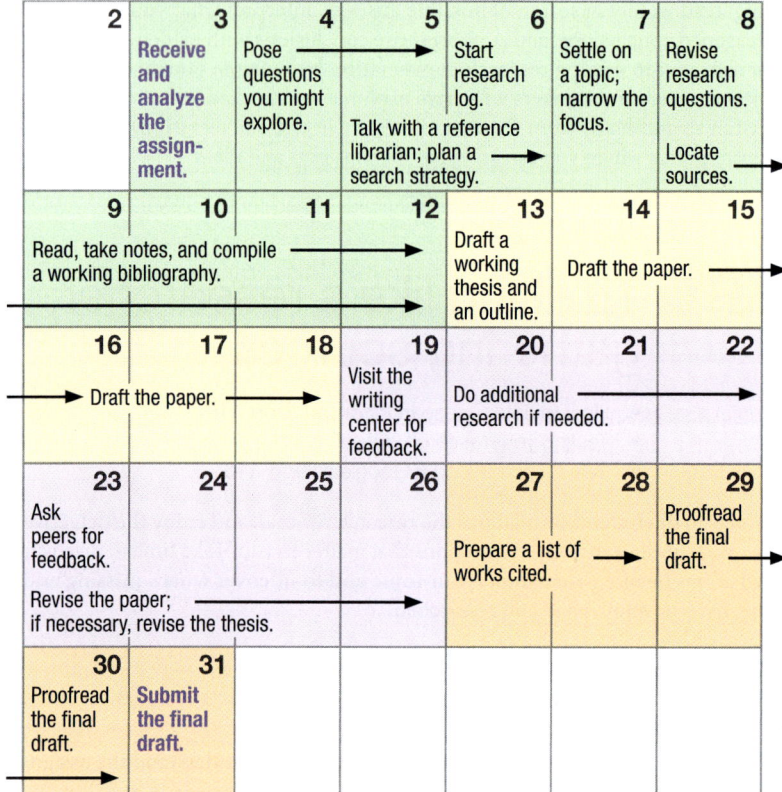

2	3	4	5	6	7	8
	Receive and analyze the assignment.	Pose questions you might explore. →	→ Talk with a reference librarian; plan a → search strategy.	Start research log.	Settle on a topic; narrow the focus.	Revise research questions. Locate sources. →

9	10	11	12	13	14	15
Read, take notes, and compile a working bibliography. → →				Draft a working thesis and an outline.	Draft the paper.	→

16	17	18	19	20	21	22
→ Draft the paper. →			Visit the writing center for feedback.	Do additional → research if needed.		→

23	24	25	26	27	28	29
Ask peers for feedback. Revise the paper; → if necessary, revise the thesis.				Prepare a list of works cited. →		Proofread the final draft. →

30	31					
Proofread the final draft. →	Submit the final draft.					

Getting the big picture

As you consider a possible research topic, take time to read a few sources to gain an overview of your topic. Ask yourself questions such as these:

- What aspects of the topic are generating the most debate?
- Why and how are people disagreeing?
- Which arguments and approaches seem worth exploring?

Keeping a research log

Research is a process. As your topic evolves, you may find yourself asking new questions that require you to create a new search strategy, find additional sources, or revise your initial assumptions. A research log — a hard-copy notebook or a digital file — helps you maintain records of the sources you read and your questions and ideas about those sources.

R1-b Pose questions worth exploring.

Every research project starts with questions. Try using *who, what, when, where, how,* and *why* to form research questions for your project.

- **Who** is responsible for the contaminated drinking water in Flint, Michigan?
- **What** happens to the arts without public funding?
- **How** can nutritional food labels be redesigned so that they inform rather than confuse consumers?
- **Why** are boys diagnosed with attention deficit disorder more often than girls are?

Choosing a focused question

If your initial question is too broad, given the length of the paper you plan to write, look for ways to narrow and focus your question.

TOO BROAD	NARROWER
What are the benefits of higher tariffs on imported cars?	**How** will higher tariffs on imported cars create new auto industry jobs and help US carmakers become more profitable?

Choosing a debatable question

Your research paper will be more interesting to both you and your audience if you ask a question that is open to debate, not a question that leads to a report or a list of facts. A *why* or *how* question most often leads to a researched argument and engages you and your readers in a debate with multiple perspectives.

TOO FACTUAL	DEBATABLE
What percentage of state police departments use body cameras?	**How** has the widespread use of body cameras changed encounters between officers and civilians?

Choosing a question grounded in evidence

For most college courses, the central argument of a research paper should be grounded in evidence, not in personal preferences or opinions. Your question should lead you to evidence, not to a defense of your beliefs.

TOO DEPENDENT ON PERSONAL OPINION	GROUNDED IN EVIDENCE
Do medical scientists have the right to experiment on animals?	**How** have technical breakthroughs made medical experiments on animals increasingly unnecessary?

Enter a research conversation

A college research project asks you to be in conversation with writers and researchers who have studied your topic — responding to their ideas and arguments and contributing your own insights to move the conversation forward. As you ask preliminary research questions, you may wonder where and how to step into a research conversation.

1 **Identify the experts and ideas in the conversation.** Ask: Who are the major writers and most influential people researching your topic? What are their credentials? What positions have they taken? How and why do the experts disagree?

2 **Identify any gaps in the conversation.** What is missing? Where are the gaps in the existing research? What questions haven't been asked yet? What positions need to be challenged?

3 **Try using sentence starters** to help you find a point of entry.

- *On one side of the debate is position X, and on the other side is Y, but there is a middle position: _____.*

- *The conventional view about the problem needs to be challenged because _____.*

- *Key details in this debate that have been overlooked are _____.*

- *Researchers have drawn conclusion X from the evidence, but one could also draw a different conclusion: _____.*

Writing for an audience

Follow your curiosity, but think about your readers, too. Ask yourself: *How will my research question engage readers? Why will readers think the question is worth asking? How might my research help readers understand a topic they care about?* Frame your research question to show readers why it needs to be asked — and why the answer matters to them.

Testing your research question

Once you have a tentative research question, check to see that it is interesting, provocative, and flexible enough to pursue.

- Does your question allow you to research a topic that interests you?

- Does your question give you (and your readers) an opportunity to think about your topic in a new way?

- Is the question debatable and flexible enough to allow for many possible answers?

- Can you answer the "So what?" question (see p. 9) to show why the question needs to be asked and why the answer is worth knowing?

> **How can I find a gap in a research debate?**
>
> ⭐ **NOTE TO SELF**
>
> * Study the debate around my topic; identify the big burning questions others have asked.
> * Think like a mediator: Is there any common ground that can bridge the disagreements?
> * Think like a scientist: Is there a group of people the research doesn't address?
> * Think like a lawyer: Look closely at the evidence to see whether there are assumptions or definitions I can challenge or question.

R1-c Map out a search strategy.

Before you search for sources, think about what kinds of sources will be appropriate for your project. Considering the kinds of sources you need will help you develop a search strategy — a systematic plan for locating sources. Try to cast a wide net in your search strategy to learn about what aspects of your topic are generating the most debate.

No single search strategy works for every topic. For some topics, it may be useful to search for information in newspapers, government publications, films, and websites. For others, the best sources might be scholarly journals and books, research reports, and specialized reference works. Still other topics might be enhanced by field research — interviews, surveys, or observation.

With the help of a librarian, each of the students whose research essays appear in this handbook constructed a search strategy appropriate for his or her research question.

Researcher Sophie Harba
(See her full paper in MLA-5b.)

CAIA Image/Sam Edwards/Getty Images

Research question Why should (or why shouldn't) the government enact laws to regulate healthy eating choices?

Search strategy

- Search the web to locate current news, government publications, and information from organizations that focus on government regulation of food.
- Check a library database for current peer-reviewed research articles.
- Use the library catalog to search for a recently published book that was cited by a source.

Researcher April Bo Wang (See her full paper in APA-5b.)

Research question How can technology facilitate a shift from teacher-delivered to student-centered learning?

Search strategy

- Search Google Scholar and *CQ Researcher* to see which aspects of the question are generating debate.
- View a TED talk to deepen her understanding of education technology.
- Use specialized databases related to education and technology to search for studies and scholarly articles.

Researcher Ned Bishop (See pages from his paper in CMS-5b.)

Research question To what extent should Major General Nathan Bedford Forrest be held accountable for the massacre of Union troops at Fort Pillow?

Search strategy

- Locate books through the library's online catalog.

- Use specialized history databases to locate scholarly articles and newspaper articles from 1864.

- Use the Library of Congress site and other websites to track down additional primary documents mentioned in his sources.

R1-d Search efficiently; master a few shortcuts to finding good sources.

You can save yourself time by becoming an efficient searcher of library databases and the web.

Distinguishing between primary and secondary sources

As you search for sources, determine whether you are looking at a primary or a secondary source.

Primary source   letter, diary, film, legislative bill, laboratory study, field research report, speech, eyewitness account, poem, short story, novel

Secondary source   commentary on or review or interpretation of a primary source by another writer

Although a primary source is not necessarily more reliable than a secondary source, it has the advantage of being a firsthand account. You can better evaluate what a secondary source says if you have read any primary source it discusses.

Using the library

The website hosted by your college library links to databases and other references containing articles, studies, and reports written by key researchers. Use your library's resources, designed for academic researchers, to find the most authoritative sources for your project.

Using the web

When conducting searches, use terms that are as specific as possible. The keywords you use will determine the quality of the results you see. Use clues in what you find (such as websites of organizations or government agencies that seem informative) to refine your search.

Using bibliographies and citations as shortcuts

Scholarly books and articles list the works the author has cited, usually at the end. Skimming these lists is a useful shortcut for finding additional reliable sources on your topic. Let one source lead you to the next. Following the trail of citations may lead you to helpful sources and a network of relevant research about your topic.

Check URLs for clues about sponsorship

Sometimes a web search brings you to a page that looks useful, but you find it difficult to tell whether it's legitimate. You may find it useful to shorten a longer URL to its root address — one that ends with .org, .gov, .edu, or .com, for example — so that you can make a better judgment about the usefulness of the content of the website or web page.

R1-e Write a research proposal.

One effective way to manage your project and focus your thinking is to write a research proposal. A proposal gives you an opportunity to look back — to remind yourself why you chose your topic — and to look forward — to predict any difficulties or obstacles that might arise during your project.

The following questions will help you organize your proposal.

- **Research question:** What question will you be exploring? Why does this question need to be asked? What do you hope to learn from the project?
- **Research conversation:** What have you learned so far about the debate or the specific research conversation you will enter? What entry point have you found to offer your own insights and ideas?

- **Search strategy:** What kinds of sources will you use to explore your question? What sources will be most useful, and why? How will you locate a variety of sources (primary/secondary, textual/visual)?
- **Research challenges:** What challenges, if any, do you anticipate (locating sufficient sources, managing the project, finding a position to take)? What resources are available to help you meet these challenges?

R1-f Conduct field research, if appropriate.

Your own field research can enhance or be the focus of a writing project. For a composition class, for example, you might interview a local politician about a current issue, such as the initiation of a city bike-share program. For a sociology class, you might conduct a survey about campus trends in community service.

NOTE: Colleges and universities often require researchers to submit projects to an institutional review board (IRB) if the research involves human subjects outside a classroom setting. Before administering a survey or conducting other fieldwork, check with your instructor to see whether IRB approval is required.

Interviewing

Interviews can often shed new light on a topic. Look for an expert who has firsthand knowledge of the subject, or seek out a key participant whose personal experience will provide a valuable perspective on your topic. Ask open questions that lead to facts, anecdotes, and vivid details that will add a meaningful dimension to your paper.

Using sources responsibly   When quoting your source (the interviewee), be accurate and fair. Do not change the meaning of your interviewee's words or take them out of context. If your interviewee grants permission, record your interview so you can review the accuracy of any quotations and the context in which they were spoken.

Conducting a survey

For some topics, you may find it useful to survey opinions or practices through a written questionnaire, a phone or email poll, or questions posted on a social media site. Many people resist long questionnaires, so for a good response rate, limit your questions with your purpose in mind.

Surveys with yes/no questions or multiple-choice options can be completed quickly, and the results are easy to tally, but you may also want to ask a few open-ended questions to invite more individual responses.

Go beyond a Google search

You might start with Google to gain an overview of your topic, but relying on the search engine to choose your sources isn't a research strategy. Good research involves going beyond the information available from a quick Google search. To locate reliable, authoritative sources, be strategic about *how* and *where* to search.

1 **Familiarize yourself with the research conversation.** Identify the current debate about the topic you have chosen and the most influential writers and experts in the debate. Where is the research conversation happening? In scholarly sources? Government agencies? The popular media?

2 **Generate keywords to focus your search.** Use specific words and combinations to search. Add words such as *debate*, *disagreements*, *proponents*, or *opponents* to track down the various positions in the research conversation. Use a journalist's questions — Who? When? Where? What? How? Why? — to refine a search.

3 **Search discipline-specific databases available through your school library** to locate carefully chosen scholarly (peer-reviewed) content that doesn't appear in search results on the open web. Use databases such as JSTOR and Academic Search Premier, designed for academic researchers, to locate sources in the most influential publications.

4 **If your topic has been in the news, try *CQ Researcher*,** available through most college libraries. Its brief articles provide pro/con arguments on current controversies in criminal justice, law, environment, technology, health, and education.

5 **Explore the Pew Research Center** (pewresearch.org), which sponsors original research and nonpartisan discussions of findings and trends in a wide range of academic fields.

R2 Managing information; taking notes responsibly

- Information to collect for a working bibliography **118**
- How to avoid plagiarizing from the web **119**
- How to take notes responsibly **123**

An effective researcher is a good record keeper. Whether you decide to keep records on paper or on a computer or mobile device, you will need methods for managing information: maintaining a working bibliography (see R2-a), keeping track of source materials (see R2-b), and taking notes without plagiarizing your sources (see R2-c).

R2-a Maintain a working bibliography.

Keep a record of sources you read, listen to, or view. This record, called a *working bibliography*, will help you keep track of publication information for the sources you might use so that you can easily refer to them as you write and also compile a list of works cited. The format of this list depends on the documentation style you are using (for MLA style, see MLA-4; for APA style, see APA-4; for CMS style, see CMS-4). See R3-d for advice on using your working bibliography as the basis for an annotated bibliography.

R2-b Keep track of source materials.

Save a copy of each potential source as you conduct your research. Many database services will allow you to email, text, save, or print citations or full texts, and you can easily download, copy, or take screen shots of information from the web. It is always a good idea to use browser bookmarks and make a folder for your research assignment to save sources.

Working with hard copies, screen shots, or files — as opposed to relying on memory or hastily written notes — lets you annotate each source as you read. You also reduce the chances of unintentional plagiarism since you will be able to compare your use of a source in your paper with the actual source, not just with your notes.

Information to collect for a working bibliography

For an article

- All authors of the article
- Title and subtitle of the article
- Title of the journal, magazine, or newspaper
- Date; volume, issue, page, or other numbers
- Date you accessed the source (for an online source that lists no publication date)

For an article retrieved from a database (in addition to preceding information)

- Name of the database
- Accession number or other number assigned by the database
- Digital object identifier (DOI), if there is one
- URL of the database home page or of the journal's home page, if there is no DOI

For a web source (including visual, audio, and multimedia sources)

- All authors, editors, or contributors to the source
- Title and subtitle of the source
- Title of the longer work, if the source is contained in a longer work
- Title of the website
- Print publication information for the source, if available
- Online page or paragraph numbers or other retrieval information (such as a time stamp or slide number)
- Date of online publication or latest update
- Sponsor or publisher of the site
- Date you accessed the source (for an undated source)
- URL or permalink for the page on which the source appears

For an entire book

- All authors; any editors or translators
- Title and subtitle
- Edition, if not the first
- Publication information: city, publisher, date, and format
- Date you accessed the source (for an undated online book)

Avoid plagiarizing from the web

1 **Understand what plagiarism is.** When you use another author's intellectual property (language, visuals, or ideas) in your own writing without giving proper credit, you engage in a kind of academic dishonesty called *plagiarism*.

2 **Treat online sources as someone else's intellectual property.** Language, data, or images that you find on the web must be cited, even if the material is publicly accessible on free sites or social media, is on a government website, or is in the public domain (which includes older works no longer protected by copyright law).

3 **Keep track of words and ideas borrowed from sources.** When you copy and paste passages from online sources, put quotation marks around any text that you have copied. Develop a system for distinguishing your words and ideas from anything you've summarized, paraphrased, or quoted.

4 **Create a complete bibliographic entry for each source to keep track of publication information.** From the start of your research project, maintain accurate records for all online sources you read, listen to, or view.

R2-c As you take notes, avoid unintentional plagiarism.

Plagiarism, using someone's words or ideas without giving credit, is often accidental. After spending so much time thinking through your topic and reading sources, it's easy to forget where a helpful idea came from or that the idea wasn't yours to begin with. Even if you half-copy an author's sentences — either by mixing the author's phrases with your own without using quotation marks or by plugging your synonyms into an author's sentence structure — you are plagiarizing.

To take notes responsibly, make sure you grasp the ideas in the source. Circle words or terms that you don't understand and look them up. Ask these questions: What is the meaning of the source? What is the argument? What is the evidence? Then, resist the temptation to look at the source as you take notes — except when you are quoting. Keep the source close by so that you can check for accuracy, but don't try to put ideas in your own words with the source's sentences in front of you. When you need to quote a source, make sure you copy the words exactly and put quotation marks around them.

Summarizing and paraphrasing ideas and quoting exact language are three ways of taking notes without unintentionally plagiarizing. See A1-c for how to write a summary and MLA-3a for how to paraphrase. Also see MLA-3 for when to summarize, paraphrase, or quote.

SUMMARIZING:
A summary, written in your own words, condenses information and captures main ideas, reducing a chapter to a short paragraph or a paragraph to a single sentence.

A summary captures the main idea of a source.

PARAPHRASING:
Like a summary, a paraphrase is written in your own words, but it restates information in roughly the same number of words as in the original source, using different sentence structure.

A paraphrase represents a source in a writer's own words and sentence structures.

QUOTING:
A quotation consists of the exact words from a source. Put all quoted material in quotation marks.

A quotation represents a source exactly.

Below is a passage about marine pollution from a National Oceanic and Atmospheric Administration (NOAA) website. Following the passage are a student's annotations — in other words, notes and questions that help him figure out meaning — and then examples of a summary, a paraphrase, and a quotation related to the original source.

ORIGINAL SOURCE

A question that is often posed to the NOAA Marine Debris Program (MDP) is "How much debris is actually out there?" The MDP has recognized the need for this answer as well as the growing interest and value of citizen science. To that end, the MDP is developing and testing two types of monitoring and assessment protocols: 1) rigorous scientific survey and 2) volunteer at-sea visual survey. These types of monitoring programs are necessary in order to compare marine debris composition, abundance, distribution, movement, and impact data on national and global scales.

> — NOAA Marine Debris Program. "Efforts and Activities Related to the 'Garbage Patches.'" *Marine Debris*, 2012, pm22100.net/ docs/pdf/enercoop/pollutions/noaa-plastiques.pdf

ORIGINAL SOURCE WITH STUDENT ANNOTATIONS

╭ by whom?   ocean ⌐   ╭ trash
A question that is often posed to the NOAA Marine Debris

Program (MDP) is "How much debris is actually out there?" The

MDP has recognized the need for this answer as well as the

                    aha
growing interest and value of citizen science. To that end, the MDP

is developing and testing two types of monitoring and assessment
            ways of gathering information
protocols: 1) rigorous scientific survey and 2) volunteer at-sea visual

survey. These types of monitoring programs are necessary in order
            kinds of materials ⌐   ╭ how much?
to compare marine debris composition, abundance, distribution,
            ╭ why it matters
movement, and impact data on national and global scales.

SUMMARY

Having to field citizens' questions about the size of debris fields in Earth's oceans, the Marine Debris Program, an arm of the US National Oceanic and Atmospheric Administration, is currently implementing methods to monitor and draw conclusions about our oceans' patches of pollution (NOAA).

PARAPHRASE

Citizens concerned and curious about the amount, makeup, and locations of debris patches in our oceans have been pressing NOAA's Marine Debris Program for answers. In response, the organization is preparing to implement plans and standards for expert study and nonexpert observation, both of which will yield results that will be helpful in determining the significance of the pollution problem (NOAA).

QUOTATION

The NOAA Marine Debris Program has noted that, as our oceans become increasingly polluted, surveillance is "necessary in order to compare marine debris composition, abundance, distribution,movement, and impact data on national and global scales."

NOTE: Because the source is from an unpaginated website, the in-text citation includes only the author's name placed either in parentheses (as in the first two examples above) or in a signal phrase (as in the third example).

In a second pass through the source, the student would engage more with the ideas and start to plan next steps for his research. He might write annotations such as these:

Find out what kind of debris is most harmful

Seems like a good idea to get citizens involved — marine debris is vast

Quote these words from source to show why surveillance is necessary

Take notes responsibly

1 **Understand the ideas in the source.** Start by determining the purpose and meaning of the source. Focus on the overall ideas in the source. Ask: What is the argument? What is the evidence?

2 **Keep the source close by to check for accuracy,** but resist the temptation to look at the source as you take notes — except when you are quoting.

3 **Use quotation marks around any borrowed words or phrases.** Copy the borrowed words exactly and keep complete bibliographic information for each source.

4 **Develop an organized system** to distinguish your insights and ideas from those of the source. Take time to note how you might use a source and what it will contribute to answering your research question.

5 **Create a method to label and identify** when you have summarized a text or its data or paraphrased or quoted an author's words.

6 **Record complete bibliographic information for each source** so you can give credit to the source, cite it accurately, and find it again easily.

R3 Evaluating sources

You will often locate far more potential sources on your topic than you will have time to read. Your challenge then is to determine what kinds of sources you need and what you need these sources to do — and to select a reasonable number of trustworthy sources. This kind of decision making is referred to as *evaluating sources.*

R3-a Evaluate the reliability and usefulness of a source.

Using reliable sources adds to your credibility and authority as a writer. The following questions will help you judge the reliability and usefulness of sources you might use to support your research project. Ideally, you want to choose sources that are relevant, current, credible, and bias-free.

Relevance Is the source clearly related to your research topic and your argument? Will your readers understand why you've included the source in your paper? What does the source add to your understanding of the research conversation? How does it help you answer your research question?

Currency How recent is the source? Is the information up to date? Does your research topic require current information? Will your research benefit from consulting older sources, including primary sources from a historical period?

Credibility Where does the source come from? Who is the author? What are the author's credentials? How accurate and trustworthy is the information? Who published the source? Is it an academic, peer-reviewed source? If the source is authored by an organization, what research has the organization done to support its claims? Are the source's ideas and research cited by other writers?

Bias Does the author endorse political or religious views that could affect objectivity? Are evidence and counterevidence presented in a fair and objective way? Is the author engaging in a scholarly debate or giving a personal point of view?

Detect false and misleading sources

Sources can distort information or spread misinformation by taking information out of context or by promoting opinions as facts. As you evaluate sources, determine authenticity: Can the information be verified? Is the source reliable? You can verify facts and quotations by reading multiple sources and gathering a variety of perspectives. Because information and misinformation live side by side on the web, you need to read critically to determine the truth.

1 **Consider the source.** Is more than one source covering the topic? Is the author anonymous or named? What can you learn about the author's credentials and the mission of a site from checking the "About Us" tab? Does the site present only one side of an issue? Be skeptical if the source is the only one reporting the story.

2 **Examine the source's language.** Is the language informal? Does the source overuse superlatives such as *most*, *best*, or *worst*? Does it use the second-person pronoun *you*?

3 **Question the seriousness of the source.** Is the source attempting to mimic a reliable source? Is it possible that the source is satirical and humorous and is not intended to be read as factual?

4 **Fact-check the information.** Can the facts be objectively verified? If the conclusions of a research study are cited, find the study to verify; if an authority is quoted, research the original source of the quotation, if possible, to see whether the quotation was taken out of context. Also, be skeptical if a source reports a research study but doesn't quote the study's principal investigator or other respected researchers.

5 **Pay attention to the URL.** Among the more credible sites are those sponsored by higher education (.edu), nonprofit groups (.org), and government agencies (.gov). Established news organizations have standard domain names. Fake sites often use web addresses such as "Newslo" or "com.co" that imitate the addresses of real sites, and they package information with misinformation to make themselves look authentic.

6 **Note your biases.** If an article makes you angry or challenges your beliefs, or if it confirms your beliefs by ignoring evidence to the contrary, take notice, and try to be as objective as possible. Learn about an issue from reliable sources and from multiple perspectives.

Determining whether a source is scholarly

Scholarly sources are written by experts for a knowledgeable audience and usually go into more depth than books and articles written for a general audience. Scholarly sources are sometimes called *refereed* or *peer-reviewed* because the work is evaluated by experts in the field before publication.

To determine whether a source is scholarly, look for the following:

- Formal language and presentation
- Authors who are academics or scientists
- Footnotes or a bibliography documenting the works cited in the source
- Original research and interpretation (rather than a summary of other people's work)

R3-b Read with an open mind and a critical eye.

As you begin reading the sources you have chosen, keep an open mind. Do not let your personal beliefs or an initial working thesis statement prevent you from listening to new ideas and opposing viewpoints. Be curious about the wide range of positions in the research conversation you are entering. Your research question should guide you as you read your sources.

Reading like a researcher

To read like a researcher is to read with an open, curious mind, to find out not only what has been written about a topic but also what is missing from the research conversation.

- **Read carefully.** Read to understand and summarize the main ideas of a source and an author's point of view. Ask questions: What does the source say? What is the author's central claim or thesis? What evidence does the author use to support the thesis? What are the strengths of the source?
- **Read skeptically.** Read to examine an author's assumptions, evidence, and conclusions and to pose counterarguments. Ask questions: Are any of the author's arguments or conclusions problematic? Is the author's evidence persuasive and sufficient? Does the author make leaps in logic? Note *how* and *why* you agree or disagree with an author.

Reading like a researcher, *continued*

- **Read evaluatively.** Read to judge the usefulness of a source for your research project. You may disagree with an author's argument or use of evidence, but refuting the author's ideas will help you clarify your position. Ask questions: Is the author an expert on the topic? Will the source provide background information, lend authority, explain a concept, or offer counterevidence for your claims?

- **Read responsibly.** Take time to read the entire source and to understand its author's arguments, assumptions, and conclusions. Avoid taking quotations from the first few pages of a source before you understand whether the ideas are representative of the work as a whole.

R3-c Assess web sources with special care.

Before using a web source in your paper, make sure you know who created the material and for what purpose. Sources with reliable information can stand up to scrutiny. As you evaluate sources, ask questions about their reliability and purpose.

Evaluating a website: Checking reliability

1 This page on Internet monitoring and privacy appears on a website sponsored by the National Conference of State Legislatures (NCSL). The NCSL is a bipartisan group that functions as a clearinghouse of ideas and research of interest to state lawmakers. It is also a lobby for state issues before the US government. The URL ending .org marks this sponsor as a nonprofit organization.

2 A clear date of publication shows currency.

3 An "About Us" page confirms that this is a credible organization whose credentials can be verified.

Evaluating a website: Checking purpose

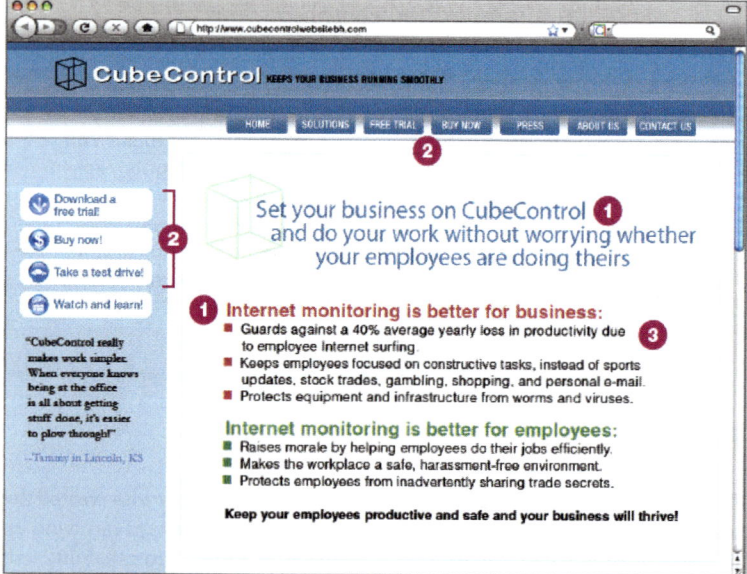

1 The site is sponsored by a company that specializes in employee-monitoring software.

2 Repeated links for trial downloads and purchase suggest the site's intended audience: consumers seeking to purchase software (probably not researchers seeking detailed information about employees' use of the Internet in the workplace).

3 The site appears to provide information and even shows statistics from studies, but ultimately the purpose of the site is to sell a product.

R3-d Construct an annotated bibliography.

Constructing an annotated bibliography allows you to summarize, evaluate, and record publication information for your sources before drafting your research paper. You summarize each source to understand its main ideas; you evaluate each source to assess how it contributes to your research project; and you record bibliographic information to keep track of publication details for each source.

NOTE TO SELF

What kinds of sources will help me answer my research question?

* Look for evidence to support my argument, but also find evidence that challenges my thinking (counterarguments).
* Use a source that will help me define any key terms.
* Think about how much background information my argument needs. Do I need a source for that?
* Figure out what roles I need my sources to play. Sources have to do more than just provide words to quote.

Tips for evaluating sources

Check for signs of bias

- Does the author or publisher endorse political or religious views that could affect objectivity?
- Is the author or publisher associated with a special-interest group, such as People for the Ethical Treatment of Animals (PETA) or the National Rifle Association (NRA), that might emphasize one side of an issue?
- Are alternative views presented and addressed? How fairly does the author treat opposing views?
- Does the author's language show signs of bias?

Bias doesn't always render a source not useful. Acknowledging bias when you see it helps you place the source in the context of the debate and in the context of your own purpose and audience.

Assess the writer's (or organization's) argument

- What is the author's central claim or thesis?
- How does the author support this claim — with relevant and sufficient evidence or with just a few anecdotes or emotional examples?
- Are statistics consistent with those you encounter in other sources? Does the author explain where the statistics come from?
- Are any of the author's assumptions questionable? Is the logic flawed?
- Does the author consider opposing arguments and refute them persuasively?

You want to find sources that both support your argument and present other arguments, but it helps to try to determine whether a source's argument has merit and is based on evidence.

Constructing an annotated bibliography focuses your attention on the most promising sources you've located, providing you with an opportunity to assess the usefulness of these sources as you reflect on *how* and *why* they will help you answer your research question. Take the following steps for each source in your annotated bibliography.

RECORD   Using whatever style your assignment requires, record the publication information for your source.

SUMMARIZE   Start by identifying the purpose and thesis of the source and the author's credentials. Summarize the source's main ideas and the evidence used to support these ideas. Summarizing gives you an opportunity to test your understanding of the source's meaning.

EVALUATE   Ask yourself what role a source might play and how it will contribute to your argument. Did it shape your thinking? Provide key evidence? Lend authority? Offer a counterargument? Evaluate how and why the source can help you answer your research question and support your position.

SAMPLE ANNOTATED BIBLIOGRAPHY ENTRY (MLA STYLE)

Resnik, David. "Trans Fat Bans and Human Freedom."

   American Journal of Bioethics, vol. 10, no. 3, Mar.   **citation**

   2010, pp. 27–32.

Type of source; author's name and credentials	In this scholarly article, bioethicist David Resnik argues that bans on unhealthy foods threaten our personal freedom. He claims that researchers
Summary presents the author's ideas and shows the student's understanding of the main points.	don't have enough evidence to know whether banning trans fats will save lives or money; all we know is that such bans restrict dietary choices. Resnik explains why most Americans oppose food restrictions, noting our multiethnic and regional food traditions as well as our resistance to government limitations on personal freedoms.
Evaluation judges the source's reliability and shows how the source contributes to the student's research.	Resnik offers a well-reasoned argument, but he goes too far by insisting that all proposed food restrictions will do more harm than good. This article contributes important perspectives on resistance to government intervention in food choice to advance public health.

summary

evaluation

How to write an annotated bibliography

Creating an **annotated bibliography** gives you an opportunity to summarize, evaluate, and record publication information for your sources before drafting your research paper. You summarize each source to understand its main ideas, and you evaluate each source for accuracy, quality, and relevance. Finally, you reflect, asking yourself how the source will contribute to your research project.

Key features

- **The list of sources, arranged in alphabetical order by author,** includes complete bibliographic information for each source.

- **A brief annotation or note for each source,** typically one hundred to two hundred words, is written in paragraph form and contains a summary and an evaluation.

- **The summary** of each source states the work's main ideas and key points briefly and accurately. The summary is written in the present tense, third person, directly and concisely. Summarizing helps you test your understanding of a source and restate its meaning responsibly.

- **The evaluation** of the source's role and usefulness in your project includes an assessment of the source's strengths and limitations, the author's qualifications and expertise, and the function of the source in your project. Evaluating a source helps you analyze how the source fits into your project and separate the source's ideas from your own.

Thinking ahead: Presenting or publishing

You may be asked to submit your annotated bibliography electronically. If this is the case, be sure that any entries for web sources include functioning links to the sources so that your reader can easily access them, if necessary.

Writing your annotated bibliography

1 Explore

For each source, begin by brainstorming responses to questions such as the following.

- What is the purpose of the source? Who is the author's intended audience?
- What is the author's thesis? What evidence supports the thesis?

- What qualifications and expertise does the author bring? Does the author have any biases or make any questionable assumptions?
- Why do you think this source is useful for your project?
- How does this source relate to the other sources in your bibliography?

❷ Draft

The following tips can help you draft one or more entries in your annotated bibliography.

- Arrange the sources in alphabetical order by author (or by title for works with no author).
- Provide consistent bibliographic information for each source. For the exact bibliographic format, see MLA-4b, APA-4b, or CMS-4c.
- Start your summary by identifying the thesis and purpose of the source as well as the credentials of the source's author.
- Keep your research question in mind. How does this source contribute to your project? How does it help you take your place in the conversation?

❸ Revise

Ask reviewers for specific feedback. Here are some questions to guide their comments.

- Is each source summarized clearly? Have you identified the author's main idea?
- For each source, have you made a clear judgment about how and why the source is useful for your project?
- Have you used quotation marks around exact words from a source?

MLA

MLA Style

MLA MLA Style

List of MLA in-text citation models

List of MLA works cited models

List of MLA works cited models, *continued*

MLA Style

In English and other humanities courses, you may be asked to use the Modern Language Association (MLA) system for documenting sources. When writing a research paper based on sources, you will follow three important conventions:

1. supporting a thesis statement (MLA-1)
2. citing your sources accurately and avoiding plagiarism (MLA-2)
3. integrating source material effectively (MLA-3)

Examples in this tabbed section are drawn from one student's research. Sophie Harba's research essay, in which she argues that state governments have the responsibility to set health policies and to regulate healthy eating choices, appears in section MLA-5b.

 MLA-1 Supporting a thesis

- Testing your thesis statement 138
- Sample graphic organizer for a researched argument 139

Once you have read a range of sources, considered your subject from different perspectives, and chosen an entry point in the research conversation (see R1-b), you are ready to focus your research paper by forming a thesis statement and supporting that thesis with well-organized evidence. (See also C1-c.)

MLA-1a Form a working thesis statement.

A thesis statement expresses your informed answer to your research question — an answer about which people might disagree. Start by developing a working thesis statement to help you narrow your ideas and clarify your purpose. As your ideas develop, you'll revise your working thesis to make it more specific and focused.

Here, for example, are student writer Sophie Harba's research question and working thesis statement.

RESEARCH QUESTION

Good start: It provides an answer to the question but doesn't show why the thesis matters.

Should state governments enact laws to regulate healthy eating choices?

WORKING THESIS STATEMENT

State governments have the responsibility to regulate healthy eating choices because of the rise of chronic diseases.

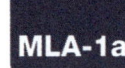

After you have written a rough draft and perhaps done more reading, you may decide to revise your thesis, as Harba did, to give it a sharper focus and to offer a "So what?" to show readers why the thesis matters. (See C1-c.)

More focused
thesis
announces a
clear position
and shows
readers why the
position matters.

REVISED THESIS STATEMENT

In the name of public health and safety, state governments have the responsibility to shape health policies and to regulate healthy eating choices, especially since doing so offers a potentially large social benefit for a relatively small cost.

In a research essay, readers are accustomed to seeing the thesis statement at the end of the first or second paragraph. Here is Harba's thesis in the context of her introduction. (See MLA-5b for the entire MLA paper.)

SAMPLE INTRODUCTION WITH THESIS STATEMENT

Introduction
opens with
a question
to engage
and hook
readers.

Should the government enact laws to regulate healthy eating choices? Many Americans would answer an emphatic "No," arguing that what and how much we eat should be left to individual choice rather than unreasonable laws. Others might argue that it would be unreasonable for the government not to enact legislation, given the rise of chronic diseases that result from harmful diets. In this debate, both the definition of reasonable regulations and the role of government to legislate food choices

Harba
introduces
a research
conversation
to show the
debate before
stating her
position.

Thesis
answers
the opening
question
and states
Harba's
position.

are at stake. In the name of public health and safety, state governments have the responsibility to shape health policies and to regulate healthy eating choices, especially since doing so offers a potentially large social benefit for a relatively small cost.

Testing your thesis statement

An effective thesis argues for a position in a debate. Keep the following guidelines in mind to develop an effective thesis statement.

- A thesis should be your answer to a question and should take a position that needs to be argued and supported. It should not be a statement of fact or a description. Make sure your position is debatable by anticipating opposing viewpoints and counterarguments.
- A thesis should match the scope of the research project. If your thesis is too broad, explore a subtopic of your original topic. If your thesis is too narrow, ask a research question that has more than one answer.

> **Testing your thesis statement,** *continued*
>
> - A thesis should be focused. Avoid vague words such as *interesting* or *good*. Use concrete language and make sure your thesis lets readers know your position.
> - A thesis should stand up to the "So what?" test. Ask yourself why readers should be interested in your essay and care about your thesis.

MLA-1b Organize ideas with a rough outline.

The body of your paper will consist of evidence in support of your thesis. Try sketching an informal plan to focus and organize your ideas. Sophie Harba, for example, used this simple plan to outline the structure of her argument.

INFORMAL OUTLINE

- Debates about the government's role in regulating food have a long history in the United States.
- Some experts argue that we should focus on the dangers of unhealthy eating habits and on preventing chronic diseases linked to diet.
- But food regulations are not a popular solution because many Americans object to government restrictions on personal choice.
- Food regulations designed to prevent chronic disease don't ask Americans to give up their freedom; they ask Americans to see health as a matter of public good.

After you have written a rough draft, a formal outline can help you test and fine-tune the organization of your argument. See C1-d to read Harba's formal outline.

To help organize your ideas, you might want to experiment with graphic organizers before and during the drafting of your paper. A fairly typical way for research writers to proceed is shown here, but of course your own assignment, purpose, audience, argument, and sources will determine the most effective way to organize and develop your paper.

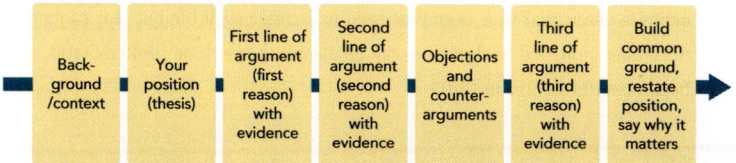

| Background /context | Your position (thesis) | First line of argument (first reason) with evidence | Second line of argument (second reason) with evidence | Objections and counter-arguments | Third line of argument (third reason) with evidence | Build common ground, restate position, say why it matters |

MLA-1c Consider how sources will contribute to your essay.

The source materials you have gathered can play many different roles to support your thesis and develop your argument. As you consider using a source, ask yourself what you learned from the source and how it might function to answer your research question.

HOW CAN SOURCES INFORM AND SUPPORT AN ARGUMENT?

Sources can provide context or background information	Sources can explain terms and concepts	Sources can support your claims	Sources can lend authority to your argument	Sources can help you understand and counter objections

Providing context or background information

Readers need some context and background information to anchor their understanding of your topic and the debate around it. Describing a research study or offering statistics can help readers grasp your topic's significance. Student writer Sophie Harba uses a source to give context for her topic, the benefits of laws designed to prevent chronic disease.

> To give just one example, Marion Nestle, New York University professor of nutrition and public health, notes that "a 1% reduction in intake of saturated fat across the population would prevent more than 30,000 cases of coronary heart disease annually and save more than a billion dollars in health care costs" (7).

Explaining terms or concepts

If readers are unfamiliar with a term or concept, you will want to define or explain it; or if your argument depends on a term with multiple meanings, you will want to explain your use of the term. Quoting or paraphrasing a source can help you define terms and concepts in accessible language. Harba defines the term *refined grains* as part of her claim that the typical American diet is getting less healthy over time.

> A diet that is low in nutritional value and high in sugars, fats, and refined grains — grains that have been processed to increase shelf life but that contain little fiber, iron, and B vitamins — can be damaging over time (United States, Department of Agriculture 36).

Supporting your claims

As you develop your argument, back up your assertions with facts, examples, and other evidence from your research. (See also A4-f.) Harba, for example, uses factual evidence to support her claim that the typical American diet is damaging.

> Michael Pollan, who has written extensively about Americans' unhealthy eating habits, notes that "[t]he Centers for Disease Control estimates that fully three quarters of US health care spending goes to treat chronic diseases, most of which are preventable and linked to diet: heart disease, stroke, type 2 diabetes, and at least a third of all cancers."

Lending authority to your argument

Expert opinion can add weight and credibility to your argument. (See also A4-f.) But don't rely on experts to make your argument for you. State your ideas in your own words and, when appropriate, cite the judgment of an authority in the field to support your position.

> Debates surrounding the government's role in regulating food have a long history in the United States. According to Lorine Goodwin, a food historian, nineteenth-century reformers who sought to purify the food supply were called "fanatics" and "radicals" by critics who argued that consumers should be free to buy and eat what they want (77).

Anticipating and countering objections

Do not ignore sources that seem contrary to your position. Instead, use them to give voice to opposing points of view and to state potential objections to your argument before you counter them (see A-4g). By anticipating her readers' argument that many Americans oppose laws that limit what they eat, Sophie Harba creates an opportunity to counter that objection and build common ground with her readers.

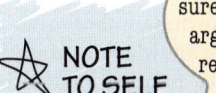
How can I make sure my researched argument doesn't read like a list?

NOTE TO SELF

* Avoid using only sources that support my thesis. I don't want the essay to be boring and one-dimensional.
* Try to round out my essay by using sources that touch on other positions in the debate.
* Don't forget that sources might help me define key terms or give context or background info.

> Why is the public largely resistant to laws that would limit unhealthy choices or penalize those choices with so-called fat taxes? Many consumers and civil rights advocates find such laws to

be an unreasonable restriction on individual freedom of choice. As health policy experts Mello and colleagues point out, opposition to food and beverage regulation is similar to the opposition to early tobacco legislation: the public views the issue as one of personal responsibility rather than one requiring government intervention (2602). In other words, if a person eats unhealthy food and becomes ill as a result, that is his or her choice. But those who favor legislation claim that freedom of choice is a myth because of the strong influence of food and beverage industry marketing on consumers' dietary habits.

Citing sources; avoiding plagiarism

- Writing for an audience **143**
- How to be a responsible research writer **144**

In a research paper, you draw on the work of other writers, and you must document their contributions by citing your sources. As an academic writer, you'll cite sources for two reasons:

1. to tell readers where your information comes from — so that they can assess its reliability and, if interested, find and read the original source
2. to give credit to the writers from whom you have borrowed words and ideas

You must include a citation when you quote from a source, when you summarize or paraphrase, and when you borrow facts that are not common knowledge. Borrowing another writer's language, sentence structure, or ideas without proper acknowledgment is plagiarism. The only exception is common knowledge — information that your readers may know or could easily locate in any number of general sources.

MLA-2a Understand how the MLA system works.

MLA style requires you to acknowledge your sources by using an in-text citation — a citation placed in parentheses within the body of your paper — to indicate the source of a quotation, paraphrase, or summary. The in-text citation points readers to a list of works cited at the end of your paper. There is a direct connection between the in-text citation and the alphabetical entry in your works cited list.

IN-TEXT CITATION

In-text citation points readers to the "Works Cited" list.

Bioethicist David Resnik emphasizes that such policies, despite their potential to make our society healthier, "open the door to excessive government control over food, which could restrict dietary choices, interfere with cultural, ethnic, and religious traditions, and exacerbate socioeconomic inequalities" (31).

Signal phrase names the author and gives credentials.

Material being cited is followed by a page number in parentheses (unless the source is unpaginated), followed by a period.

Works cited list at the end of the paper gives complete publication information for the source.

ENTRY IN THE LIST OF WORKS CITED

Resnik, David. "Trans Fat Bans and Human Freedom." *The American Journal of Bioethics*, vol. 10, no. 3, Mar. 2010, pp. 27–32.

MLA-2b Understand what plagiarism is.

In a research paper, you draw on the work of other writers. To be fair and responsible, you must document their contributions by citing your sources. When you acknowledge and document your sources, you avoid *plagiarism*, a form of academic dishonesty. The only exception to this requirement is common knowledge. When in doubt about what is or isn't common knowledge, acknowledge your source.

In general, these three acts are considered plagiarism:

1. failing to cite quotations and borrowed ideas
2. failing to enclose borrowed language in quotation marks
3. failing to put summaries and paraphrases in your own words and sentence structure

Definitions of plagiarism may vary; it's a good idea to find out how your school defines academic dishonesty.

Writing for an audience

You demonstrate your credibility, your *ethos*, by choosing the most trustworthy and reliable sources and showing readers how to find them. When your citations guide readers quickly to the sources of quoted, paraphrased, and summarized ideas, you show respect for your audience's interest in your research. Ask yourself two questions: How can I make my documentation useful to my readers? What would readers need to know to find each source themselves?

Be a responsible research writer

Using good citation habits is the best way to avoid plagiarizing sources and to demonstrate that you are a responsible researcher.

1 **Cite your sources as you write drafts.** Don't wait until your final draft is complete to add citations. Include a citation when you quote from a source, when you summarize or paraphrase, and when you borrow facts that are not common knowledge.

2 **Place quotation marks around direct quotations,** both in your notes and in your drafts.

3 **Check each quotation, summary, and paraphrase against the source** to make certain you aren't misrepresenting the source. For paraphrases, be sure that your language and sentence structure differ from those in the original passage.

4 **Provide a full citation in your works cited list.** It is not sufficient to cite a source only in the body of your paper; you must also provide complete publication information for each source in a list of works cited.

MLA-2c Use quotation marks around borrowed language.

To indicate that you are using a source's exact phrases or sentences, you must enclose them in quotation marks unless they have been set off from the text by indenting (see MLA-3b). To omit the quotation marks is to claim — falsely — that the language is your own, as in the following example. Such an omission is plagiarism even if you have cited the source.

ORIGINAL SOURCE

Although these policies may have a positive impact on human health, they open the door to excessive government control over food, which could restrict dietary choices, interfere with cultural, ethnic, and religious traditions, and exacerbate socioeconomic inequalities.

— David Resnik, "Trans Fat Bans and Human Freedom," p. 31

PLAGIARISM

Bioethicist David Resnik points out that government policies to ban trans fats may have a positive impact on human health, but they open the door to excessive government control over food, which could restrict dietary choices and interfere with cultural, ethnic, and religious traditions (31).

BORROWED LANGUAGE IN QUOTATION MARKS

Bioethicist David Resnik emphasizes that government policies to ban trans fats, despite their potential to make our society healthier, "open the door to excessive government control over food, which could restrict dietary choices [and] interfere with cultural, ethnic, and religious traditions" (31).

MLA-2d Put summaries and paraphrases in your own words.

A summary condenses information from a source; a paraphrase conveys the information using roughly the same number of words as the original source. When you summarize or paraphrase, it is not enough to name the source. You must restate the source's meaning using your own words and sentence structure. (See also R2-c and, if English is not your first language, M6.) Half-copying the author's sentences either by using the author's phrases in your own sentences without quotation marks or by plugging synonyms into the author's sentence structure (sometimes called *patchwriting*) is a form of plagiarism.

The first paraphrase of the following source is plagiarized, even though the source is cited, because the paraphrase borrows too much of its language from the original. The highlighted strings of words have been copied exactly (without quotation marks), and the writer has closely echoed the sentence structure of the source, merely substituting some synonyms.

ORIGINAL SOURCE

[A]ntiobesity laws encounter strong opposition from some quarters on the grounds that they constitute paternalistic intervention into lifestyle choices and enfeeble the notion of personal responsibility. Such arguments echo those made in the early days of tobacco regulation.
> — Michelle M. Mello et al., "Obesity — the New Frontier of Public Health Law," p. 2602

PLAGIARISM: UNACCEPTABLE BORROWING

Borrows too much language from the original and follows the sentence structure too closely.

Health policy experts Mello and colleagues argue that ==antiobesity laws encounter strong opposition from some quarters== because they interfere with ==lifestyle choices== and decrease the feeling of ==personal responsibility.== These arguments ==mirror those made in the early days of tobacco regulation== (2602).

To avoid plagiarizing an author's language, resist the temptation to look at the source while you are summarizing or paraphrasing. After you have read the passage you want to paraphrase, set the source aside. Ask yourself, "What is the author's meaning?" In your own words, state your understanding of the author's ideas. Then return to the source and check that you haven't used the author's language or sentence structure or misrepresented the author's ideas. Following these steps will help you avoid plagiarizing the source.

ACCEPTABLE PARAPHRASE

Student uses her own language and sentence structure in her paraphrase.

As health policy experts Mello and colleagues point out, opposition to food and beverage regulation is similar to the opposition to early tobacco legislation: the public views the issue as one of personal responsibility rather than one requiring government intervention (2602).

MLA-3 # Integrating sources

- How to paraphrase effectively **148–149**
- Using signal phrases in MLA papers **153**
- Using sentence guides to integrate sources **156–157**

Quotations, summaries, paraphrases, and facts will help you develop your argument, but they cannot speak for you. You need to find a balance between the words of your sources and your own voice, so that readers always know who is speaking in your paper. You can use several strategies to integrate sources into your paper while maintaining your own voice.

- Use sources as concisely as possible so that your own thinking and voice aren't lost (MLA-3a and MLA-3b).

- Use signal phrases to help you avoid dropping quotations into your paper without indicating the boundary between your words and the source's words (MLA-3c).

- Use language that shows readers how each source supports your argument and how the sources relate to one another (MLA-3d).

MLA-3a Summarize and paraphrase effectively.

In your academic writing, keep the emphasis on your ideas and your language; use your own words to summarize and paraphrase sources and to explain your points. Whether you choose to summarize or paraphrase a source depends on your purpose.

Summarizing

When you summarize a source, you express another writer's ideas in your own words, condensing the author's key points and using fewer words than the author.

WHEN TO SUMMARIZE

- When you want to state the source's main ideas simply and briefly in your own words

- When you want to compare arguments or ideas from various sources

- When you want to provide readers with an understanding of the source's argument before you respond to it or launch your own

Paraphrasing

When you paraphrase, you express an author's ideas in your own words and sentence structure, using approximately the same number of words and details as in the source.

WHEN TO PARAPHRASE

- When the ideas and information are important but the author's exact words are not needed

- When you want to restate the source's ideas in your own words

- When you need to simplify or explain a technical or complicated source

Paraphrase effectively

A paraphrase shows your readers that you understand a source and can explain it to them. When you choose to paraphrase a passage, you use the information and ideas of a source for your own purpose — to provide background information, explain a concept, or advance your argument — and yet maintain your voice. It is challenging to write a paraphrase that isn't a word-for-word translation of the original source and doesn't imitate the source's sentence structure. These strategies will help you paraphrase effectively. The examples in this box are in MLA style.

1 **Understand the source.** Identify the source's key points and argument. Test your understanding by asking questions: What is being said? Why and how is it being said? Look up words you don't know to help you understand whole ideas, not just the words.

ORIGINAL

People's vision of the world has broadened with the advent of global media such as television and the Internet. Those thinking about going elsewhere can see what the alternatives are and appear to have fewer inhibitions about resettling.

> — Darrell M. West, *Brain Gain: Rethinking U.S. Immigration Policy,* Brookings Institution Press, 2011, p. 5

STUDENT'S NOTES

—*TV and Internet have opened our eyes, our minds*

—*We can imagine making big moves (country to country) as we never could before; the web offers a preview*

—*"resettling" = moving to a new location, out of the familiar region*

—*Lessens the anxiety about starting over in a new place*

2 **Use your own vocabulary and sentence structure** to convey the source's information. Check to make sure there is no overlap in vocabulary or sentence structure with the original.

Since TV and the web can offer a preview of life in other places, people feel less uncertainty and anxiety about making moves from one area of the world to another.

3 **Use a signal phrase to identify the source** (*According to X,* or *X argues that* _____).

> West argues that since TV and the web can offer a preview of life in other places, people feel less uncertainty and anxiety about making moves from one area of the world to another.

4 **Include a citation to give credit to the source.** Even though the words are yours, you need to give credit for the idea. Here, the author's name and the page number on which the original passage appeared are listed.

> West argues that since TV and the web can offer a preview of life in other places, people feel less uncertainty and anxiety about making moves from one area of the world to another (5).

NOTE: If you choose to use exact language from the source in a paraphrase, be sure to put quotation marks around any borrowed words or phrases.

> West argues that since TV and the web can offer a preview of life in other places, people "have fewer inhibitions" about making moves from one area of the world to another (5).

MLA-3b Use quotations effectively.

When you quote a source, you borrow some of the author's exact words and enclose them in quotation marks. Quotation marks show your readers that both the idea and the words belong to the author.

WHEN TO USE QUOTATIONS

- When language is especially vivid or expressive
- When exact wording is needed for technical accuracy
- When it is important to let the debaters of an issue explain their positions in their own words
- When the words of an authority lend weight to an argument
- When the language of a source is the topic of your discussion

Limiting your use of quotations

Keep the emphasis on your own ideas, and, as much as possible, keep your ideas in your own voice. It is not always necessary to quote full sentences from a source. Often you can integrate words and phrases from a source into your own sentence structure quite effectively.

> Resnik acknowledges that his argument relies on "slippery slope" thinking, but he insists that "social and political pressures" regarding food regulation make his concerns valid (31).

For the use of signal phrases in integrating quotations, see MLA-3c.

Using the ellipsis mark

To condense a quoted passage, you can use the ellipsis mark — a series of three spaced periods — to indicate that you have omitted words. What remains must be grammatically complete.

> In Mississippi, legislators passed "a ban on bans — a law that forbids . . . local restrictions on food or drink" (Conly A23).

The writer has omitted the words *municipalities to place,* which appear before *local restrictions* in the original source, to condense the quoted material.

If you want to leave out one or more full sentences, use a period before the ellipsis.

> Legal scholars Gostin and Gostin argue that "individuals have limited willpower to defer immediate gratification for longer-term health benefits. . . . A person understands that high-fat foods or a sedentary lifestyle will cause adverse health effects, or that excessive spending or gambling will cause financial hardship, but it is not always easy to refrain" (217).

Ordinarily, do not use an ellipsis mark at the beginning or at the end of a quotation. Your readers will understand that you have taken the quoted material from a longer passage. The only exception occurs when you have dropped words at the end of the final quoted sentence. In such cases, put an ellipsis before the closing quotation mark and parenthetical reference.

Using sources responsibly   Make sure omissions and ellipsis marks do not distort the meaning of your source.

Using brackets   Brackets allow you to insert your own words into quoted material to clarify a confusing reference or to keep a sentence grammatical in your context. You also use brackets to indicate that you are changing a letter from capital to lowercase (or vice versa) to fit into your sentence. In the following example, the writer inserted words in brackets to clarify the meaning of *help*.

> Neergaard and Agiesta argue that "a new poll finds people are split on how much the government should do to help [find solutions to the national health crisis] — and most draw the line at attempts to force healthier eating."

To indicate an error such as a misspelling in a quotation, insert the word "sic" in brackets right after the error.

> "While people of every race and ethnicity are affected, diabetes disproportionately effects [sic] Black adults in the US."

Setting off long quotations

When you quote more than four typed lines of prose or more than three lines of poetry, set off the quotation by indenting it one-half inch from the left margin and use the normal right margin.

Long quotations should be introduced by an informative sentence, usually followed by a colon. Quotation marks are unnecessary because the indented format tells readers that the passage is taken word-for-word from the source.

> In response to critics who claim that laws aimed at stopping us from eating whatever we want are an assault on our freedom of choice, Conly offers a persuasive counterargument:
>
>> [L]aws aren't designed for each one of us individually. Some of us can drive safely at 90 miles per hour, but we're bound by the same laws as the people who can't, because individual speeding laws aren't practical. Giving up a little liberty is something we agree to when we agree to live in a democratic society that is governed by laws. (A23)

NOTE: At the end of an indented quotation, the parenthetical citation goes outside the final mark of punctuation.

Quotation marks with other punctuation

Integrating sources smoothly into your own sentences is easier when you follow guidelines about using periods, commas, and question marks with quotation marks.

Quotation with no page number, author mentioned in sentence

The ban, according to MacMillan, "gave consumers a healthier default option."

The ban "gave consumers a healthier default option," according to MacMillan.

NOTE: Place periods and commas inside quotation marks.

Quotation with no page number, author name in parentheses

The ban "gave consumers a healthier default option" (Macmillan).

Quotation with page number

Fortin notes that instead of a ban, the FDA "took a more moderate approach" (113).

Quotation within a writer's own question

Why did the FDA choose "a more moderate approach" (Fortin 113)?

Quotation that is itself a question

Fortin begins with a key question: "Why do we have food laws?" (3).

Long quotation

Hilts argues that Americans have faith in the FDA:

> The Roper Organization has tracked the FDA and government issues consistently, and found that among all government agencies, the FDA has been among the most popular, and routinely number one among regulatory agencies. (295)

NOTE: For a quotation of four lines or more, indent the quoted words, do not use quotation marks, and place the parenthetical citation outside of the final punctuation.

MLA-3c Use signal phrases to integrate sources.

When you include a paraphrase, summary, or direct quotation of another writer's work in your paper, prepare your readers for it with introductory words called a *signal phrase*. A signal phrase usually names the author of the source, provides some context for the source material — such as the author's credentials — and helps readers distinguish your ideas from those of the source.

When you write a signal phrase, choose a verb that fits with the way you are using the source (see MLA-1c). Are you using the source to support a claim, for example, or to refute an argument? The signal phrase you choose shows readers how you want them to think about the source.

WEAK VERB	Lorine Goodwin, a food historian, says, "..."
STRONGER VERB	Lorine Goodwin, a food historian, rejects the claim: "..."
WEAK VERB	Bioethicist David Resnik mentions ...
STRONGER VERB	Bioethicist David Resnik argues ...

NOTE: MLA style calls for verbs in the present tense or present perfect tense (*argues* or *has argued*) to introduce source material unless you include a date that specifies the time of the original author's writing.

Using signal phrases in MLA papers

To avoid monotony, try to vary both the language and the placement of your signal phrases.

Model signal phrases

Michael Pollan, who has written extensively about Americans' unhealthy eating habits, argues that "..."

As health policy experts Mello and colleagues point out, "..."

Marion Nestle, New York University professor of nutrition and public health, notes ...

Bioethicist David Resnik acknowledges that his argument ...

In response to critics, Conly offers a persuasive counterargument: "..."

Verbs in signal phrases

acknowledges	comments	endorses	points out
adds	compares	explains	reasons
admits	confirms	grants	refutes
agrees	contends	illustrates	rejects
argues	declares	implies	reports
asserts	denies	insists	responds
believes	disputes	notes	suggests
claims	emphasizes	observes	writes

Marking boundaries

Readers need to move smoothly from your words to the words of a source. Avoid dropping a quotation into the text without warning. Provide a clear signal phrase, including at least the author's name, to indicate the boundary between your words and the source's words. The signal phrase is highlighted in the second example.

DROPPED QUOTATION

Laws designed to prevent chronic disease by promoting healthier food and beverage consumption also have potentially enormous benefits. "[A] 1% reduction in intake of saturated fat across the population would prevent more than 30,000 cases of coronary heart disease annually and save more than a billion dollars in health care costs" (Nestle 7).

QUOTATION WITH SIGNAL PHRASE

Laws designed to prevent chronic disease by promoting healthier food and beverage consumption also have potentially enormous benefits. Marion Nestle, New York University professor of nutrition and public health, notes that "a 1% reduction in intake of saturated fat across the population would prevent more than 30,000 cases of coronary heart disease annually and save more than a billion dollars in health care costs" (7).

Establishing authority

The first time you mention a source, include in the signal phrase the author's title, credentials, or experience to help your readers recognize the source's authority and your own credibility (*ethos*) as a responsible researcher who has located reliable sources. Signal phrases are highlighted in the next two examples.

SOURCE WITH NO CREDENTIALS

No clues given about the source's authority.

Michael Pollan notes that "[t]he Centers for Disease Control estimates that fully three quarters of US health care spending goes to treat chronic diseases, most of which are preventable and linked to diet: heart disease, stroke, type 2 diabetes, and at least a third of all cancers."

SOURCE WITH CREDENTIALS

Credentials and authority of the source are established.

Journalist Michael Pollan, who has written extensively about Americans' eating habits, notes that "[t]he Centers for Disease Control estimates that fully three quarters of US health care spending goes to treat chronic diseases, most of which are preventable and linked to diet: heart disease, stroke, type 2 diabetes, and at least a third of all cancers."

Introducing summaries and paraphrases

Introduce most summaries and paraphrases with a signal phrase that names the author and places the material in the context of your argument. Readers will then understand that everything between the signal phrase and the parenthetical citation summarizes or paraphrases the cited source.

Without the signal phrase, readers might think that only the quotation at the end is being cited; in fact the whole paragraph is based on the source.

To improve public health, advocates such as Bowdoin College philosophy professor Sarah Conly contend that it is the government's duty to prevent people from making harmful choices whenever feasible and whenever public benefits outweigh the costs. In response to critics who claim that laws aimed at stopping us from eating whatever we want are an assault on our freedom of choice, Conly asserts that "laws aren't designed for each one of us individually" (A23).

There are times when a summary or a paraphrase does not require a signal phrase naming the author. When the context makes clear where the cited material begins, you may omit the signal phrase and include the author's last name in parentheses.

Integrating statistics and other facts

When you cite a statistic or another specific fact, a signal phrase is often not necessary. Readers usually will understand that the citation refers to the statistic or fact and not the whole paragraph.

Seventy-five percent of Americans are opposed to laws that restrict or put limitations on access to unhealthy foods (Neergaard and Agiesta).

There is nothing wrong, however, with using a signal phrase to introduce a statistic or another fact.

Putting source material in context

Readers should not have to guess why source material appears in your paper. A signal phrase can help you connect your own ideas with those of another writer by clarifying how the source will contribute to your paper.

If you use another writer's words, you must explain how they relate to your argument. Quotations don't speak for themselves; you must create a context for readers. Sandwich each quotation between sentences of your own, introducing the quotation with a signal phrase and following it with comments that link the quotation to your paper's argument.

QUOTATION WITH EFFECTIVE CONTEXT (QUOTATION SANDWICH)

Quotation is introduced with a signal phrase naming the author.

In response to critics who claim that laws aimed at stopping us from eating whatever we want are an assault on our freedom of choice, Conly offers a persuasive counterargument:

Long quotation is set off from the text; quotation marks are omitted.

> [L]aws aren't designed for each one of us individually. Some of us can drive safely at 90 miles per hour, but we're bound by the same laws as the people who can't, because individual speeding laws aren't practical. Giving up a little liberty is something we agree to when we agree to live in a democratic society that is governed by laws. (A23)

Analysis connects the source to the student's argument.

As Conly suggests, it's important to move from either/or thinking (either we have complete freedom of choice *or* we have government regulations and lose our freedom) to seeing health as a matter of public good, not individual liberty.

Using sentence guides to integrate sources

You build your credibility (*ethos*) by accurately representing the ideas of others and by integrating these ideas into your paper. An important way to present the ideas of others before agreeing or disagreeing with them is to use sentence guides. These guides act as academic sentence starters; they show you how to use signal phrases in sentences to make clear to your reader whose ideas you're presenting — your own or those you have encountered in a source.

Presenting others' ideas. As an academic writer, you will be expected to demonstrate your understanding of a source by summarizing the views or arguments of its author. The following language will help you to do so:

X argues that _____.

X and Y emphasize the need for _____.

NOTE: The examples in this box are shown in MLA style. If you were writing in APA style, you would include the year of publication after the source's name and typically use past tense or present perfect tense (*emphasized* or *has emphasized*).

Presenting direct quotations. To introduce the exact words of a source because their accuracy and authority are important for your argument, you might try phrases like these:

X describes the problem this way: "_____"

Y argues in favor of the policy, pointing out that "_____."

Using sentence guides to integrate sources, *continued*

Presenting alternative ideas. At times you will have to synthesize the ideas of multiple sources before you introduce your own.

> While X and Y have asked an important question, Z suggests that we should be asking a different question: _____.

> X has argued that Y's research findings rest upon questionable assumptions _____ and _____.

Presenting your own ideas by agreeing or extending. You may agree with the author of a source but want to add your own voice to extend the point or go deeper. The following phrases could be useful:

> X's argument is convincing because _____.

> Y claimed that _____. But isn't it also true that _____?

Presenting your own ideas by disagreeing and questioning. College writing assignments encourage you to show your understanding of a subject but also to question or challenge ideas and conclusions about the subject. This language can help:

> X's claims about _____ are misguided.

> Y insists that _____, but perhaps she is asking the wrong question.

Presenting and countering objections to your argument. To anticipate objections that readers might make, try the following sentence guides:

> Not everyone will endorse this argument; some may argue instead that _____.

> Some will object to this proposal on the grounds that _____.

MLA-3d Synthesize sources.

When you synthesize multiple sources in a research paper, you create a conversation about your research topic. You show readers that your argument is based on your analysis and integration of ideas and is not just a series of quotations and paraphrases strung together. Your synthesis will show how your sources relate to one another; one source may support, extend, or counter the ideas of another. Not every source has to "speak" to another in a research paper, but readers should understand how each source functions in your argument.

Considering how sources relate to your argument

Before you integrate sources and show readers how they relate to one another, consider how each source might contribute to your own argument. As student writer Sophie Harba became more informed about her research topic, she asked herself these questions:

- What have I learned from my sources?
- Which sources might support my ideas or illustrate the points I want to make?
- What counterarguments do I need to address to strengthen my position?

She annotated a passage from one of her sources — a nonprofit group's assertion that our choices about food are skewed by marketing messages.

STUDENT NOTES ON THE ORIGINAL SOURCE

The food and beverage industry spends approximately $2 billion per year marketing to children.
— "Facts on Junk Food"

Could use this fact to counter the personal choice point in Mello.

Placing sources in conversation

You can show readers how the ideas of one source relate to those of another by connecting and analyzing the ideas in your own voice. After all, you've done the research and thought through the issues, so you should control the conversation. Keep the emphasis on your own writing. The thread of your argument should be easy to identify and to understand, with or without your sources.

SAMPLE SYNTHESIS (MLA STYLE)

Student writer Sophie Harba sets up her synthesis with a question.

Why is the public largely resistant to laws that would limit unhealthy choices or penalize those choices with so-called fat taxes? Many consumers and civil rights advocates find such laws to be an unreasonable restriction on individual freedom of choice. As health policy experts Mello and colleagues point out, opposition to food and beverage regulation is similar to the opposition to early tobacco legislation: the public views the issue as one of personal responsibility rather than one requiring government intervention (2602). In other words, if a person eats unhealthy food and becomes ill as a result, that is his or her choice. But those who favor legislation claim that freedom of choice is a myth because of the strong influence of food and beverage industry marketing

Student writer

Signal phrase indicates how the source contributes to Harba's argument and shows that the idea that follows is not her own.

Source 1

Harba interprets a paraphrased source.

Student writer

Harba uses a source to support her counterargument.

on consumers' dietary habits. According to one nonprofit health advocacy group, food and beverage companies spend roughly two billion dollars per year marketing directly to children. As a result, kids see nearly four thousand ads per year encouraging them to eat unhealthy food and drinks ("Facts"). As was the case with antismoking laws passed in recent decades, taxes and legal restrictions on junk food sales could help to counter the strong marketing messages that promote unhealthy products.

Source 2

Student writer

Harba extends the argument and follows it with an interpretive comment.

The United States has a history of state and local public health laws that have successfully promoted a particular behavior by punishing an undesirable behavior. The decline in tobacco use as a result of antismoking taxes and laws is perhaps the most obvious example. Another example is legislation requiring the use of seat belts, which have significantly reduced fatalities in car crashes. One government agency reports that seat belt use saved an average of more than fourteen thousand lives per year in the United States between 2000 and 2010 (United States, Department of Transportation 231). Perhaps seat belt laws have public support because the cost of wearing a seat belt is small, especially when compared with the benefit of saving fourteen thousand lives per year.

Source 3

Student writer

In this synthesis, Harba uses her own analysis to shape the conversation among her sources. She does not simply string quotations together or allow them to overwhelm her writing. She guides readers through a conversation about laws that could promote and have promoted public health. She finds points of intersection among her sources, acknowledges the contributions of others, and shows readers, in her voice, how the sources support her argument.

When synthesizing sources, use the following guidelines:

- Be sure your sources address your research question.

- Think about how your sources converse with each other. In other words, how do they support, extend, or counter each other?

- Be sure that your synthesis is more than a series of quotations and paraphrases strung together. You can do this by connecting and analyzing sources in your own voice.

- Ask: Is my own argument easy to identify and to understand, with or without my sources? The answer should be yes.

Reviewing an MLA paper: Use of sources

Use of quotations

- Have you used quotation marks around quoted material (unless it has been set off from the text)? (See MLA-2c.)
- Have you checked that quoted language is word-for-word accurate? If it is not, do ellipsis marks or brackets indicate the omissions or changes? (See MLA-3b.)
- Does a clear signal phrase (usually naming the author) prepare readers for each quotation and for the purpose the quotation serves? (See MLA-3c.)
- Does a parenthetical citation follow each quotation? (See MLA-4a.)
- Is each quotation put in context? (See MLA-3c.)

Use of summaries and paraphrases

- Are summaries and paraphrases free of plagiarized wording — not copied or half-copied from the source? (See MLA-2d.)
- Are summaries and paraphrases documented with parenthetical citations? (See MLA-4a.)
- Do readers know where the cited material begins? In other words, does a signal phrase mark the boundary between your words and the summary or paraphrase? (See MLA-3c.)
- Does a signal phrase prepare readers for the purpose the summary or paraphrase has in your argument? (See MLA-3c.)

Use of statistics and other facts

- Are statistics and facts (other than common knowledge) documented with parenthetical citations? (See MLA-3c.)
- If there is no signal phrase, will readers understand exactly which facts are being cited? (See MLA-3c.)

MLA-4 Documenting sources

In English and other humanities classes, you may be asked to use the MLA (Modern Language Association) system for documenting sources, which is set forth in the *MLA Handbook*, 9th edition (MLA, 2021).

MLA recommends in-text citations that refer readers to a list of works cited. A typical in-text citation names the author of the source, often in a signal phrase, and gives a page number in parentheses. At the end of the paper, the list of works cited provides publication information about the source; the list is alphabetized by authors' last names (or by titles for works without authors). There is a direct connection between the in-text citation and the alphabetical listing. In the following example, that connection is highlighted.

IN-TEXT CITATION

Bioethicist David ==Resnik== emphasizes that such policies, despite their potential to make our society healthier, "open the door to excessive government control over food, which could restrict dietary choices, interfere with cultural, ethnic, and religious traditions, and exacerbate socioeconomic inequalities" (31).

ENTRY IN THE LIST OF WORKS CITED

==Resnik==, David. "Trans Fat Bans and Human Freedom." *The American Journal of Bioethics*, vol. 10, no. 3, Mar. 2010, pp. 27–32.

For a list of works cited that includes this entry, see MLA-5b.

MLA-4a MLA in-text citations

MLA in-text citations are made with a combination of signal phrases and parenthetical references. A signal phrase introduces information taken from a source (a quotation, summary, paraphrase, or fact); usually the signal phrase includes the author's name. The parenthetical reference comes after the cited material, often at the end of the sentence. It includes at least a page number (except for unpaginated sources, such as those found on the web). In the models in MLA-4a, the elements of the in-text citation are highlighted.

IN-TEXT CITATION

==Resnik== acknowledges that his argument relies on "slippery slope" thinking, but he insists that "social and political pressures" regarding food regulation make his concerns valid ==(31)==.

Readers can look up the author's last name in the alphabetized list of works cited, where they will learn the work's title and other publication information. If readers decide to consult the source, the page number will take them straight to the cited passage.

General guidelines for signal phrases and page numbers

Items 1–5 explain how the MLA system usually works for all sources — in print, on the web, in other media, and with or without authors and page numbers. Items 6–25 give variations on the basic guidelines.

1. Author named in a signal phrase   Ordinarily, introduce the material being cited with a signal phrase that includes the author's name. In addition to preparing readers for the source, the signal phrase allows you to keep the parenthetical citation brief.

> According to Lorine Goodwin, a food historian, nineteenth-century reformers who sought to purify the food supply were called "fanatics" and "radicals" by critics who argued that consumers should be free to buy and eat what they want (77).

The signal phrase *According to Lorine Goodwin* names the author; the parenthetical citation gives the number of the page on which the quoted words may be found.

Notice that the period follows the parenthetical citation. When a quotation ends with a question mark or an exclamation point, leave the end punctuation inside the quotation mark and add a period at the end of your sentence, after the parenthetical citation.

> Burgess asks a critical question: "How can we think differently about food labeling?" (51).

2. Author named in parentheses   If you do not give the author's name in a signal phrase, put the last name in parentheses with the page number (if the source has one). Use no punctuation between the name and the page number: (Moran 351).

> Seventy-five percent of Americans are opposed to laws that restrict or put limitations on access to unhealthy foods (Neergaard and Agiesta).

3. Author unknown   If a source has no author, the works cited entry will begin with the title. In your in-text citation, either use the complete title in a signal phrase or use a short form of the title in parentheses. Titles of books and other long works are italicized; titles of articles and other short works are put in quotation marks.

> As a result, kids see nearly four thousand ads per year encouraging them to eat unhealthy food and drinks ("Facts").

NOTE: If the author is a corporation or a government agency, see items 8 and 16.

4. Source with no page numbers   Do not include a page number if a source does not provide page numbers. Do not use page numbers from a printout from a website. (When the pages of a web source are stable, as in PDF files, supply a page number in your in-text citation.)

> Michael Pollan points out that "cheap food" actually has "significant costs — to the environment, to public health, to the public purse, even to the culture."

If a source has numbered paragraphs or sections, use "par." (or "pars.") or "sec." (or "secs.") in the parentheses: (Smith, par. 4). Notice that a comma follows the author's name. If you cite an audiovisual source (such as an online video), include a time stamp for the material you have used: (00:08:31–40).

5. One-page source   If a source is only one page long, do not include the page number in your in-text citation. You should, however, include the page number in your works cited list entry.

> **IN-TEXT CITATION FOR ONE-PAGE SOURCE**
>
> Sarah Conly uses John Stuart Mill's "harm principle" to argue that citizens need their government to intervene to prevent them from harmful actions — such as driving fast or buying unhealthy foods — out of ignorance of the harm they can do.

> **ENTRY IN THE WORKS CITED LIST**
>
> Conly, Sarah. "Three Cheers for the Nanny State." *The New York Times*, 25 Mar. 2013, p. A23.

Variations on the general guidelines

This section describes the MLA guidelines for handling a variety of situations not covered in items 1–5.

6. Two authors   Name both authors in a signal phrase, as in the following example, or include their last names in the parenthetical reference: (Gostin and Gostin 214).

> As legal scholars Gostin and Gostin explain, "[I]nterventions that do not pose a truly significant burden on individual liberty" are justified if they "go a long way towards safeguarding the health and well-being of the populace" (214).

7. Three or more authors   In a parenthetical citation, give the first author's name followed by "et al." (Latin for "and others"). In a signal phrase, give the first author's name followed by a phrase such as "and others."

> The clinical trials were extended for two years, and only after results were reviewed by an independent panel did the researchers publish their findings (Blaine et al. 35).

> Researchers Blaine and colleagues note that clinical trial results were reviewed by an independent panel (35).

8. Organization as author   When the author is a corporation or an organization, name that author either in the signal phrase or in the parenthetical citation. (For a government agency as author, see item 16.)

> The American Diabetes Association estimates that the cost of diagnosed diabetes in the United States in 2012 was $245 billion.

In the list of works cited, the American Diabetes Association is treated as the author and alphabetized under *A*. When you give the organization name in the text, spell out the name; when you use it in parentheses, shorten the name to the first noun and any preceding adjectives, removing any articles (*A, An, The*).

> The cost of diagnosed diabetes in the United States in 2012 has been estimated at $245 billion (American Diabetes).

9. Authors with the same last name   If your list of works cited includes works by two or more authors with the same last name, include the author's first name in the signal phrase or first initial in the parentheses.

> One approach to the problem is to introduce nutrition literacy at the elementary level in public schools (E. Chen 15).

10. Two or more works by the same author   Mention the title of the work in the signal phrase or include a short version of the title in the parentheses.

> The American Diabetes Association tracks trends in diabetes across age groups. In 2012, more than 200,000 children and adolescents had diabetes ("Fast Facts"). Because of an expected dramatic increase in diabetes in young people over the next forty years, the association encourages "strategies for implementing childhood obesity prevention programs and primary prevention programs for youth at risk of developing type 2 diabetes" ("Number").

Titles of articles and other short works are placed in quotation marks; titles of books and other long works are italicized.

In the rare case when both the author's name and a short title must be given in parentheses, separate them with a comma.

> Researchers have estimated that "the number of youth with type 2 [diabetes] could quadruple and the number with type 1 could triple" by 2050, "with an increasing proportion of youth with diabetes from minority populations" (American Diabetes, "Number").

11. Two or more works in one citation   To cite more than one source in the parentheses, list the authors (or titles) in alphabetical order and separate them with semicolons.

> The prevalence of early-onset type 2 diabetes has been well documented (Finn 68; Sharma 2037; Whitaker 118).

12. Repeated citations from the same source   If you cite a source more than once in a paragraph, you may omit the author's name after the first mention as long as it is clear that you are still referring to the same source. Later citations may include only the page number.

> Family expectations are at the heart of *Everything I Never Told You*, a debut novel in which a daughter shrinks from a mother who forces her to read books on science and medicine "to inspire her, to show her what she could accomplish" (Ng 73). But teenage Lydia commits herself to standing up to her overbearing mother, promising that "she will tell her mother: enough" (274).

13. Encyclopedia or dictionary entry   When an encyclopedia or dictionary entry does not have an author, mention the word or entry and give the number(s) of the page on which the entry may be found.

> The word *crocodile* has a complex etymology ("Crocodile" 139–40).

14. Entire work   Use the author's name in a signal phrase or a parenthetical citation. There is no need to use a page number.

> Michael Pollan explores the issues surrounding food production and consumption from a political angle.

15. Selection in an anthology or a collection   Put the name of the author of the selection (not the editor of the anthology) in the signal phrase or the parentheses.

> In "How to Write Iranian-America, or the Last Essay," Khakpour details degrading experiences with English language instructors "who look to you with the shine of love but the stench of pity" (3).

In the list of works cited, the work is alphabetized under *Khakpour*, the author of the essay, not under the name of the editor of the anthology. (See item 28 in MLA-4b.)

16. Government document   In a signal phrase, include the name of the agency or governing body as given in the works cited list. In a parenthetical citation, shorten the name.

> In fact, the amount of money the United States spends to treat chronic illnesses is increasing so rapidly that the Centers for Disease Control has labeled chronic disease "the public health challenge of the 21st century" (National Center 1).

If you cite more than one agency or department from the same government in your essay, you may choose to standardize the names by beginning with the government name (see item 56 in MLA-4b). In that case, when shortening names of government agencies, give enough of the name to differentiate the authors: (United States, Department of Transportation); (United States, Environmental Protection). See MLA-5b for an essay that uses standardized government authors.

17. Historical document   Titles of constitutions are italicized, but the titles of other historical documents, such as the Emancipation Proclamation, are not. Provide relevant article and section numbers. In parenthetical citations, use abbreviations such as "art." and "sec."

> While the *Constitution* provides for the formation of new states (art. 4, sec. 3), it does not explicitly allow or prohibit the secession of states.

Cite other historical documents as you would any other work, by the first element in the works cited entry (see item 57 in MLA-4b).

18. Legal source   For a legislative act (law) or court case, name the act or case either in a signal phrase or in parentheses. Italicize the names of cases but not the names of acts. (See also items 58 and 59 in MLA-4b.)

> The CARES Act of 2020 provided loans for small businesses.

> *Dred Scott v. Sandford*, which concluded that both free and enslaved Black people could not be citizens of the United States, may have been the Supreme Court's worst decision.

19. Visual such as a table, a chart, or another graphic   To cite a visual that has a figure number in the original source, use the abbreviation "fig." and the original figure number in place of a page number in your parenthetical citation: (Manning, fig. 4). If you refer to the figure in your text, spell out the word "figure."

To cite a visual that appears in a print source without a figure number, use the visual's title or a description in your text and cite the author and page number as for any other source.

For a visual not in a print source, identify the visual in your text and then in parentheses use the first element in the works cited entry: the artist's or photographer's name or the title of the work. (See items 51–55 in MLA-4b.)

Photographs such as *Woman Aircraft Worker* (Bransby) and *Women Welders* (Parks) demonstrate the US government's attempt to document the contributions of women during World War II.

20. Personal communication and social media   Cite personal letters, personal interviews, e-mail messages, and social media posts by the name listed in the works cited entry, as you would for any other source. Identify the type of source in your text if you think it is necessary for clarity. (See items 37 and 60–62 in MLA-4b.)

21. Web source   Your in-text citation for a source from the web should follow the same guidelines as for other sources. If the source lacks page numbers but has numbered paragraphs, sections, or divisions, use those numbers with the appropriate abbreviation in your parenthetical citation: "par.," "sec.," "ch.," "pt.," and so on. Do not add such numbers if the source itself does not use them; simply give the author or title in your in-text citation.

Sanjay Gupta, CNN chief medical correspondent, explains that "limited access to fresh, affordable, healthy food" is one of America's most pressing health problems.

22. Indirect source (source quoted in another source)   When a writer's or a speaker's quoted words appear in a source written by someone else, begin the parenthetical citation with the abbreviation "qtd. in." In the following example, Gostin and Gostin are the authors of the source given in the works cited list; their work contains a quotation by Beauchamp.

Public health researcher Dan Beauchamp has said that "public health practices are communal in nature, and concerned with the well-being of the community as a whole and not just the well-being of any particular person" (qtd. in Gostin and Gostin 217).

Literary works and sacred texts

Literary works and sacred texts are usually available in a variety of editions. Your list of works cited will specify which edition you are using, and your in-text citation will usually consist of a page number from the edition you consulted as for any other work. When possible, give additional information — such as book parts, play divisions, or line numbers — so that readers can locate the cited passage in any edition of the work.

23. Literary work or play   If a literary work has numbered divisions, include the page number followed by a semicolon and the section, part, or chapter number(s). For a play, include the act and/or scene numbers after the page number: (37; sc. 1).

In utter despair, Dostoyevsky's character Mitya wonders aloud about the "terrible tragedies realism inflicts on people" (376; bk. 8, ch. 2).

24. Verse play or poem   For verse plays, give act, scene, and line numbers that can be located in any edition of the work. Use arabic numerals and separate the numbers with periods.

> In Shakespeare's *King Lear,* Gloucester learns a profound lesson from a tragic experience: "A man may see how this world goes / with no eyes" (4.2.148–49).

For a poem, cite the part, stanza, and line numbers, if it has them, separated by periods.

> The Green Knight claims to approach King Arthur's court "because the praise of you, prince, is puffed so high, / And your manor and your men are considered so magnificent" (1.12.258–59).

For poems that are not divided into numbered parts or stanzas, use line numbers. For the first reference, use the word "lines": (lines 5–8). Thereafter use just the numbers: (12–13).

25. Sacred text   The first time you cite the work, give the title of the work as in the works cited entry, followed by the book, chapter, and verse (or their equivalent), separated with periods. Common abbreviations for books of the Bible are acceptable in a parenthetical citation. Omit the work's title from the parentheses in all citations after the first.

> Consider the words of Solomon: "If your enemy is hungry, give him bread to eat; and if he is thirsty, give him water to drink" (*Oxford Annotated Bible,* Prov. 25.21).

The title of a sacred work is italicized when it refers to a specific edition of the work, as in the preceding example. If you refer to the book in a general sense in your text, neither italicize it nor put it in quotation marks.

> The Bible and the Qur'an provide allegories that help readers understand how to lead a moral life.

MLA-4b MLA list of works cited

- How to answer the basic question "Who is the author?" **175**
- How to cite a source reposted from another source **192**

Your list of works cited, which you will place at the end of your paper, guides readers to the sources you have quoted, summarized, and paraphrased. Ask yourself: *What would readers need to know to find this source for themselves?* Usually, you will provide basic information common to most sources, such as author, title, publisher, publication date, and location (page numbers or URL, for example).

Throughout this section of the book, you'll find models organized by type (article, book, website, multimedia source, and so on). But even if you aren't sure exactly what type of source you have (*Is this a blog post or an article?*), you can follow two general principles:

Gather key publication information about the source — the citation elements.

Organize the basic information about the source using what MLA calls "containers."

The author's name and the title of the work are needed for many (though not all) sources and are the first two pieces of information to gather. For the remaining pieces of information, you might find it helpful to think about whether the work is contained within one or more larger works. Some sources are self-contained. Others are nested in larger containers.

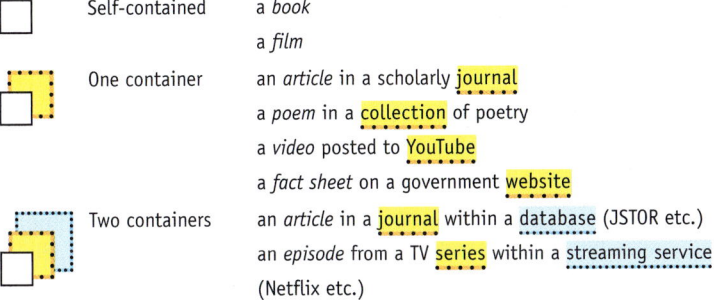

Keep in mind that most sources won't include all of the following pieces of information, so gather only those that are relevant to and available for your source.

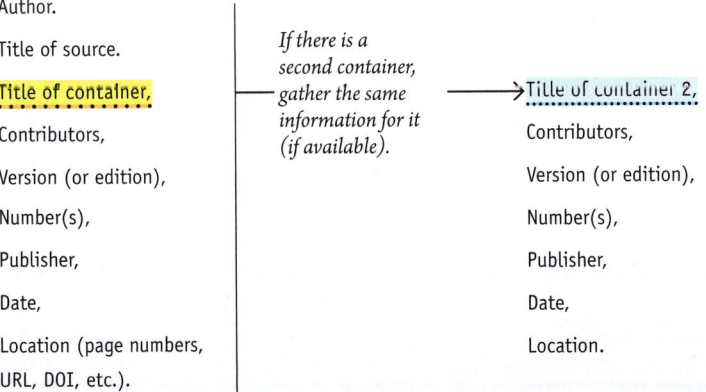

WORKS CITED ENTRY, ONE CONTAINER (SELECTION IN AN ANTHOLOGY)

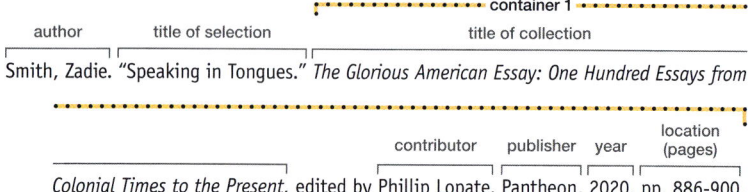

author	title of selection		title of collection

Smith, Zadie. "Speaking in Tongues." *The Glorious American Essay: One Hundred Essays from*

		contributor	publisher	year	location (pages)

Colonial Times to the Present, edited by Phillip Lopate, Pantheon, 2020, pp. 886-900.

WORKS CITED ENTRY, TWO CONTAINERS (ARTICLE IN A JOURNAL IN A DATABASE)

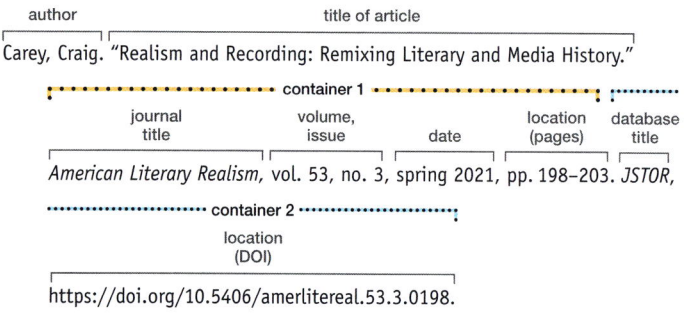

author	title of article

Carey, Craig. "Realism and Recording: Remixing Literary and Media History."

container 1

journal title	volume, issue	date	location (pages)	database title

American Literary Realism, vol. 53, no. 3, spring 2021, pp. 198–203. *JSTOR,*

container 2

location (DOI)

https://doi.org/10.5406/amerlitereal.53.3.0198.

Once you've gathered the relevant and available information about a source, you will organize the elements using the list above as your guideline. Note the punctuation after each element in that list. In this section you will find many examples of how elements and containers are combined to create works cited entries.

- List of MLA works cited models, **135–136**
- General guidelines for the works cited list, **172–173**

General guidelines for listing authors

The formatting of authors' names in items 1–11 applies to all sources — books, articles, websites — in print, on the web, or in other media. For more models of specific source types, see items 12–64.

1. Single author

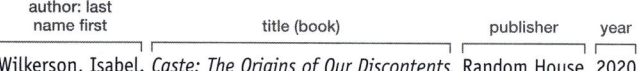

author: last name first	title (book)	publisher	year

Wilkerson, Isabel. *Caste: The Origins of Our Discontents.* Random House, 2020.

2. Two authors

first author: last name first	second author: in normal order	title (book)	publisher	year

Albertalli, Becky, and Adam Silvera. *What If It's Us.* HarperTeen, 2020.

3. Three or more authors   Name the first author followed by "et al." (Latin for "and others"). For in-text citations, see item 7 in MLA-4a.

first author: "et al." for
last name first   other authors   title (book)   publisher   year

Cunningham, Stewart, et al. *Media Economics.* Palgrave Macmillan, 2015.

4. Organization or company as author   Begin with the organization name, omitting any initial articles (*A*, *An*, or *The*). Your in-text citation also should treat the organization as the author (see item 8 in MLA-4a).

author: organization
name, not abbreviated   title (book)   publisher   year

Human Rights Watch. *World Report of 2015: Events of 2014.* Seven Stories Press, 2015.

5. No author listed

article title   publication title   date

"CEO Activism in America Is Risky Business." *The Economist,* 17 Apr. 2021,

URL

www.economist.com/business/2021/04/14/ceo-activism-in-america-is-risky-business.

NOTE: In web sources, an author's name can be hard to find. It may appear at the end of a web page or on another page of the site, such as the home page. Also, an organization or a government may be the author (see items 4 and 56).

6. Two or more works by the same author or group of authors   First alphabetize the works by title (ignoring but not omitting the article *A*, *An*, or *The* at the beginning of a title). Use the author's name or authors' names for the first entry; for subsequent entries, use three hyphens and a period. The three hyphens must stand for exactly the same name or names, in the same order, that appear in the first entry.

Coates, Ta-Nehisi. *Between the World and Me.* Spiegel and Grau, 2015.

---. *We Were Eight Years in Power: An American Tragedy.* One World, 2018.

Eaton-Robb, Pat, and Susan Haigh. "Pandemic May Lead to Long-Term Changes
     in School Calendar." *AP News,* 15 Apr. 2021, apnews.com/article/
     pandemics-connecticut-ned-lamont-975d41076ae6b985030c133614685f33.

---. "Rock Star Van Zandt Helping Connecticut Students Re-engage." *AP News,* 20 Apr.
     2021, apnews.com/article/health-music-education-arts-and-entertainment-
     entertainment-5b038c218b30863d76031134db46fa5d.

General guidelines for the works cited list

In the list of works cited, include only sources that you have quoted, summarized, or paraphrased in your paper. MLA's guidelines apply to a wide variety of sources. You can adapt the guidelines and models in this section to source types you encounter in your research.

Gathering information and organizing entries

The elements needed for a works cited entry are the following:

- The author (if a work has one)
- The title
- The title of the larger work in which the source is located, if it is contained in a larger work (MLA calls the larger work a "container" — a collection, a journal, a magazine, a website, and so on)
- As much of the following information as is available about the source and the container:

Editor, translator, director, performer	Number(s)
	Publisher
Version or edition	Date of publication

Location of the source: page numbers, URL, DOI, and so on

Not all sources will require every element. See specific models in this section for more details.

Authors

- Arrange the list alphabetically by authors' last names or by titles for works with no authors.
- For the first author, list the last name first, followed by a comma and the first name. Put a second author's name in typical order (first name followed by last name). For three or more authors, use "et al." after the first author's name.
- If the author is an organization, give the name in typical order. If the name begins with *A*, *An*, or *The*, omit it.
- Spell out "editor," "translator," "edited by," and so on.

Titles

- In titles of works, capitalize all words except articles (*a*, *an*, *the*), prepositions, coordinating conjunctions, and the *to* in infinitives — unless the word is first or last in the title or subtitle.
- Use quotation marks for titles of articles and other short works. Place single quotation marks around a quoted term or a title of a short work that appears within an article title; italicize a term or title that is normally italicized.
- Italicize titles of books and other long works, including websites. If a book title contains another title that is normally italicized, neither italicize the internal title nor place it in quotation marks. If the title within the title is normally put in quotation marks, retain the quotation marks and italicize the entire book title.

General guidelines for the works cited list, *continued*

Publication information

- Use the complete version of publishers' names, except for terms such as *Inc.* and *Co.*; retain terms such as *Books* and *Press*. For university publishers, use *U* and *P* for *University* and *Press*.
- For a book, take the name of the publisher from the title page (or from the copyright page if it is not on the title page). For a website, the publisher might be at the bottom of a page or on the "About" page. If a work has two or more publishers, separate the names with slashes.
- If the title of a website and the publisher are the same or similar, give the title of the site but omit the publisher.

Dates

- For a book, give the most recent year found on the title page or the copyright page.
- For an article from a periodical like a journal or a magazine, use the most specific date given, whether it is a month and year, a full date, or a season (*spring 2021*).
- For a web source, use the posting date, the copyright date, or the most recent update date. Use the complete date as listed in the source. If a web source has no date, give your date of access at the end: Accessed 4 Feb. 2020.
- Abbreviate all months except May, June, and July, and give the date in inverted form: 13 Mar. 2021.

Page numbers

- For most articles and other short works, give page numbers when they are available, preceded by "pp." (or "p." for only one page).
- Do not use the page numbers from a printout of a web source.
- If a short work does not appear on consecutive pages, give the number of the first page followed by a plus sign: 35+.

URLs and DOIs

- Give a DOI (digital object identifier) if a source has one. Include the protocol and host (*https://doi.org/*).
- If a source has no DOI, include a permalink if possible. Copy the permalink provided by the website.
- If a source does not have a permalink or a DOI, include the full URL for the source. Copy the URL directly from your browser. You may remove the protocol (*http://* or *https://*) when you do not need to provide live links for your readers. Do not insert any line breaks or hyphens into the URL.
- If a URL is longer than three lines on the works cited page, you may shorten it, leaving at least the website host (for example, *cnn.com* or *www.usda.gov*) in the entry.
- Always copy a URL directly from your browser. If the entire URL moves to another line, creating a short line, you may leave it that way.

7. Editor or translator   Begin with the editor's or translator's name. After the name, add "editor" or "translator." Use "editors" or "translators" for two or more (see also items 2 and 3 for how to handle multiple contributors).

first editor:
last name first

second editor:
in normal order

title (book)

Horner, Avril, and Anne Rowe, editors. *Living on Paper: Letters from Iris Murdoch, 1934–1995.*

publisher   year

Princeton UP, 2016.

8. Author with editor or translator   Begin with the name of the author. Place the editor's or translator's name after the title.

author: last
name first

title (book)

translator:
in normal order

Ullmann, Regina. *The Country Road: Stories.* Translated by Kurt Beals,

publisher   year

New Directions Publishing, 2015.

9. Graphic narrative or other illustrated work   If a work has both an author and an illustrator, the order in your citation will depend on which contributor's work you emphasize in your essay.

Gaiman, Neil. *The Sandman: Overture.* Illustrated by J. H. William III, DC Comics, 2015.

Martínez, Hugo, illustrator. *Wake: The Hidden History of Women-Led Slave Revolts.* By Rebecca Hall, Simon and Schuster, 2021.

10. Author using a pseudonym (pen name)   Use the author's name as it appears in the source, followed by the author's real name in brackets, if you know it. Alternatively, if the author's real name is more well-known, you may start with the real name followed by *published as*, italicized, and the pen name in brackets.

North, Claire [Catherine Webb]. *The Pursuit of William Abbey.* Orbit, 2019.

Franklin, Benjamin [*published* as Richard Saunders]. "Poor Richard, 1773." 1773. *Founders Online*, National Archives, founders.archives.gov/documents/ Franklin/01-01-02-0093.

11. Screen name or social media account   Start with the account display name, followed by the screen name or handle (if available) in brackets. If the account name is a first and last name, invert it. If the account name and handle are very similar (for example, ACLU SoCal and @ACLU_SoCal), you may omit the handle.

Gay, Roxane[@rgay]. "The shortness of cultural memory is always astonishing." *Twitter*, 25 Apr. 2021, twitter.com/rgay/status/1386507940601995274?.

Partlycloudy. Comment on "Is This the End?" *The New York Times*, 25 Nov. 2012, nyti .ms/3nPkY5j#permid=7726753.

Answer the basic question "Who is the author?"

Problem: Sometimes when you need to cite a source, it's not clear who the author is. This is especially true for sources on the web and other nonprint sources, which may have been created by one person and uploaded by a different person or an organization. Whom do you cite as the author in such a case? How do you determine who *is* the author?

Example: The video "Surfing the Web on the Job" (see below) was uploaded to YouTube by CBSNewsOnline. Is the person or organization that uploads the video the author of the video? Not necessarily.

Strategy: After you view or listen to the source a few times, ask yourself whether you can tell who is chiefly responsible for creating the content in the source. It could be an organization. It could be an identifiable individual. This video consists entirely of reporting by Daniel Sieberg, so in this case the author is Sieberg.

Surfing the Web on The Job

CBSNewsOnline · 42,491 videos

Subscribe   85,736

Uploaded on Nov 12, 2009
As the Internet continues to emerge as a critical facet of everyday life, CBS News' Daniel Sieberg reports that companies are cracking down on employees' personal Web use.

Citation: To cite the source, you would use the basic MLA guidelines for an online video (item 42).

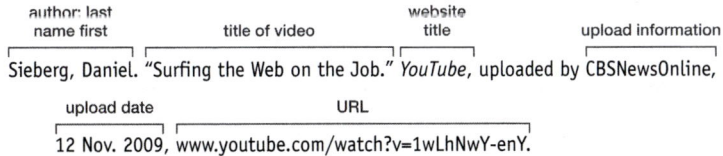

Sieberg, Daniel. "Surfing the Web on the Job." *YouTube*, uploaded by CBSNewsOnline,
12 Nov. 2009, www.youtube.com/watch?v=1wLhNwY-enY.

Articles and other short works

- Citation at a glance: Article in an online journal, 178
- Citation at a glance: Article from a database, 179

12. Basic format for an article or other short work

a. Print

author:
last name first   article title   journal title   volume, issue

Tilman, David. "Food and Health of a Full Earth." *Daedalus*, vol. 144, no. 4,

date   page(s)

fall 2015, pp. 5–7.

b. Web

author:
last name first   title of short work

Florez, Nina. "Chicago Rally Held in Support of Colombian Protesters."

title of website   date   URL

NBC 5 Chicago, 9 May 2021, www.nbcchicago.com/news/local/

chicago-rallies-held-in-support-of-colombian-protesters/2505612.

c. Database
If a database provides a DOI or a permalink, use that at the end of your citation. Otherwise, provide the URL to the article in the database.

first author: last name first   second author: in normal order   article title

Harris, Ashleigh May, and Nicklas Hållén. "African Street Literature: A Method for an

journal title

Emergent Form Beyond World Literature." *Research in African Literatures,*

volume, issue   date   page(s)   database title   DOI

vol. 51, no. 2, summer 2020, pp. 1–26. *JSTOR,* https://doi.org/10.2979/

reseafrilite.51.2.01.

13. Article in a journal

a. Print

<table>
<tr><td>author: last
name first</td><td>article title</td><td>journal
title</td></tr>
</table>

Matchie, Thomas. "Law versus Love in *The Round House*." *The Midwest Quarterly,*

<table>
<tr><td>volume,
issue</td><td>date</td><td>page(s)</td></tr>
</table>

vol. 56, no. 4, summer 2015, pp. 353–64.

b. Online journal

<table>
<tr><td>author: last
name first</td><td>article title</td></tr>
</table>

McGuire, Meg. "Women, Healing, and Social Community: Cyberfeminist Activities on Reddit."

<table>
<tr><td>journal
title</td><td>volume,
issue</td><td>date</td><td>URL</td></tr>
</table>

Kairos, vol. 25, no. 2, spring 2021, kairos.technorhetoric.net/25.2/topoi/mcguire/

index.html.

c. Database

<table>
<tr><td>author: last
name first</td><td>article title</td><td>journal
title</td></tr>
</table>

Maier, Jessica. "'A True Likeness': The Renaissance City Portrait." *Renaissance Quarterly,*

<table>
<tr><td>volume,
issue</td><td>date</td><td>page(s)</td><td>database
title</td><td>DOI</td></tr>
</table>

vol. 65, no. 3, fall 2012, pp. 711–52. *JSTOR*, https://doi.org/10.1086/668300.

14. Article in a magazine

<table>
<tr><td>author: last
name first</td><td>article title</td><td>magazine title</td><td>date</td><td>page(s)</td></tr>
</table>

Owusu, Nadia. "Head Wraps." *The New York Times Magazine*, 7 Mar. 2021, p. 20.

<table>
<tr><td>author: last
name first</td><td>article title</td></tr>
</table>

Stuart, Tessa. "New Study Suggests Burning Fossil Fuels Contributed to 1 in 5 Deaths in

<table>
<tr><td>website
title</td><td>date</td><td>URL</td></tr>
</table>

2018." *Rolling Stone*, 17 Feb. 2021, www.rollingstone.com/politics/politics-news/

fossil-fuels-air-pollution-premature-deaths-statistics-1127586/.

Citation at a glance: Article in an online journal

To cite an article in an online journal in MLA style, include the following elements:

1 Author(s) of article
2 Title and subtitle of article
3 Title of journal
4 Volume and issue numbers
5 Date of publication (including month or season, if any)
6 Page number(s) of article, if given
7 Location of source (DOI, permalink, or URL)

ONLINE JOURNAL ARTICLE

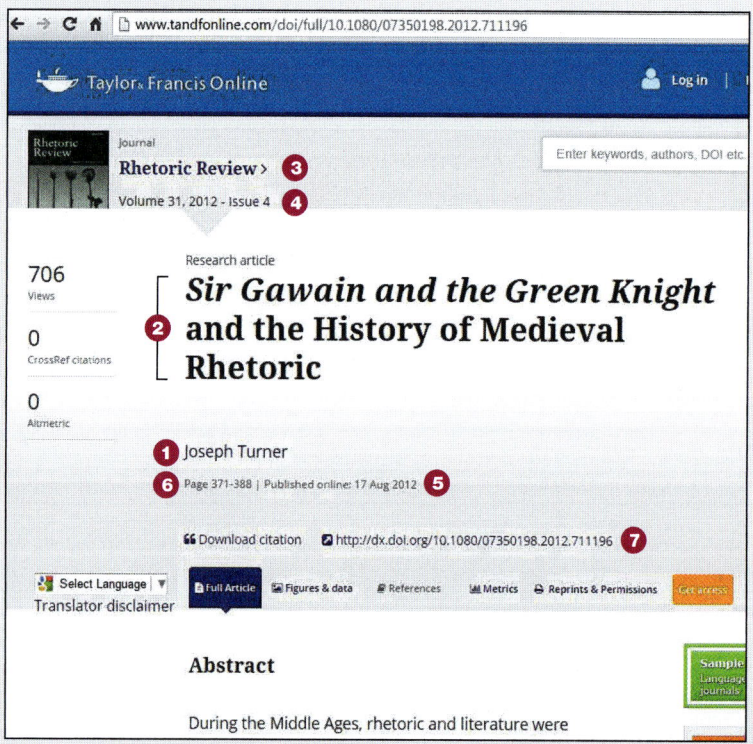

WORKS CITED ENTRY FOR AN ARTICLE IN AN ONLINE JOURNAL

      1   2

Turner, Joseph. "*Sir Gawain and the Green Knight* and the History of Medieval Rhetoric."

         3   4   5   6   7

    Rhetoric Review, vol. 31, no. 4, 17 Aug. 2012, pp. 371–88, http://dx.doi.org/

10.1080/07350198.2012.711196.

For more on citing online articles in MLA style, see item 12.

Citation at a glance: Article from a database

To cite an article from a database in MLA style, include the following elements:

1. Author(s) of article
2. Title and subtitle of article
3. Title of journal, magazine, or newspaper
4. Volume and issue numbers (for journal)
5. Date of publication (including month or season, if any)
6. Page number(s) of article, if any
7. Name of database
8. DOI or permalink, if available; otherwise, URL to article

DATABASE RECORD

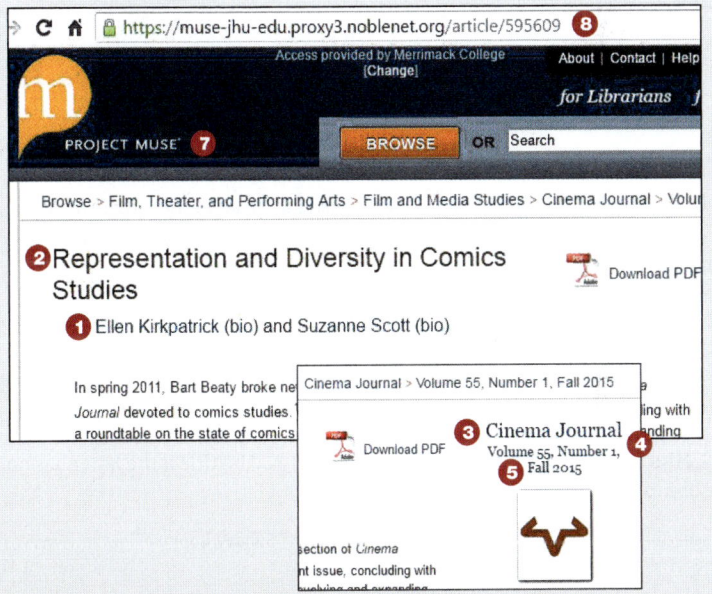

WORKS CITED ENTRY FOR AN ARTICLE FROM A DATABASE

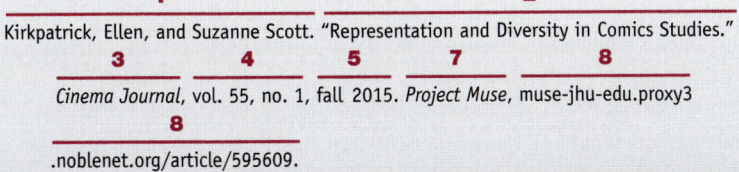

Kirkpatrick, Ellen, and Suzanne Scott. "Representation and Diversity in Comics Studies."

Cinema Journal, vol. 55, no. 1, fall 2015. *Project Muse*, muse-jhu-edu.proxy3

.noblenet.org/article/595609.

For more on citing articles from a database in MLA style, see items 12 and 13.

15. Article in a newspaper
Include the full publication date and the section and page number, if available.

author: last
name first   article title   newspaper title

Bray, Hiawatha. "As Toys Get Smarter, Privacy Issues Emerge." *The Boston Globe*,

           date   page(s)

       10 Dec. 2015, p. C1.

author: last
name first   article title

Jones, Ayana. "Chamber of Commerce Program to Boost Black-Owned Businesses."

       website title   date   URL

      The Philadelphia Tribune, 21 Apr. 2021, www.phillytrib.com/news/business/

      chamber-of-commerce-program-to-boost-black-owned-businesses/

      article_6b14ae2f-5db2-5a59-8a67-8bbf974da451.html.

16. Editorial or opinion
List the author as it appears in the source. Add the word "Editorial" or "Op-ed" to the end of the entry if it is not clear from the author or title of the source.

Kansas City Star Editorial Board. "Kansas Considers Lowering Concealed Carry

    Age to 18. Why It's Wrong for Many Reasons." *The Kansas City Star*, 9 Mar. 2021,

    www.kansascity.com/opinion/editorials/article249793143.html.

17. Letter to the editor
Use the label "Letter" as the title if the letter has no title or headline.

Carasso, Roger. Letter. *The New York Times*, 4 Apr. 2021, Sunday Book Review sec., p. 5.

18. Comment on an online article
List the author's name as it appears on the comment (see item 11). After the name, include "Comment on" followed by the article's publication information. Include the URL directly to the comment, if possible; otherwise, use the URL for the article.

author:
screen name   article title and author   website title   date and time

satch. Comment on "No Compassion," by Roy Edroso. *Alicublog*, 20 Mar. 2021, 9:50 a.m.,

      URL

    disq.us/p/2fu0ulk.

19. Book review If the review is untitled, use the label "Review of" and the title and author of the work reviewed.

Jopanda, Wayne Silao. Review of *America is Not the Heart*, by Elaine Castillo. *Alon: Journal for Filipinx American and Diasporic Studies*, vol. 1, no. 1, Mar. 2021, pp. 106–08. *eScholarship*, escholarship.org/uc/item/0d44t8wx.

Della Subin, Anna. "It Has Burned My Heart." *London Review of Books*, 22 Oct. 2015, www.lrb.co.uk/v37/n20/anna-della-subin-it-has-burned-my-heart.

20. Film review, performance review, or other review If the review is untitled, use the label "Review of" and the title and director/performer/etc. of the work reviewed. If the review has a title, do not add the label "Review" or other supplemental information.

Bramesco, Charles. "Honeyland Couches an Apocalyptic Warning in a Beekeeping Documentary." *The A.V. Club*, G/O Media, 23 July 2019, film.avclub.com/honeyland-couches-an-apocalyptic-warning-in-a-beekeepin-1836624795.

Stout, Gene. "The Ebullient Florence + the Machine Give KeyArena a Workout." *The Seattle Times*, 28 Oct. 2015, www.seattletimes.com/entertainment/music/the-ebullient-florence-the-machine-give-keyarena-a-workout.

21. Interview Begin with the person interviewed. Include the name of the interviewer after the title (or after the interviewee if the interview is untitled). If you conduct the interview personally, follow the third example.

Harjo, Joy. "The First Native American U.S. Poet Laureate on How Poetry Can Counter Hate." Interview by Olivia B. Waxman. *Time*, 22 Aug. 2019, time.com/5658443/joy-harjo-poet-interview/.

Kendi, Ibram X. Interview by Eric Deggans. *Life Kit*, NPR, 24 Oct. 2020.

Akufo, Rosa. Interview with the author. 10 Nov. 2020.

22. Article in a dictionary or an encyclopedia (including a wiki) List the author of the entry (if there is one), the title of the entry, and publication information for the reference work. For an online source that is continually updated, such as a wiki entry, use the most recent update date.

Robinson, Lisa Clayton. "Harlem Writers Guild." *Africana: The Encyclopedia of the African and African American Experience*, edited by Kwame Anthony Appiah and Henry Louis Gates Jr., 2nd ed., Oxford UP, 2005, p. 163.

"House Music." *Wikipedia: The Free Encyclopedia*, Wikimedia Foundation, 8 Apr. 2021, en.wikipedia.org/wiki/House_music.

23. Letter in a collection List the title as it appears in the collection (or, if untitled, "Letter to" and the recipient), followed by the date of the letter. End with the title and publication information for the collection.

Murdoch, Iris. Letter to Raymond Queneau. 7 Aug. 1946. *Living on Paper: Letters from Iris Murdoch, 1934–1995*, edited by Avril Horner and Anne Rowe, Princeton UP, 2016, pp. 76–78.

Oblinger, Maggie. "Letter from Maggie Oblinger to Charlie Thomas, March 31, 1895." 31 Mar. 1895. *Prairie Settlement: Nebraska Photographs and Family Letters, 1862–1912*, Library of Congress / American Memory, memory.loc.gov/cgi-bin/query/r?ammem/ps:@field(DOCID+l306)#l3060001.

Books and other long works

- Citation at a glance: Book, 183
- Citation at a glance: Selection from an anthology or a collection, 186

24. Basic format for a book

a. Print book or e-book If you have used an e-book, indicate "e-book ed." before the publisher's name.

author: last · book
name first · title · publisher · year

Porter, Max. *Lanny*. Graywolf Press, 2019.

Cabral, Amber. *Allies and Advocates: Creating an Inclusive and Equitable Culture*. E-book ed., Wiley, 2021.

b. Web Give whatever print publication information is available for the work, followed by the title of the website and the URL.

author: last
name first · book title · translator: in normal order

Piketty, Thomas. *Capital in the Twenty-First Century*. Translated by Arthur Goldhammer,

publisher · year · website title · URL

Harvard UP, 2014. *Google Books*, books.google.com/books?isbn=0674369556.

c. Audiobook After the title, include the phrase "Narrated by" followed by the narrator's full name. If the author and narrator are the same, include only the last name. Then include "audiobook ed.," the publisher, and the year of release.

de Hart, Jane Sherron. *Ruth Bader Ginsburg: A Life*. Narrated by Suzanne Toren, audiobook ed., Random House Audio, 2018.

Citation at a glance: Book

To cite a print book in MLA style, include the following elements:

1 Author(s)
2 Title and subtitle
3 Publisher
4 Year of publication (latest year)

TITLE PAGE

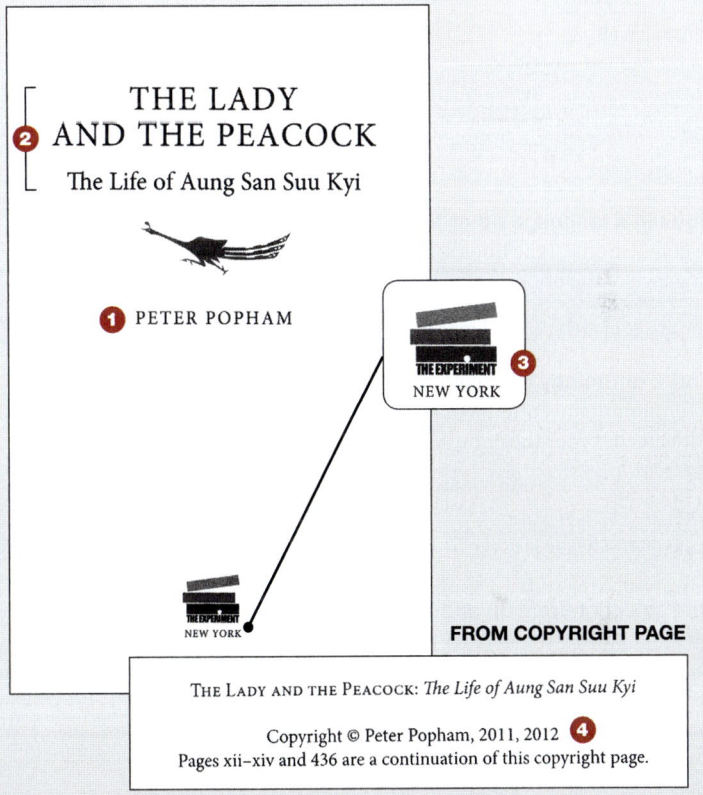

FROM COPYRIGHT PAGE

THE LADY AND THE PEACOCK: *The Life of Aung San Suu Kyi*

Copyright © Peter Popham, 2011, 2012 **4**
Pages xii–xiv and 436 are a continuation of this copyright page.

WORKS CITED ENTRY FOR A PRINT BOOK

   1   **2**   **3**

Popham, Peter. *The Lady and the Peacock: The Life of Aung San Suu Kyi*. The Experiment,

   4

2012.

For more on citing books in MLA style, see items 24–32.

25. Parts of a book (foreword, introduction, preface, or afterword)

author of book part: last name first	book part	book title	author of book: in normal order	publisher

Coates, Ta-Nehisi. Foreword. *The Origin of Others*, by Toni Morrison, Harvard UP,

       year   page(s)

      2017, pp. vii–xvii.

Sullivan, John Jeremiah. "The Ill-Defined Plot." Introduction. *The Best American*

      Essays 2014, edited by Sullivan, Houghton Mifflin Harcourt, 2014,

      pp. xvii–xxvi.

26. Book in a language other than English
Capitalize the title according to the conventions of the book's language. If your readers are not familiar with the language of the book, include a translation of the title in brackets.

Vargas Llosa, Mario. *El sueño del celta* [*The Dream of the Celt*]. Alfaguara Ediciones, 2010.

27. Entire anthology or collection
An anthology is a collection of works on a common theme, often with different authors for the selections and usually with an editor for the entire volume.

editor: last name first	title of anthology	publisher	year

Ooi, Yen, editor. *Ab Terra 2020: A Science Fiction Anthology*. Brain Mill Press, 2020.

28. One selection from an anthology or a collection

author of selection	title of selection	title of anthology

Symanovich, Alaina. "Compatibility." *Ab Terra 2020: A Science Fiction Anthology*, edited

editor(s) of anthology	publisher	year	page(s)

      by Yen Ooi, Brain Mill Press, 2020, pp. 116–23.

29. Two or more selections from an anthology or a collection
Provide an entry for the entire anthology (see item 27) and a shortened entry for each selection. Alphabetize the entries by authors' or editors' last names. Here, the Challinor and Symanovich selections appear in Ooi's *Science Fiction Anthology*.

author of selection	title of selection	editor(s) of anthology	page(s)

Challinor, Nels. "Porch Light." Ooi, pp. 107–15.

editor of anthology   title of anthology   publisher   year

Ooi, Yen, editor. *Ab Terra 2020: A Science Fiction Anthology.* Brain Mill Press, 2020.

author of selection   title of selection   editor(s) of anthology   page(s)

Symanovich, Alaina. "Compatibility." Ooi, pp. 116–23.

30. Edition other than the first If the book has a translator or an editor in addition to the author, give the name of the translator or editor before the edition number (see item 8 for a book with an editor or a translator).

Eagleton, Terry. *Literary Theory: An Introduction.* 3rd ed., U of Minnesota P, 2008.

31. Multivolume work Include the total number of volumes at the end of the entry, using the abbreviation "vols." If the volumes were published over several years, give the inclusive dates of publication.

Cather, Willa. *Willa Cather: The Complete Fiction and Other Writings.* Edited by Sharon
    O'Brien, Library of America, 1987–92. 3 vols.

If you cite only one volume in your essay, include the volume's title (if the volumes are individually titled) and number before the publisher and give the date of publication for that volume.

Cather, Willa. *Willa Cather: Later Novels.* Edited by Sharon O'Brien, Library of
    America,1990. Vol. 2 of *Willa Cather: The Complete Fiction and Other Writings.*

32. Sacred text Give the title of the edition (taken from the title page), italicized; the editor's or translator's name (if any); and publication information. Add the name of the version, if there is one, before the publisher.

The Oxford Annotated Bible with the Apocrypha. Edited by Herbert G. May and Bruce M.
    Metzger, Revised Standard Version, Oxford UP, 1965.

Quran: The Final Testament. Translated by Rashad Khalifa, Authorized English Version
    with Arabic Text, Universal Unity, 2000.

33. Dissertation

Kabugi, Magana J. *The Souls of Black Colleges: Cultural Production, Ideology, and Identity
    at Historically Black Colleges and Universities.* 2020. Vanderbilt U, PhD dissertation.
    Vanderbilt University Institutional Repository, hdl.handle.net/1803/16103.

Citation at a glance: Selection from an anthology or a collection

To cite a selection from an anthology in MLA style, include the following elements:

1 Author(s) of selection
2 Title and subtitle of selection
3 Title and subtitle of anthology
4 Editor(s) of anthology

5 Publisher
6 Year of publication
7 Page number(s) of selection

FIRST PAGE OF SELECTION

TITLE PAGE OF ANTHOLOGY

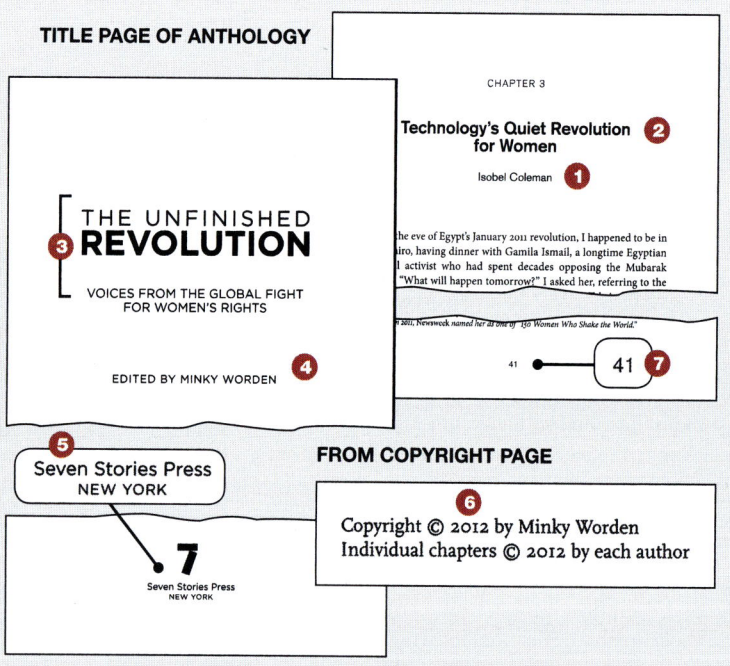

FROM COPYRIGHT PAGE

WORKS CITED ENTRY FOR A SELECTION FROM AN ANTHOLOGY

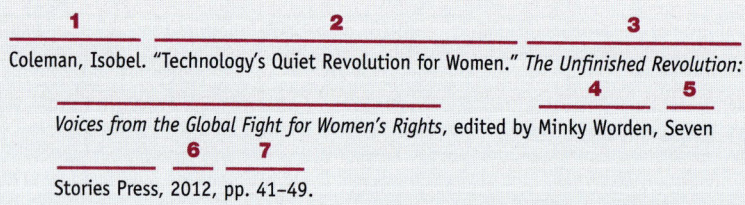

For more on citing selections from anthologies in MLA style, see items 27–29.

Web sources

● Citation at a glance: Work from a website, 188

34. An entire website   Include the website's sponsor or publisher and the update date. If the website name is the same or similar to the publisher, do not include it; if no date is provided, include the date you accessed the source.

title of
website   publisher
⌐‾‾‾‾‾⌐   ⌐‾‾⌐
Lift Every Voice. Library of America / Schomburg Center for Research in Black Culture,

update
date   URL
⌐‾‾⌐   ⌐‾‾‾‾‾‾‾‾‾‾‾‾‾‾‾‾‾‾‾⌐
2020, africanamericanpoetry.org/.

The Newton Project. 2021, www.newtonproject.ox.ac.uk/.

35. Work from a website

a. Short works (article, individual web page)

Place the title in quotation marks. If there is no posting date or update date, include the date you accessed the source.

author: last   title of
name first   title of short work   website   date
⌐‾‾‾‾‾‾‾‾⌐ ⌐‾‾‾‾‾‾‾‾‾‾‾‾‾‾‾‾‾‾‾‾‾‾‾‾‾⌐ ⌐‾‾‾‾‾‾‾⌐ ⌐‾‾‾‾‾‾‾‾‾⌐
Enzinna, Wes. "Syria's Unknown Revolution." *Pulitzer Center*, 24 Nov. 2015,

URL
⌐‾‾⌐
pulitzercenter.org/projects/middle-east-syria-enzinna-war-rojava.

title of
author   article   title of website   URL
⌐‾‾‾‾⌐ ⌐‾‾‾‾‾‾‾⌐ ⌐‾‾‾‾‾‾‾‾‾‾⌐ ⌐‾‾‾‾‾‾‾‾‾‾‾‾‾‾‾‾‾‾‾‾‾‾‾‾‾‾‾‾‾‾‾⌐
Bali, Karan. "Shashikala." *Upperstall*, upperstall.com/profile/shashikala/.

access date for
undated site
⌐‾‾‾‾‾‾‾‾‾‾‾‾‾‾⌐
Accessed 22 Apr. 2021.

MLA

Citation at a glance: Work from a website

To cite a work from a website in MLA style, include the following elements:

1 Author(s) of work, if any
2 Title and subtitle
3 Title of website
4 Publisher of website (unless it is the same as the title of site)
5 Update date
6 URL of page
7 Date of access (if no update date on site)

INTERNAL PAGE FROM A WEBSITE

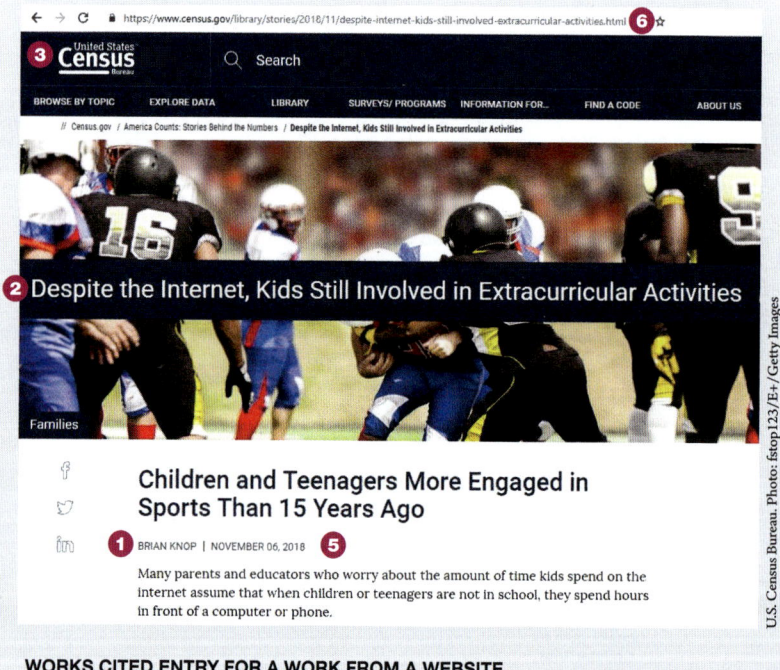

U.S. Census Bureau. Photo: fstop123/E+/Getty Images

WORKS CITED ENTRY FOR A WORK FROM A WEBSITE

Knop, Brian. "Despite the Internet, Kids Still Involved in Extracurricular Activities."

United States Census Bureau, 6 Nov. 2018, www.census.gov/library/stories

/2018/11/despite-internet-kids-still-involved-extracurricular-activities.html.

For more on citing sources from websites in MLA style, see item 35.

35. Work from a website *(cont.)*

b. Long works (book, report) If a book's original publication date is not available, include the date of online publication.

> author   title of long work   other publication information
>
> Euripides. *The Trojan Women.* Translated by Gilbert Murray, Oxford UP, 1915.
>
> title of website   URL
>
> *Internet Sacred Text Archive,* www.sacred-texts.com/cla/eurip/trojan.htm.

36. Blog post

Cite a blog post as you would a work from a website (see item 35), with the title of the post in quotation marks. (To cite a comment on a blog, follow the guidelines in item 18.)

> author: last name first   title of blog post   title of blog   publisher   update date
>
> Horgan, John. "My Quantum Experiment." *Cross-Check,* Scientific American, 5 June 2020,
>
> URL
>
> blogs.scientificamerican.com/cross-check/my-quantum-experiment/.
>
> author   title of blog post   title of blog   date   URL
>
> Edroso, Roy. "No Compassion." *Alicublog,* 18 Mar. 2021, alicublog.blogspot.com/2021/03/
>
> no-compassion.html.

37. Social media post

Cite as a work from a website (see item 34). Begin with the author (see item 11 for citing screen names). Use the caption or full text of the post as the title, if brief; if the post is long, use the first few words followed by an ellipsis. If the post has no text, or if you focus on a visual element in your paper, provide a description of the post.

> Abdurraqib, Hanif [@NifMuhammad]. "Tracy Chapman really one of the greatest Ohio writers." *Twitter,* 30 Mar. 2021, twitter.com/NifMuhammad/status/1377086355667320836.
>
> ACLU. "Public officials have. . . ." *Facebook,* 10 May 2021, www.facebook.com/aclu/photos/a.74134381812/10157852911711813.
>
> Rosa, Camila [camixvx]. Illustration of nurses in masks with fists raised. *Instagram,* 28 Apr. 2020, www.instagram.com/p/B_h62W9pJaQ/.

Audio, visual, and multimedia sources

38. Podcast series or episode

```
                          series
     episode title         title              host
```
"Childish Gambino: *Because the Internet.*" *Dissect*, hosted by Cole Cuchna,

```
                                           method of
   season, episode    distributor   date     access
```
season 7, episode 1, Spotify, Sep. 2020. *Spotify* app.

Dolly Parton's America. Hosted by Jad Abumrad, produced and reported by Shima Oliaee,
WNYC Studios, 2019, www.wnycstudios.org/podcasts/dolly-partons-america.

39. Stand-alone audio segment

"The Past Returns to Gdańsk." Written and narrated by Michael Segalov, *BBC*, 26 Apr.
2021, www.bbc.co.uk/sounds/play/m000vh4f.

40. Film
Generally, begin the entry with the title, followed by the director, as in the first example. If your essay emphasizes one or more people involved with the film, you may begin with those names, as in the second example. If you viewed the film on a streaming service, include the app or website name and URL.

```
                                                          release
        film title              director   distributor     date
```
Judas and the Black Messiah. Directed by Shaka King Warner Bros. Pictures, 2021.

Kubrick, Stanley, director. *A Clockwork Orange.* Hawk Films / Warner Bros. Pictures, 1971.
Netflix, www.netflix.com

41. Supplementary material accompanying a film
Begin with the title of the supplementary material, in quotation marks, and the names of any important contributors. End with information about the film, as in item 40, and about the location of the supplementary material.

"Sweeney's London." Produced by Eric Young. *Sweeney Todd: The Demon Barber of Fleet
Street*, directed by Tim Burton, DreamWorks, 2007, disc 2. DVD.

42. Online video
If the video is viewed on a video sharing site such as *YouTube* or *Vimeo*, put the name of the uploader after the name of the website. If the video emphasizes a single speaker or presenter, as TED Talks often do, list that person as the author.

"The Art of Single Stroke Painting in Japan." *YouTube*, uploaded by National Geographic,
13 July 2018, www.youtube.com/watch?v=g7H8IhGZnpM.

speaker   title of video

Kundu, Anindya. "The 'Opportunity Gap' in US Public Education—and How to Close It."

website
title   date   URL

TED, May 2019, www.ted.com/talks/anindya_kundu_the_opportunity_gap_in_us_

public_education_and_how_to_close_it.

43. Video game List the developer or author of the game (if any); the title, italicized; the version, if there is one; and the distributor and date of publication. If the game can be played on the web, add information as for a work from a website (see item 35).

Gearbox Software. *Borderlands 3: Deluxe Edition.* 2K Games, 2019.

44. Computer software or app Provide whatever information is available about the version, distributor, and date.

NYT Cooking. Version 4.36, The New York Times, 2021.

45. TV or radio episode or program After the episode and/or series title, provide relevant information about the program, such as contributors; the episode number (if any); the network, distributor, or production company; and the date of broadcast or upload. If you viewed the program on a website or in an app, include that information.

title of episode   program title   narrator (host or speaker)   network   date

"Umbrellas Down." *This American Life,* hosted by Ira Glass, WBEZ, 10 July 2020.

"Shock and Delight." *Bridgerton,* season 1, episode 2, Shondaland / *Netflix,* 2020.
     Netflix, www.netflix.com.

Hillary. Directed by Nanette Burstein, Propagate Content / *Hulu,* 2020. *Hulu* app.

Cite a source reposted from another source

Problem: Some sources that you find online, particularly on blogs or on video-sharing sites, did not originate with the person who uploaded or published the source online. In such a case, how do you give proper credit to the source?

Example: Say you need to cite President John F. Kennedy's inaugural address. You have found a video on YouTube that provides footage of the address (see image). The video was uploaded by PaddyIrishMan2 on October 29, 2006. But clearly, PaddyIrishMan2 is not the author of the video or of the address.

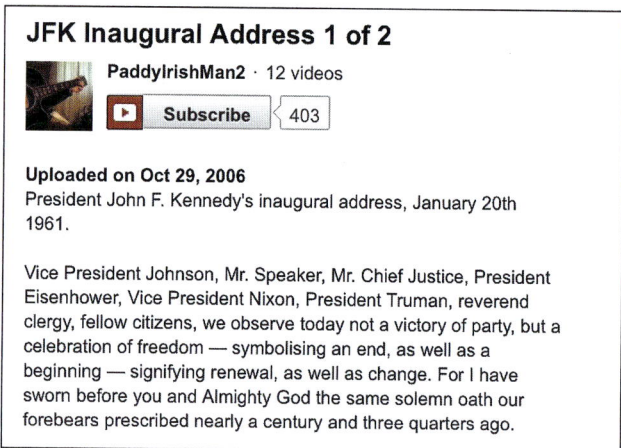

JFK Inaugural Address 1 of 2

PaddyIrishMan2 · 12 videos

▶ Subscribe   ⟨ 403

Uploaded on Oct 29, 2006
President John F. Kennedy's inaugural address, January 20th 1961.

Vice President Johnson, Mr. Speaker, Mr. Chief Justice, President Eisenhower, Vice President Nixon, President Truman, reverend clergy, fellow citizens, we observe today not a victory of party, but a celebration of freedom — symbolising an end, as well as a beginning — signifying renewal, as well as change. For I have sworn before you and Almighty God the same solemn oath our forebears prescribed nearly a century and three quarters ago.

Strategy: Start with what you know. The source is a video that you viewed on the web. For this particular video, John F. Kennedy is the speaker and the author of the inaugural address. PaddyIrishMan2 is identified as the person who uploaded the source to YouTube.

Citation: To cite the source, you can follow the basic MLA guidelines for an online video (see item 42).

author/speaker: website
last name first   title of video   title   upload information

Kennedy, John F. "JFK Inaugural Address: 1 of 2." *YouTube*, uploaded by PaddyIrishMan2,

       upload
       date   URL

29 Oct. 2006, www.youtube.com/watch?v=xE0iPY7XGBo.

NOTE: If your work calls for a primary source, you should try to find the original source of the video; a reference librarian can help.

46. Transcript Cite the source (interview, radio or television program, video, and so on), and add the label "Transcript" at the end of the entry.

Kundu, Anindya. "The 'Opportunity Gap' in US Public Education — and How to Close It."
  TED, May 2019, www.ted.com/talks/anindya_kundu_the_opportunity_gap_in_us_
  public_education_and_how_to_close_it/transcript. Transcript.

47. Live performance Begin with either the title of the work performed, or the author, composer, or main performer if relevant. Include relevant contributors; the theater, ballet, or opera company, if any; the date of the performance; and the location.

Beethoven, Ludwig van. *Piano Concerto No. 3*. Conducted by Andris Nelsons, performed by
  Paul Lewis and Boston Symphony Orchestra, 9 Oct. 2015, Symphony Hall, Boston.

Schreck, Heidi. *What the Constitution Means to Me*. Directed by Oliver Butler, 16 June
  2019, Helen Hayes Theater, New York City.

48. Lecture or public address Begin with the speaker's name, the title of the lecture, the sponsoring organization, the date, and the location. If you viewed the lecture on the web, cite as you would an online video (see item 42). If the lecture or address has no title, use the label "Lecture" or "Address" after the speaker's name.

Gay, Roxane. "Difficult Women, Bad Feminists and Unruly Bodies." Beatty Lecture Series,
  18 Oct. 2018, McGill University.

49. Musical score Begin with the composer's name; the title of the work, italicized; and the date of composition. For a print source, give the publisher and date. For an online source, give the title of the website, the publisher, the date, and the URL.

Beethoven, Ludwig van. *Symphony no. 5 in C Minor, Opus 67*. 1807. Center for Computer
  Assisted Research in the Humanities, 2008, scores.ccarh.org/beethoven/
  sym/beethoven-sym5-1.pdf.

50. Music recording   Begin with the name of the person you want to emphasize: the composer, conductor, or performer. After the song and/or album title, give the names of relevant performers, the record company, and the date. If you accessed the recording on a website or app, include that information.

Bach, Johann Sebastian. *Bach: Violin Concertos*. Performances by Itzhak Perlman,

    Pinchas Zukerman, and English Chamber Orchestra, EMI, 2002.

Bad Bunny. "Vete." *YHLQMDLG*, Rimas, 2020. *Apple Music* app.

51. Artwork, photograph, or other visual art   Begin with the artist and the title of the work, italicized. If you viewed the original work, give the date of composition followed by a comma and the location. If you viewed the work online, give the date of composition followed by a period and the website title, publisher (if any), and URL. If you viewed the work reproduced in a book, cite as a work in an anthology or a collection (item 28), giving the date of composition after the title.

Bradford, Mark. *Let's Walk to the Middle of the Ocean*. 2015, Museum of Modern Art, New York.

Lange, Dorothea. *Migrant Mother, Nipomo, California*. Mar. 1936. *MOMA*, www.moma.org/

    collection/works/50989.

Kertész, André. *Meudon*. 1928. *Street Photography: From Atget to Cartier-Bresson*, by

    Clive Scott, Tauris, 2011, p. 61.

52. Visual such as a table, a chart, or another graphic   Cite a visual as you would a short work within a longer work. Add a descriptive label at the end if the type of visual is not clear from the title or if it is important for your work.

"New COVID-19 Cases Worldwide." *Coronavirus Resource Center*, Johns Hopkins U and

    Medicine, 3 May 2021, coronavirus.jhu.edu/data/new-cases. Chart.

"Number of Measles Cases Reported by Year 2010–2019." *Centers for Disease Control and

    Prevention*, 22 Feb. 2019, www.cdc.gov/measles/cases-outbreaks.html. Table.

53. Cartoon or comic strip   Give the cartoonist's name; the title of the cartoon, if it has one, in quotation marks, or the label "Cartoon" or "Comic strip"
without quotation marks in place of a title; and publication information. Cite
an online cartoon as a work from a website (item 35).

Shiell, Mike. Cartoon. *The Saturday Evening Post*, Jan.–Feb. 2021, p. 8.

Munroe, Randall. "Heartbleed Explanation." *xkcd*, xkcd.com/1354/. Accessed
    10 Oct. 2020.

54. Advertisement   If the advertisement has no title, begin with the label
"Advertisement for" and what is being advertised, followed by the publication
information for the source in which the advertisement appears. For special
advertisement formats, end with a descriptive label, such as "Billboard."

Advertisement for Better World Club. *Mother Jones*, Mar.–Apr. 2021, p. 2.

"The Whole Working-from-Home Thing — Apple." *YouTube*, uploaded by Apple, 13 July
    2020, /www.youtube.com/watch?v=6_pru8U2RmM.

55. Map   Cite a map as you would a short work within a longer work. If the
map is published on its own, cite it as a book or another long work. Use the
label "Map" at the end if it is not clear from the title or source information.

"Australia." *Perry-Castañeda Library Map Collection*, U of Texas Libraries, 2016, legacy.lib.
    utexas.edu/maps/cia16/australia_sm_2016.gif.

Government and legal documents

56. Government document   Treat the government agency as the author. In
most situations, give the name of the author as presented by the source, as in
the first example. If you are using several government sources, you may want
to standardize your list of works cited by listing the name of the government,
spelled out, followed by the name of any agencies and subagencies, as in the
second example.

U.S. Bureau of Labor Statistics. "Consumer Expenditures Report 2019." *BLS Reports*,
    Dec. 2020, www.bls.gov/opub/reports/consumer-expenditures/2019/home.htm.

government   department   agency (or agencies)
United States, Department of Transportation, Federal Highway Administration.

                                        title of work
    Environmental Justice Analysis in Transportation Planning and Programming: State
                        date   URL
    of the Practice. Feb. 2019, www.fhwa.dot.gov/environment/environmental_justice/

    publications/tpp/fhwahep19022.pdf.

57. Historical document The titles of most historical documents are neither italicized nor put in quotation marks. For the titles of constitutions, use italics (*Constitution of the United States*).

Emancipation Proclamation. 1863. *National Archives*, www.archives.gov/exhibits/fea-
tured-documents/emancipation-proclamation/transcript.html.

58. Legislative act (law) Begin with the name of the legislative body and the act's Public Law number. Then give the publication information for the source in which you found the act.

United States, Congress. Public Law 116–136. *United States Statutes at Large*, 134,
2019, pp. 281–615. *U.S. Government Publishing Office*, www.govinfo.gov/content/
pkg/PLAW-116publ136/uslm/PLAW-116publ136.xml.

59. Court case List the name of the court. Then provide the title of the case, the date of the decision, and publication information.

United States, Supreme Court. *Miller v. Alabama*. 25 June 2012. *Legal Information
Institute*, Cornell Law School, www.law.cornell.edu/supremecourt/text/10-9646

Personal communication and course materials

60. Personal letter

Nadir, Abdul. Letter to the author. 6 May 2019. Typescript.

61. E-mail message

Lewis-Truth, Antoine. E-mail to the Office of Student Financial Assistance. 30 Aug. 2020.

62. Text message

Primak, Shoshana. Text message to the author. 9 Mar. 2021.

63. Course materials For materials posted to an online learning manage-
ment system, include as much information as is available about the source (author, title or description, and any publication information); then give the course, instructor, platform, institution name, date of posting, and URL. For materials delivered in a print or PDF coursepack, include author and title of the work; the words "Course pack for" with the course number and name; "compiled by" with the instructor's name; the term; and the institution name.

Rose, Mike. "Blue-Collar Brilliance." *Introduction to College Writing*, taught by Melanie Li. *Blackboard*, Merrimack College, 9 Sept. 2020, blackboard.merrimack.edu/ultra/ courses/_25745_1/cl/readings.

MLA-4c MLA information notes (optional)

Researchers who use the MLA system of parenthetical documentation may also use information notes for one of two purposes:

1. to provide additional material that is important but might interrupt the flow of the paper
2. to refer to several sources that support a single point or to provide comments on sources

Information notes may be either footnotes or endnotes. Footnotes appear at the foot of the page; endnotes appear on a separate page at the end of the paper, just before the list of works cited. For either style, the notes are numbered consecutively throughout the paper. The text of the paper contains a raised arabic numeral that corresponds to the number of the note.

TEXT

In the past several years, employees have filed a number of lawsuits against employers because of online monitoring practices.[1]

NOTE

[1] For a discussion of federal law applicable to electronic surveillance in the workplace, see Kesan 293.

 **MLA-5**   # MLA format; sample research paper

The following guidelines are consistent with advice given in the *MLA Handbook*, 9th edition (MLA, 2021), and with typical requirements for student papers. For a sample MLA research paper, see MLA-5b.

MLA-5a MLA format

Formatting the paper: The basics

Papers written in MLA style should be formatted as follows.

Heading includes the student's name, instructor's name, course, and date.

Sophie Harba

Professor Baros-Moon

Engl 1101

9 November 2018

Harba 1

Student's last name and the **page number** appear in the right-hand corner of every page.

Center the **title**. Add no extra space above or below it, and use no quotation marks or italics.

What's for Dinner? Personal Choices vs. Public Health

Should the government enact laws to regulate healthy eating choices? Many Americans would answer an emphatic "No," arguing that what and how much we eat should be left to individual choice rather than unreasonable laws. Others might argue that it would be unreasonable for the government not to enact legislation, given the rise of chronic diseases that result from harmful diets. In this debate, both the definition of reasonable regulations and the role of government to legislate food choices are at stake. In the name of public health and safety, state governments have the responsibility to shape health policies and to regulate healthy eating choices, especially since doing so offers a potentially large social benefit for a relatively small cost.

Debates surrounding the government's role in regulating food have a long history in the United States. According to Lorine Goodwin, a food

Use Times New Roman or another easy-to-read **font**.

Use a **1-inch margin** on all sides of the page, and **double-space** the text.

Formatting the paper: Other concerns

Group projects   If you are writing a group project, create a title page with all members' names, the instructor's name, the course, and the date, all aligned left on separate double-spaced lines. Center the title on a new line a few spaces down. Starting on the first text page, include all members' last names and the page number, aligned top and right, on every page. If all last names will not fit on a single line, include only the page number.

Capitalization, italics, and quotation marks   In titles of works, capitalize all words except articles (*a, an, the*), prepositions (*to, from, between*), coordinating conjunctions (*and, but, or, for*), and the *to* in infinitives — unless the word is first or last in the title or subtitle. Follow these guidelines in your paper even if the title appears in all capital or all lowercase letters in the source.

In your text, when a complete sentence follows a colon, lowercase the first word following the colon.

Italicize the titles of books, journals, magazines, and other long works, such as websites. Use quotation marks around the titles of articles, short stories, poems, and other short works.

Long quotations   When a quotation is longer than four typed lines of prose or three lines of poetry, set it off from the text by indenting the entire quotation one-half inch from the left margin. Do not use quotation marks when a quotation has been set off from the text by indenting. See MLA-3b for an example.

Headings   While headings are generally not needed for brief essays, readers may find them helpful for long or complex essays. Place each heading in the same style and size. Place main headings at the left margin, in boldface without any indent. If you need subheadings (level 2, level 3), be consistent in styling them. Capitalize headings as you would titles.

Visuals   MLA classifies visuals as tables and figures (figures include graphs, charts, maps, photographs, and drawings). Place visuals in your essay as near as possible to the relevant text. Label each table with an arabic numeral ("Table 1") and provide a clear title. Capitalize as you would the title of a work (see above). Place the table number and title on separate lines above the table, flush with the left margin.

For a table that you have borrowed or adapted, give the source below the table in a note like the following:

Source: Boris Groysberg and Michael Slind, "Leadership Is a Conversation," *Harvard Business Review*, June 2012, p. 83.

All other visuals should be labeled "Figure" (abbreviated "Fig."), numbered, and captioned. The label and caption should appear on the same line, aligned left, underneath the visual. Capitalize the caption as you would a sentence; include source information following the caption. If your caption includes full publication information and you do not cite the source anywhere else in your essay, it is not necessary to include an entry in your list of works cited. Refer to visuals in your text (*see table 1; as shown in figure 2*), indicating how each contributes to a point you are making. See MLA-5b for an example of a figure in a paper.

Preparing the list of works cited

Begin the list of works cited on a new page at the end of the paper. Center the title "Works Cited" one inch from the top of the page. Double-space throughout. See the student essays in A4-h and MLA-5b for sample lists of works cited.

Alphabetizing the list   Alphabetize the list by the last names of the authors (or editors); if a work has no author or editor, alphabetize by the first word of the title other than *A*, *An*, or *The*.

Indenting   Do not indent the first line of each works cited entry, but indent any additional lines one-half inch. This technique, called a hanging indent, highlights the names of the authors, making it easy for readers to scan the alphabetized list. See the works cited list in MLA-5b.

URLs and DOIs   Do not insert line breaks, spaces, or hyphens into URLs or DOIs in works cited entries. If the entire URL moves to another line, creating a short line, you may leave it that way. See also the guidelines on page 173 for treating URLs and DOIs.

MLA-5b Sample MLA research paper

On the following pages is a research paper on the topic of the role of government in legislating food choices, written by Sophie Harba, a student in a composition class. Harba's paper is documented with in-text citations and a list of works cited in MLA style. Annotations in the margins of the paper draw your attention to Harba's use of MLA style and her effective writing.

Harba 1

Sophie Harba

Professor Baros-Moon

Engl 1101

9 November 2018

What's for Dinner? Personal Choices vs. Public Health

Should the government enact laws to regulate healthy eating

choices? Many Americans would answer an emphatic "No," arguing that

what and how much we eat should be left to individual choice rather than

unreasonable laws. Others might argue that it would be unreasonable for

the government not to enact legislation, given the rise of chronic diseases

that result from harmful diets. In this debate, both the definition of

reasonable regulations and the role of government to legislate food choices

are at stake. In the name of public health and safety, state governments

have the responsibility to shape health policies and to regulate healthy

eating choices, especially since doing so offers a potentially large social

benefit for a relatively small cost.

Debates surrounding the government's role in regulating food have

a long history in the United States. According to Lorine Goodwin, a food

historian, nineteenth-century reformers who sought to purify the food

supply were called "fanatics" and "radicals" by critics who argued that

consumers should be free to buy and eat what they want (77). Thanks to

regulations, though, such as the 1906 federal Pure Food and Drug Act,

food, beverages, and medicine are largely free from toxins. In addition, to

prevent contamination and the spread of disease, meat and dairy products

are now inspected by government agents to ensure that they meet health

requirements. Such regulations can be considered reasonable because

they protect us from harm with little, if any, noticeable consumer cost. It

is not considered an unreasonable infringement on personal choice that

contaminated meat or arsenic-laced cough drops are *un*available at our

local supermarket. Rather, it is an important government function to stop

such harmful items from entering the marketplace.

Even though our food meets current safety standards, there is a need

for further regulation. Not all food dangers, for example, arise from obvious

toxins like arsenic and *E. coli*. A diet that is low in nutritional value and

high in sugars, fats, and refined grains—grains that have been processed

to increase shelf life but that contain little fiber, iron, and B vitamins—can

Title is
centered.

Opening question
engages readers.

Writer highlights
the research
conversation.

Thesis answers
the question
and presents
main point.

Signal phrase
names the
author. Page
number is in
parentheses.

Harba provides
historical
background
and introduces
a key term,
reasonable.

Harba
establishes
common ground
with the reader.

Transition
helps readers
move from one
paragraph to
the next.

Marginal annotations indicate MLA-style formatting and effective writing.

Harba 2

be damaging over time (United States, Department of Agriculture 36).
A graph from the government's *Dietary Guidelines for Americans, 2010*
shows that Americans consume about three times more fats and sugars
and twice as many refined grains as is recommended but only half of the
recommended foods (see fig. 1).

Harba uses a graph to illustrate Americans' poor nutritional choices.

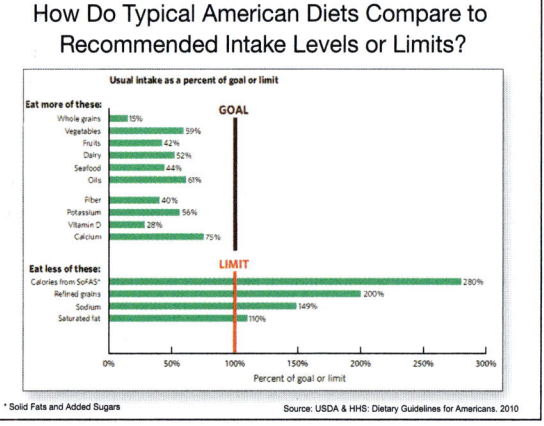

Visual includes a caption with a figure number and source information.

Fig. 1. United States, Department of Agriculture, fig. 5-1.

Michael Pollan, who has written extensively about Americans'
unhealthy eating habits, notes that "[t]he Centers for Disease Control
estimates that fully three quarters of US health care spending goes to
treat chronic diseases, most of which are preventable and linked to diet:
heart disease, stroke, type 2 diabetes, and at least a third of all cancers."
In fact, the amount of money the United States spends to treat chronic
illnesses is increasing so rapidly that the Centers for Disease Control has
labeled chronic disease "the public health challenge of the 21st century"
(United States, Department of Health 1). In fighting this epidemic, the
primary challenge is not the need to find a cure; the challenge is to
prevent chronic diseases from striking in the first place.

No page number is available for this web source.

Harba emphasizes the urgency of her argument.

Legislation, however, is not a popular solution when it comes to
most Americans and the food they eat. According to a nationwide poll,
seventy-five percent of Americans are opposed to laws that restrict or

Harba treats both sides fairly.

Harba 3

put limitations on access to unhealthy foods (Neergaard and Agiesta). When New York mayor Michael Bloomberg proposed a regulation in 2012 banning the sale of soft drinks in servings greater than twelve ounces in restaurants and movie theaters, he was ridiculed as "Nanny Bloomberg." In California in 2011, legislators failed to pass a law that would impose a penny-per-ounce tax on soda, which would have funded obesity prevention programs. And in Mississippi, legislators passed "a ban on bans—a law that forbids . . . local restrictions on food or drink" (Conly).

> No page number is needed for a one-page source.

Why is the public largely resistant to laws that would limit unhealthy choices or penalize those choices with so-called fat taxes? Many consumers and civil rights advocates find such laws to be an unreasonable restriction on individual freedom of choice. As health policy experts Mello and others point out, opposition to food and beverage regulation is similar to the opposition to early tobacco legislation: the public views the issue as one of personal responsibility rather than one requiring government intervention (2602). In other words, if a person eats unhealthy food and becomes ill as a result, that is his or her choice. But those who favor legislation claim that freedom of choice is a myth because of the strong influence of food and beverage industry marketing on consumers' dietary habits. According to one nonprofit health advocacy group, food and beverage companies spend roughly two billion dollars per year marketing directly to children. As a result, kids see nearly four thousand ads per year encouraging them to eat unhealthy food and drinks ("Facts"). As was the case with antismoking laws passed in recent decades, taxes and legal restrictions on junk food sales could help to counter the strong marketing messages that promote unhealthy products.

> Harba anticipates objections to her idea. She counters opposing views and supports her argument.

> Shortened title provided in parentheses for a source with no named author.

The United States has a history of state and local public health laws that have successfully promoted a particular behavior by punishing an undesirable behavior. The decline in tobacco use as a result of antismoking taxes and laws is perhaps the most obvious example. Another example is legislation requiring the use of seat belts, which have significantly reduced fatalities in car crashes. One government agency reports that seat belt use saved an average of more than fourteen thousand lives per year in the United States between 2000 and 2010 (United States, Department of Transportation 231). Perhaps seat belt laws have public support because the cost of wearing a seat belt

> Analogy extends Harba's argument.

> A government or organization author's name is shortened in parentheses.

Harba 4

is small, especially when compared with the benefit of saving fourteen thousand lives per year.

Laws designed to prevent chronic disease by promoting healthier food and beverage consumption also have potentially enormous benefits. To give just one example, Marion Nestle, New York University professor of nutrition and public health, notes that "a 1% reduction in intake of saturated fat across the population would prevent more than 30,000 cases of coronary heart disease annually and save more than a billion dollars in health care costs" (7). Few would argue that saving lives and dollars is not an enormous benefit. But three-quarters of Americans say they would object to the costs needed to achieve this benefit—the regulations needed to reduce saturated fat intake.

Why do so many Americans believe there is a degree of personal choice lost when regulations such as taxes, bans, or portion limits on unhealthy foods are proposed? Some critics of anti-junk-food laws believe that even if state and local laws were successful in curbing chronic diseases, they would still be unacceptable. Bioethicist David Resnik emphasizes that such policies, despite their potential to make our society healthier, "open the door to excessive government control over food, which could restrict dietary choices, interfere with cultural, ethnic, and religious traditions, and exacerbate socioeconomic inequalities" (31). Resnik acknowledges that his argument relies on "slippery slope" thinking, but he insists that "social and political pressures" regarding food regulation make his concerns valid (31). Yet the social and political pressures that Resnik cites are really just the desire to improve public health, and limiting access to unhealthy, artificial ingredients seems a small price to pay. As legal scholars L. O. Gostin and K. G. Gostin explain, "[I]nterventions that do not pose a truly significant burden on individual liberty" are justified if they "go a long way towards safeguarding the health and well-being of the populace" (214).

To improve public health, advocates such as Bowdoin College philosophy professor Sarah Conly contend that it is the government's duty to prevent people from making harmful choices whenever feasible and whenever public benefits outweigh the costs. In response to critics who claim that laws aimed at stopping us from eating whatever we want are an assault on our freedom of choice, Conly offers a persuasive counterargument:

> [L]aws aren't designed for each one of us individually. Some of us
> can drive safely at 90 miles per hour, but we're bound by the same
> laws as the people who can't, because individual speeding laws

Annotations (left margin):

Harba introduces a quotation with a signal phrase and shows readers why she chose to use the source.

Harba acknowledges critics and counterarguments.

Including the source's credentials makes Harba more credible.

Signal phrase names the author.

Harba 5

aren't practical. Giving up a little liberty is something we agree
to when we agree to live in a democratic society that is governed
by laws.

As Conly suggests, it is important to move from *either/or* thinking
(either we have complete freedom of choice *or* we have government
regulations and lose our freedom) to seeing health as a matter of public
good, not individual liberty. Proposals such as Mayor Bloomberg's that seek
to limit portions of unhealthy beverages aren't about giving up liberty;
they are about asking individuals to choose substantial public health
benefits at a very small cost.

Despite arguments in favor of regulating unhealthy food as a means
to improve public health, public opposition has stood in the way of
legislation. Americans freely eat as much unhealthy food as they want, and
manufacturers and sellers of these foods have nearly unlimited freedom
to promote such products and drive increased consumption, without
any requirements to warn the public of potential hazards. Yet mounting
scientific evidence points to unhealthy food as a significant contributing
factor to chronic disease, which is straining our health care system,
decreasing Americans' quality of life, and leading to unnecessary premature
deaths. Americans must consider whether to allow the costly trend of rising
chronic disease to continue in the name of personal choice or whether to
support the regulatory changes and public health policies that will reverse
that trend.

Long quotation is set off from the text. Quotation marks are omitted.

Quotation is followed by comments that connect the source to Harba's argument.

Conclusion sums up Harba's argument and provides closure.

Harba 6

Works Cited

Conly, Sarah. "Three Cheers for the Nanny State." *The New York Times*, 25 Mar. 2013, p. A23.

"The Facts on Junk Food Marketing and Kids." *Prevention Institute*, www.preventioninstitute.org/focus-areas/were-not-buying-it-get-involved/were-not-buying-it-the-facts-on-junk-food-marketing-and-kids. Accessed 16 Oct. 2018.

Goodwin, Lorine Swainston. *The Pure Food, Drink, and Drug Crusaders, 1879–1914*. McFarland, 2006.

Gostin, L. O., and K. G. Gostin. "A Broader Liberty: J. S. Mill, Paternalism, and the Public's Health." *Public Health*, vol. 123, no. 3, Mar. 2009, pp. 214–21, https://doi.org/10.1016/j.puhe.2008.12.024.

Mello, Michelle M., et al. "Obesity—the New Frontier of Public Health Law." *The New England Journal of Medicine*, vol. 354, no. 24, 15 June 2006, pp. 2601–10, https://doi.org/10.1056/NEJMhpr060227.

Neergaard, Lauran, and Jennifer Agiesta. "Obesity's a Crisis but We Want Our Junk Food, Poll Shows." *The Huffington Post*, 4 Jan. 2013, www.huffingtonpost.com/2013/01/04/obesity-junk-food-government-intervention-poll_n_2410376.html.

Nestle, Marion. *Food Politics: How the Food Industry Influences Nutrition and Health*. U of California P, 2013.

Pollan, Michael. "The Food Movement, Rising." *The New York Review of Books*, 10 June 2010, www.nybooks.com/articles/2010/06/10/food-movement-rising.

Resnik, David. "Trans Fat Bans and Human Freedom." *The American Journal of Bioethics*, vol. 10, no. 3, Mar. 2010, pp. 27–32.

United States, Department of Agriculture and Department of Health and Human Services. *Dietary Guidelines for Americans, 2010*, health.gov/dietaryguidelines/dga2010/dietaryguidelines2010.pdf.

---, Department of Health and Human Services, Centers for Disease Control and Prevention, National Center for Chronic Disease Prevention and Health Promotion. *The Power of Prevention*, 2009, www.cdc.gov/chronicdisease/pdf/2009-Power-of-Prevention.pdf.

---, Department of Transportation, National Highway Traffic Safety Administration. *Traffic Safety Facts 2010: A Compilation of Motor Vehicle Crash Data from the Fatality Analysis Reporting System and the General Estimates System*. 2010, www.nrd.nhtsa.dot.gov/Pubs/811659.pdf.

Works cited list begins on a new page. Heading is centered.

Access date used for an undated online source.

List is alphabetized by authors' last names (or by title if no author).

First line of each entry is at the left margin; extra lines are indented ½".

Double-spacing is used throughout.

Author names are standardized for multiple government sources.

APA
CMS

APA Style and CMS Style

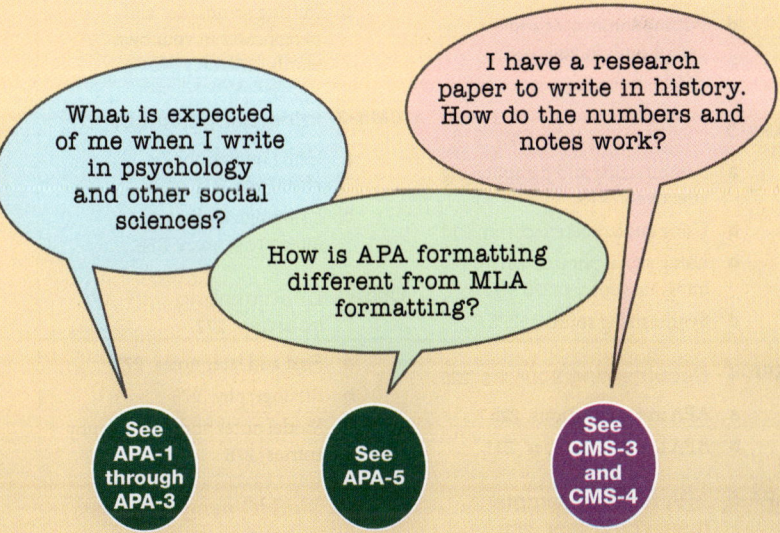

What is expected of me when I write in psychology and other social sciences?

I have a research paper to write in history. How do the numbers and notes work?

How is APA formatting different from MLA formatting?

See APA-1 through APA-3

See APA-5

See CMS-3 and CMS-4

APA CMS APA Style and CMS Style

List of APA in-text citation models

List of APA reference list models

List of APA reference list models, *continued*

List of CMS-style notes and bibliography entries is on page 265.

This tabbed section shows how to document sources in APA style for the social sciences and fields such as nursing and business, and in CMS (*Chicago*) style for history and some humanities classes. It also includes discipline-specific advice on three important topics: supporting a thesis, citing sources and avoiding plagiarism, and integrating sources.

NOTE: For advice on finding and evaluating sources and on managing information in courses across the disciplines, see the tabbed section R, Researching.

APA Style

Most instructors in the social sciences and some instructors in other disciplines will ask you to document your sources with the American Psychological Association (APA) system of in-text citations and references described in APA-4. When writing an APA-style paper that draws on sources, you face three main challenges:

1. supporting a thesis (APA-1)
2. citing your sources and avoiding plagiarism (APA-2)
3. integrating source material effectively (APA-3)

Examples in this section are drawn from one student's research for a review of the literature on technology's role in the shift to student-centered learning. April Wang's paper appears in APA-5b.

 ## Supporting a thesis

Most research assignments ask you to form a thesis, or main idea, and to support that thesis with well-organized evidence. In a paper reviewing the literature on a topic, the thesis analyzes the conclusions drawn by a variety of researchers.

APA-1a Form a working thesis.

Once you have read a range of sources, considered your issue from different perspectives, and chosen an entry point in the research conversation (see R1-b), you are ready to focus your research paper by forming a working thesis: a one-sentence (or occasionally a two-sentence) statement of your central idea. (See also C1-c.) The working thesis expresses more than your opinion; it expresses your informed, reasoned answer to your research question — an answer about which people might disagree. As you learn more about your subject, your ideas may change, and you can revise your thesis as you draft. Here, for example, is a research question posed by April Wang, a student in an education class, followed by her thesis in response.

RESEARCH QUESTION

Can educational technology improve student learning and solve the problem of teacher shortages?

WORKING THESIS

Educational technology can help solve teacher shortages by shifting the focus from teachers to students.

The thesis usually appears at the end of the introductory paragraph. To read April Wang's thesis in the context of her introduction, see APA-5b.

See MLA-1a for guidelines for testing your working thesis statement.

APA-1b Organize your ideas.

The American Psychological Association encourages the use of headings to help readers follow the organization of a paper. For an original research report, the major headings often follow a standard model: "Method," "Results," "Discussion." The introduction does not have a heading; it consists of the material between the title of the paper and the first heading.

For a literature review, headings will vary. Student writer April Wang used three questions to focus her research (see her final paper in APA-5b); the questions then became headings in her paper:

In what ways is student-centered learning effective?

Can educational technology help students drive their own learning?

How can public schools effectively combine teacher talent and educational technology?

APA-1c Consider how sources will contribute to your essay.

The source materials you have gathered can play many different roles and will help you support and develop your argument.

Providing background information or context

Readers need some background information and context to anchor their understanding of your topic. Describing a research study or offering facts and statistics, as student writer April Wang does, can help readers grasp your topic's significance.

> In the United States, most public school systems are struggling with teacher shortages, which are projected to worsen as the number of applicants to education schools decreases (Donitsa-Schmidt & Zuzovsky, 2014, p. 420). Citing federal data, *The New York Times* reported a 30% drop in "people entering teacher preparation programs" between 2010 and 2014 (Rich, 2015, para. 10).

Explaining terms or concepts

If readers are unfamiliar with a term or concept important to your topic, you will want to define or explain it; or if your argument depends on a term with multiple meanings, you will want to explain your use of the term. Quoting or paraphrasing a source can help you define terms and concepts in accessible language. April Wang uses a source to define a key concept, student-centered learning.

> According to the International Society for Technology in Education (2016), "Student-centered learning moves students from passive receivers of information to active participants in their own discovery process (What Is It? section)."

Supporting your claims

As you draft, make sure to back up your assertions with facts, examples, and other evidence from your research (see also A4-f). April Wang, for example, uses one source's findings to support her claim that a combination of teachers and educational technology can promote student-centered learning.

> Many schools have already effectively paired a reduced faculty with educational technology to support successful student-centered learning. For example, Watson (2008) offered a case study of the Cincinnati Public Schools Virtual High School, which brought students together in a physical school building to work with an assortment of online learning programs. Although there were only 10 certified teachers in the building, students were able to engage in highly individualized instruction according to their own needs, strengths, and learning styles, using the 10 teachers as support (p. 7).

Lending authority to your argument

Expert opinion can add credibility to your argument (see also A4-f). But don't rely on experts to make your points for you. State your ideas in your own words and, when appropriate, cite the judgment of an authority in the field to support your position.

> Horn and Staker (2011) concluded that the chief benefit of technological learning was that it could adapt to the individual student in a way that whole-class delivery by a single teacher could not. Their study examined various schools where technology enabled student-centered learning.

Anticipating and countering alternative perspectives

Do not ignore sources that contradict your position. Instead, use them to state potential objections to your argument before you counter them (see A4-g). Readers often have objections in mind already, whether or not they agree with you. Wang uses a source to acknowledge that some teachers oppose student instruction driven by technology.

> Some researchers have expressed doubt that schools are ready for student-centered learning—or any type of instruction—that is driven by technology. In a recent survey conducted by the Nellie Mae Education Foundation, Moeller and Reitzes (2011) reported not only that many teachers lacked confidence in their ability to incorporate technology in the classroom but that 43% of polled high school students said that they lacked confidence in their technological proficiency going into college and careers.

 # Citing sources; avoiding plagiarism

In a research paper, you draw on the work of other researchers and writers, and you must document their contributions by citing your sources. Sources are cited for two reasons:

1. to tell readers where your information comes from — so that they can assess its reliability and, if interested, find and read the original source
2. to give credit to the writers from whom you have borrowed words and ideas

You must cite anything you borrow from a source, including direct quotations; statistics and other facts; visuals such as tables and graphs; and summaries and paraphrases. Borrowing without proper acknowledgment is a form of dishonesty known as plagiarism. The only exception is common knowledge — information that your readers may know or could easily locate in any number of reference sources.

APA-2a Understand how the APA system works.

The American Psychological Association recommends an author-date system of citation. The following describes that system.

1. The source is introduced by a signal phrase that includes the last name of the author followed by the date of publication in parentheses.
2. The material being cited is followed by a page number or other locator in parentheses (for a direct quotation).
3. At the end of the paper, an alphabetized list of references gives complete publication information for the source.

In APA style, a page number or other locator (paragraph number, section title) need not be included for a summary or a paraphrase, but check with your instructors to make sure you understand their requirements.

IN-TEXT CITATION

Bell (2010) reported that students engaged in this kind of learning performed better on both project-based assessments and standardized tests (pp. 39–40).

ENTRY IN THE LIST OF REFERENCES

Bell, S. (2010). Project-based learning for the 21st century: Skills for the future. *The Clearing House, 83*(2), 39–43.

This basic APA format varies for different types of sources. For a detailed discussion and other models, see APA-4.

APA-2b Understand what plagiarism is.

In a research paper, you draw on the work of other writers. To be fair and responsible, you must document their contributions by citing your sources. When you acknowledge and document your sources, you avoid plagiarism, a serious academic offense.

Three different acts are considered plagiarism:

1. failing to cite quotations and borrowed ideas
2. failing to enclose borrowed language in quotation marks
3. failing to put summaries and paraphrases in your own words

Definitions of plagiarism may vary; it's a good idea to find out how your school defines and addresses academic dishonesty.

APA-2c Use quotation marks around borrowed language.

To indicate that you are using a source's exact phrases or sentences, you must enclose them in quotation marks unless they have been set off from the text by indenting (see APA-3b). To omit the quotation marks is to claim — falsely — that the language is your own. Such an omission is plagiarism even if you have cited the source.

ORIGINAL SOURCE

Student-centered learning, or student centeredness, is a model which puts the student in the center of the learning process.

— Z. Çubukçu, "Teachers' Evaluation of Student-Centered Learning Environments" (2012), p. 50

PLAGIARISM

According to Çubukçu (2012), student-centered learning . . . is a model which puts the student in the center of the learning process (p. 50).

The student writer has cited the source, Çubukçu; however, the writer has not put quotation marks around the definition of "student centered learning," which is taken word-for-word from the source.

BORROWED LANGUAGE IN QUOTATION MARKS

According to Çubukçu (2012), "student-centered learning . . . is a model which puts the student in the center of the learning process" (p. 50).

NOTE: Quotation marks are not used when quoted sentences are set off from the text by indenting (see APA-3b).

APA-2d Put summaries and paraphrases in your own words.

A summary condenses information; a paraphrase conveys the information using roughly the same number of words as the original source. When you summarize or paraphrase, it is not enough to name the source; you must present the source's meaning using your own words and sentence structure. (See also R2-c.) You are plagiarizing when you "patchwrite" — half-copy the author's sentences, either by mixing the author's phrases with your own without using quotation marks or by plugging synonyms into the author's sentence structure.

The following paraphrases are plagiarized — even though the source is cited — because their language or sentence structure is too close to that of the source.

ORIGINAL SOURCE

Student-centered teaching focuses on the student. Decision-making, organization and content are determined for most by taking individual students' needs and interests into consideration. Student-centered teaching provides opportunities to develop students' skills of transferring knowledge to other situations, triggering retention, and adapting a high motivation for learning.

— Z. Çubukçu, "Teachers' Evaluation of Student-Centered Learning Environments" (2012), p. 52

UNACCEPTABLE BORROWING OF PHRASES

Borrows too much language from the original

According to Çubukçu (2012), student-centered teaching takes into account the needs and interests of each student, making it possible to foster students' skills of transferring knowledge to new situations and triggering retention (p. 52).

UNACCEPTABLE BORROWING OF STRUCTURE

Follows the structure of the original too closely

According to Çubukçu (2012), this new model of teaching centers on the student. The material and flow of the course are chosen by considering the students' individual requirements. Student-centered teaching gives a chance for students to develop useful, transferable skills, ensuring they'll remember material and stay motivated (p. 52).

To avoid plagiarizing an author's language, resist the temptation to look at the source while you are summarizing or paraphrasing. After you have read the passage you want to paraphrase, set the source aside. Ask yourself, "What is the author's meaning?" In your own words, state your understanding of the author's basic point. Return to the source and check that you haven't used the author's language or sentence structure or misrepresented the author's ideas. When you fully understand another writer's meaning, you can more easily and accurately present those ideas in your own words.

ACCEPTABLE PARAPHRASE

In his research, Çubukçu (2012) has documented the numerous benefits of student-centered teaching in putting the student at the center of teaching and learning. When students are given the option of deciding what they learn and how they learn, they are motivated to apply their learning to new settings and to retain the content of their learning (p. 52).

Note that APA does not require a page number or other locator for a paraphrase, but you can choose to include one when doing so might help a reader locate the passage in the source.

APA-3 Integrating sources

Summaries, paraphrases, quotations, and data will help you support your argument, but they cannot speak for you. You need to find a balance between the words of your sources and your own voice, so that readers always know who is speaking in your paper. You can use several strategies to integrate sources into your paper while maintaining your own voice.

APA-3a Summarize and paraphrase effectively.

In your academic writing, keep the emphasis on your ideas and your language; use your own words to summarize and to paraphrase your sources and to explain your points. How you choose to use a source — as summary or paraphrase — depends on your purpose.

Summarizing

When you summarize a source, you express another writer's ideas in your own words, condensing the author's key points and using fewer words than the author. Even though a summary is in your own words, the original ideas remain the intellectual property of the author, so you must include a citation. Summarizing allows you to state the source's main idea simply before you respond to or counter it.

See "When to summarize" (MLA-3a) for more advice.

Paraphrasing

When you paraphrase, you express an author's ideas in your own words and sentence structure, using approximately the same number of words and details as in the source. Even though the words are your own, the original ideas are the author's intellectual property, so you must give a citation. Paraphrasing allows you to capture a source's ideas but perhaps simplify or reorder them.

See "When to paraphrase" (MLA-3a) for more advice.

APA-3b Use quotations effectively.

When you quote a source, you borrow some of the author's exact words and enclose them in quotation marks. Quotation marks show your readers that both the idea and the words belong to the author.

See "When to use quotations" (MLA-3b) for more advice.

Limiting your use of quotations

Keep the emphasis on your own ideas. Although it is tempting to insert many quotations in your paper and to use your own words only for connecting passages, do not quote excessively. It is almost impossible to integrate numerous long quotations smoothly into your own text.

It is not always necessary to quote full sentences from a source. You can often integrate language from a source into your own sentence structure.

> Citing federal data, *The New York Times* reported a 30% drop in "people entering teacher preparation programs" between 2010 and 2014 (Rich, 2015, para. 10).

> Bell (2010) has argued that the chief benefit of student-centered learning is that it can connect students with "real-world tasks," thus making learning more engaging as well as more comprehensive (p. 39).

Using the ellipsis mark

To condense a quoted passage, you can use the ellipsis mark (a series of three spaced periods) to indicate that you have omitted words. What remains must be grammatically complete.

> Demski (2012) noted that "personalized learning . . . acknowledges and accommodates the range of abilities, prior experiences, needs, and interests of each student" (p. 33).

The writer has omitted the phrase "a student-centered teaching and learning model that" from the source.

If you leave out one or more full sentences, use a period before the three ellipsis dots.

> According to Demski (2012), "In any personalized learning model, the student—not the teacher—is the central figure. . . . Personalized learning may finally allow individualization and differentiation to actually happen in the classroom" (p. 34).

Ordinarily, do not use an ellipsis mark at the beginning or at the end of a quotation. Your readers will understand that you have taken the quoted material from a longer passage. The only exception occurs when you feel it is necessary, for clarity, to indicate that your quotation begins or ends in the middle of a sentence.

Using sources responsibly   Make sure omissions and ellipsis marks do not distort the meaning of your source.

Using brackets

Brackets allow you to insert your own words into quoted material to clarify a confusing reference or to keep a sentence grammatical in your context.

> Demski's (2012) research confirms that "implement[ing] a true personalized learning model on a national level" is difficult for a number of reasons (p. 36).

To indicate an error such as a misspelling in a quotation, insert "[*sic*]," italicized and with brackets around it, right after the error. (See P6-b.)

Setting off long quotations

When you quote forty or more words from a source, set off the quotation by indenting it one-half inch from the left margin. Use the normal right margin and do not single-space the quotation.

Long quotations should be introduced by an informative sentence, usually followed by a colon. Quotation marks are unnecessary because the indented format tells readers that the passage is taken word-for-word from the source.

> According to Svokos (2015), some educational technology resources entertain students while supporting student-centered learning:
>
>> GlassLab, a nonprofit that was launched with grants from the Bill & Melinda Gates and MacArthur Foundations, creates educational games that are now being used in more than 6,000 classrooms across the country. Some of the company's games are education versions of existing ones—for example, its first release was SimCity EDU—while others are originals. Teachers get real-time updates on students' progress as well as suggestions on what subjects they need to spend more time perfecting.
>> (5. Educational Games section)

The parenthetical citation with a locator (page number, paragraph number, or section title) goes outside the final mark of punctuation. (When a quotation is run into your text, the opposite is true. See the sample citations presented earlier in APA-3b.)

APA-3c Use signal phrases to integrate sources.

Whenever you include a paraphrase, summary, or direct quotation of another writer's work in your paper, prepare your readers for it with a signal phrase— or what APA calls a "narrative citation." A signal phrase usually names the author of the source, gives the publication year in parentheses, and often provides some context. It is generally acceptable in APA style to call authors by their last name only, even on a first mention. If your paper refers to two authors with the same last name, use their initials as well.

When you write a signal phrase, choose a verb that fits with the way you are using the source (see APA-1c). Are you providing background, explaining a concept, supporting a claim, lending authority, or refuting an argument? See the chart in this section for a list of verbs commonly used in signal phrases.

NOTE: APA requires using verbs in the past tense or present perfect tense ("explained" or "has explained") to introduce source material. Use the present tense only for discussing the applications or effects of your own results ("the data suggest") or knowledge that has been clearly established ("researchers agree").

Marking boundaries

Readers need to move smoothly from your words to the words of a source. Avoid dropping a direct quotation into your text without warning. Provide a clear signal phrase, including at least the author's name and the year of publication. A signal phrase marks the boundary between source material and your own words and can also tell readers why a source is worth quoting. (The signal phrase is highlighted in the second example.)

DROPPED QUOTATION

Many educators have been intrigued by the concept of blended learning but have been unsure how to define it. "Blended learning is a formal education program in which a student learns at least in part through online delivery of content and instruction with some element of student control over time, place, and pace" (Horn & Staker, 2011, p. 4).

QUOTATION WITH SIGNAL PHRASE

Many educators have been intrigued by the concept of blended learning but have been unsure how to define it. As Horn and Staker (2011) have argued, "Blended learning is a formal education program in which a student learns at least in part through online delivery of content and instruction with some element of student control over time, place, and pace" (p. 4).

Using signal phrases with summaries and paraphrases

Introduce most summaries and paraphrases with a signal phrase that names the author and the year and places the material in the context of your argument. Readers will then understand that everything between the signal phrase and the parenthetical citation summarizes or paraphrases the cited source.

Without the signal phrase (highlighted) in the following example, readers might think that only the last sentence is being cited, when in fact the whole paragraph is based on the source.

Watson (2008) reported that for American postsecondary students, technology is integral to their academic lives. Nearly three-quarters own their own laptops, and 83% have used a course management system for an online component of a class. Watson pointed out that online and blended learning models are even more widespread outside of the United States (p. 15).

There are times, however, when a summary or a paraphrase does not require a signal phrase naming the author. When the context makes clear where the cited material begins, you may omit the signal phrase and include the author's name and the year in parentheses.

Using signal phrases in APA papers

To avoid monotony, try to vary both the language and the placement of your signal phrases.

Model signal phrases

In the words of Mitra (2013), "..."

As Bell (2010) has noted, "..."

Donitsa-Schmidt and Zuzovsky (2014) pointed out that "..."

"...," claimed Çubukçu (2012, Introduction section).

"...," explained Demski (2012), "..."

Horn and Staker (2011) have offered a compelling argument for this view: "..."

Moeller and Reitzes (2011) answered objections with the following analysis: "..."

Verbs in signal phrases

admitted	contended	pointed out
agreed	declared	reasoned
argued	denied	refuted
asserted	emphasized	rejected
believed	explained	reported
claimed	insisted	responded
compared	noted	suggested
confirmed	observed	wrote

Integrating statistics and other data

When you cite a statistic or other data, a signal phrase may be used but is often not necessary. In most cases, readers will understand that the citation refers to the data and not the whole paragraph.

> Of polled high school students, 43% said that they lacked confidence in their technological proficiency going into college and careers (Moeller & Reitzes, 2011).

Putting source material in context

Readers should not have to guess why source material appears in your paper; you must put the source in context. If you use another writer's words, you must explain how they relate to your point. It's a good idea to sandwich a quotation between sentences of your own, introducing it with a signal phrase and following it with comments that link the quotation to your paper's argument. (See also APA-3d.)

QUOTATION WITH EFFECTIVE CONTEXT

> According to the International Society for Technology in Education (2016), "Student-centered learning moves students from passive receivers of information to active participants in their own discovery process. What students learn, how they learn it and how their learning is assessed are all driven by each individual student's needs and abilities" (What Is It? section). The results of student-centered learning have been positive, not only for academic achievement but also for student self-esteem. In this model of instruction, the teacher acts as a facilitator, and the students actively participate in the process of learning and teaching.

APA-3d Synthesize sources.

When you synthesize multiple sources in a research paper, you create a conversation about your research topic. You show readers how the ideas of one source relate to those of another by connecting and analyzing the ideas in the context of your argument. Keep the emphasis on your own writing. The thread of your argument should be easy to identify and to understand, with or without your sources.

SAMPLE SYNTHESIS

Student writer April Wang begins with a claim that needs support.

Student writer

It is clear that educational technology will continue to play a role in student and school performance.

Source 1

Horn and Staker (2011) acknowledged that they focused on programs in which integration of educational technology

Signal phrase indicates how the source contributes to Wang's paper and shows that the ideas that follow are not her own.

led to improved student performance. In other schools, technological learning is simply distance learning—watching a remote teacher—and not student-centered learning that allows students to partner with teachers to develop enriching learning experiences. That said, many educators seem

Student writer

convinced that educational technology has the potential to help them transition from traditional teacher-driven learning to student-centered learning. All four schools in

Source 2

Wang extends the argument and sets up two additional sources.

the Stanford study heavily relied on technology (Friedlaender et al., 2014). And indeed, Demski (2012) argued that

Source 3

technology is not supplemental but instead is "central" to student-centered learning (p. 33). Rather than turning to

Student writer

a teacher as the source of information, students are sent to investigate solutions to problems by searching online, emailing experts, collaborating with one another in a wiki

Wang closes the paragraph by interpreting the source and connecting it to her claim.

space, or completing online practice. Rather than turning to a teacher for the answer to a question, students are driven to perform—driven to use technology to find those answers themselves.

In this synthesis, Wang uses her own analyses to shape the conversation among her sources. She does not simply string quotations and statistics together or allow her sources to overwhelm her writing. The final sentence, written in her own voice, gives her an opportunity to explain to readers how her sources support and extend her argument.

When synthesizing sources, ask yourself these questions:

- How do your sources address your research question?

- How do your sources respond to each other's ideas?

- Have you varied the functions of sources — to provide background, explain concepts, lend authority, and anticipate counterarguments? Do your signal phrases indicate these functions?

- Do you connect and analyze sources in your own voice?

- Is your own argument easy to identify and to understand, with or without your sources?

Documenting sources

In most social science classes, you will be asked to use the APA system for documenting sources, which is set forth in the *Publication Manual of the American Psychological Association*, 7th ed. (APA, 2020).

APA recommends in-text citations that refer readers to a list of references. An in-text citation gives the author of the source (often in a signal phrase), the year of publication, and often a page number or other locator in parentheses. At the end of the paper, a list of references provides publication information about the source; the list is alphabetized by authors' last names (or by titles for works with no authors). The direct link between the in-text citation and the entry in the reference list is highlighted in the following example.

IN-TEXT CITATION

Bell (2010) reported that students engaged in this kind of learning performed better on both project-based assessments and standardized tests (pp. 39–40).

ENTRY IN THE LIST OF REFERENCES

Bell, S. (2010). Project-based learning for the 21st century: Skills for the future. *The Clearing House, 83*(2), 39–43.

For a reference list that includes this entry, see APA-5b.

APA-4a APA in-text citations

APA's in-text citations provide the author's last name and the year of publication, usually before the cited material, and a page number in parentheses directly after the cited material. In the following models, the elements of the in-text citation are highlighted.

NOTE: APA style requires the use of the past tense or the present perfect tense in signal phrases introducing cited material: Smith (2020) reported; Smith (2020) has argued.

1. Basic format for a quotation   Ordinarily, introduce the quotation with a signal phrase that includes the author's last name followed by the year of publication in parentheses. Put the page number (preceded by "p.," or "pp." for more than one page) in parentheses after the quotation. For sources from the web without page numbers, see item 3 in this section.

Çubukçu (2012) argued that for a student-centered approach to work, students must maintain "ownership for their goals and activities" (p. 64).

If the author is not named in the signal phrase, place the author's name, the year, and the page number in parentheses after the quotation: (Çubukçu, 2012, p. 64). (See items 7 and 15 for citing sources that lack authors.)

NOTE: Do not include a month in an in-text citation, even if the entry in the reference list includes the month.

2. Basic format for a summary or a paraphrase   As for a quotation (see item 1), include the author's last name and the year either in a signal phrase introducing the material or in parentheses following it. A page number or other locator is not required for a summary or a paraphrase, but include one if it would help readers find the information or if your instructor requires it.

Watson (2008) offered a case study of the Cincinnati Public Schools Virtual High School, in which students were able to engage in highly individualized instruction according to their own needs, strengths, and learning styles, using 10 teachers as support (p. 7).

The Cincinnati Public Schools Virtual High School brought students together to engage in highly individualized instruction according to their own needs, strengths, and learning styles, using 10 teachers as support (Watson, 2008, p. 7).

3. Quotation from a source without page numbers   If your source does not include page numbers, include another locator — information from the source such as a section heading, paragraph number, figure or table number, slide number, or time stamp — to help readers find the cited passage:

Lopez (2020) has noted that ". . ." (Symptoms section).

Myers (2019) extolled the benefits of humility (para. 5).

Brezinski and Zhang (2017) traced the increase . . . (Figure 3).

The American Immigration Council has recommended that ". . ." (Slide 5).

In a recent TED Talk, Gould (2019) argued that ". . ." (13:27).

Do not include location numbers for sources in e-book format. If you shorten a long heading, place it in quotation marks: ("How to Apply" section).

4. Specific section of a source   To cite a specific section of a source, such as a portion of an audio or video recording, a slide in a set of lecture slides, or a dedication, preface, foreword, afterword, or chapter from a book, name the section in your in-text citation.

In a dedication written while he was in hiding, Salman Rushdie (1991) included an acrostic of his son's name: SAFAR.

If the section was written by someone other than the author, include the section author's name in your in-text citation.

> In his foreword to Anthony Ray Hinton's moving book (2018), Bryan Stevenson wrote . . . (p. iv).

In your reference list, include a citation for the work as a whole.

5. Work with two authors   Name both authors in the signal phrase or in parentheses each time you cite the work. In the parentheses, use "&" between the authors' names; in the signal phrase, use "and."

> According to Donitsa-Schmidt and Zuzovsky (2014), "demographic growth in the school population" can lead to teacher shortages (p. 426).

> In the United States, most public school systems are struggling with teacher shortages, which are projected to worsen as the number of applicants to education schools decreases (Donitsa-Schmidt & Zuzovsky, 2014, p. 420).

6. Work with three or more authors   Use the first author's name followed by "et al." (Latin for "and others") in either a signal phrase or a parenthetical citation.

> In 2013, Harper et al. studied teachers' perceptions of project-based learning (PBL) before and after participating in a PBL pilot program.

> Researchers studied teachers' perceptions of project-based learning (PBL) before and after participating in a PBL pilot program (Harper et al., 2013).

7. Work with an unknown or anonymous author   If the author is unknown, include the work's title (shortened if more than a few words) in the in-text citation.

> Collaboration increases significantly among students who own or have regular access to a laptop ("Tech Seeds," 2015).

All titles in in-text citations are set in title case: Capitalize the first and last words of a title and subtitle, all significant words, and any words of four letters or more. For books and most stand-alone works (except websites), italicize the title; for most articles and other parts of larger works, set the title in quotation marks.

Only in rare cases, when "Anonymous" is specified as the author, use the word "Anonymous" in the author position: (Anonymous, 2020). (Also use the word "Anonymous" at the start of the reference list entry.)

NOTE: Titles are treated differently in reference list entries. See APA-4b.

8. Organization as author   If the author is an organization or a government agency, name the organization in the signal phrase or in the parentheses the first time you cite the source.

> According to the International Society for Technology in Education (2016), "Student-centered learning moves students from passive receivers of information to active participants in their own discovery process" (What Is It? section).

For an organization with a long name, you may abbreviate the name of the organization in citations after the first.

> **FIRST CITATION**   (Texas Higher Education Coordinating Board [THECB], 2019)
>
> **LATER CITATIONS**   (THECB, 2019)

For a work by a government agency or large organization with multiple, nested departments, list the most specific agency or department as the author, as in the reference list (see item 33 in APA-4b).

9. Authors with the same last name   To avoid confusion use initials with the last names in your in-text citations. If authors share the same initials, spell out each author's first name.

> Research by E. Smith (2019) revealed that . . .
>
> One 2018 study contradicted . . . (R. Smith, p. 234).

10. Two or more works by the same author in the same year   In your reference list, you will use lowercase letters ("a," "b," and so on) with the year to order the entries (see item 8 in APA-4b). Use those same letters with the year in the in-text citations.

> Research by Durgin (2013b) has yielded new findings about the role of smartphones in the classroom.

11. Two or more works in the same parentheses   Put the works in the same order that they appear in the reference list, separated by semicolons: (Nazer, 2015; Serrao et al., 2014).

12. Multiple citations to the same work in one paragraph   If you give the author's name in the text of your paper (not in parentheses) and you mention that source again in the text of the same paragraph, give only the author's name, not the date, in the later citation. If any subsequent reference in the same paragraph is in parentheses, include both the author and the date in the parentheses.

> Bell (2010) has argued that the chief benefit of student-centered learning is that it can connect students with "real-world tasks," thus making learning

more engaging as well as more comprehensive (p. 42). For example, Bell observed a group of middle-school students who wanted to build a social justice monument for their school. Students engaged in this kind of learning performed better on both project-based assessments and standardized tests (Bell, 2010).

13. Part of a source (chapter, figure)   To cite a specific part of a source, such as a whole chapter or a figure or table, identify the element in parentheses. Don't abbreviate terms such as "Figure," "Chapter," and "Section"; "page" is abbreviated "p." (or "pp." for more than one page).

The data support the finding that peer relationships are difficult to replicate in a completely online environment (Hanniman, 2010, Figure 8-3).

14. Indirect source (source quoted in another source)   When a published source is quoted in a source written by someone else, cite the original source first; include "as cited in" before the author and date of the source you read. In the following example, Chow is the author of the source in the reference list; that source contains a quotation by Brailsford.

Brailsford (1990) commended the writer and educator's "sure understanding of the thoughts of young people" (as cited in Chow, 2019, para. 9).

15. Web source   Cite sources from the web as you would cite any other source, giving the author and the year when they are available.

Atkinson (2011) found that children who spent at least four hours a day engaged in online activities in an academic environment were less likely to want to play video games or watch TV after school.

Usually a page number is not available; occasionally a web source will lack an author or a date (see 15a–15c).

a. No page numbers   When quoting a web source that lacks stable numbered pages, include a paragraph number or a section heading, or both, to help readers locate the passage being cited.

Some sources have numbered paragraphs; if a source lacks both numbered paragraphs and headings, count the paragraphs manually. When quoting an audio or video source, use a time stamp to indicate the start of the quotation.

Crush and Jayasingh (2015) pointed out that several other school districts in low-income areas had "jump-started their distance learning initiatives with available grant funds" (Funding Change section, para. 6).

If a heading in a source is long, you may use a shortened version of the heading in quotation marks: (Gregor, 2017, "What Happens When" section).

15. Web source (*cont.*)

b. Unknown author   If no author is named in the source, mention the title of the source in a signal phrase or give the first word or two of the title in parentheses (see also item 7). (If an organization serves as the author, see item 8.)

> A student's IEP may, in fact, recommend the use of mobile technology ("Considerations," 2012).

c. Unknown date   When the source does not give a date, use the abbreviation "n.d." (for "no date").

> Administrators believe 1-to-1 programs boost learner engagement (Magnus, n.d.).

16. An entire website   If you mention an entire website from which you did not pull specific information, give the URL in the text of your paper but do not include it in the reference list.

> The Berkeley Center for Teaching and Learning website (https://teaching .berkeley.edu/) shares ideas for using mobile technology in the classroom.

17. Personal communication   Interviews that you conduct, memos, letters, email messages, and similar communications that would be difficult for your readers to retrieve should be cited in the text only, not in the reference list. (Use the first initial with the last name either in your text sentence or in parentheses.)

> One of Yim's colleagues, who has studied the effect of social media on children's academic progress, has contended that the benefits of this technology for children under 12 years old are few (F. Johnson, personal communication, October 20, 2013).

18. Course materials   Cite lecture notes from your instructor or your own class notes as personal communication (see item 17). If your instructor's material contains publication information, cite as you would the appropriate source. See also item 56 in APA-4b.

19. Work available in multiple versions   If you consulted a reprinted, republished, or translated work, include both the date of original publication and the date of the version you used, and separate the dates with a slash: (Padura, 2009/2014).

20. Sacred or classical text   Identify the book (specifying the version or edition you used), the publication date(s), and the relevant part (chapter, verse, line). It is not necessary to include the source in the reference list.

> Peace activists have long cited the biblical prophet's vision of a world without war: "And they shall beat their swords into plowshares, and their spears into pruning hooks; nation shall not lift up sword against nation, neither shall they learn war any more" (*Holy Bible Revised Standard Edition*, 1952/2004, Isaiah 2:4).

APA-4b APA list of references

As you gather sources for an assignment, you will likely find sources in print, on the web, and in other places. The information you will need for the reference list at the end of your paper will differ slightly for some sources, but the main principles apply to all sources: You should identify an author, a creator, or a producer whenever possible; give a title; and provide the date on which the source was produced. In most cases, you will provide page numbers or other locator or retrieval information.

- General guidelines for the reference list, 232–234

Section APA-4b provides specific requirements for and examples of many of the sources you are likely to encounter. When you cite sources, your goals are to show that the sources you've used are reliable and relevant to your work, to provide your readers with enough information so that they can find your sources easily, and to provide that information in a consistent way according to APA conventions.

In the list of references, include only sources that you quote, summarize, or paraphrase in your paper.

General guidelines for listing authors

The formatting of authors' names in items 1–11 applies to all sources in print and on the web — books, articles, websites, and so on. For more models of specific source types, see items 12–59.

1. Single author

author: last name + initial(s) | year (book) | title (book) | publisher

Yanagihara, H. (2015). *A little life.* Doubleday.

2. Two to twenty authors
List up to twenty authors by last names followed by initials. Use an ampersand (&) before the name of the last author. (See items 5 and 6 in APA-4a for citing works with multiple authors in the text of your paper.)

all authors: last name + initial(s) | year (journal) | title (article)

Kim, E. H., Hollon, S. D., & Olatunji, B. O. (2016). Clinical errors in cognitive-behavior

journal title | volume, issue | page(s) | DOI

therapy. *Psychotherapy, 53*(3), 325–330. https://doi.org/10.1037/pst0000074

3. Twenty-one or more authors List the first nineteen authors, followed by an ellipsis mark (...) and the last author's name.

Sharon, G., Cruz, N. J., Kang, D.-W., Gandal, M. J., Wang, B., Kim, Y.-M., Zink, E. M.,
Casey, C. P., Taylor, B. C., Lane, C. J., Bramer, L. M., Isern, N. G., Hoyt, D. W.,
Noecker, C., Sweredoski, M. J., Moradian, A., Borenstein, E., Jansson, J. K., Knight,
R., ... Mazmanian, S. K. (2019). Human gut microbiota from autism spectrum
disorder promote behavioral symptoms in mice. *Cell, 177*(6), 1600–1618.
https://doi.org/10.1016/j.cell.2019.05.004

General guidelines for the reference list

In APA style, the alphabetical list of works cited, which appears at the end of the paper, is titled "References." In general, an APA-style reference consists of four parts:

- the **author**'s (or authors') name(s)
- the **date** of publication
- the **title** of the work
- the **source** of the work (the retrieval information)

Insert a period following each of these four parts.

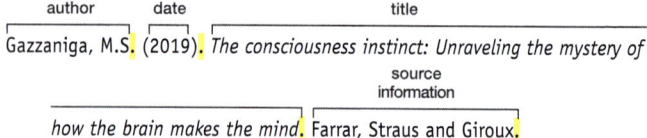

The first two elements typically appear in both the in-text citation and the reference list entry. In general, the title and source information appear only in the reference list entry.

Authors and dates

- The author is the person or people most responsible for the work: For a book or article, for example, the author is the person or people who wrote it; for a movie, the person most responsible is the director; for a government report, the author might be the specific agency that produced the work.
- Alphabetize entries in the list of references by authors' last names; if a work has no author, alphabetize it by its title.
- For all authors' names, put the last name first, followed by a comma; use initials for the first and middle names.
- With two or more authors separate the names with commas. Include names for up to twenty authors, with an ampersand (&)

General guidelines for the reference list, *continued*

before the last author's name. For twenty-one or more authors, list the first nineteen authors, three ellipsis dots, and the last author.

- If the author is a company or an organization, give the name in normal order.
- Put the date of publication immediately after the first element of the citation. Enclose the date in parentheses, followed by a period (outside the parentheses).
- Use the date as given in the publication. Generally, give the year for books and journals (2019); the year and month for monthly magazines (2019, April); and the year, month, and day for weekly magazines and for newspapers (2019, April 9). Use the season when a publication gives the season. For web sources use the date of posting, if it is available. Use "(n.d.)" if no date is given.

Titles

- Italicize the titles and subtitles of books, journals, and other stand-alone works. If a book title contains another book title or an article title, do not italicize the internal title and do not put quotation marks around it.
- Use no italics or quotation marks for the titles of articles. If an article title contains another article title or a term usually placed in quotation marks, use quotation marks around the internal title or term. If it contains a title or term usually italicized, place the title or term in italics.
- For books and articles, capitalize only the first word of the title and subtitle and all proper nouns.
- For the titles of journals, magazines, and newspapers, capitalize all words of four letters or more (and all nouns, pronouns, verbs, adjectives, and adverbs of any length).

Source information

- In publishers' names, omit business designations such as "Inc." or "Ltd." Otherwise, write the publisher's name exactly how it appears in the source.
- For online sources, list the name of the website in the publisher position: Twitter; YouTube; U.S. Census Bureau.
- If the publisher is the same as the author, do not repeat the name in the publisher position.
- Provide locations only for works associated with a single location (such as a conference presentation).

General guidelines for the reference list, *continued*

- Include the volume and issue numbers for any journals, magazines, or other periodicals that have them. Italicize the volume number and put the issue number, not italicized, in parentheses: *26*(2).

- When an article appears on consecutive pages, provide the range of pages: 87–96. When an article does not appear on consecutive pages, give all page numbers: A1, A17.

- Use "p." and "pp." only before page numbers for selections in edited books. Do not use "p." and "pp." with magazines, journals, and newspapers.

URLs, DOIs, and other retrieval information

- For articles and books from the web, use the DOI (digital object identifier) if the source has one. If a source does not have a DOI, give the URL.

- If a URL or DOI is long, you may use a permalink (if the website provides one) or create one using a shortening service such as shortdoi.org or bitly.com.

- Use a retrieval date for a web source only if the content is likely to change (such as content on a website's home page or in a social media profile).

4. Organization as author

author:
organization name   year   title (book)

American Psychiatric Association. (2013). *Diagnostic and statistical manual of mental*

edition

disorders (5th ed.).

5. Unknown author   Begin the entry with the work's title.

title (article)   year + month + day (weekly publication)   magazine title   volume, issue   page(s)

Pushed out. (2019, August 24). *The Economist, 432*(9157), 19–20.

6. Author using a screen name, pen name, or stage name   Use the author's real name, if known, and give the screen name or pen name in brackets exactly as it appears in the source. If only the screen name is known, begin

with that name and do not use brackets. (See also items 58 and 59 on citing screen names in social media.)

```
      screen name    year + month + day
                     (daily publication)              text of comment
    dr.zachary.smith. (2019, October 3). What problem are they trying to solve?
                                                          title of
                            label                        publication
    [Comment on the article "Georgia is purging voter rolls again"]. Slate.
            URL
    https://fyre.it/sjSPFyza.4
```

If the author uses just a single name ("Prince," "Sophocles") or a two-part name in which the two parts are essential ("Cardi B"), give the name with no abbreviations or alterations.

7. Two or more works by the same author   Use the author's name for all entries. List the entries by year, the earliest first.

Abdurraqib, H. (2017). *They can't kill us until they kill us.* Two Dollar Radio.

Abdurraqib, H. (2019). *Go ahead in the rain: Notes to A Tribe Called Quest.* University of Texas Press.

8. Two or more works by the same author in the same year   List the works by date. In the parentheses, add "a," "b," and so on after the year. (Use these same letters when giving the year in the in-text citations.) If the works have identical dates, list the works alphabetically by title. (See also item 10 in APA-4a.)

Conover, E. (2019a, June 8). Gold's origins tied to collapsars. *Science News, 195*(10), 10. https://bit.ly/31JTgKD

Conover, E. (2019b, June 22). Space flames may hold secrets to soot-free fire. *Science News, 195*(11), 5. https://bit.ly/2p0Xj89

9. Editor   Begin with the name(s) of the editor(s); place the abbreviation "Ed." (or "Eds." for more than one editor) in parentheses following the names.

Yeh, K.-H. (Ed.). (2019). *Asian indigenous psychologies in the global context.* Palgrave Macmillan.

10. Author and editor   Begin with the author and the date. After the title, place the name(s) of the editor(s) and the abbreviation "Ed." or "Eds." in parentheses.

Sontag, S. (2018). *Debriefing: Collected stories* (B. Taylor, Ed.). Picador.

11. Translator Begin with the name of the author. After the title, in parentheses place the name of the translator (in normal order) and the abbreviation "Trans." (for "Translator"). Add the original date of publication at the end of the entry.

Calasso, R. (2019). *The unnamable present* (R. Dixon, Trans.). Farrar, Straus and Giroux.
(Original work published 2017)

Articles and other short works

- Citation at a glance: Online article in a journal or magazine, 238
- Citation at a glance: Article from a database, 239

12. Article in a journal If an article from the web has no DOI, include the URL for the article. If an article from a database has no DOI, do not include a URL.

a. Print

all authors:
last name + initial(s) year article title

Ganegoda, D. B., & Bordia, P. (2019). I can be happy for you, but not all the time:

A contingency model of envy and positive empathy in the workplace.

journal title volume, issue page(s)

Journal of Applied Psychology, 104(6), 776–795.

b. Web

author:
last name +
initial(s) year article title

Bruns, A. (2019). The third shift: Multiple job holding and the incarceration of women's

journal title volume, issue page(s) DOI

partners. *Social Science Research, 80*(1), 202–215. https://doi.org/dfgj

all authors: last
name + initial(s) year article title

Vicary, A. M., & Larsen, A. (2018). Potential factors influencing attitudes toward

veterans who commit crimes: An experimental investigation of PTSD in the legal

journal title volume, issue URL for article

system. *Current Research in Social Psychology, 26*(2). https://www.uiowa.edu/crisp

/sites/uiowa.edu.crisp/files/crisp_vol_26_2.pdf

c. Database

author	year	article title

Maftsir, S. (2019). Emotional change: Romantic love and the university in postcolonial

	journal title	volume, issue	page(s)	DOI

Egypt. *Journal of Social History, 52*(3), 831–859. https://doi.org/10.1093/jsh/shx155

13. Article in a magazine   If an article from the web has no DOI, use the
URL for the article. If an article from a database has no DOI, do not include
a URL.

a. Print

author	year + month (monthly magazine)	article title

Andersen, R. (2019, April). The intention machine: A new generation of brain-machine

	magazine title	volume, issue	page(s)

interface can deduce what a person wants. *Scientific American, 320*(4), 24–31.

b. Web

author	date of posting (when available)	article title	magazine title

Srinivasan, D. (2019, June 4). How digital advertising markets really work. *The American*

	URL for article

Prospect. https://prospect.org/article/how-digital-advertising-markets-really-work

c. Database

author	year + month (monthly magazine)	article title

Greengard, S. (2019, August). The algorithm that changed quantum machine learning.

	magazine title	volume, issue	page(s)	DOI

Communications of the ACM, 62(8), 15–17. https://doi.org/10.1145/3339458

14. Article in a newspaper

a. Print

author	year + month + day	article title

Finucane, M. (2019, September 25). Americans still eating too many low-quality carbs.

newspaper title	page(s)

The Boston Globe, B2.

Citation at a glance: Online article in a journal or magazine

To cite an online article in a journal or magazine in APA style, include the following elements:

1 Author(s)
2 Year of publication for journal; complete date for magazine
3 Title and subtitle of article
4 Name of journal or magazine
5 Volume and issue numbers
6 DOI (digital object identifier), if article has one; otherwise, URL for article

ONLINE ARTICLE

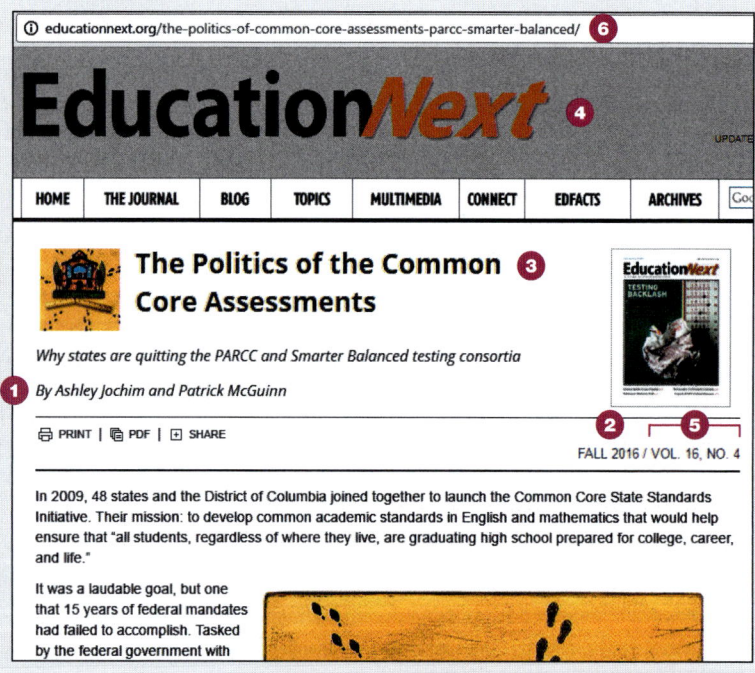

REFERENCE LIST ENTRY FOR AN ONLINE ARTICLE IN A JOURNAL OR MAGAZINE

Jochim, A., & McGuinn, P. (2016, Fall). The politics of the Common Core assessments.

Education Next, 16(4). https://www.educationnext.org/the-politics-of-common

-core-assessments-parcc-smarter-balanced/

For more on citing online articles in APA style, see items 12–14.

Citation at a glance: Article from a database

To cite an article from a database in APA style, include the following elements:

1 Author(s)
2 Year of publication for journal; complete date for magazine or newspaper
3 Title and subtitle of article
4 Name of periodical
5 Volume and issue numbers
6 Page number(s)
7 DOI (digital object identifier)

DATABASE RECORD

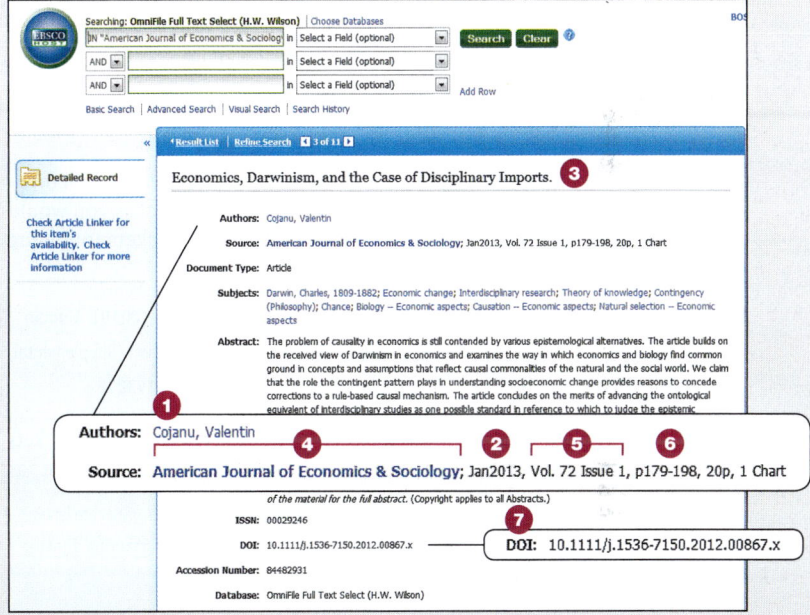

REFERENCE LIST ENTRY FOR AN ARTICLE FROM A DATABASE

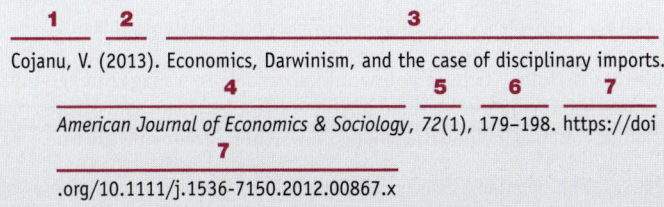

    1   **2**   **3**

Cojanu, V. (2013). Economics, Darwinism, and the case of disciplinary imports.

         4   **5**   **6**   **7**

American Journal of Economics & Sociology, 72(1), 179–198. https://doi

        7

.org/10.1111/j.1536-7150.2012.00867.x

For more on citing articles from a database in APA style, see items 12–13.

14. Article in a newspaper (*cont.*)

b. Web

author year + month + day   article title

Daly, J. (2019, August 2). Duquesne's med school plan part of national trend to train

                                         newspaper title   shortened URL

more doctors. *Pittsburgh Post-Gazette.* http://bit.ly/2CbUZOX

15. Comment on an online article   Include the first twenty words of the comment, followed by the title of the source article in brackets.

lollyl2. (2019, September 25). My husband works in IT in a major city down South. He
    is a permanent employee now, but for years [Comment on the article "The Google
    workers who voted to unionize in Pittsburgh are part of tech's huge contractor
    workforce"]. *Slate.* https://fyre.it/0RT8HmeL

16. Supplemental material   If an article on the web contains supplemental material that is not part of the main article, cite the material as you would an article and add the label "Supplemental material" in brackets following the title.

Blasi, D. E., Moran, S., Moisik, S. R., Widmer, P., Dediu, D., & Bickel, B. (2019). Human
    sound systems are shaped by post-Neolithic changes in bite configuration [Supplemental
    material]. *Science, 363*(6432). https://doi.org/10.1126/science.aav3218

17. Letter to the editor   Insert the words "Letter to the editor" in brackets after the title of the letter. If the letter has no title, use [Letter to the editor] as the title.

Doran, K. (2019, October 11). When the homeless look like grandma or grandpa [Letter
    to the editor]. *The New York Times.* https://nyti.ms/33foDOK

18. Editorial or other unsigned article

Gavin Newsom wants to stop rent gouging. Will lawmakers finally stand up for tenants?
    [Editorial]. (2019, September 4). *Los Angeles Times.* https://lat.ms/2lBlRm1

19. Newsletter article   Cite as you would an article in a magazine, giving whatever retrieval information is available. If it will not be clear that you are citing a newsletter, you may include the label "[Newsletter]" following the title.

Bond, G. (2018, Fall). Celebrities as epidemiologists. *American College of Epidemiology
    Online Member Newsletter.* https://www.acepidemiology.org/assets/ACE
    _Newsletter_Fall_2018%20FINAL.pdf

20. Review In brackets, give the type of work reviewed, the title, and the director for a film or the author for a book. If the review has no author or title, use the description in brackets as the title.

Douthat, R. (2019, October 14). A hustle gone wrong [Review of the film *Hustlers*, by L. Scafaria, Dir.]. *National Review, 71*(18), 47.

Hall, W. (2019). [Review of the book *How to change your mind: The new science of psychedelics*, by M. Pollan]. *Addiction, 114*(10), 1892–1893. https://doi.org /10.1111/add.14702

21. Published interview

Remnick, D. (2019, July 1). Robert Caro reflects on Robert Moses, L.B.J., and his own career in nonfiction. *The New Yorker.* https://bit.ly/2Lukm3X

22. Article in a reference work (encyclopedia, dictionary, wiki) When referencing an online, undated reference work entry, include the retrieval date. When referencing a work with archived versions, like *Wikipedia*, use the date and URL of the archived version you read.

Brue, A. W., & Wilmshurst, L. (2018). Adaptive behavior assessments. In B. B. Frey (Ed.), *The SAGE encyclopedia of educational research, measurement, and evaluation* (pp. 40–44). SAGE Publications. https://doi.org/10.4135/9781506326139.n21

Merriam-Webster. (n.d.). Adscititious. In *Merriam-Webster.com dictionary*. Retrieved September 5, 2019, from https://www.merriam-webster.com/dictionary /adscititious

Behaviorism. (2019, October 11). In *Wikipedia*. https://en.wikipedia.org/w/index .php?title=Behaviorism&oldid=915544724

23. Paper or poster presented at a conference or meeting (unpublished)

Wood, M. (2019, January 3–6). *The effects of an adult development course on students' perceptions of aging* [Poster session]. Forty-First Annual National Institute on the Teaching of Psychology, St. Pete Beach, FL, United States. https://nitop.org /resources/Documents/2019%20Poster%20Session%20II.pdf

Books and other long works

- Citation at a glance: Book, 243

24. Basic format for a book

a. Print

author(s):
last name
+ initial(s)   year   book title

Treuer, D. (2019). *The heartbeat of Wounded Knee: Native America from 1890 to the*

               publisher

    present. Riverhead Books.

b. Web (or online library)   Give the URL for the page where you accessed the book.

author(s)
or editor(s)   year   book title publisher   URL

Obama, M. (2018). *Becoming.* Crown. https://books.google.com/books?id=YbtNDwAAQBAJ

c. E-book   Include the DOI or, if a DOI is not available, the URL for the page from which you downloaded the book.

Coates, T.-N. (2017). *We were eight years in power: An American tragedy.* One World.

    https://www.amazon.com/dp/B01MT734OD/

d. Database   If the book has a DOI, include it. If not, do not list a URL or database name.

Kilby, P. (2019). *The green revolution: Narratives of politics, technology and gender.*

    Routledge. http://doi.org/dfgt

25. Edition other than the first   Include the edition number (abbreviated) in parentheses after the title.

Dessler, A. E., & Parson, E. A. (2019). *The science and politics of global climate change: A*

    guide to the debate (3rd ed.). Cambridge University Press.

26. Selection in an anthology or a collection   An anthology is a collection of works on a common theme, often with different authors for the selections and usually with an editor for the entire volume.

a. Entire anthology

       editor(s)   year   title of anthology

Lindert, J., & Marsoobian, A. T. (Eds.). (2018). *Multidisciplinary perspectives on genocide*

            publisher

    and memory. Springer.

Citation at a glance: Book

To cite a print book in APA style, include the following elements:

1 Author(s)
2 Year of publication
3 Title and subtitle
4 Publisher

TITLE PAGE

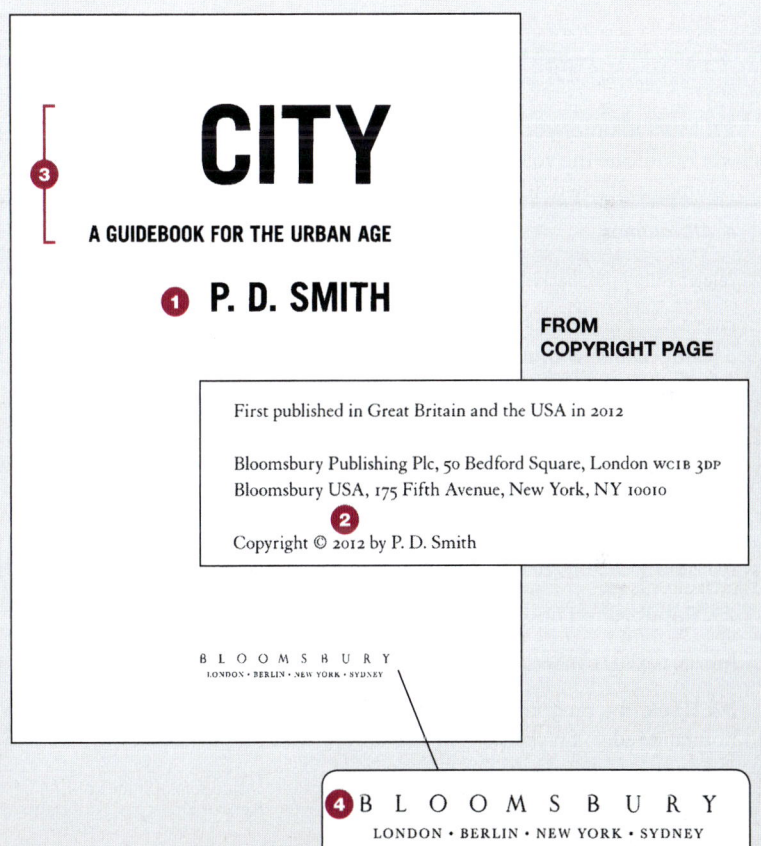

CITY

A GUIDEBOOK FOR THE URBAN AGE

❶ P. D. SMITH

FROM COPYRIGHT PAGE

First published in Great Britain and the USA in 2012

Bloomsbury Publishing Plc, 50 Bedford Square, London WC1B 3DP
Bloomsbury USA, 175 Fifth Avenue, New York, NY 10010

Copyright © 2012 by P. D. Smith

BLOOMSBURY
LONDON · BERLIN · NEW YORK · SYDNEY

❹ BLOOMSBURY
LONDON · BERLIN · NEW YORK · SYDNEY

REFERENCE LIST ENTRY FOR A PRINT BOOK

1   **2**   **3**   **4**

Smith, P. D. (2012). *City: A guidebook for the urban age*. Bloomsbury.

For more on citing books in APA style, see items 24–30.

26. Selection in an anthology or a collection (*cont.*)

b. Selection in an anthology

author of
selection   year   title of selection

Pettigrew, D. (2018). The suppression of cultural memory and identity in Bosnia and

                                        editors of anthology   title of anthology

Herzegovina. In J. Lindert & A. T. Marsoobian (Eds.), *Multidisciplinary perspectives*

                          page numbers
                          of selection   publisher

on genocide and memory (pp. 187–198). Springer.

27. Multivolume work   If you have used only one volume of a multivolume work, indicate the volume number after the title of the complete work; if the volume has its own title, add that title after the volume number.

a. All volumes

Zeigler-Hill, V., & Shackelford, T. K. (Eds.). (2018). *The SAGE handbook of personality and individual differences* (Vols. I–III). SAGE Publications.

b. One volume, with title

Zeigler-Hill, V., & Shackelford, T. K. (Eds.). (2018). *The SAGE handbook of personality and individual differences: Vol. II. Origins of personality and individual differences*. SAGE Publications.

28. Dictionary or other reference work

Leong, F. T. L. (Ed.). (2008). *Encyclopedia of counseling* (Vols. 1–4). SAGE Publications.

29. Republished book

Fremlin, C. (2017). *The hours before dawn*. Dover Publications. (Original work published 1958)

30. Book in a language other than English   Place the English translation, not italicized, in brackets.

Carminati, G. G., & Méndez, A. (2012). *Étapes de vie, étapes de soins* [Stages of life, stages of care]. Médecine & Hygiène.

31. Dissertation

Bacaksizlar, N. G. (2019). *Understanding social movements through simulations of anger contagion in social media* [Doctoral dissertation, University of North Carolina at Charlotte]. ProQuest Dissertations & Theses.

32. Conference proceedings

Srujan Raju, K., Govardhan, A, Padmaja Rani, B., Sridevi, R., & Ramakrishna Murty, M. (Eds.) (2018). *Proceedings of the third international conference on computational intelligence and informatics*. Springer.

33. Government document If no author is listed, begin with the department that produced the document. Any broader organization listed can be included as the publisher of the document, as in the first example below. If a specific report number is provided, include it after the title.

National Park Service. (2019, April 11). *Travel where women made history: Ordinary and extraordinary places of American women*. U.S. Department of the Interior. https://www.nps.gov/subjects/travelwomenshistory/index.htm

Berchick, E. R., Barnett, J. C., & Upton, R. D. (2019, September 10). *Health insurance coverage in the United States: 2018* (Report No. P60-267). U.S. Census Bureau. https://www.census.gov/library/publications/2019/demo/p60-267.html

34. Report from a private organization

Ford Foundation International Fellowships Program. (2019). *Leveraging higher education to promote social justice: Evidence from the IFP alumni tracking study*. https://p.widencdn.net/kei61u/IFP-Alumni-Tracking-Study-Report-5

35. Legal source The title of a court case is italicized in an in-text citation, but it is not italicized in the reference list.

Sweatt v. Painter, 339 U.S. 629 (1950). http://www.law.cornell.edu/supct/html/historics/USSC_CR_0339_0629_ZS.html

36. Sacred or classical text Cite sacred and classical texts as books, using the title, year, and editor/translator (if any) of the version you are using. If an original date is known, include it at the end of the citation. If the year is approximate, include "ca." (for "circa"); use "B.C.E." for ancient texts.

The Holy Bible 1611 edition: King James version. (2006). Hendrickson Publishers. (Original work published 1611)

Homer. (2018). *The odyssey* (E. Wilson, Trans.). W. W. Norton & Company. (Original work published ca. 725–675 B.C.E.)

Websites and parts of websites

- Citation at a glance: Page from a website, 247

37. Entire website If you retrieved specific information from the home page of a website, include the website name, retrieval date, and URL in your reference list entry. If you only mention the website in the body of your paper, do not include it in your reference list. See items 15 and 16 in APA-4a for advice about how to cite websites in the text of your paper.

38. Page from a website   Use one of the models below only when your source doesn't fit into any other category. These models are for content found on an interior page of a website and not published elsewhere. The website name follows the page title unless the author and website name are the same.

National Institute of Mental Health. (2016, March). *Seasonal affective disorder*. National

　　Institutes of Health. https://www.nimh.nih.gov/health/topics/seasonal

　　-affective-disorder/index.shtml

BBC News. (2019, October 31). *California fires: Goats help save Ronald Reagan*

　　Presidential Library. https://www.bbc.com/news/world-us-canada-50248549

39. Document on a website   Most documents published on websites fall into other categories, such as an article, a government document, or a report from an organization (items 12, 33, and 34).

　　　　　author(s): last
　　　　　name + initials　　　　year　　　　　document title

Tahseen, M., Ahmed, S., & Ahmed, S. (2018). *Bullying of Muslim youth: A review*

　　　　　　　　　　　　　　　　　　　　　　website

of research and recommendations. The Family and Youth Institute.

　　　　　　　　　　　　　　　URL

http://www.thefyi.org/wp-content/uploads/2018/10/FYI-Bullying-Report.pdf

40. Blog post   Cite a blog post as you would an article in a periodical.

Fister, B. (2019, February 14). Information literacy's third wave. *Library Babel Fish*.

　　https://www.insidehighered.com/blogs/library-babel-fish/information-literacy

　　%E2%80%99s-third-wave

Treat a comment on a blog post as you would a comment on an online article (see item 15). Use a screen name if the writer's real name is not given.

Mollie F. (2019, February 14). It's a daunting task, isn't it? Last year, I got a course

　　on Scholarly Communication and Information Literacy approved for [Comment on

　　the blog post "Information literacy's third wave"]. *Library Babel Fish*. http://disq

　　.us/p/1zr92uc

Audio, visual, and multimedia sources

41. Podcast

a. Series

Abumrad, J., & Krulwich, R. (Hosts). (2002–present). *Radiolab* [Audio podcast]. WNYC

　　Studios. https://www.wnycstudios.org/podcasts/radiolab/podcasts

Citation at a glance: Page from a website

To cite a page from a website in APA style, include the following elements:

1 Author(s)

2 Date of publication or most recent update ("n.d." if there is no date)

3 Title of web page

4 Name of website (if not the same as author)

5 URL of web page

PAGE FROM A WEBSITE

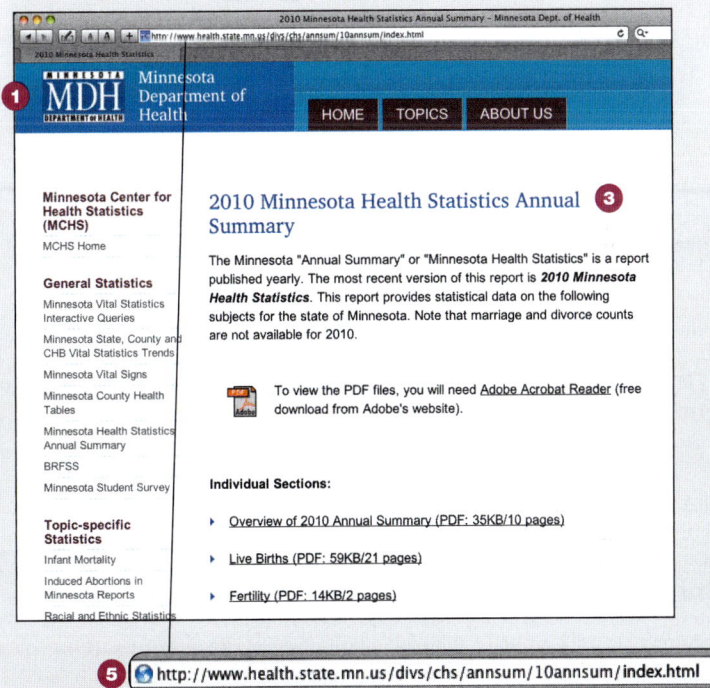

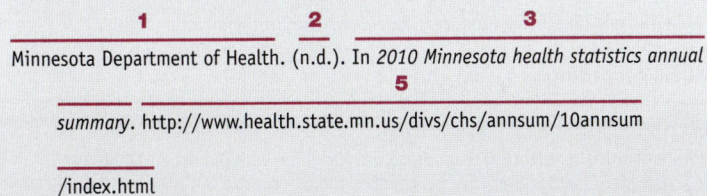

REFERENCE LIST ENTRY FOR A PAGE FROM A WEBSITE

        1   **2**   **3**

Minnesota Department of Health. (n.d.). In *2010 Minnesota health statistics annual*

                          5

summary. http://www.health.state.mn.us/divs/chs/annsum/10annsum

/index.html

For more on citing documents from websites in APA style, see items 37–39.

41. Podcast (cont.)

b. Episode

Longoria, J. (Host & Producer). (2019, April 19). Americanish [Audio podcast episode].
In J. Abumrad & R. Krulwich (Hosts), *Radiolab*. WNYC Studios. https://www
.wnycstudios.org/podcasts/radiolab/articles/americanish

42. Video or audio on the web (YouTube, TED Talk)

The New York Times. (2018, January 9). *Taking a knee and taking down a monument*
[Video]. YouTube. https://www.youtube.com/watch?v=qY34DQCdUvQ

Wray, B. (2019, May). *How climate change affects your mental health* [Video].
TED Conferences. https://www.ted.com/talks/britt_wray_how_climate_change
_affects_your_mental_health

43. Transcript of an audio or video file

Gopnik, A. (2019, July 10). *A separate kind of intelligence* [Video transcript]. Edge.
https://www.edge.org/conversation/alison_gopnik-a-separate-kind-of-intelligence

44. Film If the film is a special version, such as an extended cut, include that
information in brackets after the title.

Peele, J. (Director). (2017). *Get out* [Film]. Universal Pictures.

Hitchcock, A. (Director). (1959). *The essentials collection: North by northwest* [Film;
special ed. on DVD]. Metro-Goldwyn-Mayer; Universal Pictures Home Entertainment.

45. TV or radio series or episode

Waller-Bridge, P., Williams, H., & Williams, J. (Executive Producers). (2016–2019).
Fleabag [TV series]. Two Brothers Pictures; BBC.

Waller-Bridge, P. (Writer), & Bradbeer, H. (Director). (2019, March 18). The provocative
request (Season 2, Episode 3) [TV series episode]. In P. Waller-Bridge, H. Williams,
& J. Williams (Executive Producers), *Fleabag*. Two Brothers Pictures; BBC.

46. Music recording

Nielsen, C. (2014). *Carl Nielsen: Symphonies 1 & 4* [Album recorded by New York
Philharmonic Orchestra]. Dacapo Records. (Original work published 1892–1916)

Carlile, B. (2018). The mother [Song]. On *By the way, I forgive you*. Low Country Sound;
Elektra.

47. Lecture, speech, address, or recorded interview Cite the speaker or interviewee as the author.

Warren, E. (2019, September 16). *Senator Elizabeth Warren speech in Washington Square Park* [Speech video recording]. C-SPAN. https://www.c-span.org/video/?464314-1 /senator-elizabeth-warren-campaigns-york-city

48. Data set or graphic representation of data (chart, table)

Reid, L. (2019). *Smarter homes: Experiences of living in low carbon homes 2013–2018* [Data set]. UK Data Service. https://doi.org/10.5255/UKDA-SN-853485

Pew Research Center. (2018, November 15). *U.S. public is closely divided about overall health risk from food additives* [Chart]. https://www.pewresearch.org/science /2018/11/19/public-perspectives-on-food-risks/

49. Mobile app Begin with the developer of the app, if known.

Google. (2019). *Google Earth* (Version 9.3.3) [Mobile app]. App Store. https://apps .apple.com/us/app/google-earth/id293622097

50. Video game

ConcernedApe. (2016). *Stardew Valley* [Video game]. Chucklefish.

51. Map

Desjardins, J. (2017, November 17). *Walmart nation: Mapping the largest employers in the U.S.* [Map]. Visual Capitalist. https://www.visualcapitalist.com /walmart-nation-mapping-largest-employers-u-s/

52. Advertisement

America's Biopharmaceutical Companies [Advertisement]. (2018, September). *The Atlantic, 322*(2), 2.

Centers for Disease Control and Prevention. (n.d.). *A tip from a former smoker: Beatrice* [Advertisement]. U.S. Department of Health and Human Services. https://www.cdc.gov /tobacco/campaign/tips/resources/ads/pdf-print-ads/beatrices-tip-print-ad-7x10.pdf

53. Work of art or photograph

O'Keeffe, G. (1931). *Cow's skull: Red, white, and blue* [Painting]. Metropolitan Museum of Art, New York, NY, United States. https://www.metmuseum.org/art/collection /search/488694

Browne, M. (1963). *The burning monk* [Photograph]. Time. http://100photos.time.com /photos/malcolm-browne-burning-monk

54. Brochure or fact sheet

National Council of State Boards of Nursing. (2018). *A nurse manager's guide to substance use disorder in nursing* [Brochure].

World Health Organization. (2019, July 15). *Immunization coverage* [Fact sheet]. https://www.who.int/news-room/fact-sheets/detail/immunization-coverage

55. Press release

New York University. (2019, September 5). *NYU Oral Cancer Center awarded $2.5 million NIH grant to study cancer pain* [Press release]. https://www.nyu.edu/about /news-publications/news/2019/september/nyu-oral-cancer-center-awarded--2-5-million-nih-grant-to-study-c.html

56. Lecture notes or other course materials Cite posted materials as you would a document on a website (see item 39). Cite material from your instructor that is not available to others as personal communication in the text of your paper (see item 17 in APA-4a).

Chatterjee, S., Constenla, D., Kinghorn, A., & Mayora, C. (2018). *Teaching vaccine economics everywhere: Costing in vaccine planning and programming* [Lecture notes and slides]. Department of Population, Family, and Reproductive Health, Johns Hopkins University. http://ocw.jhsph.edu/index.cfm/go/viewCourse/course /TeachVaccEconCosting/coursePage/lectureNotes/

Social media

57. Email Email messages, letters, and other personal communication are not included in the list of references. See item 17 in APA-4a for citing these sources in the text of your paper.

58. Social media post (Twitter, Instagram) If the writer's real name and screen name are given, put the real name first, followed by the screen name in brackets. If only the screen name is known, begin with the screen name without brackets. For the title, include up to the first twenty words (including hashtags or emojis) of the title, caption, or post. After the title, list any attachments (such as a photo or link) and the type of post in separate brackets. List the website or app in the publisher position. Include the URL for the post. Cite posts that are not accessible to all readers as personal communication in the text of your paper.

National Science Foundation [@NSF]. (2019, October 13). *Understanding how forest structure drives carbon sequestration is important for ecologists, climate modelers and forest managers, who are working on* [Thumbnail with link attached] [Tweet]. Twitter. https://twitter.com/NSF/status/1183388649263652864

Georgia Aquarium. (2019, June 25). *True love* ❤ *Charlie and Lizzy are a bonded pair of African penguins who have been together for more than* [Image attached] [Status update]. Facebook. https://www.facebook.com/GeorgiaAquarium /photos/a.163898398123/10156900637543124/?type=3&theater

Smithsonian [@smithsonian]. (2019, October 7). *You're looking at a ureilite meteorite under a microscope. When illuminated with polarized light, they appear in dazzling colors, influenced* [Photograph]. Instagram. https://www.instagram.com/p /B3VI27yHLQG/

59. Social media profile or highlight   Because profiles are designed to change over time, include the date you viewed the webpage.

National Science Foundation [@NSF]. (n.d.). *Tweets* [Twitter profile]. Twitter. Retrieved October 15, 2019, from https://twitter.com/NSF

Smithsonian [@smithsonian]. (n.d.). *#Apollo50* [Highlight]. Instagram. Retrieved January 5, 2020, from https://www.instagram.com/stories/highlights /17902787752343364/

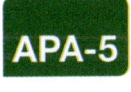

APA format; sample research paper

The guidelines in this section are consistent with advice given in the *Publication Manual of the American Psychological Association*, 7th ed. (APA, 2020), and with typical requirements for undergraduate papers.

APA-5a APA format

Formatting the paper

The guidelines in this section describe APA's recommendations for formatting the text of a paper written for an undergraduate college course and for preparing the reference list.

Font   If your instructor does not require a specific font, use one that is standard and easy to read (such as 12-point Times New Roman).

Title page   Put the page number 1 at the right margin one-half inch from the top of the page. A few lines down the page, center the full title of your paper in bold. After a blank line, include your name, and then add the following assignment details on separate lines: the department and the school, the course code and name, your instructor's name, and the due date. See APA-5b for a sample title page.

Page numbers   Starting with the title page, number all pages in the upper right corner one-half inch from the top of the page.

Margins, line spacing, and paragraph indents   Use margins of one inch on all sides of the page. Left-align the text.

Double-space throughout the paper. Indent the first line of each paragraph one-half inch.

Capitalization, italics, and quotation marks   In headings and in titles of works that appear in the text of the paper, capitalize all words of four letters or more (and all nouns, pronouns, verbs, adjectives, and adverbs of any length). Capitalize the first word following a colon in a title or a heading, and capitalize the first word following a colon in the body of your paper if the word begins a complete sentence.

In the body of your paper, italicize the titles of books, journals, magazines, and other long works, including websites. Use quotation marks around the titles of articles, short stories, and other short works named in the body of your paper.

NOTE: APA has different requirements for titles in the reference list. See page 254.

Long quotations   When a quotation is forty or more words, indent it one-half inch from the left margin. Double-space the quotation. Do not use quotation marks around it. (See APA-5b for an example. See also APA-3b for more information about integrating long quotations.)

Footnotes   Insert footnotes using the footnote function in your word processing program. The callout number in the text should immediately follow a word or any mark of punctuation except a dash. The text of the footnote should be single-spaced.

Abstract   If your assignment requires an abstract — a 150-to-250-word summary paragraph — include it on a new page after the title page. Center the word "Abstract" (in bold) one inch from the top of the page. Double-space the abstract and do not indent the first or subsequent lines.

Headings   Although headings are not always necessary, their use is encouraged in the social sciences. For most undergraduate papers, one level of heading is usually sufficient. (See APA-5b.)

First-level headings are centered and boldface. In research papers and laboratory reports, the major headings are "Method," "Results," and "Discussion." In other types of papers, the major headings should be informative and concise, conveying the structure of the paper.

Second-level headings are left-aligned and boldface. Third-level headings are left-aligned, italic and boldface.

In all three levels of headings, capitalize the first and last words and all words of four or more letters (and nouns, pronouns, verbs, adjectives, and adverbs of any length).

First-Level Heading Centered

Second-Level Heading Aligned Left

Third-Level Heading Aligned Left

Visuals   APA classifies visuals as tables and figures (figures include graphs, charts, drawings, and photographs). Place each visual immediately after the paragraph in which it is called out, or place it on the following page if it does not fit on the same page as the callout.

Tables   Number each table (Table 1, Table 2, and so on) and provide a clear title. The label and title should appear on separate lines above the table, flush left and double-spaced. Type the table number in bold font; italicize the table title.

Table 2

Effect of Nifedipine (Procardia) on Blood Pressure in Women

If you have used data from an outside source or have taken or adapted the table from a source, give the source information in a note below the table. Begin with the word "Note," italicized and followed by a period. If you use lettered footnotes to explain specific data in the table, those footnotes begin on a new line after the source information.

Figures   As with tables, number each figure in bold and include a title in italic font. If you have taken or adapted the figure from an outside source, give the source information in a note underneath the figure, starting with the word "Note" in italics and followed by a period. Use the term "From" or "Adapted from" before the source information. Notes can also give additional information or context for the figure.

Preparing the list of references

Begin your list of references on a new page at the end of the paper. Center the title "References" in bold one inch from the top of the page. Double-space throughout. For a sample reference list, see APA-5b.

Indenting entries   Type the first line of each entry at the left margin and indent any additional lines one-half inch.

Alphabetizing the list   Alphabetize the reference list by the last names of the authors (or editors) or by the first word of an organization name (if the author is an organization). When a work has no author or editor, alphabetize by the first word of the title other than "A," "An," or "The."

If your list includes two or more works by the same author, arrange the entries by year, the earliest first. If your list includes two or more works by the same author in the same year, arrange the works alphabetically by title. Add the letters "a," "b," and so on within the parentheses after the year. For journal articles, use only the year and the letter: (2012a). For articles in magazines and newspapers, use the full date and the letter in the reference list: (2012a, July 7); use only the year and the letter in the in-text citation.

Authors' names   Invert all authors' names and use initials instead of first names. Separate the names with commas. For two to twenty authors, use an ampersand (&) before the last author's name. For twenty-one or more authors, give the first nineteen authors, followed by three ellipsis dots and the last author (see item 3 in APA-4b).

Titles of books and articles   In the reference list, italicize the titles and subtitles of books. Do not italicize or use quotation marks around the titles of articles and other stand-alone works. For both books and articles, capitalize only the first word of the title and subtitle (and all proper nouns). Capitalize names of journals, magazines, and newspapers as you would capitalize them normally (see P8-c).

Abbreviations for page numbers   Abbreviations for "page" and "pages" ("p." and "pp.") are used before page numbers of selections in anthologies and other edited books (see item 26 in APA-4b). Do not use "p." or "pp." before page numbers of articles in journals and magazines (see items 12 and 13 in APA-4b).

Breaking a URL or DOI   Do not insert any line breaks into a URL or DOI (digital object identifier). Any line breaks that your word processor makes automatically are acceptable. Do not add a period at the end of a URL or DOI.

APA-5b Sample APA research paper

On the following pages is a research paper on the use of educational technology in the shift to student-centered learning, written by April Wang, a student in an education class. Wang's assignment was to write a literature review paper documented with APA-style citations and references.

1

Technology and the Shift From Teacher-Delivered to Student-Centered Learning: A Review of the Literature

April Bo Wang

Department of Education, Glen County Community College

EDU 107: Education, Technology, and Media

Dr. Julien Gomez

October 29, 2019

Marginal annotations indicate APA-style formatting and effective writing.

2

Technology and the Shift From Teacher-Delivered to

Student-Centered Learning: A Review of the Literature

In the United States, most public school systems are struggling with teacher shortages, which are projected to worsen as the number of applicants to education schools decreases (Donitsa-Schmidt & Zuzovsky, 2014, p. 420). Citing federal data, *The New York Times* reported a 30% drop in "people entering teacher preparation programs" between 2010 and 2014 (Rich, 2015, para. 10). Especially in science and math fields, the teacher shortage is projected to escalate in the next 10 years (Hutchison, 2012). In recent decades, instructors and administrators have viewed the practice of student-centered learning as one promising solution. Unlike traditional teacher-delivered (also called "transmissive") instruction, student-centered learning allows students to help direct their own education by setting their own goals and selecting appropriate resources for achieving those goals. Though student-centered learning might once have been viewed as an experimental solution in understaffed schools, it is gaining credibility as an effective pedagogical practice. What is also gaining momentum is the idea that technology might play a significant role in fostering student-centered learning. This literature review will examine three key questions:

1. In what ways is student-centered learning effective?
2. Can educational technology help students drive their own learning?
3. How can public schools effectively combine teacher talent and educational technology?

In the face of mounting teacher shortages, public schools should embrace educational technology that promotes student-centered learning in order to help all students become engaged and successful learners.

In What Ways Is Student-Centered Learning Effective?

According to the International Society for Technology in Education (2016), "Student-centered learning moves students from passive receivers of information to active participants in their own discovery process. What students learn, how they learn it, and how their learning is assessed are all driven by each individual student's needs and abilities" (What Is It? section). The results of student-centered learning have been positive, not only for academic achievement but also for student self-esteem. In this model

---

Sources provide background information and context.

In-text citation for a quotation from a source without page numbers includes a paragraph number or another locator.

Wang sets up her organization by posing three questions.

Wang states her thesis.

Headings, centered and boldface, help readers follow the organization.

Wang uses a source to define the key term "student-centered learning."

3

of instruction, the teacher acts as a facilitator, and the students actively participate in the process of learning and teaching. With guidance, students decide on the learning goals most pertinent to themselves, they devise a learning plan that will most likely help them achieve those goals, they direct themselves in carrying out that learning plan, and they assess how much they learned (Çubukçu, 2012, Introduction section). The major differences between student-centered learning and instructor-centered learning are summarized in Table 1.

> Locator (section title) is included for a paraphrase to help readers find the source in a long article without page numbers.

Bell (2010) has argued that the chief benefit of student-centered learning is that it can connect students with "real-world tasks," thus making learning more engaging as well as more comprehensive (p. 42). For example, Bell observed a group of middle-school students who wanted to build a social justice monument for their school. They researched social justice issues, selected several to focus on, and then designed a three-dimensional playground to represent those issues. In doing so, they achieved learning goals in the areas of social studies, physics, and mathematics and practiced research and teamwork. Students engaged in this kind of learning performed better on both project-based assessments and standardized tests (Bell, 2010).

> Page number or other locator is not necessary for a paraphrase from a short article.

A Stanford study came to a similar conclusion; researchers examined four schools that had moved from teacher-driven instruction to student-centered learning (Friedlaender et al., 2014). The study focused on students from a mix of racial, cultural, and socioeconomic backgrounds, with varying levels of English-language proficiency. The researchers predicted that this mix of students, representing differing levels of academic ability, would benefit from a student-centered approach. Through interviews, surveys, and classroom observations, the researchers identified key characteristics of the new student-centered learning environments at the four schools:

> In a citation of a work with three or more authors, the first author's name, followed by "et al.," is given in parentheses or in a signal phrase.

- teachers who prioritized building relationships with students
- support structures for teachers to improve and collaborate on instruction
- a shift in classroom activity from lectures and tests to projects and performance-based assessments (pp. 5–7)

After the schools designed their curriculum to be personalized to individual students rather than standardized across a diverse student body and to be inclusive of skills such as persistence as well as traditional academic skills, students outperformed peers on state tests and increased their rates of high school and college graduation (Friedlaender et al., 2014, p. 3).

> Authors and year are given earlier in the paragraph, so only page numbers are provided at the end of the paraphrase.

4

Wang creates a
table to compare
and contrast two
key concepts for
her readers.

Table 1

Comparison of Two Approaches to Teaching and Learning

Teaching and learning period	Instructor-centered approach	Student-centered approach
Before class	• Instructor prepares lecture/instruction on new topic. • Students complete homework on previous topic.	• Students read and view new material, practice new concepts, and prepare questions ahead of class. • Instructor views student practice and questions, identifies learning opportunities.
During class	• Instructor delivers new material in a lecture or prepared discussion. • Students—unprepared—listen, watch, take notes, and try to follow along with the new material.	• Students lead discussions of the new material or practice applying the concepts or skills in an active environment. • Instructor answers student questions and provides immediate feedback.
After class	• Instructor grades homework and gives feedback about the previous lesson. • Students work independently to practice or apply the new concepts.	• Students apply concepts/skills to more complex tasks, some of their own choosing, individually and in groups. • Instructor posts additional resources to help students.

Note. Adapted from *The Flipped Class Demystified*, by New York University, n.d. (https://www.nyu.edu/faculty/teaching-and-learning-resources/instructional-technology-support/instructional-design-assessment/flipped-classes/the-flipped-class-demystified.html).

Can Educational Technology Help Students Drive Their Own Learning?

When students engage in self-directed learning, they rely less on teachers to deliver information and require less face-to-face time with teachers. For content delivery, many school districts have begun to use educational technology resources that, in recent years, have become more available, more affordable, and easier to use. For the purposes of this paper, the term "educational technology resources" encompasses the following: distance learning, by which students learn from a remote instructor online; other online education programming such as slide shows

5

and video or audio lectures; interactive online activities, such as quizzing or games; and the use of computers, tablets, smartphones, SMART Boards, or other such devices for coursework.

Much like student-centered learning, the use of educational technology began in many places as a temporary measure to keep classes running despite teacher shortages. A Horn and Staker study (2011) examined the major patterns over time for students who subscribed to distance learning, for example. A decade ago, students who enrolled in distance learning often fell into one of the following categories: They lived in a rural community that had no alternative for learning; they attended a school where there were not enough qualified teachers to teach certain subjects; or they were homeschooled or homebound. But faced with tighter budgets, teacher shortages, increasingly diverse student populations, and rigorous state standards, schools recognized the need and the potential for distance learning across the board.

As the teacher shortage has intensified, educational technology resources have become more tailored to student needs and more affordable. Pens that convert handwritten notes to digital text and organize them, backpacks that charge electronic devices, and apps that create audiovisual flash cards are just a few of the more recent innovations. According to Svokos (2015), some educational technology resources entertain students while supporting student-centered learning:

> GlassLab, a nonprofit that was launched with grants from the Bill & Melinda Gates and MacArthur Foundations, creates educational games that are now being used in more than 6,000 classrooms across the country. Some of the company's games are education versions of existing ones—for example, its first release was SimCity EDU—while others are originals. Teachers get real-time updates on students' progress as well as suggestions on what subjects they need to spend more time perfecting. (5. Educational Games section)

Many of the companies behind these products offer institutional discounts to schools where such devices are used widely by students and teachers.

Horn and Staker (2011) concluded that the chief benefit of technological learning was that it could adapt to the individual student in a way that whole-class delivery by a single teacher could not. Their study examined various schools where technology enabled student-centered learning. For example, Carpe Diem High School in Yuma, Arizona, hired only six certified subject teachers and then outfitted its classrooms with 280 computers connected to

---

Marginal annotations:

Wang develops her thesis.

In a signal phrase, the word "and" links the names of two authors; the date is given in parentheses.

Quotation of 40 or more words is indented without quotation marks.

Locator (section title) is used for a direct quotation from an online source with no page numbers.

6

online learning programs. The programs included software that offered "continual feedback, assessment, and incremental victory in a way that a face-to-face teacher with a class of 30 students never could. After each win, students continue to move forward at their own pace" (p. 9). Students alternated between personalized 55-minute courses online and 55-minute courses with one of the six teachers. The academic outcomes were promising. Carpe Diem ranked first in its county for student math and reading scores. Similarly, Rocketship Education, a charter network that serves low-income, predominantly Latino students, created a digital learning lab, reducing the need to hire more teachers. Rocketship's academic scores ranked in the top 15 of all California low-income public schools.

Wang uses her own analysis to shape the conversation among her sources in this synthesis paragraph.

It is clear that educational technology will continue to play a role in student and school performance. Horn and Staker (2011)acknowledged that they focused on programs in which integration of educational technology led to improved student performance. In other schools, technological learning is simply distance learning—watching a remote teacher—and not student-centered learning that allows students to partner with teachers to develop enriching learning experiences. That said, many educators seem convinced that educational technology has the potential to help them transition from traditional teacher-driven learning to student-centered learning. All four schools in the Stanford study heavily relied on technology (Friedlaender et al., 2014). And indeed, Demski (2012) argued that technology is not supplemental but instead is "central" to student-centered learning (p. 33). Rather than turning to a teacher as the source of information, students are sent to investigate solutions to problems by searching online, emailing experts, collaborating with one another in a wiki space, or completing online practice. Rather than turning to a teacher for the answer to a question, students are driven to perform—driven to use technology to find those answers themselves.

How Can Public Schools Effectively Combine Teacher Talent and Educational Technology?

Some researchers have expressed doubt that schools are ready for student-centered learning—or any type of instruction—that is driven by technology. In a recent survey conducted by the Nellie Mae Education Foundation, Moeller and Reitzes (2011) reported not only that many teachers lacked confidence in their ability to incorporate technology in the classroom but that 43% of polled high school students said that they lacked confidence

7

in their technological proficiency going into college and careers. The study concluded that technology alone would not improve learning environments. Yet others argued that students adapt quickly to even unfamiliar technology and use it to further their own learning. For example, Mitra (2013) caught the attention of the education world with his study of how to educate students in the slums of India. He installed an Internet-accessible computer in a wall in a New Delhi urban slum and left it there with no instructions. Over a few months, many of the children had learned how to use the computer, how to access information over the Internet, how to interpret information, and how to communicate this information to one another. Mitra's experiment was "not about making learning happen. [It was] about letting it happen" (16:31). He concluded that in the absence of teachers, even in developing countries less inundated by technology, a tool that allowed access to an organized database of knowledge (such as a search engine) was sufficient to provide students with a rewarding learning experience.

> Wang uses a source to introduce a counterargument.

> Brackets indicate Wang's change in the quoted material.

> For a direct quotation from a video, a time stamp indicates the start of the quotation.

According to the Stanford study, however, the presence of teachers is still crucial (Friedlaender et al., 2014). Their roles will simply change from distributors of knowledge to facilitators and supporters of self-directed student-centered learning. The researchers asserted that teacher education and professional development programs can no longer prepare their teachers in a single instructional mode, such as teacher-delivered learning; they must instead equip teachers with a wide repertoire of skills to support a wide variety of student learning experiences. The Stanford study argued that since teachers would be partnering with students to shape the learning experience, rather than designing and delivering a curriculum on their own, the main job of a teacher would become relationship building. The teacher would establish a relationship with each student so that the teacher could support whatever learning the student pursues.

Many schools have already effectively paired a reduced faculty with educational technology to support successful student-centered learning. For example, Watson (2008) offered a case study of the Cincinnati Public Schools Virtual High School, which brought students together in a physical school building to work with an assortment of online learning programs. Although there were only 10 certified teachers in the building, students were able to engage in highly individualized instruction according to their own needs, strengths, and learning styles, using the 10 teachers as support (p. 7). Commonwealth Connections Academy (CCA), a public school in

8

Pennsylvania, also brings students into a physical school building to engage in digital curriculum. However, rather than having students identify their own learning goals and design their own curriculum around those goals, CCA uses educational technology as an assessment tool to identify areas of student weakness. It then partners students with teachers to address those areas (pp. 8–9).

Conclusion

Tone of the conclusion is objective and presents answers to Wang's three organizational questions.

Public education faces the opportunity for a shift from the model of teacher-delivered instruction that has characterized American public schools since their foundation to a student-centered learning model. Not only has student-centered learning proved effective in improving student academic and developmental outcomes, but it can also synchronize with technological learning for widespread adaptability across schools. Because it relies on student direction rather than an established curriculum, student-centered learning supported by educational technology can adapt to the different needs of individual students and a variety of learning environments—urban and rural, well funded and underfunded. Similarly, when student-centered learning relies on technology rather than a corps of uniformly trained teachers, it holds promise for schools that would otherwise suffer from a lack of human or financial resources.

9

References

Bell, S. (2010). Project-based learning for the 21st century: Skills for the future. *The Clearing House, 83*(2), 39–43.

Çubukçu, Z. (2012). Teachers' evaluation of student-centered learning environments. *Education, 133*(1).

Demski, J. (2012, January). This time it's personal. *THE Journal (Technological Horizons in Education), 39*(1), 32–36.

Donitsa-Schmidt, S., & Zuzovsky, R. (2014). Teacher supply and demand: The school level perspective. *American Journal of Educational Research, 2*(6), 420–429. https://doi.org/10.12691 /education-2-6-14

Friedlaender, D., Burns, D., Lewis-Charp, H., Cook-Harvey, C. M., & Darling-Hammond, L. (2014). *Student-centered schools: Closing the opportunity gap* [Research brief]. Stanford Center for Opportunity Policy in Education. https://edpolicy.stanford.edu/sites/default /files/scope-pub-student-centered-research-brief.pdf

Horn, M. B., & Staker, H. (2011). *The rise of K-12 blended learning.* Innosight Institute. http://www.christenseninstitute.org /wp-content/uploads/2013/04/The-rise-of-K-12-blended -learning.pdf

Hutchison, L. F. (2012). Addressing the STEM teacher shortage in American schools: Ways to recruit and retain effective STEM teachers. *Action in Teacher Education, 34*(5/6), 541–550. https://doi.org/10.1080/0162 6620.2012.729483

International Society for Technology in Education. (2016). *Student-centered learning.* http://www.iste.org/connected/standards/ essential-conditions/student-centered-learning

Mitra, S. (2013, February). *Build a school in the cloud* [Video]. TED. https://www.ted.com/talks/sugata_mitra_build_a_school_in_ the_cloud?language=en

Moeller, B., & Reitzes, T. (2011, July). *Integrating technology with student-centered learning.* Nellie Mae Education Foundation. http://www.nmefoundation.org/research/personalization /integrating-technology-with-student-centered-learn

Rich, M. (2015, August 9). Teacher shortages spur a nationwide hiring scramble (credentials optional). *The New York Times.* https://nyti .ms/1WaaV7a

List of references begins on a new page. Heading is centered and boldface.

List is alphabetized by authors' last names. All authors' names are inverted.

First line of an entry is at the left margin; subsequent lines indent 1/2".

Double-spacing is used throughout.

10

Svokos, A. (2015, May 7). 5 innovations from the past decade that aim to change the American classroom *Huffpost*. https://www.huffpost.com /entry/technology-changes-classrooms_n_7190910

Watson, J. (2008, January). *Blended learning: The convergence of online and face-to-face education*. North American Council for Online Learning. http://www.inacol.org/wp-content/uploads/2015/02 /NACOL_PP-BlendedLearning-lr.pdf

List of CMS-style notes and bibliography entries

CMS (*Chicago*) Style

Most history instructors and some humanities instructors will ask you to document sources with footnotes or endnotes based on *The Chicago Manual of Style*, 17th ed. (University of Chicago Press, 2017). When writing a research paper based on sources, you will follow three important conventions:

1. supporting a thesis statement (CMS-1)
2. citing your sources and avoiding plagiarism (CMS-2)
3. integrating source material effectively (CMS-3)

Examples in this section appear in CMS (*Chicago*) style and are drawn from one student's research on the Fort Pillow massacre, which occurred during the Civil War. Sample pages from Ned Bishop's paper are in section CMS-5b.

CMS-1 Supporting a thesis statement

Most assignments based on reading or research — such as those assigned in history or other humanities classes — ask you to form a thesis, or main idea, and to support that thesis with well-organized evidence.

CMS-1a Form a working thesis statement.

Once you have read a range of sources, considered your issue from different perspectives, and chosen an entry point in the research conversation, you are ready to focus your research paper by forming a working thesis: a one-sentence (or occasionally a two-sentence) statement of your central idea. (See also C1-c.) Because it is a working, or tentative, thesis, you can remain flexible and revise it as your ideas develop. Ultimately, the thesis will express your informed answer to your research question — an answer about which people might disagree (see R1-b). Here, for example, are student writer Ned Bishop's research question and working thesis statement.

RESEARCH QUESTION

To what extent was Confederate Major General Nathan Bedford Forrest responsible for the massacre of Union troops at Fort Pillow?

WORKING THESIS

By encouraging racism among his troops, Nathan Bedford Forrest was directly responsible for the massacre of Union troops at Fort Pillow.

Notice that the thesis expresses a view on a debatable issue. The writer's job is to persuade such readers that this view is worth taking seriously. To read Ned Bishop's thesis in the context of his introduction, see CMS-5b.

CMS-1b Organize your ideas.

The body of your paper will consist of evidence in support of your thesis. Try sketching an informal plan to focus and organize your ideas. Ned Bishop, for example, used a simple outline to structure his ideas. In the paper, the points in the outline became headings that help readers follow his line of argument.

> What happened at Fort Pillow?
>
> Did Forrest order the massacre?
>
> Can Forrest be held responsible for the massacre?

CMS-1c Consider how sources will contribute to your essay.

Used thoughtfully, your source materials will make your argument more complex and convincing for readers. Sources can support your thesis by playing several different roles.

Providing background information or context

You can use facts and statistics to support generalizations or to establish the importance of your topic, as student writer Ned Bishop does near the beginning his paper.

> Fort Pillow, Tennessee, which sat on a bluff overlooking the Mississippi River, had been held by the Union for two years. It was garrisoned by 580 men, 292 of them from United States Colored Heavy and Light Artillery regiments, 285 from the white Thirteenth Tennessee Cavalry. Nathan Bedford Forrest commanded about 1,500 troops.[1]

Explaining terms or concepts

If readers are unlikely to be familiar with a word, a phrase, or an idea important to your topic, you must explain it for them. Quoting or paraphrasing a source can help you define terms and concepts clearly and concisely.

> The Civil War practice of giving no quarter to an enemy—in other words, "denying [an enemy] the right of survival"—defied Lincoln's mandate for humane and merciful treatment of prisoners.[9]

Supporting your claims

As you draft, make sure to back up your assertions with facts, examples, and other evidence from your research (see also A4-f). Ned Bishop, for example, uses an eyewitness report of the racially motivated violence perpetrated by Nathan Bedford Forrest's troops.

> The slaughter at Fort Pillow was no doubt driven in large part by racial hatred. . . . A Southern reporter traveling with Forrest makes clear that the discrimination was deliberate: "Our troops maddened by the excitement, shot down the ret[r]eating Yankees, and not until they had attained t[h]e water's edge and turned to beg for mercy, did any prisoners fall in [t]o our hands—Thus the whites received quarter, but the negroes were shown no mercy."[19]

Lending authority to your argument

Expert opinion can give weight to your argument (see also A4-f). But don't rely on experts to make your argument for you. Construct your argument in your own words and, when appropriate, cite the judgment of an authority in the field for support.

> Fort Pillow is not the only instance of a massacre or threatened massacre of black soldiers by troops under Forrest's command. Biographer Brian Steel Wills points out that at Brice's Cross Roads in June 1864, "black soldiers suffered inordinately" as Forrest looked the other way and Confederate soldiers deliberately sought out those they termed "the damned negroes."[21]

Anticipating and countering alternative perspectives

Do not ignore sources that seem contrary to your position or that offer arguments different from your own. Instead, use them to give voice to opposing points of view and alternative interpretations before you counter them (see A4-g). Your readers will often have opposing points of view in mind already, whether or not they agree with you. Ned Bishop, for example, presents conflicting evidence to acknowledge that some readers may give Nathan Bedford Forrest credit for stopping the massacre. In doing so, Bishop creates an opportunity to counter their objections and persuade those readers that Forrest can be held accountable.

> Hurst suggests that the temperamental Forrest "may have ragingly ordered a massacre and even intended to carry it out—until he rode inside the fort and viewed the horrifying result" and ordered it stopped.[15] While this is an intriguing interpretation of events, even Hurst would probably admit that it is merely speculation.

CMS-2 Citing sources; avoiding plagiarism

In a research paper, you draw on the work of other writers, and you must document their contributions by citing your sources. Sources are cited for two reasons:

1. to tell readers where your information comes from — so that they can assess its reliability and, if interested, find and read the original source
2. to give credit to the writers from whom you have borrowed words and ideas

You must cite anything you borrow from a source, including direct quotations; statistics and other specific facts; visuals such as tables, graphs, and diagrams; and any ideas you present in a summary or paraphrase. Borrowing another writer's language, sentence structures, or ideas without proper acknowledgment is a form of dishonesty known as plagiarism. The only exception is common knowledge — information that your readers may know or could easily locate in any number of reference sources.

CMS-2a Use the CMS (*Chicago*) system for citing sources.

CMS citations consist of superscript numbers in the text of the paper that refer readers to notes with corresponding numbers either at the foot of the page (footnotes) or at the end of the paper (endnotes).

TEXT

Governor John Andrew was not allowed to recruit black soldiers from out of state. "Ostensibly," writes Peter Burchard, "no recruiting was done outside Massachusetts, but it was an open secret that Andrew's agents were working far and wide."[1]

NOTE

1. Peter Burchard, *One Gallant Rush: Robert Gould Shaw and His Brave Black Regiment* (New York: St. Martin's, 1965), 85.

For detailed advice on using CMS-style notes, see CMS-4. When you use footnotes or endnotes, you will usually need to provide a bibliography as well.

BIBLIOGRAPHY ENTRY

Burchard, Peter. *One Gallant Rush: Robert Gould Shaw and His Brave Black Regiment*. New York: St. Martin's, 1965.

CMS-2b Understand what plagiarism is.

In a research paper, you draw on the work of other writers. To be fair and responsible, you must document their contributions by citing your sources. Failure to give proper credit for another writer's intellectual property (words, ideas, or visuals) is a form of academic dishonesty known as *plagiarism*.

Three different acts are generally considered plagiarism:

1. failing to cite quotations and borrowed ideas
2. failing to enclose borrowed language in quotation marks
3. failing to put summaries and paraphrases in your own words

Definitions of plagiarism may vary; it's a good idea to find out how your school defines and addresses academic dishonesty.

CMS-2c Use quotation marks around borrowed language.

To indicate that you are using a source's exact phrases or sentences, you must enclose them in quotation marks unless they have been set off from the text by indenting (see CMS-3a). To omit the quotation marks is to claim — falsely — that the language is your own. Such an omission is plagiarism even if you have cited the source.

ORIGINAL SOURCE

For many Southerners it was psychologically impossible to see a black man bearing arms as anything but an incipient slave uprising complete with arson, murder, pillage, and rapine.

— Dudley Taylor Cornish, *The Sable Arm*, p. 158

PLAGIARISM

According to Civil War historian Dudley Taylor Cornish, for many Southerners it was psychologically impossible to see a black man bearing arms as anything but an incipient slave uprising complete with arson, murder, pillage, and rapine.[2]

BORROWED LANGUAGE IN QUOTATION MARKS

According to Civil War historian Dudley Taylor Cornish, "For many Southerners it was psychologically impossible to see a black man bearing arms as anything but an incipient slave uprising complete with arson, murder, pillage, and rapine."[2]

NOTE: Long quotations are set off from the text by indenting and do not need quotation marks (see the example at the end of CMS-3a).

CMS-2d Put summaries and paraphrases in your own words.

A summary condenses information; a paraphrase conveys the information using roughly the same number of words as the original source. When you summarize or paraphrase, it is not enough to name the source; you must present the source's meaning using your own language and sentence structure. (See also R2-c.) You are plagiarizing when you *patchwrite* — half-copy the author's sentences, either by mixing the author's phrases with your own without using quotation marks or by plugging synonyms into the author's sentence structure.

The first paraphrase of the following source is plagiarized — even though the source is cited — because too much of its language is borrowed from the original. The highlighted strings of words have been copied exactly (without quotation marks). In addition, the writer has closely followed the sentence structure of the original source, merely making a few substitutions (such as *Fifty percent* for *Half* and *angered and perhaps frightened* for *enraged and perhaps terrified*).

ORIGINAL SOURCE

Half of the force holding Fort Pillow were Negroes, former slaves now enrolled in the Union Army. Toward them Forrest's troops had the fierce, bitter animosity of men who had been educated to regard the colored race as inferior and who for the first time had encountered that race armed and fighting against white men. The sight enraged and perhaps terrified many of the Confederates and aroused in them the ugly spirit of a lynching mob.

— Albert Castel, "The Fort Pillow Massacre," pp. 46–47

PLAGIARISM: UNACCEPTABLE BORROWING

Albert Castel suggests that much of the brutality at Fort Pillow can be traced to racial attitudes. Fifty percent of the troops holding Fort Pillow were Negroes, former slaves who had joined the Union Army. Toward them Forrest's soldiers displayed the savage hatred of men who had been taught the inferiority of blacks and who for the first time had confronted them armed and fighting against white men. The vision angered and perhaps frightened the Confederates and aroused in them the ugly spirit of a lynching mob.[3]

To avoid plagiarizing an author's language, resist the temptation to look at the source while you are summarizing or paraphrasing. After you have read the passage you want to paraphrase, set the source aside. Ask yourself, "What is the author's meaning?" In your own words, state your understanding of the author's basic point. Return to the source and check that you haven't used the author's language or sentence structure or misrepresented the author's ideas. Following these steps will help you avoid plagiarizing the source. When you fully understand another writer's meaning, you can more easily and accurately present those ideas in your own words.

ACCEPTABLE PARAPHRASE

Albert Castel suggests that much of the brutality at Fort Pillow can be traced to racial attitudes. Nearly half of the Union troops were blacks, men whom the Confederates had been raised to consider their inferiors. The shock and perhaps fear of facing armed ex-slaves in battle for the first time may well have unleashed the fury that led to the massacre.[3]

CMS-3 Integrating sources

Quotations, summaries, paraphrases, and facts will help you develop your argument, but they cannot speak for you. You need to find a balance between the words of your sources and your own voice, so that readers always know who is speaking in your paper. You can use several strategies to integrate sources into your paper while maintaining your own voice.

CMS-3a Use quotations effectively.

When you quote a source, you borrow some of the author's exact words and enclose them in quotation marks. Quotation marks show your readers that both the idea and the words belong to the author.

WHEN TO USE QUOTATIONS

- When language is especially vivid or expressive
- When exact wording is needed for technical accuracy
- When it is important to let the debaters of an issue explain their positions in their own words
- When the words of an authority lend weight to an argument
- When the language of a source is the topic of your discussion

Limiting your use of quotations

Keep the emphasis on your own ideas. Although it is tempting to insert many quotations in your paper and to use your own words only for connecting passages, do not quote excessively. It is almost impossible to integrate numerous quotations smoothly into your own text.

It is not always necessary to quote full sentences from a source. To reduce your reliance on the words of others, you can often integrate language from a source into your own sentence structure.

Union surgeon Dr. Charles Fitch testified that after he was in custody, he "saw" Confederate soldiers "kill every negro that made his appearance dressed in Federal uniform."[20]

Using the ellipsis mark

To condense a quoted passage, you can use the ellipsis mark (a series of three spaced periods) to indicate that you have left words out. What remains must be grammatically complete.

> Union surgeon Fitch's testimony that all women and children had been evacuated from Fort Pillow before the attack conflicts with Forrest's report: "We captured . . . about 40 negro women and children."[6]

The writer has omitted several words not relevant to the issue at hand: *164 Federals, 75 negro troops, and.*

When you want to leave out one or more full sentences, use a period before the three ellipsis dots. For an example, see the long quotation at the end of this section.

Ordinarily, do not use an ellipsis mark at the beginning or at the end of a quotation. Your readers will understand that you have taken the quoted material from a longer passage. The only exception occurs when you have dropped words at the end of the final quoted sentence. In such cases, put an ellipsis before the closing quotation mark.

....

Using sources Make sure omissions and ellipsis marks do not distort the
responsibly meaning of your source.

....

Using brackets

Brackets allow you to insert your own words into quoted material to clarify a confusing reference or to keep a sentence grammatical in your context.

> According to Albert Castel, "It can be reasonably argued that he [Forrest] was justified in believing that the approaching steamships intended to aid the garrison [at Fort Pillow]."[7]

NOTE: Use the word *sic*, italicized and in brackets, to indicate that an error in a quoted sentence appears in the original source. (An example appears in the next section.) Do not overuse *sic* to call attention to errors in a source. Sometimes paraphrasing is a better option.

Setting off long quotations

CMS style allows you some flexibility in deciding whether to set off a long quotation or run it into your text. For emphasis, you may want to set off a quotation of more than four or five typed lines of text; almost certainly you should set off quotations of ten or more lines. To set off a quotation, indent it one-half inch from the left margin and use the normal right margin. Double-space the indented quotation.

Long quotations should be introduced by an informative sentence, usually followed by a colon. Quotation marks are unnecessary because the indented format tells readers that the passage is taken word-for-word from the source.

> In a letter home, Confederate officer Achilles V. Clark recounted what
> happened at Fort Pillow:
>
>> Words cannot describe the scene. The poor deluded negroes would run up to
>> our men fall upon their knees and with uplifted hands scream for mercy but
>> they were ordered to their feet and then shot down. The whitte [*sic*] men
>> fared but little better. . . . I with several others tried to stop the butchery
>> and at one time had partially succeeded, but Gen. Forrest ordered them shot
>> down like dogs, and the carnage continued.[8]

CMS-3b Use signal phrases to integrate sources.

Whenever you include a paraphrase, summary, or direct quotation of another writer's work in your paper, prepare your readers for it with introductory words called a *signal phrase*. A signal phrase usually names the author of the source, provides some context for the source material — such as the author's credentials — and helps readers distinguish your ideas from those of the source.

When you write a signal phrase, choose a verb that fits with the way you are using the source (see CMS-1c). Are you providing background, explaining a concept, supporting a claim, lending authority, or refuting an argument? The signal phrase you choose shows readers how you want them to think about the source. See the chart in this section for a list of verbs commonly used in signal phrases.

Note that CMS style calls for verbs in the present tense or present perfect tense (*points out* or *has pointed out*) to introduce source material unless you include a date that specifies the time of the original author's writing.

The first time you mention an author, use the full name: *Shelby Foote argues* . . . When you refer to the author again, you may use the last name only: *Foote raises an important question.*

Marking boundaries

Readers need to move smoothly from your words to the words of a source. Avoid dropping a quotation into your text without warning. Provide a clear signal phrase, usually including the author's name, to indicate the boundary between your words and the source's words. The signal phrase is highlighted in the second example.

DROPPED QUOTATION

Not surprisingly, those testifying on the Union and Confederate sides recalled events at Fort Pillow quite differently. Unionists claimed that their troops had abandoned their arms and were in full retreat. "The Confederates, however, all agreed that the Union troops retreated to the river with arms in their hands."[9]

QUOTATION WITH SIGNAL PHRASE

Not surprisingly, those testifying on the Union and Confederate sides recalled events at Fort Pillow quite differently. Unionists claimed that their troops had abandoned their arms and were in full retreat. "The Confederates, however," writes historian Albert Castel, "all agreed that the Union troops retreated to the river with arms in their hands."[9]

Using signal phrases with summaries and paraphrases

Introduce most summaries and paraphrases with a signal phrase that names the author and places the material in the context of your argument. Readers will then understand that everything between the signal phrase and the parenthetical citation summarizes or paraphrases the cited source.

Without the signal phrase (highlighted) in the following example, readers might think that only the last sentence is being cited, when in fact the whole paragraph is based on the source.

According to Jack Hurst, official Confederate policy was that black soldiers were to be treated as runaway slaves; in addition, the Confederate Congress decreed that white Union officers commanding black troops be killed. Confederate Lieutenant General Kirby Smith went one step further, declaring that he would kill all captured black troops. Smith's policy never met with strong opposition from the Richmond government.[10]

Integrating statistics and other facts

When you cite a statistic or another specific fact, a signal phrase is often not necessary. In most cases, readers will understand that the citation refers to the statistic or fact and not the whole paragraph.

Of 289 white troops garrisoned at Fort Pillow, 168 were taken prisoner. Black troops fared worse, with only 58 of 262 captured and most of the rest presumably killed or wounded.[12]

Using signal phrases in CMS papers

To avoid monotony, try to vary both the language and the placement of your signal phrases.

Model signal phrases

In the words of historian James M. McPherson, "..."[1]

As Dudley Taylor Cornish has argued, "..."[2]

In a letter to his wife, a Confederate soldier who witnessed the massacre wrote that "..."[3]

"...," claims Benjamin Quarles.[4]

"...," writes Albert Castel, "..."[5]

Shelby Foote offers an intriguing interpretation: "..."[6]

Verbs in signal phrases

admits	compares	explains	refutes
agrees	confirms	insists	rejects
argues	contends	notes	reports
asserts	declares	observes	responds
believes	denies	points out	suggests
claims	emphasizes	reasons	writes

There is nothing wrong, however, with using a signal phrase to introduce a statistic or another fact.

> Shelby Foote notes that of 289 white troops garrisoned at Fort Pillow, 168 were taken prisoner but that black troops fared worse, with only 58 of 262 captured and most of the rest presumably killed or wounded.[12]

Putting source material in context

Readers should not have to guess why source material appears in your paper. A signal phrase can help you connect your own ideas with those of another writer by clarifying how the source will contribute to your paper.

If you use another writer's words, you must explain how they relate to your argument. Quotations don't speak for themselves; you must create a context for readers. Sandwich each quotation between sentences of your own, introducing the quotation with a signal phrase and following it with comments that link the quotation to your paper's argument.

QUOTATION WITH EFFECTIVE CONTEXT

In a respected biography of Nathan Bedford Forrest, Hurst suggests that the temperamental Forrest "may have ragingly ordered a massacre and even intended to carry it out—until he rode inside the fort and viewed the horrifying result" and ordered it stopped.[11] While this is an intriguing interpretation of events, even Hurst would probably admit that it is merely speculation.

NOTE: When you bring other sources into a conversation about your research topic, you are synthesizing. For more on synthesis, see MLA-3d.

CMS-4 Documenting sources

In history and some other humanities courses, you may be asked to use the documentation system of *The Chicago Manual of Style*, 17th ed. (University of Chicago Press, 2017). In CMS style, superscript numbers (like this[1]) in the text of the paper refer readers to notes with corresponding numbers either at the foot of the page (footnotes) or at the end of the paper (endnotes). A bibliography is often required as well; it appears at the end of the paper and gives publication information for all the works cited in the notes.

TEXT

As Jack Hurst points out and Forrest must have known, in this twenty-minute battle, "Federals running for their lives had little time to concern themselves with a flag."[6]

FOOTNOTE OR ENDNOTE

6. Jack Hurst, *Nathan Bedford Forrest: A Biography* (New York: Knopf, 1993), 174.

BIBLIOGRAPHY ENTRY

Hurst, Jack. *Nathan Bedford Forrest: A Biography*. New York: Knopf, 1993.

CMS-4a First and later notes for a source

The first time you cite a source, the note should include publication information for that work as well as the page number for the passage you are citing.

1. Peter Burchard, *One Gallant Rush: Robert Gould Shaw and His Brave Black Regiment* (New York: St. Martin's, 1965), 85.

For later references to a source you have already cited, you may simply give the author's last name, a short form of the title, and the page or pages cited. A short form of the title of a book or another long work is italicized; a short form of the title of an article or another short work is put in quotation marks.

4. Burchard, *One Gallant Rush*, 31.

When you have two notes in a row from the same source, give the author's last name and the page or pages cited.

> 6. Jack Hurst, *Nathan Bedford Forrest: A Biography* (New York: Knopf, 1993), 174.

> 7. Hurst, 182.

CMS-4b CMS-style bibliography

A bibliography at the end of your paper lists the works you have cited in your notes; it may also include works you consulted but did not cite. See CMS-5a for how to construct the list; see CMS-5b for a sample bibliography.

NOTE: If you include a bibliography, *The Chicago Manual of Style* suggests that you shorten all notes, including the first reference to a source, as described in CMS-4a. Check with your instructor, however, to see whether using an abbreviated note for a first reference to a source is acceptable.

CMS-4c Model notes and bibliography entries

The following models are consistent with guidelines in *The Chicago Manual of Style*, 17th ed. For each type of source, a model note appears first, followed by a model bibliography entry. The note shows the format you should use when citing a source for the first time. For subsequent, or later, citations of a source, use shortened notes (see CMS-4a).

Some sources on the web, typically periodical articles, use a permanent locator called a digital object identifier (DOI). Use the DOI, when it is available, in place of a URL in your citations.

When a URL or a DOI must break across lines, do not insert a hyphen or break at a hyphen if the URL or DOI contains one. Instead, break after a colon or a double slash or before any other mark of punctuation.

General guidelines for listing authors

1. One author

> 1. Salman Rushdie, *Two Years Eight Months and Twenty-Eight Nights* (New York: Random House, 2015), 73.

Rushdie, Salman. *Two Years Eight Months and Twenty-Eight Nights*. New York: Random House, 2015.

2. Two or three authors For a work with two or three authors, give all authors' names in both the note and the bibliography entry.

> 2. Bill O'Reilly and Martin Dugard, *Killing Reagan: The Violent Assault That Changed a Presidency* (New York: Holt, 2015), 44.

O'Reilly, Bill, and Martin Dugard. *Killing Reagan: The Violent Assault That Changed a Presidency*. New York: Holt, 2015.

3. Four or more authors For a work with four or more authors, in the note give the first author's name followed by "et al." (for "and others"); in the bibliography entry, list all authors' names.

> 3. Lynn Hunt et al., *The Making of the West: Peoples and Cultures*, 5th ed. (Boston: Bedford/St. Martin's, 2015), 541.

> Hunt, Lynn, Thomas R. Martin, Barbara H. Rosenwein, and Bonnie G. Smith. *The Making of the West: Peoples and Cultures*. 5th ed. Boston: Bedford/St. Martin's, 2015.

4. Organization as author

> 4. The Big Horn Basin Foundation, *Wyoming's Dinosaur Discoveries* (Charleston, SC: Arcadia Publishing, 2015), 24.

> The Big Horn Basin Foundation. *Wyoming's Dinosaur Discoveries*. Charleston, SC: Arcadia Publishing, 2015.

5. Unknown author

> 5. *The Men's League Handbook on Women's Suffrage* (London, 1912), 23.

> *The Men's League Handbook on Women's Suffrage*. London, 1912.

6. Multiple works by the same author In the bibliography, arrange the entries alphabetically by title. Use six hyphens in place of the author's name in the second and subsequent entries.

> Kolbert, Elizabeth. *Field Notes from a Catastrophe: Man, Nature, and Climate Change*. New York: Bloomsbury USA, 2006.

> ------. *The Sixth Extinction: An Unnatural History*. New York: Holt, 2014.

7. Editor

> 7. Teresa Carpenter, ed., *New York Diaries: 1609–2009* (New York: Modern Library, 2012), 316.

> Carpenter, Teresa, ed. *New York Diaries: 1609–2009*. New York: Modern Library, 2012.

8. Editor with author

> 8. Susan Sontag, *As Consciousness Is Harnessed to Flesh: Journals and Notebooks, 1964–1980*, ed. David Rieff (New York: Farrar, Straus and Giroux, 2012), 265.

> Sontag, Susan. *As Consciousness Is Harnessed to Flesh: Journals and Notebooks, 1964–1980*. Edited by David Rieff. New York: Farrar, Straus and Giroux, 2012.

9. Translator with author

> 9. Karin Wieland, *Dietrich and Riefenstahl: Hollywood, Berlin, and a Century in Two Lives*, trans. Shelley Frisch (New York: Liveright, 2015), 52.

> Wieland, Karin. *Dietrich and Riefenstahl: Hollywood, Berlin, and a Century in Two Lives*. Translated by Shelley Frisch. New York: Liveright, 2015.

Books and other long works

- Citation at a glance: Book, 281

10. Basic format for a book

a. Print

10. David Leatherbarrow, *Topographical Studies in Landscape and Architecture* (Philadelphia: University of Pennsylvania Press, 2015), 45.

Leatherbarrow, David. *Topographical Studies in Landscape and Architecture*. Philadelphia: University of Pennsylvania Press, 2015.

b. E-book

10. Atul Gawande, *Being Mortal: Medicine and What Matters in the End* (New York: Metropolitan, 2014), chap. 3, NOOK.

Gawande, Atul. *Being Mortal: Medicine and What Matters in the End*. New York: Metropolitan, 2014. NOOK.

c. Web (or online library)

10. Charles Hursthouse, *New Zealand, or Zealandia, the Britain of the South* (1857; Hathi Trust Digital Library, n.d.), 2:356, http://catalog.hathitrust.org/Record/006536666.

Hursthouse, Charles. *New Zealand, or Zealandia, the Britain of the South*. 2 vols. 1857. Hathi Trust Digital Library, n.d. http://catalog.hathitrust.org/Record/006536666.

11. Edition other than the first

11. Judy Root Aulette and Judith Wittner, *Gendered Worlds*, 3rd ed. (Oxford: Oxford University Press, 2015), 86.

Aulette, Judy Root, and Judith Wittner. *Gendered Worlds*. 3rd ed. Oxford: Oxford University Press, 2015.

12. Volume in a multivolume work

If each volume has its own title, give the volume title first, followed by the volume number and the title of the entire work, as in the following examples. If the volumes do not have individual titles, give the volume and page number in the note (for example, 2:356) and the total number of volumes in the bibliography entry (see item 10c).

12. Robert A. Caro, *The Passage of Power*, vol. 4 of *The Years of Lyndon Johnson* (New York: Knopf, 2012), 198.

Caro, Robert A. *The Passage of Power*. Vol. 4 of *The Years of Lyndon Johnson*. New York: Knopf, 2012.

13. Work in an anthology or a collection

13. Ben Merriman, "Lessons of the Arkansas," in *City by City: Dispatches from the American Metropolis*, ed. Keith Gessen and Stephen Squibb (New York: n+1/Farrar, Straus and Giroux, 2015), 142.

Merriman, Ben. "Lessons of the Arkansas." In *City by City: Dispatches from the American Metropolis*, edited by Keith Gessen and Stephen Squibb, 142–56. New York: n+1/Farrar, Straus and Giroux, 2015.

Citation at a glance: Book

CMS

To cite a print book in CMS style, include the following elements:

1 Author(s)
2 Title and subtitle
3 City of publication

4 Publisher
5 Year of publication
6 Page number(s) cited
(for notes)

TITLE PAGE

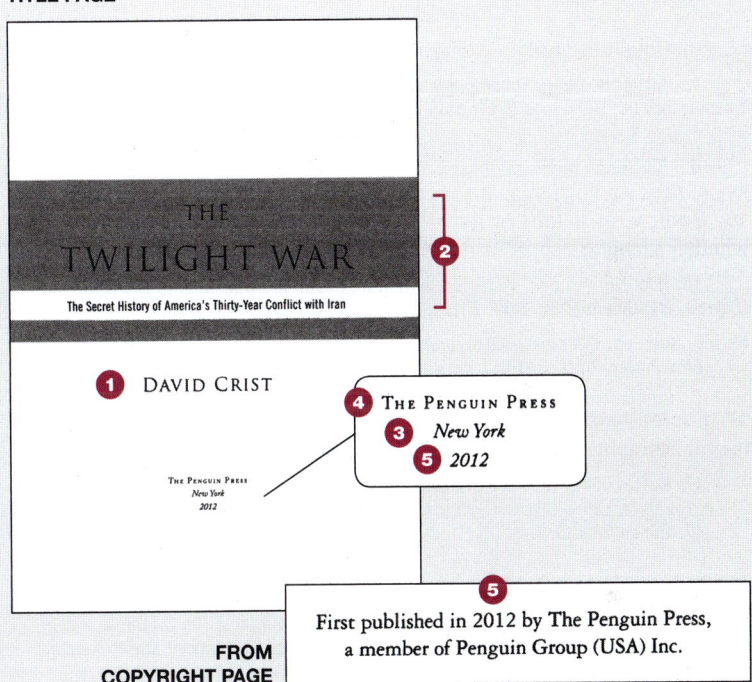

**FROM
COPYRIGHT PAGE**

NOTE

      1   **2**

   1. David Crist, *The Twilight War: The Secret History of America's Thirty-Year Conflict*
2   **3**   **4**   **5**   **6**
with Iran (New York: Penguin Press, 2012), 354.

BIBLIOGRAPHY

   1   **2**

Crist, David. *The Twilight War: The Secret History of America's Thirty-Year Conflict with*
     2   **3**   **4**   **5**
   Iran. New York: Penguin Press, 2012.

For more on citing books in CMS style, see items 10–17.

14. Introduction, preface, foreword, or afterword

14. Alice Walker, afterword to *The Indispensable Zinn: The Essential Writings of the "People's Historian,"* by Howard Zinn, ed. Timothy Patrick McCarthy (New York: New Press, 2012), 373.

Walker, Alice. Afterword to *The Indispensable Zinn: The Essential Writings of the "People's Historian,"* by Howard Zinn, 371–76. Edited by Timothy Patrick McCarthy. New York: New Press, 2012.

15. Republished book

15. Arthur M. Okun, *Equality and Efficiency: The Big Tradeoff* (1975; repr., Washington, DC: Brookings Institution Press, 2015), 26.

Okun, Arthur M. *Equality and Efficiency: The Big Tradeoff*. 1975. Reprint, Washington, DC: Brookings Institution Press, 2015.

16. Book with a title in its title   Use quotation marks around any title, whether a long or a short work, within an italicized title.

16. Noel Merino, ed., *Wilderness Adventure in Jon Krakauer's "Into the Wild"* (Detroit, MI: Greenhaven Press, 2015), 47.

Merino, Noel, ed. *Wilderness Adventure in Jon Krakauer's "Into the Wild."* Detroit, MI: Greenhaven Press, 2015.

17. Sacred text   Sacred texts such as the Bible are usually not included in the bibliography.

17. Matt. 20:4–9 (Revised Standard Version).

17. Qur'an 18:1–3.

18. Government document

18. United States Senate, Committee on Foreign Relations, *The U.S. Role in the Middle East: Hearing before the Committee on Foreign Relations, United States Senate,* 114th Cong., 1st sess. (Washington, DC: GPO, 2015), 35.

United States Senate. Committee on Foreign Relations. *The U.S. Role in the Middle East: Hearing before the Committee on Foreign Relations, United States Senate,* 114th Cong., 1st sess. Washington, DC: GPO, 2015.

19. Published proceedings of a conference   Cite as a book, adding the location and dates of the conference after the title.

19. Stacey K. Sowards et al., eds., *Across Borders and Environments: Communication and Environmental Justice in International Contexts,* University of Texas at El Paso, June 25–28, 2011 (Cincinnati, OH: International Environmental Communication Association, 2012), 114.

Sowards, Stacey K., Kyle Alvarado, Diana Arrieta, and Jacob Barde, eds. *Across Borders and Environments: Communication and Environmental Justice in International Contexts*. University of Texas at El Paso, June 25–28, 2011. Cincinnati, OH: International Environmental Communication Association, 2012.

20. Source quoted in another source (a secondary source) Sometimes you will want to use a quotation from one source that you have found in another source. In your note and bibliography entry, cite whatever information is available about the original source of the quotation, including a page number. Then add the words "quoted in" and give publication information for the source in which you found the words. In the following examples, author John Matteson quotes the words of Thomas Wentworth Higginson. Matteson's book includes a note with information about the Higginson book.

20. Thomas Wentworth Higginson, *Margaret Fuller Ossoli* (Boston: Houghton Mifflin, 1890), 11, quoted in John Matteson, *The Lives of Margaret Fuller* (New York: Norton, 2012), 7.

Higginson, Thomas Wentworth. *Margaret Fuller Ossoli*. Boston: Houghton Mifflin, 1890, 11. Quoted in John Matteson, *The Lives of Margaret Fuller* (New York: Norton, 2012), 7.

Articles and other short works

- Citation at a glance: Article in an online journal, 284–285
- Citation at a glance: Article from a database, 286–287

NOTE ON PAGE NUMBERS: For print articles, give a page number in a note and a page range in the bibliography entry. For articles on the web and in databases, if the source gives only a beginning page, do not give a page number in your note, but use a plus sign after the beginning page number in the bibliography entry: 21+. If a source has no page numbers but has headings or numbered paragraphs, you may use those locators in a note.

NOTE ON DATABASES: For articles in databases, at the end of the note and bibliography entry give one of the following pieces of information, in this order of preference: a DOI for the article; *or* the name of the database; *or* a stable URL for the article. (The DOI consists of the prefix https://doi.org/ followed by the DOI identifier or locator found in the source. See item 21b for an example.)

21. Article in a journal Include the volume and issue numbers (if the journal has them) and the date.

a. Print

21. Bernard Dubbeld, "Capital and the Shifting Ground of Emancipatory Politics: The Limits of Radical Unionism in Durban Harbor, 1974–85," *Critical Historical Studies* 2, no. 1 (2015): 86.

Dubbeld, Bernard. "Capital and the Shifting Ground of Emancipatory Politics: The Limits of Radical Unionism in Durban Harbor, 1974–85." *Critical Historical Studies* 2, no. 1 (2015): 85–112.

Citation at a glance: Article in an online journal

To cite an article in an online journal or magazine in CMS style, include the following elements:

1 Author(s)
2 Title and subtitle of article
3 Title of journal
4 Volume and issue numbers
5 Year of publication

6 Page number(s) cited (for notes); page range of article (for bibliography), if available
7 DOI, if article has one; otherwise, URL for article

ISSUE CONTENTS PAGE

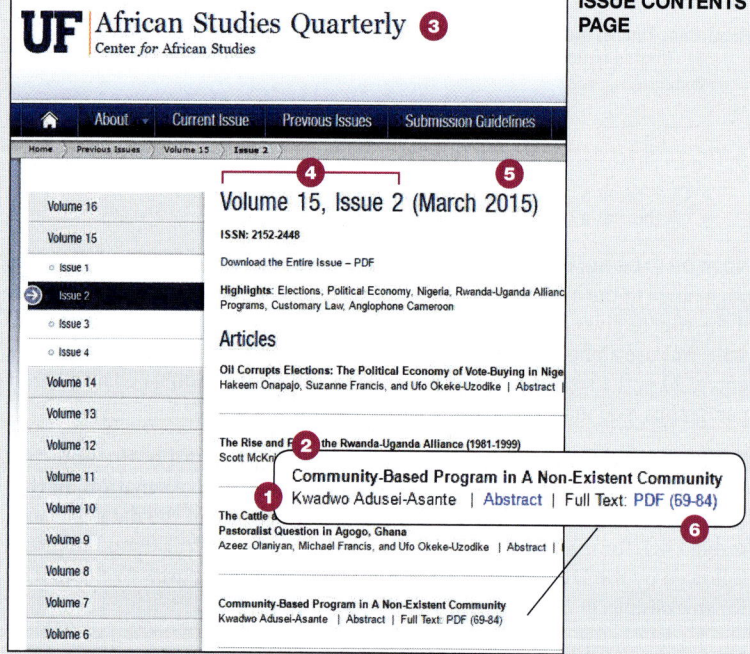

ARTICLE HOME PAGE (top) AND FULL TEXT (bottom)

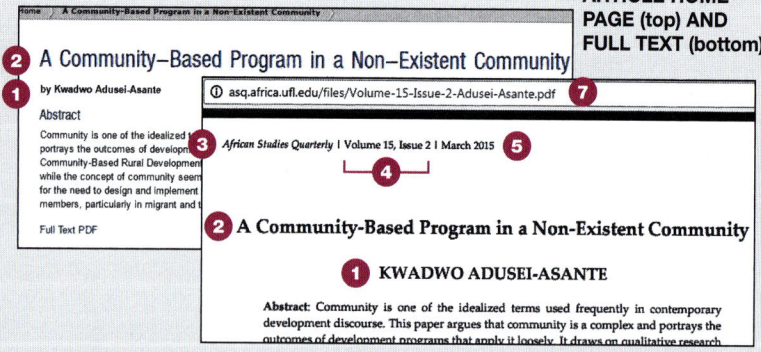

NOTE

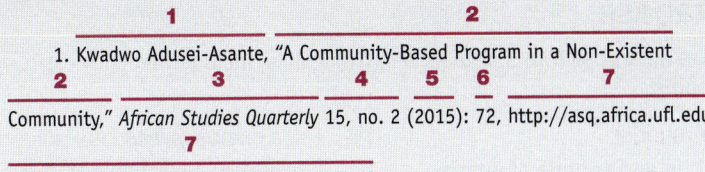

1. Kwadwo Adusei-Asante, "A Community-Based Program in a Non-Existent Community," *African Studies Quarterly* 15, no. 2 (2015): 72, http://asq.africa.ufl.edu /files/Volume-15-Issue-2-Adusei-Asante.pdf.

BIBLIOGRAPHY

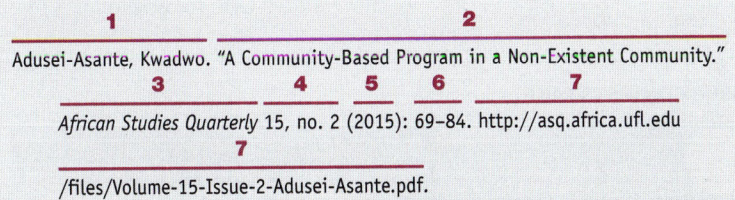

Adusei-Asante, Kwadwo. "A Community-Based Program in a Non-Existent Community." *African Studies Quarterly* 15, no. 2 (2015): 69–84. http://asq.africa.ufl.edu /files/Volume-15-Issue-2-Adusei-Asante.pdf.

For more on citing articles in CMS style, see items 21–23.

21. Article in a journal *(cont.)*

b. Web Give the complete DOI if the article has one; if there is no DOI, give the URL for the article.

> 21. Anne-Lise François, "Flower Fisting," *Postmodern Culture* 22, no. 1 (2011), https://doi.org/10.1353/pmc.2012.0004.

> François, Anne-Lise. "Flower Fisting." *Postmodern Culture* 22, no. 1 (2011). https://doi .org/10.1353/pmc.2012.0004.

c. Database For more on citing page numbers and database information, see the notes on page 283.

> 21. Estelle Joubert, "Performing Sovereignty, Sounding Autonomy: Political Representation in the Operas of Maria Antonia of Saxony," *Music and Letters* 96, no. 3 (2015): 345, https://muse.jhu.edu/article/597807.

> Joubert, Estelle. "Performing Sovereignty, Sounding Autonomy: Political Representation in the Operas of Maria Antonia of Saxony." *Music and Letters* 96, no. 3 (2015): 344–89. https://muse.jhu.edu/article/597807.

22. Article in a magazine
Give the month and year for a monthly publication; give the month, day, and year for a weekly publication. (For more on citing page numbers and database information, see the notes on p. 283.)

a. Print

> 22. Alexandra Fuller, "Haiti on Its Own Terms," *National Geographic*, December 2015, 112.

> Fuller, Alexandra. "Haiti on Its Own Terms." *National Geographic*, December 2015, 98–118.

Citation at a glance: Article from a database

To cite an article from a database in CMS style, include the following elements:

1 Author(s)

2 Title and subtitle of article

3 Title of journal

4 Volume and issue numbers

5 Year of publication

6 Page number(s) cited (for notes, if available); page range of article (for bibliography), if given

7 DOI; *or* database name; *or* stable URL for article

ISSUE CONTENTS PAGE

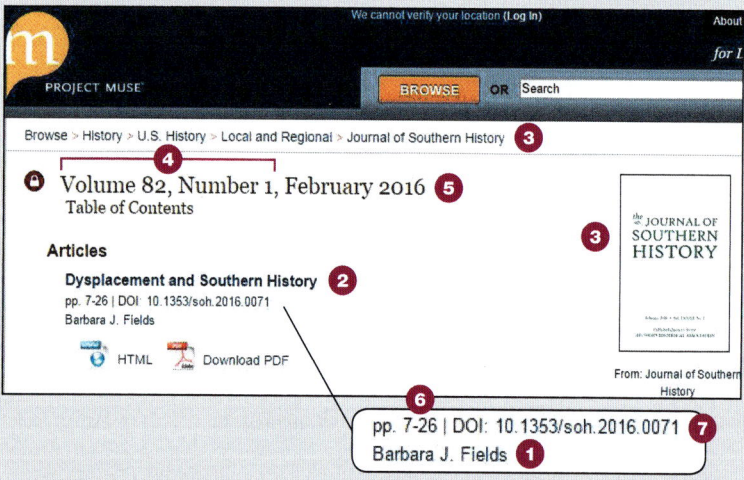

ARTICLE FIRST PAGE

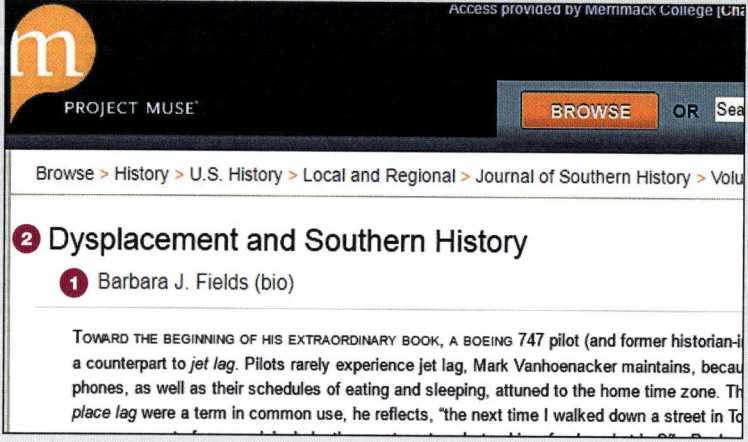

NOTE

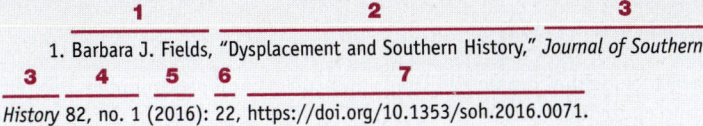

1. Barbara J. Fields, "Dysplacement and Southern History," *Journal of Southern History* 82, no. 1 (2016): 22, https://doi.org/10.1353/soh.2016.0071.

BIBLIOGRAPHY

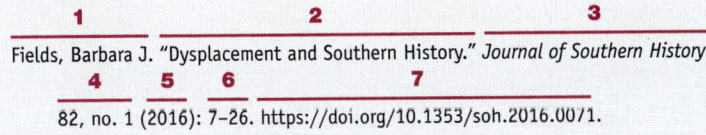

Fields, Barbara J. "Dysplacement and Southern History." *Journal of Southern History* 82, no. 1 (2016): 7–26. https://doi.org/10.1353/soh.2016.0071.

For more on citing articles from databases in CMS style, see items 21–23.

22. Article in a magazine *(cont.)*

b. Web

22. Alan Lightman, "What Came before the Big Bang?," *Harper's*, January 2016, http://harpers.org/archive/2016/01/what-came-before-the-big-bang.

Lightman, Alan. "What Came before the Big Bang?" *Harper's*, January 2016. http://harpers.org/archive/2016/01/what-came-before-the-big-bang.

c. Database

22. Ron Rosenbaum, "The Last Renaissance Man," *Smithsonian*, November 2012, 40, OmniFile Full Text Select.

Rosenbaum, Ron. "The Last Renaissance Man." *Smithsonian*, November 2012, 39–44. OmniFile Full Text Select.

23. Article in a newspaper   Page numbers are not necessary; a section letter or number, if available, is sufficient. (For more on citing page numbers and database information, see the notes on p. 283.)

a. Print

23. Neil Irwin, "Low Rates May Stay for Years After the Fed Reverses Course," *New York Times*, December 15, 2015, sec. A.

Irwin, Neil. "Low Rates May Stay for Years After the Fed Reverses Course." *New York Times*, December 15, 2015, sec. A.

23. Article in a newspaper (*cont.*)

b. Web Include the complete URL for the article. Omit page numbers, even if the source provides them.

23. Chris Mooney, "The World Just Adopted a Tough New Climate Goal. Here's How Hard It Will Be to Meet," *Washington Post*, December 15, 2015, https://www .washingtonpost.com/news/energy-environment/wp/2015/12/15/the-world-just -adopted-a-tough-new-climate-goal-heres-how-hard-it-will-be-to-meet.

Mooney, Chris. "The World Just Adopted a Tough New Climate Goal. Here's How Hard It Will Be to Meet." *Washington Post*, December 15, 2015. https://www .washingtonpost.com/news/energy-environment/wp/2015/12/15/the-world-just -adopted-a-tough-new-climate-goal-heres-how-hard-it-will-be-to-meet.

c. Database For more on citing page numbers and database information, see the notes on page 283.

23. "Safe in Sioux City at Last: Union Pacific Succeeds in Securing Trackage from the St. Paul Road," *Omaha Daily Herald*, May 16, 1889, America's Historical Newspapers.

"Safe in Sioux City at Last: Union Pacific Succeeds in Securing Trackage from the St. Paul Road." *Omaha Daily Herald*, May 16, 1889. America's Historical Newspapers.

24. Unsigned newspaper article
See item 23. In the note, begin with the title of the article. In the bibliography entry, begin with the title of the newspaper.

24. "Next President Better Be a Climate Change Believer," *Chicago Sun-Times*, June 24, 2016, https://chicago.suntimes.com/opinion/editorial-next-president-better -be-a-climate-change-believer/.

Chicago Sun-Times. "Next President Better Be a Climate Change Believer." June 24, 2016. https://chicago.suntimes.com/opinion/editorial-next-president-better-be-a-climate -change-believer/.

25. Article with a title in its title
Use italics for titles of long works such as books and for terms that are normally italicized. Use single quotation marks for titles of short works and terms that would otherwise be placed in double quotation marks.

25. Julia Hudson-Richards, " 'Women Want to Work': Shifting Ideologies of Women's Work in Franco's Spain, 1939–1962," *Journal of Women's History* 27, no. 2 (2015): 91.

Hudson-Richards, Julia. " 'Women Want to Work': Shifting Ideologies of Women's Work in Franco's Spain, 1939–1962." *Journal of Women's History* 27, no. 2 (2015): 87–109.

26. Review
If the review has a title, provide it immediately following the author of the review.

26. Philip Zozzaro, review of *Among the Ruins: The Decline and Fall of the Roman Catholic Church*, by Paul L. Williams, *San Francisco Book Review*, October 1, 2017, https://sanfranciscobookreview.com/product/among-the-ruins-the-decline-and-fall-of -the-roman-catholic-church/.

Zozzaro, Philip. Review of *Among the Ruins: The Decline and Fall of the Roman Catholic Church*, by Paul L. Williams. *San Francisco Book Review*, October 1, 2017. https:// sanfranciscobookreview.com/product/among-the-ruins-the-decline-and-fall-of-the -roman-catholic-church/.

27. Letter to the editor   Do not use the letter's title, even if the publication gives one.

27. Fredric Rolando, letter to the editor, *Economist*, December 5, 2015, http://www.economist.com/.

Rolando, Fredric. Letter to the editor. *Economist*, December 5, 2015. http://www.economist.com/.

28. Article in a dictionary or an encyclopedia (including a wiki)   Reference works such as encyclopedias do not require publication information and are usually not included in the bibliography. The abbreviation "s.v." is for the Latin *sub verbo* ("under the word").

28. *Encyclopaedia Britannica*, 15th ed. (2010), s.v. "Monroe Doctrine."

28. Wikipedia, s.v. "James Monroe," last modified December 19, 2012, http://en.wikipedia.org/wiki/James_Monroe.

28. Bryan A. Garner, *Garner's Modern American Usage*, 3rd ed. (Oxford: Oxford University Press, 2009), s.v. "brideprice."

Garner, Bryan A. *Garner's Modern American Usage*. 3rd ed. Oxford: Oxford University Press, 2009.

29. Letter in a published collection   If the letter writer's name is part of the book title, begin the note with only the last name but begin the bibliography entry with the full name.

- Citation at a glance: Letter in a published collection, 290–291

29. Reagan to Richard Nixon, July 15, 1960, in *Reagan: A Life in Letters*, ed. Kiron K. Skinner, Annelise Anderson, and Martin Anderson (New York: Free Press, 2003), 704–5.

Reagan, Ronald. *Reagan: A Life in Letters*. Edited by Kiron K. Skinner, Annelise Anderson, and Martin Anderson. New York: Free Press, 2003.

Web sources

For most websites, include an author if a site has one, the title of the site, the sponsor, the date of publication or the modified (update) date, and the site's complete URL. Do not italicize a website title unless the site is an online book or periodical. Use quotation marks for the titles of sections or pages in a website. If a site does not have a date of publication or a modified date, give the date you accessed the site ("accessed January 27, 2020").

30. An entire website

30. Chesapeake and Ohio Canal National Historical Park (website), National Park Service, last modified November 25, 2015, http://www.nps.gov/choh/index.htm.

National Park Service. Chesapeake and Ohio Canal National Historical Park (website). Last modified November 25, 2015. http://www.nps.gov/choh/index.htm.

Citation at a glance: Letter in a published collection

To cite a letter in a published collection in CMS style, include the following elements:

1 Author of letter
2 Recipient of letter
3 Date of letter
4 Title of collection
5 Editor of collection
6 City of publication
7 Publisher
8 Year of publication
9 Page number(s) cited (for notes)

TITLE PAGE OF BOOK

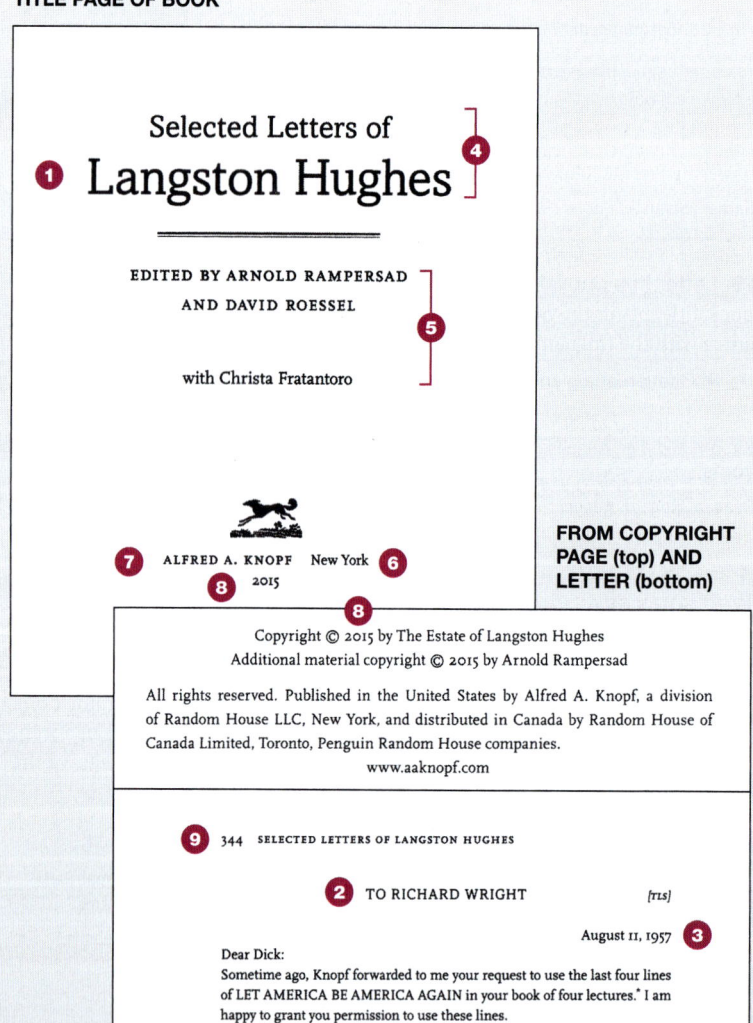

Selected Letters of

1 **Langston Hughes** **4**

EDITED BY ARNOLD RAMPERSAD
AND DAVID ROESSEL **5**

with Christa Fratantoro

7 ALFRED A. KNOPF   New York **6**
8 2015

FROM COPYRIGHT PAGE (top) AND LETTER (bottom)

8

Copyright © 2015 by The Estate of Langston Hughes
Additional material copyright © 2015 by Arnold Rampersad

All rights reserved. Published in the United States by Alfred A. Knopf, a division of Random House LLC, New York, and distributed in Canada by Random House of Canada Limited, Toronto, Penguin Random House companies.
www.aaknopf.com

9 344   SELECTED LETTERS OF LANGSTON HUGHES

2 TO RICHARD WRIGHT   [TLS]

August 11, 1957 **3**

Dear Dick:
Sometime ago, Knopf forwarded to me your request to use the last four lines of LET AMERICA BE AMERICA AGAIN in your book of four lectures.* I am happy to grant you permission to use these lines.

NOTE

1. Hughes to Richard Wright, August 11, 1957, in *Selected Letters of Langston Hughes*, ed. Arnold Rampersad, David Roessel, and Christa Fratantoro (New York: Knopf, 2015), 344–45.

BIBLIOGRAPHY

Hughes, Langston. *Selected Letters of Langston Hughes*. Edited by Arnold Rampersad, David Roessel, and Christa Fratantoro. New York: Knopf, 2015.

For another citation of a letter in CMS style, see item 29.

31. Work from a website

- Citation at a glance: Primary source from a website, 292–293

31. Alexios Mantzarlis, "How TV Fact-Checked Spain's Final Debate," Poynter, last modified December 15, 2015, https://www.poynter.org/news/how-tv-fact-checked-spains-final-debate.

Mantzarlis, Alexios. "How TV Fact-Checked Spain's Final Debate." Poynter, last modified December 15, 2015. https://www.poynter.org/news/how-tv-fact-checked-spains-final-debate.

32. Blog post

Treat as a work from a website (see item 31), but italicize the name of the blog. Insert "blog" in parentheses after the name if the word *blog* is not part of the name. If the blog is part of a larger site (such as a newspaper's or an organization's site), add the title of the site after the blog title.

32. Gregory LeFever, "Skull Fraud 'Created' the Brontosaurus," *Ancient Tides* (blog), December 16, 2012, http://ancient-tides.blogspot.com/2012/12/skull-fraud-created-brontosaurus.html.

LeFever, Gregory. "Skull Fraud 'Created' the Brontosaurus." *Ancient Tides* (blog), December 16, 2012. http://ancient-tides.blogspot.com/2012/12/skull-fraud-created-brontosaurus.html.

33. Comment on a blog post

33. OllyPye, December 12, 2015, comment on Graham Readfern, "Paris Agreement a Victory for Climate Change and Ultimate Defeat for Fossil Fuels," *Planet Oz* (blog), *Guardian*, http://www.theguardian.com/environment/planet-oz/2015/dec/12/paris-agreement-a-victory-for-climate-science-and-ultimate-defeat-for-fossil-fuels#comments-64993862.

OllyPye. December 12, 2015. Comment on Graham Readfern, "Paris Agreement a Victory for Climate Change and the Ultimate Defeat for Fossil Fuels." *Planet Oz* (blog). *Guardian*. http://www.theguardian.com/environment/planet-oz/2015/dec/12/paris-agreement-a-victory-for-climate-science-and-ultimate-defeat-for-fossil-fuels#comments-64993862.

CMS

Citation at a glance: Primary source from a website

To cite a primary source (or any other document) from a website in CMS style, include as many of the following elements as are available:

1 Author(s)
2 Title of document
3 Title of site
4 Sponsor of site

5 Publication date or modified date; date of access (if no publication date)
6 URL of document page

WEBSITE HOME PAGE

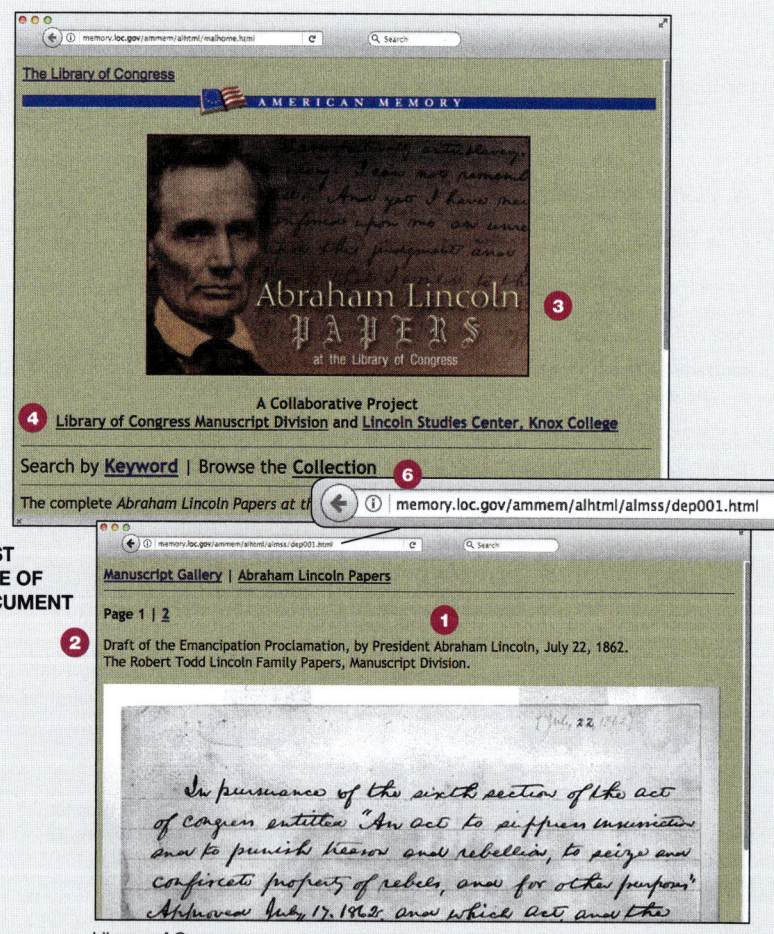

FIRST PAGE OF DOCUMENT

Library of Congress

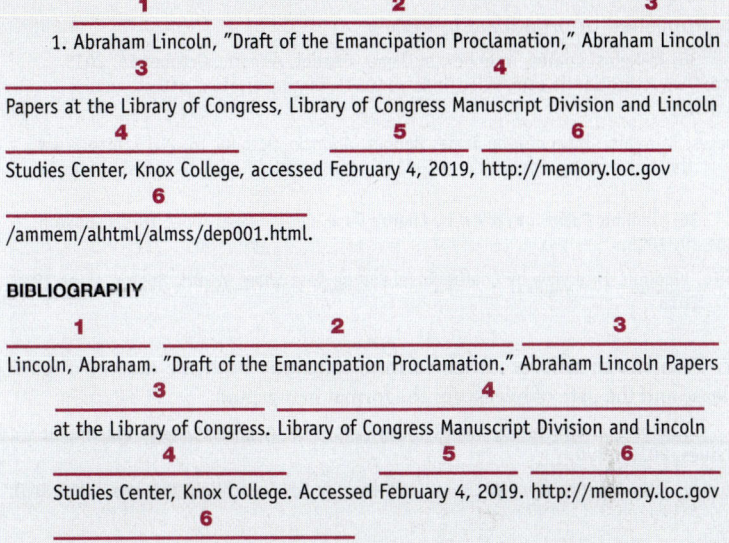

1. Abraham Lincoln, "Draft of the Emancipation Proclamation," Abraham Lincoln Papers at the Library of Congress, Library of Congress Manuscript Division and Lincoln Studies Center, Knox College, accessed February 4, 2019, http://memory.loc.gov /ammem/alhtml/almss/dep001.html.

BIBLIOGRAPHY

Lincoln, Abraham. "Draft of the Emancipation Proclamation." Abraham Lincoln Papers at the Library of Congress. Library of Congress Manuscript Division and Lincoln Studies Center, Knox College. Accessed February 4, 2019. http://memory.loc.gov /ammem/alhtml/almss/dep001.html.

For more on citing documents from websites in CMS style, see item 31.

Audio, visual, and multimedia sources

34. Podcast   Treat as a work from a website (see item 31), including the following, if available: the author, speaker, or host; title of the episode; an identifying number, if any; date of release or upload; title of the podcast (italicized); sponsor or database; time stamp; and complete URL.

34. Toyin Falola, "Creativity and Decolonization: Nigerian Cultures and African Epistemologies," Episode 96, November 17, 2015, in *Africa Past and Present*, African Online Digital Library, podcast, MP3 audio, 43:44, http://afripod.aodl.org/2015/11 /afripod-96/.

Falola, Toyin. "Creativity and Decolonization: Nigerian Cultures and African Epistemologies." Episode 96, November 17, 2015. *Africa Past and Present*. African Online Digital Library. Podcast, MP3 audio, 43:44. http://afripod.aodl .org/2015/11/afripod-96/.

35. Online audio or video   Cite as a work from a website (see item 31). If the source is downloadable, identify the format or medium before the URL.

35. Will Potter, "The Secret US Prisons You've Never Heard of Before," TED Talks, November 9, 2015, https://www.youtube.com/watch?v=xuAAPsiD768.

Potter, Will. "The Secret US Prisons You've Never Heard of Before." TED Talks, November 9, 2015. https://www.youtube.com/watch?v=xuAAPsiD768.

36. Published or broadcast interview

36. Ta-Nehisi Coates, interview by James Bennet, *Atlantic,* October 16, 2015, http://www.theatlantic.com/video/index/410815/in-conversation-with-ta-nehisi-coates/.

Coates, Ta-Nehisi. Interview by James Bennet. *Atlantic,* October 16, 2015. http://www.theatlantic.com/video/index/410815/in-conversation-with-ta-nehisi-coates/.

36. Vladimir Putin, interview by Charlie Rose, *Charlie Rose Show,* WGBH, Boston, June 19, 2015.

Putin, Vladimir. Interview by Charlie Rose. *Charlie Rose Show.* WGBH, Boston, June 19, 2015.

37. Film (DVD, BD, or other format)   Include both the date of original release and the date of release for the format being cited.

37. *Brooklyn,* directed by John Crowley (2015; Los Angeles, CA: Fox Searchlight Pictures, 2016), DVD.

Crowley, John, dir. *Brooklyn.* 2015; Los Angeles, CA: Fox Searchlight Pictures, 2016. DVD.

38. Sound recording

38. Gustav Holst, *The Planets,* Royal Philharmonic Orchestra, conducted by André Previn, recorded April 14–15, 1986, Telarc 80133, compact disc.

Holst, Gustav. *The Planets.* Royal Philharmonic Orchestra. Conducted by André Previn. Recorded April 14–15, 1986. Telarc 80133, compact disc.

38. "Work," MP3 audio, track 4 on Rihanna, *Anti,* Roc Nation, 2016.

Rihanna. "Work." *Anti.* Roc Nation, 2016, MP3 audio.

39. Musical score or composition

39. Antonio Vivaldi, *L'Estro armonico,* op. 3, ed. Eleanor Selfridge-Field (Mineola, NY: Dover, 1999).

Vivaldi, Antonio. *L'Estro armonico,* op. 3. Edited by Eleanor Selfridge-Field. Mineola, NY: Dover, 1999.

40. Work of art

40. Hope Gangloff, *Vera,* 2015, acrylic on canvas, Kemper Museum of Contemporary Art, Kansas City, MO.

Gangloff, Hope. *Vera.* 2015. Acrylic on canvas. Kemper Museum of Contemporary Art, Kansas City, MO.

41. Performance

41. Wendy Wasserstein, *The Heidi Chronicles,* directed by Vivienne Benesch, Trinity Repertory Company, Providence, RI, December 3, 2015.

Wasserstein, Wendy. *The Heidi Chronicles.* Directed by Vivienne Benesch. Trinity Repertory Company, Providence, RI, December 3, 2015.

Personal communication and social media

42. Personal communication Personal communications are not included in the bibliography.

> 42. Sara Lehman, email message to author, August 13, 2019.

43. Online posting or email If an online posting has been archived, include a URL. Emails that are not part of an online discussion are treated as personal communication (see item 42). Online postings and emails are not included in the bibliography.

> 43. Bart Dale, reply to "Which country made best science/technology contribution?," Historum General History Forums, December 15, 2015, http://historum.com/general-history/46089-country-made-best-science-technology-contribution-16.html.

44. Social media post

> 44. NASA (@nasa), "This galaxy is a whirl of color," Instagram photo, September 23, 2017, https://www.instagram.com/p/BZY8adnnZQJ/.

> NASA. "This galaxy is a whirl of color." Instagram photo, September 23, 2017. https://www.instagram.com/p/BZY8adnnZQJ/.

CMS-5 CMS (*Chicago*) format; sample pages

The following guidelines for formatting a CMS-style paper and preparing its endnotes and bibliography are based on *The Chicago Manual of Style*, 17th ed. (University of Chicago Press, 2017). For pages from a sample paper, see CMS-5b.

CMS-5a CMS format

Formatting the paper

The guidelines in this section describe recommendations for formatting the text of your paper, preparing the endnotes, and preparing the bibliography.

Font If your instructor does not require a specific font, choose one that is standard and easy to read (such as Times New Roman).

Title page Include the full title of your paper, your name, the course title, the instructor's name, and the date. See CMS-5b for a sample title page.

Pagination Using arabic numerals, number the pages in the upper right corner. Do not number the title page but count it in the manuscript numbering; that is, the first page of the text will be numbered 2. Depending on your instructor's preference, you may also use a short title or your last name before the page numbers to help identify pages.

Margins, line spacing, and paragraph indents Leave margins of at least one inch at the top, bottom, and sides of the page. Double-space the body of the paper, including long quotations that have been set off from the text. (For line spacing in notes and the bibliography, see the end of section CMS-5a.) Left-align the text.

Indent the first line of each paragraph one-half inch from the left margin.

Capitalization, italics, and quotation marks In titles of works, capitalize all words except articles (*a, an, the*), prepositions (*at, from, between*, and so on), coordinating conjunctions (*and, but, or, nor, for, so, yet*), and *to* and *as* — unless the word is first or last in the title or subtitle. Follow these guidelines in your paper even if the title is styled differently in the source.

Lowercase the first word following a colon even if the word begins a complete sentence. When the colon introduces a series of sentences or questions, capitalize the first word in all sentences in the series, including the first.

Italicize the titles of books and other long works. Use quotation marks around the titles of periodical articles, short stories, poems, and other short works.

Long quotations You can choose to set off a long quotation of five to ten typed lines by indenting the entire quotation one-half inch from the left margin. (Always set off quotations of ten or more lines.) Double-space the quotation; do not use quotation marks and do not add extra space above or below it. (See CMS-5b for a long quotation in the text of a paper; see also CMS-3a.)

Visuals CMS classifies visuals as tables and figures (graphs, drawings, photographs, maps, and charts). Keep visuals as simple as possible.

Label each table with an arabic numeral (Table 1, Table 2, and so on) and provide a clear title that identifies the table's subject. The label and the title should appear on separate lines above the table, left-aligned. For a table that you have borrowed or adapted, give its source in a note like this one, below the table:

Source: Edna Bonacich and Richard P. Appelbaum, *Behind the Label* (Berkeley: University of California Press, 2000), 145.

For each figure, place a label and a caption below the figure, left-aligned. The label and caption need not appear on separate lines. The word "Figure" may be abbreviated to "Fig."

In the text of your paper, discuss the most significant features of each visual. Place visuals as close as possible to the sentences that relate to them unless your instructor prefers that visuals appear in an appendix.

URLs and DOIs   When a URL or a DOI (digital object identifier) must break across lines, do not insert a hyphen or break at a hyphen. Instead, break after a colon or a double slash or before any other mark of punctuation. If you will post your project online or submit it electronically and you want to include live URLs for readers to click on, do not insert any line breaks.

Headings   CMS does not provide guidelines for the use of headings in student papers. If you would like to insert headings in a long essay or research paper, check first with your instructor. See CMS-5b for typical placement and formatting of headings in a CMS-style paper.

Preparing the endnotes

Begin the endnotes on a new page at the end of the paper. Center the title "Notes" about one inch from the top of the page, and number the pages consecutively with the rest of the paper. See CMS-5b for an example.

Indenting and numbering   Indent the first line of each note one-half inch from the left margin; do not indent additional lines in the note. Begin the note with the arabic numeral that corresponds to the number in the text. Put a period after the number.

Line spacing   Single-space each note and double-space between notes (unless your instructor prefers double-spacing throughout).

Preparing the bibliography

Typically, the notes in CMS-style papers are followed by a bibliography, an alphabetically arranged list of all the works cited or consulted. Center the title "Bibliography" about one inch from the top of the page. Number bibliography pages consecutively with the rest of the paper. See CMS-5b for a sample bibliography.

Alphabetizing the list   Alphabetize the bibliography by the last names of the authors (or editors); when a work has no author or editor, alphabetize it by the first word of the title other than *A, An,* or *The.*

If your list includes two or more works by the same author, arrange the entries alphabetically by title. Then use six hyphens instead of the author's name in all entries after the first. (See item 6 on p. 279.)

Indenting and line spacing   Begin each entry at the left margin, and indent any additional lines one-half inch. Single-space each entry and double-space between entries (unless your instructor prefers double-spacing throughout).

CMS-5b Sample pages from a CMS-style research paper

Following are pages from a research paper by Ned Bishop, a student in a history class. Bishop used CMS-style endnotes, bibliography, and manuscript format.

The Massacre at Fort Pillow:
Holding Nathan Bedford Forrest Accountable

| Title of paper

Ned Bishop

| Writer's name

History 214
Professor Citro
March 22, 2019

| Title of course,
instructor's
name, and
date

Marginal annotations indicate CMS-style formatting and effective writing.

Although Northern newspapers of the time no doubt exaggerated some of the Confederate atrocities at Fort Pillow, most modern sources agree that a massacre of Union troops took place there on April 12, 1864. It seems clear that Union soldiers, particularly black soldiers, were killed after they had stopped fighting or had surrendered or were being held prisoner. Less clear is the role played by Major General Nathan Bedford Forrest in leading his troops. Although we will never know whether Forrest directly ordered the massacre, evidence suggests that he was responsible for it.

Thesis asserts Bishop's main point.

What happened at Fort Pillow?

Headings, centered, help readers follow the organization.

Fort Pillow, Tennessee, which sat on a bluff overlooking the Mississippi River, had been held by the Union for two years. It was garrisoned by 580 men, 286 of them from United States Colored Heavy and Light Artillery regiments, 279 from the white Thirteenth Tennessee Cavalry. Nathan Bedford Forrest commanded about 1,500 troops.[1]

Statistics are cited with an endnote.

The Confederates attacked Fort Pillow on April 12, 1864, and had virtually surrounded the fort by the time Forrest arrived on the battlefield. At 3:30 p.m., Forrest demanded the surrender of the Union forces, sending in a message of the sort he had used before: "The conduct of the officers and men garrisoning Fort Pillow has been such as to entitle them to being treated as prisoners of war. . . . Should my demand be refused, I cannot be responsible for the fate of your command."[2] Union Major William Bradford, who had replaced Major Booth, killed earlier by sharpshooters, asked for an hour to consider the demand. Forrest, worried that vessels in the river were bringing in more troops, "shortened the time to twenty minutes."[3] Bradford refused to surrender, and Forrest quickly ordered the attack.

Quotation is cited with an endnote.

The Confederates charged to the fort, scaled the parapet, and fired on the forces within. Victory came quickly, with the Union forces running toward the river or surrendering. Shelby Foote describes the scene like this:

> Some kept going, right on into the river, where a number drowned and the swimmers became targets for marksmen on the bluff. Others, dropping their guns in terror, ran back toward the Confederates with their hands up, and of these some were spared as prisoners, while others were shot down in the act of surrender.[4]

Long quotation is set off from text by indenting. Quotation marks are omitted.

Bishop 3

In his own official report, Forrest makes no mention of the massacre. He does make much of the fact that the Union flag was not lowered by the Union forces, saying that if his own men had not taken down the flag, "few, if any, would have survived unhurt another volley."[5] However, as Jack Hurst points out and Forrest must have known, in this twenty-minute battle, "Federals running for their lives had little time to concern themselves with a flag."[6]

The federal congressional report on Fort Pillow, which charged the Confederates with appalling atrocities, was strongly criticized by Southerners. Respected writer Shelby Foote, while agreeing that the report was "largely" fabrication, points out that the "casualty figures . . . indicated strongly that unnecessary killing had occurred."[7] In an important article, John Cimprich and Robert C. Mainfort Jr. argue that the most trustworthy evidence is that written within about ten days of the battle, before word of the congressional hearings circulated and Southerners realized the extent of Northern outrage. The article reprints a group of letters and newspaper sources written before April 22 and thus "untainted by the political overtones the controversy later assumed."[8] Cimprich and Mainfort conclude that these sources "support the case for the occurrence of a massacre" but that Forrest's role remains "clouded" because of inconsistencies in testimony.[9]

Did Forrest order the massacre?

We will never really know whether Forrest directly ordered the massacre, but it seems unlikely. True, Confederate soldier Achilles Clark, who had no reason to lie, wrote to his sisters that "I with several others tried to stop the butchery . . . but Gen. Forrest ordered them [Negro and white Union troops] shot down like dogs, and the carnage continued."[10] But it is not clear whether Clark heard Forrest giving the orders or was just reporting hearsay. Many Confederates had been shouting "No quarter! No quarter!" and, as Shelby Foote points out, these shouts were "thought by some to be at Forrest's command."[11] A Union soldier, Jacob Thompson, claimed to have seen Forrest order the killing, but when asked to describe the six-foot-two general, he called him "a little bit of a man."[12]

Perhaps the most convincing evidence that Forrest did not order the massacre is that he tried to stop it once it had begun. Historian Albert Castel quotes several eyewitnesses on both the Union and

Bishop uses a primary source as well as secondary sources.

Quotation is introduced with a signal phrase.

Bishop draws attention to an article that reprints primary sources.

Topic sentence states the main idea for this section.

Writer presents a balanced view of the evidence.

Confederate sides as saying that Forrest ordered his men to stop firing.[13] In a letter to his wife three days after the battle, Confederate soldier Samuel Caldwell wrote that "if General Forrest had not run between our men & the Yanks with his pistol and sabre drawn not a man would have been spared."[14]

In a respected biography of Nathan Bedford Forrest, Hurst suggests that the temperamental Forrest "may have ragingly ordered a massacre and even intended to carry it out—until he rode inside the fort and viewed the horrifying result" and ordered it stopped.[15] While this is an intriguing interpretation of events, even Hurst would probably admit that it is merely speculation.

Can Forrest be held responsible for the massacre?

Even assuming that Forrest did not order the massacre, he can still be held accountable for it. That is because he created an atmosphere ripe for the possibility of atrocities and did nothing to ensure that it wouldn't happen. Throughout his career Forrest repeatedly threatened "no quarter," particularly with respect to black soldiers, so Confederate troops had good reason to think that in massacring the enemy they were carrying out his orders. As Hurst writes, "About all he had to do to produce a massacre was issue no order against one."[16] Dudley Taylor Cornish agrees:

> It has been asserted again and again that Forrest did not order a massacre. He did not need to. He had sought to terrify the Fort Pillow garrison by a threat of no quarter, as he had done at Union City and at Paducah in the days just before he turned on Pillow. If his men did enter the fort shouting "Give them no quarter; kill them; kill them; it is General Forrest's orders," he should not have been surprised.[17]

The slaughter at Fort Pillow was no doubt driven in large part by racial hatred. Numbers alone suggest this: of 289 white troops, 168 were taken prisoner, but of 262 black troops, only 58 were taken into custody, with the rest either dead or too badly wounded to walk.[18] A Southern reporter traveling with Forrest makes clear that the discrimination was deliberate: "Our troops maddened by the excitement, shot down the ret[r] eating Yankees, and not until they had attained t[h]e water's edge and turned to beg for mercy, did any prisoners fall in [t]o our hands—Thus the whites received quarter, but the negroes were shown no mercy."[19]

Topic sentence for this section reinforces the thesis.

Bishop 7

Notes begin on a new page.

Notes

1. John Cimprich and Robert C. Mainfort Jr., eds., "Fort Pillow Revisited: New Evidence about an Old Controversy," *Civil War History* 28, no. 4 (1982): 287–94.

First line of each note is indented ½". Note number is followed by a period. Authors' names are not inverted.

2. Quoted in Brian Steel Wills, *A Battle from the Start: The Life of Nathan Bedford Forrest* (New York: HarperCollins, 1992), 182.

3. Quoted in Wills, 183.

4. Shelby Foote, *The Civil War, a Narrative: Red River to Appomattox* (New York: Vintage, 1986), 110.

Notes are single-spaced, with double-spacing between notes. (Some instructors may prefer double-spacing throughout.)

5. Nathan Bedford Forrest, "Report of Maj. Gen. Nathan B. Forrest, C.S. Army, Commanding Cavalry, of the Capture of Fort Pillow," Shotgun's Home of the American Civil War, accessed March 6, 2019, http://www.civilwarhome.com/forrest.htm.

6. Jack Hurst, *Nathan Bedford Forrest: A Biography* (New York: Knopf, 1993), 174.

7. Foote, *Civil War*, 111.

8. Cimprich and Mainfort, "Fort Pillow," 295.

Shortened notes refer to works presented in earlier notes.

9. Cimprich and Mainfort, 305.

10. Cimprich and Mainfort, 299.

11. Foote, *Civil War*, 110.

12. Quoted in Wills, *Battle from the Start*, 187.

Writer cites an indirect source: words quoted in another source.

13. Albert Castel, "The Fort Pillow Massacre: A Fresh Examination of the Evidence," *Civil War History* 4, no. 1 (1958): 44–45.

14. Cimprich and Mainfort, "Fort Pillow," 300.

15. Hurst, *Nathan Bedford Forrest*, 177.

16. Hurst, 177.

17. Dudley Taylor Cornish, *The Sable Arm: Black Troops in the Union Army, 1861–1865* (Lawrence: University Press of Kansas, 1987), 175.

18. Foote, *Civil War*, 111.

19. Cimprich and Mainfort, "Fort Pillow," 304.

20. Quoted in Wills, *Battle from the Start*, 189.

21. Quoted in Wills, 215.

22. Quoted in Hurst, *Nathan Bedford Forrest*, 177.

23. Quoted in James M. McPherson, *Battle Cry of Freedom: The Civil War Era* (New York: Oxford University Press, 1988), 402.

24. Hurst, *Nathan Bedford Forrest*, 74.

25. Quoted in Foote, *Civil War*, 106.

Bibliography begins on a new page.

Entries are alphabetized by authors' last names.

First line of entry is at left margin; additional lines are indented ½".

Entries are single-spaced, with double-spacing between entries. (Some instructors may prefer double-spacing throughout.)

Bibliography

Castel, Albert. "The Fort Pillow Massacre: A Fresh Examination of the Evidence." *Civil War History* 4, no. 1 (1958): 37–50.

Cimprich, John, and Robert C. Mainfort Jr., eds. "Fort Pillow Revisited: New Evidence about an Old Controversy." *Civil War History* 28, no. 4 (1982): 293–306.

Cornish, Dudley Taylor. *The Sable Arm: Black Troops in the Union Army, 1861–1865.* Lawrence: University Press of Kansas, 1987.

Foote, Shelby. *The Civil War, a Narrative: Red River to Appomattox.* New York: Vintage, 1986.

Forrest, Nathan Bedford. "Report of Maj. Gen. Nathan B. Forrest, C.S. Army, Commanding Cavalry, of the Capture of Fort Pillow." Shotgun's Home of the American Civil War. Accessed March 6, 2019. http://www.civilwarhome.com/forrest.htm.

Hurst, Jack. *Nathan Bedford Forrest: A Biography.* New York: Knopf, 1993.

McPherson, James M. *Battle Cry of Freedom: The Civil War Era.* New York: Oxford University Press, 1988.

Wills, Brian Steel. *A Battle from the Start: The Life of Nathan Bedford Forrest.* New York: HarperCollins, 1992.

S

Sentence Style

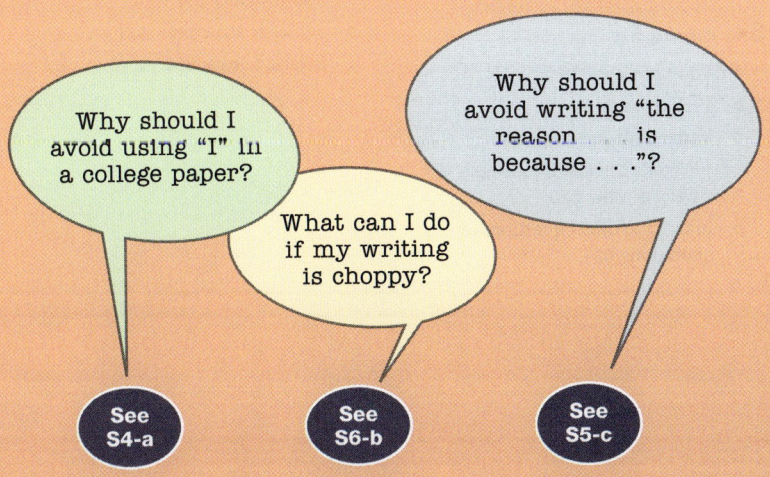

Why should I avoid using "I" in a college paper?

See S4-a

What can I do if my writing is choppy?

See S6-b

Why should I avoid writing "the reason . . . is because . . ."?

See S5-c

S Sentence Style

S1 Parallelism

If two or more ideas are parallel, they should be expressed in parallel grammatical form. Single words should be balanced with single words, phrases with phrases, clauses with clauses.

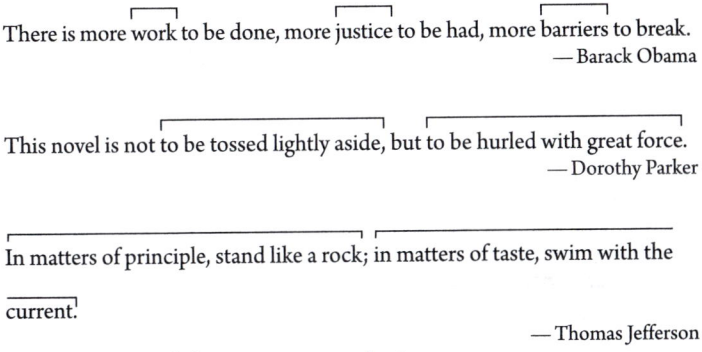

There is more work to be done, more justice to be had, more barriers to break.
— Barack Obama

This novel is not to be tossed lightly aside, but to be hurled with great force.
— Dorothy Parker

In matters of principle, stand like a rock; in matters of taste, swim with the current.
— Thomas Jefferson

Writers often use parallelism to create emphasis.

S1-a Balance parallel ideas in a series.

Readers expect items in a series to appear in parallel grammatical form. When one or more of the items violate readers' expectations, a sentence will be needlessly awkward.

▶ Children who study music also learn confidence, discipline,
creativity.
and ~~they are creative.~~
  ^

The revision presents all the items in the series as nouns: *confidence, discipline,* and *creativity.*

▶ Impressionist painters believed in focusing on ordinary

subjects, capturing the effects of light on those subjects,
using
and ~~to use~~ short brushstrokes.
  ^

The revision uses *-ing* forms for all the items in the series: *focusing, capturing,* and *using.*

In headings and lists, aim for as much parallelism as the content allows.

Headings

Headings on the same level of organization should be written in parallel form — as single words, phrases, or clauses.

PHRASES AS HEADINGS

Safeguarding Earth's atmosphere

Charting the path to sustainable energy

Conserving global forests

INDEPENDENT CLAUSES AS HEADINGS

Ask the patient to describe current symptoms.

Take a detailed medical history.

Record the patient's vital signs.

Lists

Lists are usually introduced with an independent clause followed by a colon. They are most readable when they are presented in parallel grammatical form. Like headings, lists might consist of words, phrases, or clauses. The following list consists of parallel noun phrases.

Renewable energy technologies include the following: hydroelectric power, solar power, wind energy, and geothermal energy.

S1-b   Balance parallel ideas presented as pairs.

When pairing ideas, underscore their connection by expressing them in similar grammatical form. Paired ideas are usually connected in one of these ways:

- with a coordinating conjunction such as *and, but,* or *or*
- with a correlative conjunction such as *either . . . or* or *not only . . . but also*
- with a word introducing a comparison, usually *than* or *as*

Parallel ideas linked with coordinating conjunctions

Coordinating conjunctions (*and, but, or, nor, for, so, yet*) link ideas of equal importance. When those ideas are closely parallel in content, they should be expressed in parallel grammatical form.

▶ Emily Dickinson's poetry features the use of dashes and
    the capitalization of
    ~~capitalizing~~ common words.
    ^

The revision balances the nouns *use* and *capitalization*.

▶ Many colleges are making SAT scores optional and ~~encourage~~ ^{encouraging}
  alternative admissions material.

> The revision balances the verb *making* with the verb *encouraging*.

Parallel ideas linked with correlative conjunctions

Correlative conjunctions come in pairs: *either . . . or, neither . . . nor, not only . . . but also, both . . . and, whether . . . or.* Make sure that the grammatical structure following the second half of the pair is the same as that following the first half.

▶ Thomas Edison was not only a prolific inventor but also ~~was~~ a
  successful entrepreneur

> The words *a prolific inventor* follow *not only,* so *a successful entrepreneur* should follow *but also.*

▶ The clerk told me either to change my flight or ^{to} take the train.

> *To change my flight,* which follows *either,* should be balanced with *to take the train,* which follows *or.*

Comparisons linked with *than* or *as*

In comparisons linked with *than* or *as,* the elements being compared should be expressed in parallel grammatical structure.

▶ For some situations, it is better to talk in person than ~~texting.~~ ^{to text.}

> *To talk* is balanced with *to text.*

Comparisons should also be logical and complete. (See S2-c.)

S1-c Repeat function words to clarify parallels.

Function words such as prepositions (*by, to*) and subordinating conjunctions (*that, because*) signal the grammatical nature of the word groups to follow. Although you can sometimes omit function words, be sure to include them whenever they signal parallel structures that readers might otherwise miss.

▶ **Our study revealed that left-handed students were more likely to**
that

have trouble with classroom desks and rearranging desks
^

for exam periods was useful.

A second subordinating conjunction helps readers sort out the two parallel ideas: *that* left-handed students have trouble with classroom desks and *that* rearranging desks was useful.

S2 Needed words

Sometimes writers leave out words intentionally without affecting the meaning of the sentence. But often the result is confusing or ungrammatical. Readers need to see at a glance how the parts of a sentence are connected.

S2-a Add words needed to complete compound structures.

In compound structures, words are often left out for economy: *Tom is a man who means what he says and* [*who*] *says what he means.* Such omissions are acceptable as long as the omitted words are common to both parts of the compound structure.

If a sentence defies grammar or idiom because an omitted word is not common to both parts of the compound structure, the simplest solution is to put the word back in.

▶ **Advertisers target customers whom they identify through research**
who
or have purchased their product in the past.
^

The word *who* must be included because *whom . . . have purchased* is not grammatically correct.

accepted

▶ **Mayor Davis never has and never will accept a bribe.**
^

Has . . . accept is not grammatically correct.

in

▶ **Many South Pacific islanders still believe and live by ancient laws.**
^

Believe . . . by is not idiomatic in English. (For a list of common idioms, see W5-d.)

For Multilingual Writers Languages sometimes differ in the need for certain words. In particular, be alert for missing articles, verbs, subjects, or expletives. See M2, M3-a, and M3-b.

S2-b Add the word *that* if there is any danger of misreading without it.

If there is no danger of misreading, the word *that* may be omitted when it introduces a subordinate clause (see B3-e). *The value of a principle is the number of things [that] it will explain.* When a sentence might be misread without *that*, however, include the word.

▶ In his famous obedience experiments, psychologist Stanley Milgram
    that
discovered ordinary people were willing to inflict physical pain on
    ^
strangers.

> Milgram didn't discover ordinary people; he discovered that ordinary people were willing to inflict pain on strangers. The word *that* tells readers to expect a clause, not just *ordinary people*, as the direct object of *discovered*.

S2-c Add words needed to make comparisons logical and complete.

Comparisons should be made between items that are alike. To compare unlike items is illogical and distracting.

                                                                those of
▶ The forests of North America are much more extensive than Europe.
                                                                  ^

> Forests must be compared with forests, not with all of Europe.

▶ Some music critics argue that Ella Fitzgerald's renditions of Cole
                                            singer's.
Porter's songs are better than any other ~~singer.~~
                                            ^

> Ella Fitzgerald's renditions cannot logically be compared with a singer. The revision uses the possessive form *singer's*, with the word *renditions* being implied.

Sometimes the word *other* must be inserted to make a comparison logical.

▶ **Jupiter is larger than any** $\overset{\text{other}}{\wedge}$ **planet in our solar system.**

Jupiter is a planet in our solar system, and it cannot be larger than itself.

Sometimes the word *as* must be inserted to make a comparison grammatically complete.

▶ **The city of Lowell is as old,** $\overset{\text{as}}{\wedge}$ **if not older than, the neighboring city of Lawrence.**

The construction *as old* is not complete without a second *as: as old as ... the neighboring city of Lawrence.*

Comparisons should be complete enough to ensure clarity. The reader should understand what is being compared.

INCOMPLETE	Brand X is less salty.
COMPLETE	Brand X is less salty than Brand Y.

Finally, comparisons should leave no ambiguity for readers. If a sentence lends itself to more than one interpretation, revise the sentence to state clearly which interpretation you intend.

AMBIGUOUS	Ken helped me more than my roommate.
CLEAR	Ken helped me more than *he helped* my roommate.
CLEAR	Ken helped me more than my roommate *did*.

S2-d Add the articles *a, an,* and *the* where necessary for grammatical completeness.

It is not always necessary to repeat articles with paired items: *We bought a laptop and printer.* However, if one of the items requires *a* and the other requires *an,* both articles must be included.

▶ **We bought a laptop and** $\overset{\text{an}}{\wedge}$ **e-reader.**

For Multilingual Writers   Choosing and using articles can be challenging for multilingual writers. See M2.

S3 Problems with modifiers

Modifiers, whether they are single words, phrases, or clauses, should point clearly to the words they modify. As a rule, related words should be kept together.

S3-a Put limiting modifiers in front of the words they modify.

Limiting modifiers such as *only, even, almost, nearly,* and *just* should appear in front of a verb only if they modify the verb: *At first, I couldn't even touch my toes, much less grasp them.* If they limit the meaning of some other word in the sentence, they should be placed in front of that word.

▶ Research shows that students ~~only~~ learn new vocabulary words when
_^ only
they are encouraged to read.

> *Only* limits the meaning of the *when* clause.

▶ If you ~~just~~ interview chemistry majors, your understanding of the
_^ just
student response to the new policies will be incomplete.

> The adverb *just* limits the meaning of *chemistry majors,* not *interview.*

When the limiting modifier *not* is misplaced, the sentence usually suggests a meaning the writer did not intend.

▶ In the United States in 1860, all Black southerners were ~~not~~ enslaved.
_^ not

> The original sentence says that no Black southerners were enslaved. The revision makes the writer's real meaning clear: Some (but not all) Black southerners were enslaved.

S3-b Place phrases and clauses so that readers can see at a glance what they modify.

Although phrases and clauses can appear at some distance from the words they modify, make sure your meaning is clear. When phrases or clauses are oddly placed, as in the following example, misreadings can result.

| MISPLACED | The soccer player returned to the clinic where he had undergone emergency surgery in 2012 in a limousine sent by Adidas. |
| REVISED | Traveling in a limousine sent by Adidas, the soccer player returned to the clinic where he had undergone emergency surgery in 2012. |

The revision corrects the false impression that the soccer player underwent emergency surgery in a limousine.

On the walls
▶ ~~There~~ are many pictures of comedians who have performed
   ^
at Gavin's. ~~on the walls.~~
            ^

The comedians weren't performing on the walls; the pictures were on the walls.

Occasionally the placement of a modifier leads to an ambiguity — a squinting modifier. In such a case, two revisions will be possible, depending on the writer's intended meaning.

AMBIGUOUS	The exchange students we met for coffee occasionally questioned us about our latest slang.
CLEAR	The exchange students we occasionally met for coffee questioned us about our latest slang.
CLEAR	The exchange students we met for coffee questioned us occasionally about our latest slang.

In the original sentence, it's not clear what happened occasionally, the meeting or the questioning. Both revisions eliminate the ambiguity.

S3-c Move awkwardly placed modifiers.

As a rule, a sentence should flow from subject to verb to object, without lengthy detours along the way. When a long adverbial word group separates a subject from its verb, a verb from its object, or a helping verb from its main verb, the result is often awkward.

                                              Hong Kong
▶ ~~Hong Kong,~~ after more than 150 years of British rule, was
   ^   ^
transferred back to Chinese control in 1997.

There is no reason to separate the subject, *Hong Kong*, from the verb, *was transferred*, with a long phrase.

> **For Multilingual Writers**   In English, take care not to place an
> adverb between a verb and its object. See M3-f.
>
> easily
> ▶ Yolanda lifted ~~easily~~ the fifty-pound weight.
> ^

S3-d Avoid split infinitives when they are awkward.

An infinitive consists of *to* plus the base form of a verb: *to think, to breathe, to dance.* When a modifier appears between *to* and the verb, an infinitive is said to be "split": *to carefully balance, to completely understand.*

If a split infinitive is awkward, move the modifier to another position in the sentence.

If possible, the
▶ ~~The~~ patient should try to ~~if possible~~ avoid going up and down stairs.
^

Attempts to avoid split infinitives can result in equally awkward sentences. When alternative phrasing sounds unnatural, most experts encourage splitting the infinitive.

AWKWARD	We decided actually to enforce the law.
BETTER	We decided to actually enforce the law.

At times, neither the split infinitive nor its alternative sounds particularly awkward. In such situations, it is usually better not to split the infinitive.

▶ Nursing students learn to ~~accurately~~ record a patient's vital
accurately.
signs/
^

S3-e Repair dangling modifiers.

A dangling modifier fails to refer logically to any word in the sentence. Dangling modifiers are easy to repair, but they can be hard to recognize, especially in your own writing.

Recognizing dangling modifiers

Dangling modifiers are usually introductory word groups (such as verbal phrases) that suggest but do not name an actor. When a sentence opens with such a modifier, readers expect the subject of the next clause to name the actor. If it doesn't, the modifier dangles.

▶ **Understanding the need to create checks and balances on power,** *the framers of*
the Constitution divided the government into three branches.
  ^

The framers of the Constitution (not the document itself) understood the need for checks and balances.

                                              users can easily view their
▶ **After logging into the site,** ~~users'~~ **account balances.** ~~can be easily~~
                                  ^   ^
~~viewed.~~

Users (not their account balances) log into the site.

The following sentences illustrate four common kinds of dangling modifiers. Although most readers will understand the writer's intended meaning in such sentences, the unintended humor can be distracting.

DANGLING   *Deciding to join the navy,* the recruiter enthusiastically pumped Joe's hand. [Participial phrase]

DANGLING   *Upon entering the doctor's office,* a skeleton caught my attention. [Preposition followed by a gerund phrase]

DANGLING   *To satisfy her mother,* the piano had to be practiced every day. [Infinitive phrase]

DANGLING   *Though not eligible for the clinical trial,* the doctor prescribed the drug for Ethan on compassionate grounds. [Elliptical clause with an understood subject and verb]

These dangling modifiers falsely suggest that the recruiter decided to join the navy, that the skeleton entered the doctor's office, that the piano intended to satisfy the mother, and that the doctor was not eligible for the clinical trial.

Checking for dangling modifiers

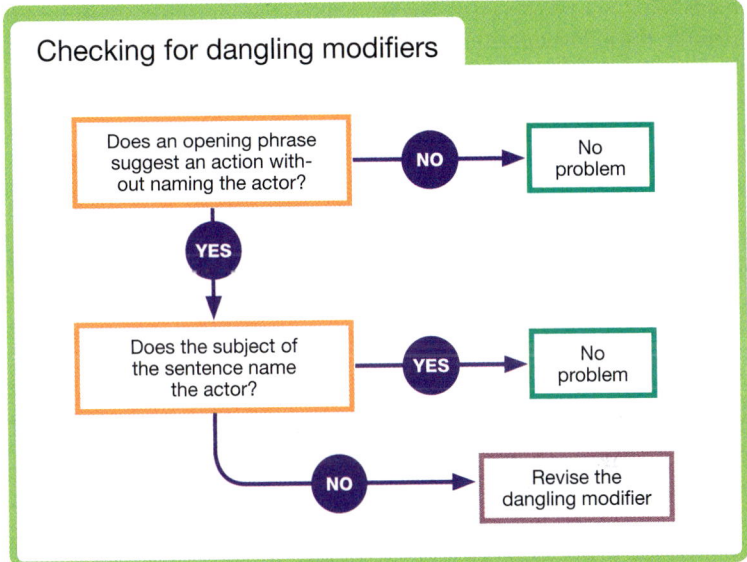

Repairing dangling modifiers

To repair a dangling modifier, you can revise the sentence in one of two ways:

- Name the actor in the subject of the sentence.
- Name the actor in the modifier.

Depending on your sentence, one of these revision strategies may be more appropriate than the other.

ACTOR NAMED IN SUBJECT

▶ Upon entering the doctor's office, a skeleton. <del>caught my attention.</del> _{I noticed}

▶ To satisfy her mother, the piano <del>had to be practiced</del> every day. _{Jing-mei had to practice}

ACTOR NAMED IN MODIFIER

▶ <del>Deciding</del> to join the navy, the recruiter enthusiastically pumped <del>Joe's</del> hand. _{When Joe decided} _{his}

▶ Though not eligible for the clinical trial, the doctor prescribed the drug for <del>Ethan</del> on compassionate grounds. _{Ethan was} _{him}

NOTE: You cannot repair a dangling modifier just by moving it. Consider, for example, the following sentence about a skeleton. If you put the modifier at the end of the sentence (*A skeleton caught my attention upon entering the doctor's office*), you are still suggesting that the skeleton entered the office. The only way to avoid the problem is to put the word *I* in the sentence, either as the subject or in the modifier.

▶ Upon entering the doctor's office, a skeleton. ~~caught my attention.~~
   I noticed

▶ ~~Upon entering~~ the doctor's office, a skeleton caught my attention.
   As I entered

S4   Shifts

This section can help you avoid unnecessary shifts that might distract or confuse your readers: shifts in point of view, in verb tense, in mood or voice, or from indirect to direct questions or quotations.

S4-a Make the point of view consistent in person and number.

The point of view of a piece of writing is the perspective from which it is written: first person (*I* or *we*), second person (*you*), or third person (*he, she, it, one,* or *they*).

The *I* (or *we*) point of view, which emphasizes the writer, is a good choice for informal letters and writing based on personal experience. The *you* point of view, which emphasizes the reader, works well for giving advice or explaining how to do something. The third-person point of view, which emphasizes the subject, is appropriate in academic and professional writing.

Writers who have trouble settling on an appropriate point of view sometimes shift confusingly from one to another and, in doing so, distract their readers. The solution is to choose a suitable perspective and stay with it.

▶ Our class practiced rescuing a victim trapped in a wrecked car. We learned to dismantle the car with the essential tools. ~~You~~ were graded on ~~your~~ speed and ~~your~~ skill in freeing the victim.
   We   *our*   *our*

The writer should have stayed with the *we* point of view. *You* is inappropriate because the writer is not addressing readers directly. *You* should not be used in a vague sense meaning "anyone." (See G3-b.)

> *You need*
> ► ~~One needs~~ a password and a credit card number to access the
> ^
> database. You will be billed at an hourly rate.

You is an appropriate choice because the writer is giving advice directly
to readers.

S4-b Maintain consistent verb tenses.

Consistent verb tenses clearly establish the time of the actions being
described. When a passage begins in one tense and then shifts without warning and for no reason to another, readers are distracted and confused.

> ► Our candidate struggled in the debate. Just as we gave up hope, she
> *soared*
> ~~soars~~ ahead in the polls.
> ^
> The writer thought that the present tense (*soars*) would convey excitement.
> But having begun in the past tense (*struggled, gave up*), the writer should follow
> through in the past tense.

Writers often encounter difficulty with verb tenses when writing about
literature. Because fictional events occur outside the time frames of real
life, the past tense and the present tense may seem equally appropriate. The
literary convention, however, is to describe fictional events consistently in the
present tense.

> ► The scarlet letter is a punishment sternly placed on Hester's breast by
> *is*
> the community, and yet it ~~was~~ a fanciful and imaginative product of
> ^
> Hester's own needlework.

S4-c Make verbs consistent in mood and voice.

Unnecessary shifts in the mood of a verb can be distracting and confusing
to readers. There are three moods in English: the *indicative*, used for facts,
opinions, and questions; the *imperative*, used for orders or advice; and the *subjunctive*, used in certain contexts to express wishes or conditions contrary to
fact (see G2-g).

Writer's Choice
Choosing a point of view

Using the *I* point of view is not grammatically wrong for college writing. As you review your options, think about your **purpose** and **audience**, as well as the **genre** (type of writing) expected. When in doubt, ask your instructor.

When you want to focus on your experience, choose the first-person point of view.

FIRST PERSON

Although initially intimidated, I found that my mentor's observations during my student teaching created opportunities for important discussions about learning.

The firsthand experience and personal tone in this sentence help the writer connect with the reader. The first-person point of view is often used in narrative and reflective writing.

When you want to focus on the reader, choose the second-person point of view.

SECOND PERSON

Although initially you may be intimidated, you may find that your mentor's observations during your student teaching create opportunities for important discussions about learning.

The tone here is instructive and establishes the writer as a guide for the reader. Use the second-person point of view when you are giving instructions or advice.

When you want to focus on the topic, choose the third-person point of view.

THIRD PERSON

Although initially they may be intimidated, many student teachers find that their mentor's observations during their student teaching create opportunities for important discussions about learning.

This sentence focuses on the topic, not on the writer or the reader. Use the third-person point of view when you are arguing a point or presenting information.

Once you make a choice, stick with it. Shifting points of view within a piece of writing confuses your reader.

The following passage shifts confusingly from the indicative to the imperative mood.

> The counselor advised us to spread out our core requirements over two or three semesters. ~~Also,~~ _{She also suggested that we} pay attention to prerequisites for elective courses.

The writer began by reporting the counselor's advice in the indicative mood (*counselor advised*) and switched to the imperative mood (*pay attention*); the revision puts both sentences in the indicative.

A verb may be in either the active voice (with the subject doing the action) or the passive voice (with the subject receiving the action). (See W3-a.) If a writer shifts without warning from one to the other, readers may be left wondering why.

> Each student completes a self-assessment~~/, The self-assessment is~~ _{gives it} ~~then given~~ to the teacher, and a copy ~~is exchanged~~ _{exchanges} with a classmate.

Because the passage began in the active voice (*student completes*) and then switched to the passive (*self-assessment is given, copy is exchanged*), readers are left wondering who gives the self-assessment to the teacher and the classmate. The active voice, which is clearer and more direct, leaves no ambiguity.

S4-d Avoid sudden shifts from indirect to direct questions or quotations.

An indirect question reports a question without asking it: *We asked whether we could visit Miriam.* A direct question asks directly: *Can we visit Miriam?* Sudden shifts from indirect to direct questions are awkward. In addition, sentences containing such shifts are impossible to punctuate because indirect questions must end with a period and direct questions must end with a question mark. (See P6-a.)

> LGBTQ business owners wonder whether their businesses are unfairly targeted and ~~can they~~ _{whether they can} reverse the trend~~?~~.

The revision poses both questions indirectly. The writer could also ask both questions directly: *Are LGBTQ-owned businesses being unfairly targeted? Can these business owners reverse the trend?*

An indirect quotation reports someone's words without quoting word for word: *Senator Kessel said that she wants to see evidence.* A direct quotation presents the exact words of a speaker or writer, set off with quotation marks: *Senator Kessel said, "I want to see evidence."* Unannounced shifts from indirect to direct quotations are distracting and confusing, especially when the writer fails to insert quotation marks, as in the following example.

▶ The patient said she had been experiencing heart palpitations and
   asked me to
   ~~please~~ run as many tests as possible to find out the problem.
   ^

The revision reports the patient's words indirectly. The writer also could quote the words directly: *The patient said, "I have been experiencing heart palpitations. Please run as many tests as possible to find out the problem."*

S5 Mixed constructions

A mixed construction contains sentence parts that do not sensibly fit together. The mismatch may be a matter of grammar or of logic.

S5-a Untangle the grammatical structure.

You should not begin a sentence with one grammatical plan and switch without warning to another. Often you must rethink the purpose of the sentence and revise.

> **MIXED**   For most drivers who have a blood alcohol content of .05 percent double their risk of causing an accident.

The writer begins the sentence with a long prepositional phrase and makes it the subject of the verb *double*. But a prepositional phrase can serve only as a modifier; it cannot be the subject of a sentence.

> **REVISED**   For most drivers who have a blood alcohol content of .05 percent, the risk of causing an accident is doubled.

> **REVISED**   Most drivers who have a blood alcohol content of .05 percent double their risk of causing an accident.

In the first revision, the writer begins with the prepositional phrase and finishes the sentence with a proper subject and verb (*risk . . . is doubled*). In the second revision, the writer stays with the original verb (*double*) and begins the sentence another way, making *drivers* the subject of *double*.

Electing
▶ ~~When the country elects~~ a president is the most important
  ^
responsibility in a democracy.

The adverb clause *When the country elects a president* cannot serve as the subject of the verb *is*. The revision replaces the adverb clause with a gerund phrase, a word group that can function as a subject. (See B3-e and B3-b.)

▶ Although the United States is a wealthy nation, ~~but~~ more than

20 percent of our children live in poverty.

The coordinating conjunction *but* cannot link a subordinate clause (*Although the United States . . .*) with an independent clause (*more than 20 percent of our children live in poverty*).

For Multilingual Writers   When writing in English, watch out for double subjects, which can happen when a noun and pronoun try to serve the same grammatical function in a sentence. Also take care not to repeat an object or adverb in an adjective clause. See M3-c and M3-d.

▶ My father ~~he~~ moved to Peru before he met my mother.

S5-b Straighten out the logical connections.

A sentence's subject and verb should make sense together; when they don't, the error is known as *faulty predication*.

Tiffany
▶ The court decided that ~~Tiffany's welfare~~ would be safer living with
  ^
her grandparents.

Tiffany, not her welfare, would be safer.

An appositive is a noun that renames a nearby noun. When an appositive and the noun it renames are not logically equivalent, the error is known as *faulty apposition*. (See B3-c.)

Tax accounting,
▶ ~~The tax accountant,~~ a lucrative profession, requires intelligence,
  ^
patience, and attention to mathematical detail.

The tax accountant is a person, not a profession.

S5-c Avoid *is when, is where*, and *reason . . . is because* constructions.

In formal English, readers sometimes object to *is when, is where,* and *reason . . . is because* constructions on grammatical or logical grounds. Grammatically, the verb *is* (as well as *are, was,* and *were*) should be followed by a noun or an adjective, not by an adverb clause beginning with *when, where,* or *because*. (See B2-b and B3-e.) Logically, the words *when, where,* and *because* suggest relations of time, place, and cause — relations that do not always make sense with *is, are, was,* or *were*.

▶ Anorexia nervosa is ~~where people~~ think they are overweight and

   often diet to the point of starvation.

a disorder suffered by people who

> *Where* refers to places. Anorexia nervosa is a disorder, not a place.

▶ The ~~reason the~~ experiment failed ~~is~~ because conditions in the lab

   were not sterile.

> The writer might have changed *because* to *that* (*The reason the experiment failed is that conditions in the lab were not sterile*), but the preceding revision is more concise.

S6 Sentence emphasis

Within each sentence, emphasize your point by expressing it in the subject and verb of an independent clause, the words that receive the most attention from readers (see S6-a to S6-e).

    Within longer stretches of prose, you can draw attention to ideas deserving special emphasis by using a variety of techniques, often involving an unusual twist or some element of surprise (see S6-f).

S6-a Coordinate equal ideas; subordinate minor ideas.

When combining two or more ideas in one sentence, you have two choices: coordination or subordination. Choose coordination to indicate that the ideas are equal or nearly equal in importance. Choose subordination to indicate that one idea is less important than another.

Coordination

Coordination draws attention equally to two or more ideas. To coordinate single words or phrases, join them with a coordinating conjunction or with a correlative conjunction: *bananas and strawberries; not only a lackluster plot but also inferior acting* (see B1-g).

To coordinate independent clauses — word groups that each express a complete thought and can stand alone as a sentence — join them with a comma and a coordinating conjunction or with a semicolon:

, and	, but	, or	, nor
, for	, so	, yet	;

The semicolon is often accompanied by a conjunctive adverb such as *furthermore, therefore,* or *however* or by a transitional phrase such as *for example, in other words,* or *as a matter of fact.* (For a longer list, see the "Using coordination" chart in S6-b.)

Subordination

To give unequal emphasis to two or more ideas, express the major idea in an independent clause and place any minor ideas in subordinate clauses or phrases. (For specific subordination strategies, see the "Using subordination" chart in S6-b.)

Let your intended meaning determine which idea you emphasize. Thinking about your purpose and your audience often helps you decide which ideas deserve emphasis.

For Multilingual Writers Conjunctions (words such as *and* and *but*) and conjunctive adverbs (words such as *therefore* and *meanwhile*) can help you express relationships between ideas when you write in English.

S6-b Combine choppy sentences.

Short sentences demand attention, so you should use them primarily for emphasis. Too many short sentences, one after the other, make for a choppy style.

If an idea is not important enough to deserve its own sentence, try combining it with a sentence close by. Put any minor ideas in subordinate structures such as phrases or subordinate clauses. (See B3.)

▶ The Parks Department keeps the use of insecticides to a
  because the
minimum/~~The~~ city is concerned about the environment.
  ^

The writer wanted to emphasize that the Parks Department minimizes its use of chemicals, so she put the reason in a subordinate clause beginning with *because.*

▶ The Chesapeake and Ohio Canal, ~~is~~ a 184-mile waterway constructed
  ^

in the 1800s~~/,~~ ~~It~~ was a major source of transportation for goods
         ^

during the Civil War.

A minor idea is now tucked into an appositive phrase (*a 184-mile waterway constructed in the 1800s*).

Although subordination is ordinarily the most effective technique for combining short, choppy sentences, coordination is appropriate when the ideas are equal in importance.

▶ On January 1, lawmakers raised the minimum wage~~/~~ **and** ~~Lawmakers~~
                                                  ^

opened doors for thousands of families.

Combining two short sentences by joining their predicates (*raised ... opened*) is an effective coordination technique.

Using coordination to combine sentences of equal importance

1. Consider using a comma and a coordinating conjunction between the sentences. (See P1-a.)

    , and   , but   , or   , nor
    , for   , so   , yet

    ▶ In Orthodox Jewish funeral ceremonies, the shroud is
                                    and the
      a simple linen vestment~~/,~~ ~~The~~ coffin is plain wood.
                              ^

2. Consider using a semicolon with a conjunctive adverb or a transitional phrase. (See P3-a.)

also	however	next
as a result	in addition	now
besides	in fact	of course
consequently	in other words	otherwise
finally	in the first place	still
for example	meanwhile	then
for instance	moreover	therefore
furthermore	nevertheless	thus

    in addition, she
    ▶ Alicia scored well on the SAT~~/;~~ ~~She also~~ had excellent grades
                                       ^
    and a record of community service.

3. Consider using a semicolon alone. (See P3-a.)

    in
    ▶ In youth we learn~~/;~~ ~~In~~ age we understand.
                        ^

Using subordination to combine sentences of unequal importance

1. Consider putting the less important idea in a subordinate clause beginning with one of the following words. (See B3-e.)

after	before	that	which
although	even though	unless	while
as	if	until	who
as if	since	when	whom
because	so that	where	whose

▶ *When* Elizabeth Cady Stanton proposed a convention to discuss the status of women in America/, Lucretia Mott agreed.

▶ My sister owes much of her recovery to a yoga program/~~She~~ *that she* began ~~the program~~ three years ago.

2. Consider putting the less important idea in an appositive phrase. (See B3-c.)

▶ Karate, is a discipline based on the philosophy of nonviolence/, ~~It~~ teaches the art of self-defense.

3. Consider putting the less important idea in a participial phrase. (See B3-b.)

▶ ~~American essayist Cheryl Peck was~~ *E*ncouraged by friends to write about her life/, *American essayist Cheryl Peck* ~~She~~ began combining humor and irony in her essays about being overweight.

For Multilingual Writers When you write in English, take care not to repeat objects or adverbs in adjective clauses. See M3-d.

▶ The apartment that we rented ~~it~~ needed repairs.

The pronoun *it* cannot repeat the relative pronoun *that*.

Writer's Choice
Positioning major and minor ideas

There are many ways to organize the ideas in a sentence. If your **purpose** is to convey one particular idea to your readers, put that major idea in the main part of the sentence, and place minor ideas in a subordinate word group to de-emphasize them. Consider these two ideas about social networking sites.

> Social networking websites offer ways for people to connect in the virtual world.

> Social networking sites do not replace face-to-face interaction.

To stress the ways that people can *connect* in the virtual world, the writer should subordinate (or de-emphasize) the idea about the limitations.

┌───────────────── MINOR IDEA ─────────────────┐ ┌─ MAJOR IDEA ─┐
Although they do not replace face-to-face interaction, social networking
──┐
websites offer ways for people to connect in the virtual world.

The writer might be arguing that joining sites such as LinkedIn is the best way to broaden the range of job opportunities for college graduates.

To focus on the *limitations* of the virtual world, the writer should subordinate the idea about the ways people connect on these websites.

┌───────────────── MINOR IDEA ──────────────────────
Although social networking websites offer ways for people to connect in the
──────────────┐ ┌─────────── MAJOR IDEA ───────────┐
virtual world, they do not replace face-to-face interaction.

The writer might be arguing that personal contact is still the best way to build professional relationships.

When you have both major and minor ideas in a sentence, put your main idea in the independent clause and tuck minor ideas into subordinate word groups.

S6-c Avoid ineffective or excessive coordination.

Coordinate structures are appropriate only when you intend to draw readers' attention equally to two or more ideas: *Professor Liu praises loudly, and she criticizes softly.* If one idea is more important than another — or if a coordinating conjunction does not clearly signal the relationship between the ideas — you should subordinate the less important idea.

INEFFECTIVE COORDINATION	Closets were taxed as rooms, and most colonists stored their clothes in chests or clothespresses.
IMPROVED WITH SUBORDINATION	Because closets were taxed as rooms, most colonists stored their clothes in chests or clothespresses.

The revision subordinates the less important idea (*closets were taxed as rooms*). Notice that the subordinating conjunction *Because* signals the relation between the ideas more clearly than the coordinating conjunction *and*.

Because it is so easy to string ideas together with *and*, writers often rely too heavily on coordination in their rough drafts. The cure for excessive coordination is simple: Look for opportunities to tuck minor ideas into subordinate clauses or phrases.

▶ ~~Four hours went by, and~~ a rescue truck finally arrived, but by that
    After four hours,
    ^
time we had been evacuated in a helicopter.

Having three independent clauses was excessive. The least important idea has become a prepositional phrase.

S6-d Do not subordinate major ideas.

If a sentence buries its major idea in a subordinate construction, readers may not give the idea enough attention. Make sure to express your major idea in an independent clause and to subordinate any minor ideas.

▶ Harry S. Truman, who was the unexpected winner of the 1948
                    defeated Thomas E. Dewey,
                    ^
presidential election/. ~~defeated Thomas E. Dewey.~~
                ^

The writer wanted to focus on Truman's unexpected victory, but the original sentence buried this information in an adjective clause. The revision puts the more important idea in an independent clause and tucks the less important idea into an adjective clause (*who defeated Thomas E. Dewey*).

> As
> ▶ I ~~was~~ driving home from my new job, heading down Ranchitos
>   ^
>   Road, ~~when~~ my car suddenly overheated.

The writer wanted to emphasize that the car overheated, not the fact of driving home. The revision expresses the major idea in an independent clause and places the less important idea in an adverb clause (*As I was driving home from my new job*).

S6-e Do not subordinate excessively.

In attempting to avoid short, choppy sentences, writers sometimes go to the opposite extreme, putting more subordinate ideas into a sentence than its structure can bear. If a sentence collapses of its own weight, occasionally it can be restructured. More often, however, such sentences must be divided.

> ▶ Some professional athletes argue that they should not be looked on
>   These athletes
>   as role models. ~~and that they~~ believe that modeling behavior is a
>   ^^
>   parent's responsibility.

By splitting the original sentence in two, the writer makes it easier for the reader to focus on the main claim, that modeling behavior is a parent's job.

S6-f Experiment with techniques for gaining emphasis.

By experimenting with certain techniques, usually involving some element of surprise, you can draw attention to ideas that deserve special emphasis. Use such techniques sparingly, however, or they will lose their punch. The writer who tries to emphasize everything ends up emphasizing nothing.

Using sentence endings for emphasis

You can highlight an idea simply by withholding it until the end of a sentence. The technique works something like a punch line. In the following example, the sentence's meaning is not revealed until its very last word.

> The only completely consistent people are the dead. — Aldous Huxley

An inverted sentence reverses the normal subject-verb order, placing the subject at the end, where it receives unusual emphasis. (See also S7-c.)

> In golden pots are hidden the most deadly poisons. — Thomas Draxe

Using parallel structure for emphasis

Parallel grammatical structure draws special attention to paired ideas or to items in a series. (See S1.) When parallel ideas are paired, the emphasis falls on words that underscore comparisons or contrasts, especially when they occur at the end of a phrase or clause.

> We must *stop talking* about the *American dream* and *start listening* to the *dreams of Americans.* —Reubin Askew

In a parallel series, the emphasis falls at the end, so it is generally best to end with the most dramatic or climactic item in the series.

> My uncle often talks about growing up in Sudan — playing soccer, eating goat stew, and dodging bullets. — Alec Hamza, student

S7 Sentence variety

When a rough draft is filled with too many sentences that begin the same way or have the same structure, try injecting some variety — as long as you can do so without sacrificing clarity or ease of reading.

S7-a Vary your sentence openings.

Most sentences in English begin with the subject, move to the verb, and continue to the object, with modifiers tucked in along the way or put at the end. For the most part, such sentences are fine. Put too many of them in a row, however, and they become monotonous.

Words, phrases, or clauses modifying the verb can often be inserted ahead of the subject.

▶ Eventually a
A few drops of sap ~~eventually~~ began to trickle into the aluminum
bucket.

Like most adverbs, *eventually* does not need to appear close to the verb it modifies (*began*).

▶ Just as the sun was coming up, a
A pair of black ducks flew over the pond. ~~just as the sun was coming up.~~

The adverb clause, which modifies the verb *flew*, is as clear at the beginning of the sentence as it is at the end.

Writer's Choice
Strengthening with variety

If you look at a whole paragraph in your draft, you may have difficulty seeing the individual sentences. If a particular passage sounds repetitive, try listing the sentences one after the other so that you can review them.

> I have always loved trains.
>
> As a young boy, I watched the trains from a hillside overlooking the rail yard.
>
> I remember the individual cars rolling down the hill.
>
> I remember how they would couple with other cars.
>
> Sometimes I would hear a loud boom, which always surprised me.

When seen in this format, the sentences look monotonous and sound dull — *I did this, I remember that.* To engage the **audience** and to bring readers into the experience, narrative writing needs variety and detail.

To reduce the repetition, try varying the sentence structure.

REVISED SENTENCES

I have always loved trains, even as a young boy.

From a hillside overlooking the rail yard, I would watch individual cars roll down the track to couple with other cars.

The *BOOM!* — the sound of two cars joining — always surprised me.

REVISED PARAGRAPH

I have always loved trains, even as a young boy. From a hillside overlooking the rail yard, I would watch individual cars roll down the track to couple with other cars. The *BOOM!* — the sound of two cars joining — always surprised me.

In the revision, the sentences don't all begin in the same way, and the writer has provided details of sight and sound so that readers can experience the memory.

When you revise for variety, keep your audience in mind. Choose details specific enough to engage the reader, and make choices that add some variety to your sentence structure.

Adjectives and participial phrases can frequently be moved to the beginning of a sentence without loss of clarity.

> Dejected and withdrawn,
> ▶ Edward/~~dejected and withdrawn,~~ nearly gave up his job search.
>   ^

TIP: When beginning a sentence with an adjective or a participial phrase, make sure that the subject of the sentence names the person or thing described in the introductory phrase. If it doesn't, the phrase will dangle. (See S3-e.)

S7-b Use a variety of sentence structures.

A writer should not rely too heavily on simple sentences and compound sentences, for the effect tends to be both monotonous and choppy. (See S6-b and S6-c.) Too many complex or compound-complex sentences, however, can be equally monotonous. If your style tends to one extreme or the other, try to achieve a better mix of sentence types.

The major sentence types are illustrated in the following sentences, all taken from Flannery O'Connor's "The King of the Birds," an essay describing the author's pet peafowl.

SIMPLE	Frequently the cock combines the lifting of his tail with the raising of his voice.
COMPOUND	Any chicken's dusting hole is out of place in a flower bed, but the peafowl's hole, being the size of a small crater, is more so.
COMPLEX	The peacock does most of his serious strutting in the spring and summer when he has a full tail to do it with.
COMPOUND-COMPLEX	The cock's plumage requires two years to attain its pattern, and for the rest of his life, this chicken will act as though he designed it himself.

For a fuller discussion of sentence types, see B4-a.

S7-c Try inverting sentences occasionally.

A sentence is inverted if it does not follow the normal subject-verb-object pattern. Many inversions sound artificial and should be avoided except in the most formal contexts. If an inversion sounds natural, though, it can provide a welcome touch of variety.

▶ <ins>Set at the top two corners of the stage were huge</ins>
~~Huge~~ lavender hearts outlined in bright white lights. ~~were set at the~~
   ^   ^
~~top two corners of the stage.~~

In the revision, the subject, *hearts*, appears after the verb, *were set*. Notice that the two parts of the verb are also inverted — and separated from each other (*Set . . . were*) — without any awkwardness or loss of meaning.

Inverted sentences are used for emphasis as well as for variety (see S6-f).

W

Word Choice

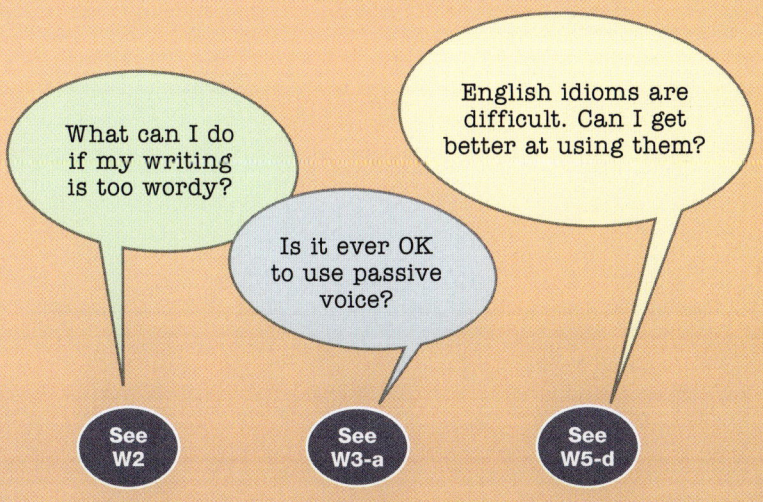

What can I do if my writing is too wordy? **See W2**

Is it ever OK to use passive voice? **See W3-a**

English idioms are difficult. Can I get better at using them? **See W5-d**

W Word Choice

W1 Glossary of usage

This glossary includes words commonly confused (such as *accept* and *except*), words commonly misused (such as *anxious*), and words and phrases that are incorrect (such as *would of*). It also lists words that may be appropriate in informal speech but are inappropriate in formal writing.

accept, except   *Accept* is a verb meaning "to receive." *Except* is usually a preposition meaning "excluding." *I will accept all the packages except that one. Except* is also a verb meaning "to exclude." *Please except that item from the list.*

advice, advise   *Advice* is a noun, *advise* a verb. *We advise you to follow John's advice.*

affect, effect   *Affect* is usually a verb meaning "to influence." *Effect* is usually a noun meaning "result." *The drug did not affect the disease, and it had adverse side effects. Effect* can also be a verb meaning "to bring about." *Only the president can effect such a dramatic change.*

agree to, agree with   *Agree to* means "to give consent to." *Agree with* means "to be in accord with" or "to come to an understanding with." *He agrees with me about the need for change, but he won't agree to my plan.*

all ready, already   *All ready* means "completely prepared." *Already* means "previously." *Susan was all ready for the concert, but her friends had already left.*

all together, altogether   *All together* means "everyone or everything in one place." *Altogether* means "entirely." *We were not altogether certain that we could bring the family all together for the reunion.*

allude   To *allude* to something is to make an indirect reference to it. Do not use *allude* to mean "to refer directly." *In his lecture, the professor referred* (not *alluded*) *to several pre-Socratic philosophers.*

allusion, illusion   An *allusion* is an indirect reference. An *illusion* is a misconception or false impression. *Did you catch my allusion to Shakespeare? Mirrors give the room an illusion of depth.*

a lot   *A lot* is two words. Do not write *alot. Sam lost a lot of weight.* See also *lots, lots of.*

among, between   See *between, among.*

amount, number   Use *amount* with quantities that cannot be counted; use *number* with those that can. *This recipe calls for a large amount of sugar. We have a large number of toads in our garden.*

anyone, any one   *Anyone*, an indefinite pronoun, means "any person at all." *Any one*, the pronoun *one* preceded by the adjective *any*, refers to a particular person or thing in a group. *Anyone from the winning team may choose any one of the prizes on display.*

anyplace   *Anyplace* is informal. In formal writing, use *anywhere.*

as   Do not use *as* to mean "because" if there is any chance of ambiguity. *We canceled the picnic because* (not *as*) *it began raining. As* here could mean either "because" or "when."

awhile, a while   *Awhile* is an adverb; it can modify a verb, but it cannot be the object of a preposition such as *for*. The two-word form *a while* is a noun preceded by an article and therefore can be the object of a preposition. *Stay awhile. Stay for a while.*

being as, being that   *Being as* and *being that* are casual expressions. Write *because* instead. *Because* (not *Being as*) *I slept late, I had to skip breakfast.*

beside, besides   *Beside* is a preposition meaning "at the side of" or "next to." *Annie sleeps with a flashlight beside her bed. Besides* is a preposition meaning "except" or "in addition to." *No one besides Terrie can have that ice cream. Besides* is also an adverb meaning "in addition." *I'm not hungry; besides, I don't like ice cream.*

between, among   Ordinarily, use *among* with three or more entities, *between* with two. *The prize was divided among several contestants. You have a choice between carrots and beans.*

bring, take   Use *bring* when an object is being transported toward you, *take* when it is being moved away. *Please bring me a glass of water. Please take these forms to Mr. Scott.*

can, may   *Can* is traditionally reserved for ability, *may* for permission. *Can you speak French? May I help you?*

capital, capitol   *Capital* refers to a city, *capitol* to a building where lawmakers meet. *Capital* also refers to wealth or resources. *The residents of the state capital protested plans to close the streets surrounding the capitol.*

cite, site   *Cite* means "to quote as an authority or example." *Site* is usually a noun meaning "a particular place." *He cited the zoning law in his argument against the proposed site of the gas station.* Locations on the Internet are usually referred to as *sites. The library's website now includes a chat feature.*

compare to, compare with   *Compare to* means "to represent as similar." *She compared him to a wild stallion. Compare with* means "to examine similarities and differences." *The study compared the language ability of apes with that of dolphins.*

complement, compliment   *Complement* is a verb meaning "to go with or complete" or a noun meaning "something that completes." As a verb, *compliment* means "to flatter"; as a noun, it means "flattering remark." *Her skill at rushing the net complements his skill at volleying. Martha's flower arrangements receive many compliments.*

conscience, conscious   *Conscience* is a noun meaning "moral principles." *Conscious* is an adjective meaning "aware or alert." *Let your conscience be your guide. Were you conscious of his love for you?*

continual, continuous   *Continual* means "repeated regularly and frequently." *She grew weary of the continual telephone calls. Continuous* means "extended or prolonged without interruption." *The broken siren made a continuous wail.*

could of   *Could of* is an incorrect version of *could have. We could have* (not *could of*) *taken the train.*

council, counsel   A *council* is a deliberative body, and a *councilor* is a member of such a body. *Counsel* usually means "advice" and can also mean "lawyer"; a *counselor* is one who gives advice or guidance. *The councilors met to draft the council's position paper. The pastor offered wise counsel to the troubled teenager.*

data   *Data* is a plural noun technically meaning "facts or propositions." But *data* is increasingly being accepted as a singular noun. *The new data suggest* (or *suggests*) *that our theory is correct.* (The singular *datum* is rarely used.)

different from, different than   Ordinarily, write *different from*. *Your sense of style is different from Jim's.* However, *different than* is acceptable to avoid an awkward construction. *Please let me know if your plans are different than* (to avoid *from what*) *they were six weeks ago.*

disinterested, uninterested   *Disinterested* means "impartial, objective"; *uninterested* means "not interested." *We sought the advice of a disinterested counselor to help us solve our problem. Mark was uninterested in anyone's opinion but his own.*

e.g.   In formal writing, replace the Latin abbreviation *e.g.* with its English equivalent: *for example* or *for instance*.

emigrate from, immigrate to   *Emigrate* means "to leave one country or region to settle in another." *In 1903, my great-grandfather emigrated from Russia to escape the religious pogroms. Immigrate* means "to enter another country and reside there." *More than fifty thousand Bosnians immigrated to the United States in the 1990s.*

etc.   Avoid ending a list with *etc.* It is more emphatic to end with an example, and in most contexts readers will understand that the list is not exhaustive. When you don't wish to end with an example, *and so on* is more graceful than *etc.*

everyone, every one   *Everyone* is an indefinite pronoun. *Every one*, the pronoun *one* preceded by the adjective *every*, means "each individual or thing in a particular group." *Every one* is usually followed by *of. Everyone wanted to go. Every one of the missing books was found.*

except   See *accept, except*.

explicit, implicit   *Explicit* means "expressed directly" or "clearly defined"; *implicit* means "implied, unstated." *I gave him explicit instructions not to go swimming. My mother's silence indicated her implicit approval.*

farther, further   *Farther* usually describes distances. *Further* usually suggests quantity or degree. *Chicago is farther from Miami than I thought. I would be grateful for further suggestions.*

fewer, less   Use *fewer* for items that can be counted; use *less* for items that cannot be counted. *Fewer people are living in the city. Please put less sugar in my tea.*

firstly   *Firstly* sounds pretentious, and it leads to the ungainly series *firstly, secondly, thirdly*, and so on. Write *first, second, third* instead.

further   See *farther, further*.

good, well   *Good* is an adjective, *well* an adverb. (See G4-a, G4-b, and G4-c.) *He hasn't felt good about his game since he sprained his wrist last season. She performed well on the uneven parallel bars.*

hanged, hung   *Hanged* is the past-tense and past-participle form of the verb *hang* meaning "to execute." *The prisoner was hanged at dawn. Hung* is the past-tense and past-participle form of the verb *hang* meaning "to fasten or suspend." *The stockings were hung by the chimney with care.*

hopefully   *Hopefully* means "in a hopeful manner." *We looked hopefully to the future.* Some usage experts object to the use of *hopefully* as a sentence adverb on grounds of clarity. To be safe, avoid using *hopefully* in sentences such as the following: *Hopefully, your son will recover soon.* Instead, indicate who is doing the hoping: *I hope that your son will recover soon.*

however   It is acceptable to start a sentence with the conjunctive adverb *however*, but be careful to place the word in your sentence according to your intended meaning and emphasis. All of the following sentences are correct. *Pam decided, however, to attend the lecture. However, Pam decided to attend the lecture.* (She had been considering other activities.) *Pam, however, decided to attend the lecture.* (Unlike someone else, Pam chose to attend the lecture.) (See P1-f.)

hung   See *hanged, hung.*

i.e.   In formal writing, use *in other words* or *that is* rather than the Latin abbreviation *i.e.* to introduce a clarifying statement. *Exposure to borax usually causes only mild skin irritation; in other words* (not *i.e.*), *it's not usually toxic.*

if, whether   Use *if* to express a condition and *whether* to express alternatives. *If you go on a trip, whether to Idaho or Italy, remember to bring identification.*

illusion   See *allusion, illusion.*

immigrate   See *emigrate from, immigrate to.*

imply, infer   *Imply* means "to suggest or state indirectly"; *infer* means "to draw a conclusion." *John implied that he knew all about databases, but the interviewer inferred that John was inexperienced.*

in, into   *In* indicates location or condition; *into* indicates movement or a change in condition. *They found the lost letters in a box after moving into the house.*

irregardless   *Irregardless* is incorrect. Use *regardless.*

kind of, sort of   Avoid using *kind of* or *sort of* to mean "somewhat." *The movie was somewhat* (not *sort of*) *boring.* Do not put *a* after either phrase. *That kind of* (not *kind of a*) *salesclerk annoys me.*

lay, lie   See *lie, lay.*

lead, led   *Lead* is a metallic element; it is a noun. *Led* is the past tense of the verb *lead. He led me to the treasure.*

less   See *fewer, less.*

lie, lay   *Lie* is an intransitive verb meaning "to recline or rest on a surface." Its forms are *lie, lay, lain. Lay* is a transitive verb meaning "to put or place." Its forms are *lay, laid, laid. I'm going to lay my phone on the picnic table and lie in the hammock.*

like, as   *Like* is a preposition, not a subordinating conjunction. It can be followed only by a noun or a noun phrase. *As* is a subordinating conjunction that introduces a subordinate clause. In casual speech, you may say *She looks like she hasn't slept.* But in formal writing, use *as. She looks as if she hasn't slept.* (See also B1-f and B1-g.)

loose, lose   *Loose* is an adjective meaning "not securely fastened." *Lose* is a verb meaning "to misplace" or "to not win." *Did you lose all your loose change?*

lots, lots of   *Lots* and *lots of* are informal substitutes for *many, much,* or *a lot.* Avoid using them in formal writing.

may   See *can, may.*

maybe, may be   *Maybe* is an adverb meaning "possibly." *Maybe the sun will shine tomorrow. May be* is a verb phrase. *Tomorrow may be brighter.*

number   See *amount, number.*

of   Use the verb *have,* not the preposition *of,* after the verbs *could, should, would, may, might,* and *must.* They must have (not *must of*) *left early.*

off of   *Off* is sufficient. Omit *of. The ball rolled off* (not *off of*) *the table.*

passed, past   *Passed* is the past tense of the verb *pass. Ann passed me another slice of cake. Past* usually means "belonging to a former time" or "beyond a time or place." *Our past president spoke until past midnight. The hotel is just past the next intersection.*

precede, proceed   *Precede* means "to come before." *Proceed* means "to go forward." *As we proceeded up the mountain path, we noticed fresh tracks in the mud, evidence that a group of hikers had preceded us.*

principal, principle   *Principal* is a noun meaning "the head of a school or an organization" or "a sum of money." It is also an adjective meaning "most important." *Principle* is a noun meaning "a basic truth or law." *The principal expelled her for three principal reasons. We believe in the principle of equal justice for all.*

quote, quotation   *Quote* is a verb; *quotation* is a noun. Avoid using *quote* as a shortened form of *quotation. Her quotations* (not *Her quotes*) *are appearing in various social media channels.*

raise, rise   *Raise* is a transitive verb meaning "to move or cause to move upward." It takes a direct object. *I raised the shades. Rise* is an intransitive verb meaning "to go up." *Heat rises.*

real, really   *Real* is an adjective; *really* is an adverb. *Real* is sometimes used informally as an adverb, but avoid this use in formal writing. *She was really* (not *real*) *angry.*

reason why   The expression *reason why* is redundant. *The reason* (not *The reason why*) *Jones lost the election is clear.*

respectfully, respectively   *Respectfully* means "showing or marked by respect." *Respectively* means "each in the order given." *He respectfully submitted his opinion to the judge. John, Tom, and Larry were a butcher, a baker, and a lawyer, respectively.*

set, sit   *Set* is a transitive verb meaning "to put" or "to place." Its past tense is *set. Sit* is an intransitive verb meaning "to be seated." Its past tense is *sat. She set the dough in a warm corner of the kitchen. The cat sat in the doorway.*

should of   *Should of* is a casual version of *should have. They should have* (not *should of*) *been home an hour ago.*

since   Do not use *since* to mean "because" if there is any chance of ambiguity. *Because* (not *Since*) *we won the game, we have been celebrating with pizza and dessert. Since* here could mean "because" or "from the time that."

site   See *cite, site.*

sometime, some time, sometimes   *Sometime* is an adverb meaning "at an indefinite time." *Some time* is the adjective *some* modifying the noun *time* and means "a period of time." *Sometimes* is an adverb meaning "at times, now and then." *I'll see you sometime soon. I haven't lived there for some time. Sometimes I see him at work.*

suppose to   *Suppose to* is an incorrect version of *supposed to. I am supposed to* (not *suppose to*) *be there by noon.*

sure and   Write *sure to. We were all taught to be sure to* (not *sure and*) *look both ways before crossing a street.*

take   See *bring, take.*

than, then   *Than* is a conjunction used in comparisons; *then* is an adverb denoting time. *That pizza is more than I can eat. Tom laughed, and then we recognized him.*

that   See *who, which, that.*

that, which   Many writers reserve *that* for restrictive clauses, *which* for nonrestrictive clauses. *Restaurants that allow pets are few in number. Restaurants, which generally don't allow pets, must follow strict health codes.* (See P1-e.)

there, their, they're   *There* is an adverb specifying place; it is also an expletive (placeholder). Adverb: *Sylvia is sitting there patiently.* Expletive: *There are two plums left. Their* is a possessive pronoun. *Fred and Jane finally washed their car. They're* is a contraction of *they are. They're later than usual today.*

to, too, two   *To* is a preposition; *too* is an adverb; *two* is a number. *Too many of your shots slice to the left, but the last two were just right.*

toward, towards   *Toward* and *towards* are generally interchangeable, although *toward* is preferred in American English.

try and   *Try and* is an informal version of *try to. The teacher asked us all to try to* (not *try and*) *write an original haiku.*

unique   Avoid expressions such as *most unique, more straight, less perfect, very round.* Either something is unique or it isn't. It is illogical to suggest degrees of uniqueness. (See G4-d.)

wait for, wait on   *Wait for* means "to be in readiness for" or "to await." *Wait on* means "to serve." *We're waiting for* (not *waiting on*) *Ruth to take us to the museum.*

weather, whether   The noun *weather* refers to the state of the atmosphere. *Whether* is a conjunction referring to a choice between alternatives. *We wondered whether the weather would clear.*

well, good   See *good, well.*

which   See *that, which* and *who, which, that.*

while   Avoid using *while* to mean "although" or "whereas" if there is any chance of ambiguity. *Although* (not *While*) *Gloria lost money in the slot machine, Tom won it at roulette.* Here *While* could mean either "although" or "at the same time that."

who, which, that   Do not use *which* to refer to persons. Use *who* instead. *That*, though generally used to refer to things, may be used to refer to a group or class of people. *The player who* (not *that* or *which*) *made the basket at the buzzer was named MVP. The team that scores the most points in this game will win the tournament.*

who, whom   *Who* is used for subjects and subject complements; *whom* is used for objects. *Who are the candidates for this year's scholarship? The candidates, whom I met with yesterday, are impressive.* (See G3-d.)

who's, whose   *Who's* is a contraction of *who is; whose* is a possessive pronoun. *Who's ready for more popcorn? Whose coat is this?* (See P4-b and P4-d.)

would of   *Would of* is a casual version of *would have. She would have* (not *would of*) *had a chance to play if she had arrived on time.*

your, you're   *Your* is a possessive pronoun; *you're* is a contraction of *you are. Is that your new bike? You're in the finals.* (See P4-b and B1-b.)

W2   Wordy sentences

Long sentences are not necessarily wordy, nor are short sentences always concise. A sentence is wordy if it can be tightened without loss of meaning.

W2-a Eliminate redundancies.

Redundancies such as *cooperate together, yellow in color,* or *basic essentials* are a common source of wordiness. There is no need to say the same thing twice.

▶ Daniel ~~is now employed~~ at a private rehabilitation center ~~working~~ as
   ^works^
   a registered physical therapist.

Though modifiers ordinarily add meaning to the words they modify, occasionally they are redundant.

▶ *The Pursuit of Happyness* tells the story of a single father determined
   ~~in his mind~~ to pull his family out of homelessness.

The word *determined* contains the idea that his resolution formed in his mind.

W2-b Avoid unnecessary repetition of words.

Though words may be repeated deliberately, for effect, repetitions will seem awkward if they are clearly unnecessary. When a more concise version is possible, choose it.

▶ His third speech, delivered in Chicago, was ~~an~~ outstanding. ~~speech.~~

▶ The best teachers help each student ~~become a better student~~ grow both academically and emotionally.

W2-c Cut empty or inflated phrases.

An empty phrase can be cut with little or no loss of meaning. Common examples are word groups that weaken a writer's authority by apologizing or hedging: *in my opinion, I think that, it seems that,* and so on.

▶ ~~In my opinion,~~ Our current immigration policy is misguided.

Readers understand without being told that they are hearing the writer's opinion.

Inflated phrases can be reduced to a word or two without loss of meaning.

▶ We are unable to provide funding ~~at this point in time.~~ now.

INFLATED	CONCISE
along the lines of	like
as a matter of fact	in fact
at the present time	now, currently
due to the fact that	because
for the purpose of	for
in order to	to
in spite of the fact that	although, though
in the final analysis	finally

W2-d Simplify the structure.

Simplifying sentences and using stronger verbs can make writing more direct. Look for opportunities to strengthen verbs.

▶ The analyst claimed that because of market conditions she could not ~~make an~~ estimate ~~of~~ the company's future profits.

The verb *estimate* is more vigorous and concise than *make an estimate of*.

The colorless verbs *is, are, was,* and *were* frequently generate excess words.

▶ Investigators ~~were involved in studying~~ **studied** the effect of classical music on unborn babies.

The revision is more direct and concise. The action (*studying*), originally appearing in a subordinate structure, has become a strong verb, *studied*.

The expletive constructions *there is* and *there are* (or *there was* and *there were*) can also lead to wordy sentences. The same is true of expletive constructions beginning with *it*.

▶ ~~There is~~ **A**nother module ~~that~~ tells the story of Charles Darwin and introduces the theory of evolution.

Finally, verbs in the passive voice may be needlessly indirect. When the active voice expresses your meaning as effectively, use it. (See W3-a.)

W2-e Reduce clauses to phrases, phrases to single words.

Word groups functioning as modifiers can often be made more compact. Look for any opportunities to reduce clauses to phrases or phrases to single words.

▶ We took a side trip to Monticello, ~~which was~~ the home of Thomas Jefferson.

▶ In ~~the~~ **this** essay, ~~that follows,~~ I argue against Kohn's claim that the grading system discourages thinking/. ~~which is a problematic claim.~~ **problematic**

W3 Active verbs

Choose an active verb whenever possible. Active verbs express meaning more vigorously than forms of the verb *be* or verbs in the passive voice. Forms of *be* (*be, am, is, are, was, were, being, been*) lack vigor because they convey no action. Passive verbs lack strength because their subjects receive the action instead of doing it.

BE VERB	A surge of power *was* responsible for the destruction of the pumps.
PASSIVE	The pumps *were destroyed* by a surge of power.
ACTIVE	A surge of power *destroyed* the pumps.

Even among active verbs, some are more vigorous and colorful than others. Carefully selected verbs can energize a piece of writing.

▶ The goalie crouched low, ~~reached~~ *swept* out his stick, and ~~sent~~ *hooked* the rebound away from the mouth of the net.

Academic English   Although you may be tempted to avoid the passive voice completely, keep in mind that some writing situations call for it, including some scientific writing. For advice about forming the passive voice, see M1-b.

W3-a Choose the active voice or the passive voice depending on your writing situation.

In the active voice, the subject does the action; in the passive voice, the subject receives the action. Although both voices are grammatically correct, the active voice is usually more effective because it is clearer and more direct.

ACTIVE	Hernando *caught* the fly ball.
PASSIVE	The fly ball *was caught* by Hernando.

In passive sentences, the actor (in this case, *Hernando*) frequently does not appear: *The fly ball was caught.*

Most of the time, you will want to emphasize the actor, so you should use the active voice. To replace a passive verb with an active one, make the actor the subject of the sentence.

▶ The settlers stripped the land of timber before realizing
~~The land was stripped of timber before the settlers realized~~ the
consequences of their actions.

The revision emphasizes the actors (*settlers*) by naming them in the subject.

The decision to use the active or the passive voice will be influenced not only by your purpose but also by your audience's expectations. In much scientific writing, for example, the passive voice properly emphasizes an experiment or a process, not a person.

Just before harvest, the tobacco plants are sprayed with a chemical to prevent the growth of suckers.

W3-b Replace *be* verbs that result in dull or wordy sentences.

Not every *be* verb needs replacing. The forms of *be* (*be, am, is, are, was, were, being, been*) work well when you want to link a subject to a noun that clearly renames it or to an adjective that describes it: *Orchard House was the home of Louisa May Alcott. The harvest will be bountiful after the summer rains.*

Be verbs also are essential as helping verbs before present participles (*is flying, are disappearing*) to express ongoing action: *Derrick was fighting the fire when his wife went into labor.* (See G2-f.)

If using a *be* verb makes a sentence needlessly wordy, consider replacing it. Often a phrase following the verb contains a noun or an adjective (such as *violation* or *resistant*) that suggests a more vigorous, active verb (*violate, resist*).

▶ Burying nuclear waste in Antarctica would violate ~~be in violation of~~ an international treaty.

Violate is less wordy and more vigorous than *be in violation of.*

▶ When Rosa Parks resisted ~~was resistant to~~ giving up her seat on the bus, she became a civil rights hero.

Resisted is stronger than *was resistant to.*

Writer's Choice
Using the active or the passive voice

You will usually choose whether to write in the active voice or the passive voice. While your instructors often expect you to use the active voice, some situations and fields of study will require you to write in the passive voice. This choice will be influenced primarily by your **purpose** but also by your **audience's expectations** and the **genre** in which you are writing (see C1-a).

To emphasize the actor and not the receiver of the action, choose the active voice.

ACTIVE State officials forced nearly 28,000 Hawaiians to leave their homes after the earthquake.

> *This sentence focuses on the government's displacing the people. Emphasizing the state's action may be better for the writer whose purpose is to make an argument about that action.*

To focus attention on the receiver of the action, choose the passive voice.

PASSIVE Nearly 28,000 Hawaiians were forced to leave their homes after the earthquake.

> *This sentence focuses on the people displaced by the earthquake. Emphasizing the number of homeless Hawaiians may be better for the writer whose purpose is to discuss how the earthquake affected residents.*

What idea are you emphasizing in your sentence? Considering your purpose and audience, what would be more effective — focusing on the actor or on the person or thing being acted on? It's your choice.

W3-c As a rule, choose a subject that names the person or thing doing the action.

In weak, unemphatic prose, both the actor and the action may be buried in sentence elements other than the subject and the verb. In the following weak sentence, for example, both the actor and the action appear in prepositional phrases, word groups that do not receive much attention from readers.

WEAK	The institution of the New Deal had the effect of reversing some of the economic inequalities of the Great Depression.
EMPHATIC	The New Deal reversed some of the economic inequalities of the Great Depression.

Consider the subjects and verbs of the two versions — *institution had* versus *New Deal reversed*. The latter expresses the writer's point more emphatically.

> P
> ~~The use of~~ pure oxygen can ~~cause~~ heal~~ing in~~ wounds that are otherwise untreatable.

In the original sentence, the subject and verb — *use can cause* — express the point blandly. *Oxygen can heal* makes the point more emphatically and directly.

W4 Appropriate language

Language is appropriate when it suits your subject, engages your audience, and blends naturally with your own voice.

W4-a Avoid jargon, except in specialized writing situations.

Jargon is specialized language used among members of a trade, discipline, or professional group. Use jargon only when readers will be familiar with it and when plain English will not do as well.

JARGON	We outsourced the work to an outfit in Ohio because we didn't have the bandwidth to tackle it in-house.
REVISED	We hired a company in Ohio because we had too few employees to do the work.

Writer's Choice
Using discipline-specific terms

In general, try to minimize jargon and instead use plain language in your writing. Some disciplines, however, have specific terminology that is not only standard but also expected. When you use a discipline's terms effectively, you show yourself to be a member of that community and increase your authority with your **audience**.

For example, the following terms have specialized meanings in chemistry and economics and are understood by readers in those disciplines.

absolute	deadweight loss	hybridization
consumer surplus	degenerate	utility

UNNECESSARY USE OF A SPECIALIZED TERM

Although America's love affair with the automobile has not diminished, more Americans have embraced automotive <mark>hybridization</mark> as their concern for the environment has grown.

In this example, hybridization is not discipline-specific. The writer has used the word to sound impressive.

NECESSARY USE OF A SPECIALIZED TERM

As shown, sp^2 <mark>hybridization</mark> leaves one nonhybridized p orbital.

Here, hybridization has a specific meaning for chemists.

When writing for a specific disciplinary audience, familiarize yourself with the language and terminology of the discipline through course readings and other materials. Use discipline-specific terms only when you know that you and your readers understand their meaning. Doing so will help you make effective word choices.

EXAMPLES OF JARGON WITH PLAIN ENGLISH TRANSLATIONS

ameliorate (improve)　　　　　　optimal (best, most favorable)
commence (begin)　　　　　　　parameters (boundaries, limits)
components (parts)　　　　　　　peruse (read, look over)
endeavor (try)　　　　　　　　　prior to (before)
facilitate (help)　　　　　　　　utilize (use)
indicator (sign)　　　　　　　　viable (workable)

Sentences with jargon are hard to read and are often wordy.

▶ The CEO should ~~dialogue~~ *talk* with investors about ~~partnering~~ *working* with clients to buy land in ~~economically deprived zones.~~ *poor neighborhoods.*

W4-b Avoid most euphemisms and doublespeak.

Euphemisms — nice-sounding words or phrases substituted for words thought to sound harsh — are sometimes appropriate. We may use euphemisms out of concern for someone's feelings. Telling parents, for example, that their daughter is "unmotivated" is more sensitive than saying she's lazy. Tact or politeness, then, can occasionally justify euphemisms, but use them sparingly.

Most euphemisms are needlessly evasive or even deceitful.

EUPHEMISM	PLAIN ENGLISH
pre-owned automobile	used car
revenue enhancers	taxes
chemical dependency	drug addiction
correctional facility	prison, jail

The term *doublespeak* applies to any deliberately evasive or deceptive language, including euphemisms. Doublespeak is especially common in politics and business. A military retreat is described as *tactical redeployment*; *enhanced interrogation* is a euphemism for "torture"; and *downsizing* really means "firing employees."

W4-c In most contexts, avoid slang.

Slang is an informal and sometimes private vocabulary that expresses the solidarity of a group such as teenagers, rap musicians, or sports fans. It is subject to more rapid change than common English. For example, the slang teenagers use to express approval changes every few years; *cool, groovy, neat, awesome, sick,* and *dope* have replaced one another within the last several decades. Sometimes slang becomes so widespread that it is accepted as standard vocabulary. *Jazz,* for example, started out as slang but is now a standard term for a style of music.

Although slang has a certain vitality, it is an informal code that not everyone understands. Avoid using it in academic writing, unless you have a specific purpose for doing so.

> *evidence*
> ▶ Without ~~the receipts~~, we can't move forward with our proposal.
>   ^

W4-d Choose an appropriate level of formality.

In deciding on a level of formality, consider both your subject and your audience. Does the subject demand a dignified treatment, or is a relaxed tone more suitable? Will readers be put off if you assume too close a relationship with them, or might you alienate them by seeming too distant?

For most academic and professional writing, some degree of formality is appropriate. In a job application letter, for example, it is a mistake to sound too breezy and informal.

TOO INFORMAL	I'd like to get that sales job you've got on the website.
MORE FORMAL	I would like to apply for the position of sales manager posted on LinkedIn.

Informal writing is appropriate for private letters, personal email and text messages, and business correspondence between close associates. Like spoken conversation, informal writing allows contractions (*don't, I'll*) and colloquial words (*kids, kinda*).

In choosing a level of formality, above all be consistent. When a writer's voice shifts from one level of formality to another, readers receive mixed messages.

> *began*
> ▶ Jorge's pitching lesson ~~commenced~~ with his famous curveball,
>   *thrown*   ^
>   ~~implemented~~ by tucking the little finger behind the ball. Next
>   ^ *revealed*
>   he ~~elucidated~~ the mysteries of the sucker pitch, a slow ball coming
>   ^
>   behind a fast windup.

Words such as *commenced* and *elucidated* are inappropriate for the subject matter, and they clash with informal terms such as *sucker pitch* and *fast windup*.

W4-e Avoid sexist and noninclusive language.

Sexist and noninclusive language stereotypes and demeans people and should be avoided. Using nonsexist and inclusive language shows respect for and

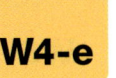

sensitivity to others. As you write for different audiences, keep in mind that words matter, and always select those that show respect for your readers.

Recognizing sexist and noninclusive language

Some objectionable language is easy to recognize because it reflects genuine contempt: referring to a woman as a "babe," for example, or calling a lawyer a "lady lawyer."

Other forms of sexist and noninclusive language are less blatant. The following practices reflect stereotypical and outdated thinking: referring to members of one profession as exclusively male or exclusively female (teachers as women or engineers as men, for instance) or deliberately using pronouns people don't identify with or don't prefer.

STEREOTYPICAL LANGUAGE

After a nursing student graduates, *she* must face a difficult state board examination. [Not all nursing students are women.]

Running for city council are Boris Stotsky, an attorney, and *Mrs.* Cynthia Jones, a professor of English and *mother of three.* [The title *Mrs.* and the phrase *mother of three* are irrelevant.]

When a student applies for federal financial aid, *he* or *she* is given an FSA ID. [Not all students identify as *he* or *she*.]

Still other forms of sexist language result from outdated traditions. The pronouns *he, him,* and *his,* for instance, were traditionally used to refer generically to persons of either sex. Current usage favors gender-neutral terms.

GENERIC PRONOUNS (SEXIST)

A journalist is motivated by *his* deadline.

A good interior designer treats *her* clients' ideas respectfully.

Both forms are sexist — for excluding one sex entirely and for making assumptions about the members of particular professions.

Similarly, terms including *man* and *men* were once used to refer generically to persons of either sex. Current usage demands gender-neutral terms.

INAPPROPRIATE	APPROPRIATE
chairman	chairperson, moderator, chair, head
congressman	member of Congress, representative, legislator
fireman	firefighter
mailman	mail carrier, postal worker, letter carrier
to man	to operate, to staff
mankind	people, humans
manpower	personnel, staff
policeman	police officer
weatherman	forecaster, meteorologist

Revising sexist and noninclusive language

Avoiding *he* as the universal pronoun and recognizing an individual's chosen pronoun usage communicates respect and audience awareness. When revising sexist language, you may be tempted to substitute *he or she* and *his or her*. This strategy is wordy and can become awkward when repeated throughout an essay. Also, some readers may think *he or she* or *his or her* excludes transgender and gender-fluid individuals. A better revision strategy is to write in the plural; yet another strategy is to recast the sentence so that problems do not arise.

> **SEXIST**
>
> A journalist is motivated by *his* deadline.
>
> A good interior designer treats *her* clients' ideas respectfully.
>
> **BETTER: USING THE PLURAL**
>
> Journalists are motivated by *their* deadlines.
>
> Good interior designers treat *their* clients' ideas respectfully.
>
> **BETTER: REVISING THE SENTENCE**
>
> A journalist is motivated by *a* deadline.
>
> A good interior designer treats clients' ideas respectfully.
>
> **BETTER: USING SINGULAR *THEY***
>
> A journalist is motivated by their deadline.
>
> A good interior designer treats their clients' ideas respectfully.

For more examples of revision strategies, see G3-a.

W5 Exact language

Two reference works will help you find words to express your meaning exactly: a good dictionary, such as *The American Heritage Dictionary* or *Merriam-Webster* online, and a collection of synonyms and antonyms, such as *Roget's International Thesaurus*.

TIP: Do not turn to a thesaurus in search of impressive words. Look instead for words that express your meaning exactly.

W5-a Select words with appropriate connotations.

In addition to their strict dictionary meanings (or *denotations*), words have *connotations*, emotional colorings that affect how readers respond to them.

The word *steel* denotes "commercial iron that contains carbon," but it also calls up images associated with steel. These associations give the word its connotations — cold, hard, smooth, unbending.

If the connotation of a word does not seem appropriate for your purpose, your audience, or your subject matter, you should change the word. When a more appropriate synonym does not come quickly to mind, consult a dictionary or a thesaurus.

▶ When American soldiers returned home after World War II, many
women ~~abandoned~~ left their jobs in favor of marriage.

The word *abandoned* is too negative for the context.

▶ As I covered the boats with marsh grass, the ~~perspiration~~ sweat I had

worked up evaporated in the wind, and the cold morning air

seemed even colder.

The term *perspiration* is too delicate for the context, which suggests vigorous exercise.

W5-b Prefer specific, concrete nouns.

Unlike general nouns, which refer to broad classes of things, specific nouns point to particular items. *Film*, for example, names a general class, *fantasy film* names a narrower class, and *The Fellowship of the Ring* is more specific still. Other examples: *team, football team, Denver Broncos; music, symphony, Beethoven's Ninth.*

Unlike abstract nouns, which refer to qualities and ideas (*justice, beauty, realism, dignity*), concrete nouns point to immediate, often sensory experiences and to physical objects (*steeple, asphalt, lilac, stone, garlic*).

Specific, concrete nouns express meaning more vividly than general or abstract ones. Although general and abstract language is sometimes necessary to convey your meaning, use specific, concrete words whenever possible.

▶ The senator spoke about the challenges of the future:
~~the environment and world peace.~~ Pollution, dwindling resources, and terrorism,

Nouns such as *thing, area, aspect, factor,* and *individual* are especially dull and imprecise.

▶ Toni Morrison's *Beloved* is about slavery, ~~among other things.~~ motherhood, and memory.

W5-c Do not misuse words.

If a word is not in your active vocabulary, you may find yourself misusing it, sometimes with embarrassing consequences. When in doubt, check the dictionary.

▶ The fans were ~~migrating~~ *climbing* up the bleachers in search of seats.

▶ The Internet has so ~~diffused~~ *permeated* our culture that it touches all segments of society.

Also be alert for misused word forms — using a noun such as *absence or significance*, for example, when your meaning requires the adjective *absent or significant*.

▶ Most dieters are not ~~persistence~~ *persistent* enough to make a permanent change in their eating habits.

W5-d Use common idioms.

Idioms are speech forms that follow no easily specified rules. The English say "Bernice went *to hospital*," an idiom strange to American ears, which are accustomed to hearing *the* in front of *hospital*. Native speakers of a language seldom have problems with idioms, but prepositions (such as *with, to, at,* and *of*) occasionally cause trouble, especially when they follow certain verbs and adjectives. When in doubt, consult a dictionary.

UNIDIOMATIC	IDIOMATIC (PREFERABLE)
angry at (a person)	angry with (a person)
off of	off
plan on doing	plan to do
sure and	sure to
think on	think of, about
try and	try to

For Multilingual Writers Because idioms follow no particular rules, it's best to learn them individually. You may find it helpful to keep a list of idioms that you frequently encounter in conversation and in reading.

W5-e Do not rely heavily on clichés.

The pioneer who first announced that he had "slept like a log" no doubt amused his companions with a fresh, unlikely comparison. Today, however, that comparison is a cliché, a saying that can no longer add emphasis or surprise.

To see just how dully predictable clichés are, put your hand over the right-hand column and then finish the phrases on the left.

beat around	the bush
busy as a	bee, beaver
crystal	clear
dead as a	doornail
light as a	feather
starting out at the bottom	of the ladder
water under the	bridge
avoid clichés like the	plague

The solution for clichés is simple: Just delete them or rewrite them.

▶ When I received a full scholarship from my second-choice
     felt pressured to settle for second best.
  school, I found myself between a rock and a hard place.
     ^

Sometimes you can write around a cliché by adding an element of surprise. One student revised a cliché about butterflies in her stomach like this:

> If all of the action in my stomach is caused by butterflies, there must be a horde of them, with horseshoes on.

The image of butterflies wearing horseshoes is fresh and unlikely, not predictable like the original cliché.

W5-f Use figures of speech with care.

A figure of speech is an expression that uses words imaginatively (rather than literally) to make abstract ideas concrete. Most often, figures of speech compare two seemingly unlike things to reveal surprising similarities.

In a *simile*, the writer makes the comparison explicitly, typically by using *like* or *as*. We use similes in everyday speech — *strong as an ox, different as night and day, solid as the ground we stand on*. One student, in describing his grandfather, used this simile: *By the time cotton had to be picked, Grandfather's neck was as red as the clay he plowed*.

In a *metaphor*, the *like* or *as* is omitted, and the comparison is implied. Historians, economists, and politicians, for example, use metaphors when they describe the future as a rocky path forward, compare the economy to a rigged game, describe a historical moment as a new chapter, or debate whether America is a melting pot. In a 2015 eulogy, President Barack Obama called church "our beating heart."

Although figures of speech are useful devices, writers can misuse them if they don't think about the images they evoke. The result is sometimes a *mixed metaphor*, the combination of two or more images that don't make sense together.

▶ Our manager decided to put all controversial issues ~~in a holding pattern~~ on a back burner until after the annual meeting.

Here the writer is mixing airplanes and stoves. Simply deleting one of the images corrects the problem.

G

Grammatical Sentences

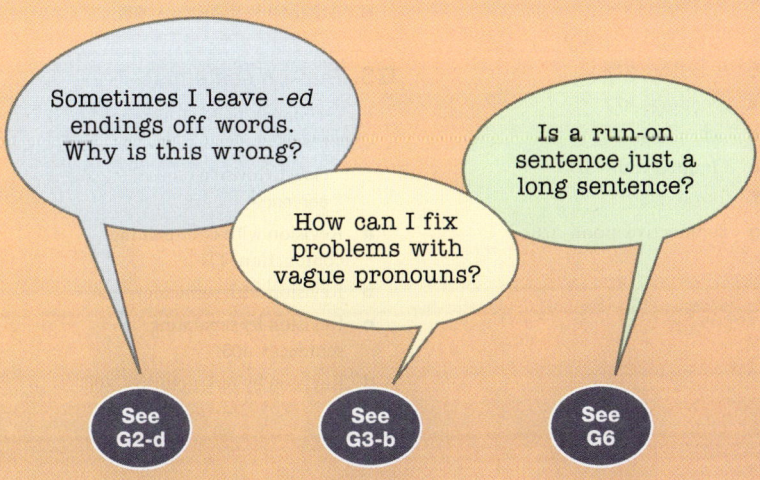

Sometimes I leave *-ed* endings off words. Why is this wrong?

See
G2-d

How can I fix problems with vague pronouns?

See
G3-b

Is a run-on sentence just a long sentence?

See
G6

G Grammatical Sentences

G1 Subject-verb agreement

In the present tense, verbs agree with their subjects in number (singular or plural) and in person (first, second, third): *I sing, you sing, she sings, we sing, they sing.* Even if your ear recognizes the subject-verb combinations in G1-a, you may encounter tricky situations such as those described in G1-b to G1-k.

G1-a Learn to recognize typical subject-verb combinations.

This section describes the basic guidelines for making present-tense verbs agree with their subjects. The present-tense ending *-s* (or *-es*) is used on a verb if its subject is third-person singular (*he, she, it,* and singular nouns); otherwise the verb takes no ending. Consider, for example, the present-tense forms of the verbs *love* and *try,* given at the beginning of the "Subject-verb agreement at a glance" chart.

The verb *be* varies from this pattern; it has special forms in *both* the present and the past tense (see the end of the chart).

If you aren't sure of the English forms, use the charts in this chapter as you proofread your work. See also G2-c on *-s* endings of regular and irregular verbs.

G1-b Make the verb agree with its subject, not with a word that comes between.

Word groups often come between the subject and the verb. Such word groups, usually modifying the subject, may contain a noun that at first appears to be the subject. By mentally stripping away such modifiers, you can isolate the noun that is in fact the subject.

The *samples* on the tray in the lab *need* testing.

▶ High levels of air pollution causes damage to the respiratory tract.

The subject is *levels,* not *pollution.* Strip away the phrase *of air pollution* to hear the correct verb: *levels cause.*

has
▶ The slaughter of pandas for their pelts ~~have~~ caused the panda
  ^
population to decline drastically.

The subject is *slaughter,* not *pandas* or *pelts.*

Subject-verb agreement at a glance

Present-tense forms of *love* and *try* (typical verbs)

	Singular		**Plural**	
FIRST PERSON	I	love	we	love
SECOND PERSON	you	love	you	love
THIRD PERSON	he/she/it*	loves	they**	love

	Singular		**Plural**	
FIRST PERSON	I	try	we	try
SECOND PERSON	you	try	you	try
THIRD PERSON	he/she/it*	tries	they**	try

Present-tense forms of *have*

	Singular		**Plural**	
FIRST PERSON	I	have	we	have
SECOND PERSON	you	have	you	have
THIRD PERSON	he/she/it*	has	they**	have

Present-tense forms of *do* (including negative forms)

	Singular		**Plural**	
FIRST PERSON	I	do/don't	we	do/don't
SECOND PERSON	you	do/don't	you	do/don't
THIRD PERSON	he/she/it*	does/doesn't	they**	do/don't

Present-tense and past-tense forms of *be*

	Singular		**Plural**	
FIRST PERSON	I	am/was	we	are/were
SECOND PERSON	you	are/were	you	are/were
THIRD PERSON	he/she/it*	is/was	they**	are/were

*And singular nouns (*child, Roger*)
**And plural nouns (*children, the Mannings*)

NOTE: Phrases beginning with expressions such as *accompanied by, in addition to, as well as, together with,* and *along with* do not make a singular subject plural: *The governor as well as his press secretary was on the plane.* To emphasize that two people were on the plane, the writer could use *and* instead: *The governor and his press secretary were on the plane.*

When to use the -*s* (or -*es*) form of a present-tense verb

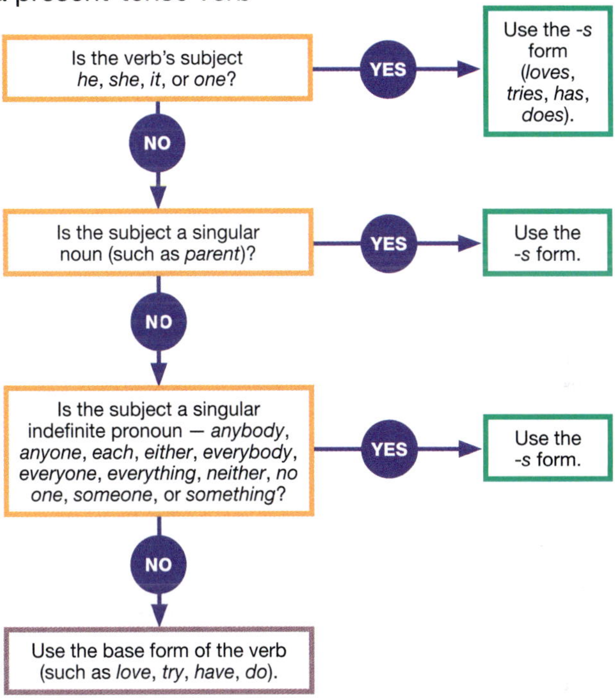

Is the verb's subject *he, she, it,* or *one*? — **YES** → Use the -*s* form (*loves, tries, has, does*).

NO ↓

Is the subject a singular noun (such as *parent*)? — **YES** → Use the -*s* form.

NO ↓

Is the subject a singular indefinite pronoun — *anybody, anyone, each, either, everybody, everyone, everything, neither, no one, someone,* or *something*? — **YES** → Use the -*s* form.

NO ↓

Use the base form of the verb (such as *love, try, have, do*).

EXCEPTION: Choosing the correct present-tense form of *be* (*am, is,* or *are*) is not quite so simple. See the chart on the previous page for both present- and past-tense forms of *be*.

TIP: Do not use the -*s* form of a verb if it follows a modal verb such as *can, must,* or *should* or another helping verb. (See M1-c.)

G1-c Treat most subjects joined with *and* as plural.

A subject with two or more parts is said to be compound. If the parts are connected with *and,* the subject is nearly always plural.

Leon and Jan often jog together.

▶ The Supreme Court's willingness to hear the case and its affirmation
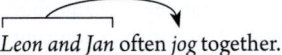
of the original decision ~~has~~ set a new precedent.

EXCEPTIONS: When the parts of the subject form a single unit or when they refer to the same person or thing, treat the subject as singular.

> Fish and chips is always on the menu.

> Sue's friend and adviser was surprised by her decision.

When a compound subject is preceded by *each* or *every*, treat it as singular.

> Each tree, shrub, and vine needs to be sprayed.

> Every car, truck, and van is required to pass inspection.

This exception does not apply when a compound subject is followed by *each*: *Alan and Marcia each have different ideas.*

G1-d With subjects joined with *or* or *nor* (or with *either . . . or* or *neither . . . nor*), make the verb agree with the part of the subject nearer to the verb.

> A driver's *license* or credit *card is* required.

> A driver's *license* or two credit *cards are* required.

▶ If an infant or a child ~~have~~ has a high fever, call a doctor.

▶ Neither the chief financial officer nor the marketing managers ~~was~~ were able to convince the client to reconsider.

The verb must be matched with the part of the subject closer to it: *child has* in the first sentence, *managers were* in the second.

NOTE: If one part of the subject is singular and the other is plural, put the plural one last to avoid awkwardness.

G1-e Treat most indefinite pronouns as singular.

Indefinite pronouns are pronouns that do not refer to specific persons or things. The following commonly used indefinite pronouns are singular.

anybody	each	everyone	nobody	somebody
anyone	either	everything	no one	someone
anything	everybody	neither	nothing	something

Many of these words appear to have plural meanings, and they are often treated as such in casual speech. In formal written English, however, they are nearly always treated as singular. (See G3-a.)

Everyone on the team *supports* the coach.

▶ Each of the essays ~~have~~ **has** been graded.

▶ Nobody who participated in the clinical trials ~~were~~ **was** given a placebo.

The subjects of these sentences are *Each* and *Nobody*. These indefinite pronouns are third-person singular, so the verbs must be *has* and *was*.

A few indefinite pronouns (*all, any, none, some*) may be singular or plural depending on the noun or pronoun they refer to.

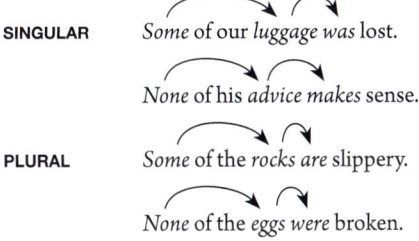

SINGULAR   *Some* of our *luggage was* lost.

None of his *advice makes* sense.

PLURAL   *Some* of the *rocks are* slippery.

None of the *eggs were* broken.

NOTE: When the meaning of *none* is emphatically "not one," *none* may be treated as singular: *None* [meaning "Not one"] *of the eggs was broken.* Using *not one* is sometimes clearer: *Not one of the eggs was broken.*

G1-f Treat collective nouns as singular unless the meaning is clearly plural.

Collective nouns such as *jury, committee, audience, crowd, troop, family,* and *couple* name a class or a group. In American English, collective nouns are nearly always treated as singular to emphasize the group as a unit. Occasionally, when there is some reason to draw attention to the individual members of the group, a collective noun may be treated as plural. (See also G3-a.)

SINGULAR   The *class respects* the teacher.

PLURAL   The *class are* debating among themselves.

To underscore the notion of individuality in the second sentence, many writers would add a clearly plural noun.

PLURAL   The class *members are* debating among themselves.

meets
▶ **The board of trustees ~~meet~~ in Denver twice a year.**
                            ^

The board as a whole meets; there is no reason to draw attention to its individual members.

were
▶ **A young couple ~~was~~ arguing about politics while holding hands.**
                        ^

The meaning is clearly plural. Only separate individuals can argue and hold hands.

NOTE: The phrase *the number* is treated as singular, *a number* as plural.

SINGULAR   *The number* of school-age children *is* declining.

PLURAL   *A number* of children *are* attending the wedding.

NOTE: In general, when a fraction or a unit of measurement is used with a singular noun, treat it as singular; when used with a plural noun, treat it as plural.

SINGULAR   *Three-fourths* of the salad *has* been eaten.

SINGULAR   Twenty *inches* of wallboard *was* covered with mud.

PLURAL   *One-fourth* of the drivers *were* texting.

PLURAL   Two *pounds* of blueberries *were* used to make the pie.

G1-g Make the verb agree with its subject even when the subject follows the verb.

Verbs ordinarily follow subjects. When this order is reversed, it is easy to become confused. Sentences beginning with *there is* or *there are* (or *there was* or *there were*) are inverted; the subject follows the verb.

There *are* surprisingly few *honeybees* left in southern China.

▶ There ~~was~~ *were* a social worker and a journalist at the meeting.

The subject, *worker and journalist*, is plural, so the verb must be *were*.

Occasionally you may decide to invert a sentence for variety or effect. When you do so, check to make sure that your subject and verb agree.

▶ Of particular concern ~~is~~ *are* penicillin and tetracycline, antibiotics used

to make animals more resistant to disease.

The subject, *penicillin and tetracycline*, is plural, so the verb must be *are*.

G1-h Make the verb agree with its subject, not with a subject complement.

One basic sentence pattern in English consists of a subject, a linking verb, and a subject complement: *Jack is a lawyer.* Because the subject complement (*lawyer*) names or describes the subject (*Jack*), it is sometimes mistaken for the subject. (See B2-b on subject complements.)

These *exercises are* a way to test your ability to perform under pressure.

▶ A tent and a sleeping bag ~~is~~ *are* the required equipment.

Tent and bag is the subject, not *equipment*.

▶ A major force in today's economy ~~are~~ *is* children — as consumers,

decision makers, and trend spotters.

Force is the subject, not *children*. If the corrected version seems too awkward, make *children* the subject: *Children are a major force in today's economy — as consumers, decision makers, and trend spotters.*

G1-i *Who, which,* and *that* take verbs that agree with their antecedents.

Like most pronouns, the relative pronouns *who, which,* and *that* have antecedents, nouns or pronouns to which they refer. A relative pronoun used as the subject of a subordinate clause takes a verb that agrees with its antecedent.

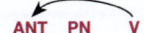
ANT PN V
Take a *course that prepares* you for classroom management.

One of the

Constructions such as *one of the students who* (or *one of the things that*) cause problems for writers. Do not assume that the antecedent must be *one*. Instead, consider the logic of the sentence.

> ► Our ability to use language is one of the things that set~~s~~ us apart
>
> from animals.
>
> The antecedent of *that* is *things*, not *one*. Several things set us apart from animals.

Only one of the

When the word *only* comes before *one*, you are safe in assuming that *one* is the antecedent of the relative pronoun.

> ► Veronica was the only one of the first-year Spanish students who
>   was
>   ~~were~~ fluent enough to apply for the exchange program.
>   ^
>   The antecedent of *who* is *one*, not *students*. Only one student was fluent enough.

G1-j Words such as *athletics, economics, mathematics, physics, politics, statistics, measles*, and *news* are usually singular, despite their plural form.

>   is
> ► Politics ~~are~~ among my mother's favorite pastimes.
>   ^

EXCEPTIONS: Occasionally some of these words, especially *mathematics, economics, politics,* and *statistics*, have plural meanings: *Office politics often sway decisions about hiring and promotion. The economics of the building plan are prohibitive.*

G1-k Treat titles of works, company names, words mentioned as words, and gerund phrases as singular.

>   describes
> ► *Lost Cities* ~~describe~~ the discoveries of fifty ancient civilizations.
>   ^
>   specializes
> ► Delmonico Brothers ~~specialize~~ in organic produce and
>   ^
>   additive-free meats.
>
>   is
> ► *Controlled substances* ~~are~~ a euphemism for illegal drugs.
>   ^

A gerund phrase consists of an *-ing* verb form followed by any objects, complements, or modifiers (see B3-b). Treat gerund phrases as singular.

> Encountering long hold times ~~make~~ ^{makes} customers impatient with
>
> telephone tech support.

G2 Verb forms, tenses, and moods

In speech, some people use verb forms and tenses that match a home dialect or variety of English. In writing, you may be expected to use the forms commonly taught in school unless you are using an English dialect or variety for authenticity or to capture a source's voice.

Except for the verb *be*, all verbs in English have five forms. The following list shows the five forms and provides a sample sentence in which each might appear.

BASE FORM	Usually I (*walk, ride*).
PAST TENSE	Yesterday I (*walked, rode*).
PAST PARTICIPLE	I have (*walked, ridden*) many times before.
PRESENT PARTICIPLE	I am (*walking, riding*) right now.
-S FORM	He/she/it (*walks, rides*) regularly.

The verb *be* has eight forms instead of the usual five: *be, am, is, are, was, were, being, been.*

G2-a Choose among the forms of irregular verbs.

For all regular verbs, the past-tense and past-participle forms are the same (ending in *-ed* or *-d*), so there is no danger of confusion. This is not true, however, for irregular verbs, such as the following.

BASE FORM	PAST TENSE	PAST PARTICIPLE
go	went	gone
break	broke	broken
fly	flew	flown

> **For Multilingual writers**   If English is not your native language, see also M1 for more help with verbs.

The past-tense form always occurs alone, without a helping verb. It expresses action that occurred entirely in the past: *I rode to work yesterday. I walked to work last Tuesday.* The past participle is used with a helping verb. It forms the perfect tenses with *has, have,* or *had;* it forms the passive voice with *be, am, is, are, was, were, being,* or *been.* (See B1-c for a list of helping verbs and G2-f for a survey of tenses.)

PAST TENSE	Last July, we *went* to Seoul.
HELPING VERB + PAST PARTICIPLE	We *have gone* to Seoul twice.

The list of common irregular verbs beginning below will help you distinguish between the past tense and the past participle. Choose the past-participle form if the verb in your sentence requires a helping verb; choose the past-tense form if the verb does not require a helping verb. (See verb tenses in G2-f.)

> saw
> ▶ Yesterday we ~~seen~~ a documentary about Isabel Allende.
>   ^

The past-tense *saw* is required because there is no helping verb.

> stolen
> ▶ The truck was apparently ~~stole~~ while the driver ate lunch.
>   ^

> fallen
> ▶ By Friday, the stock market had ~~fell~~ two hundred points.
>   ^

Because of the helping verbs *was* and *had,* the past-participle forms are required: *was stolen, had fallen.*

Common irregular verbs

BASE FORM	PAST TENSE	PAST PARTICIPLE
arise	arose	arisen
be	was, were	been
become	became	become
begin	began	begun
break	broke	broken
bring	brought	brought
build	built	built
buy	bought	bought
choose	chose	chosen

BASE FORM	PAST TENSE	PAST PARTICIPLE
come	came	come
dive	dived, dove	dived
do	did	done
drink	drank	drunk
drive	drove	driven
eat	ate	eaten
find	found	found
fly	flew	flown
forget	forgot	forgotten, forgot
get	got	gotten, got
give	gave	given
go	went	gone
hang (execute)	hanged	hanged
hang (suspend)	hung	hung
have	had	had
hide	hid	hidden
know	knew	known
lay (put)	laid	laid
let (allow)	let	let
lie (recline)	lay	lain
make	made	made
prove	proved	proved, proven
rise (get up)	rose	risen
run	ran	run
see	saw	seen
send	sent	sent
set (place)	set	set
sing	sang	sung
sink	sank	sunk
sit (be seated)	sat	sat
speak	spoke	spoken
steal	stole	stolen
swear	swore	sworn
swim	swam	swum
swing	swung	swung
take	took	taken
teach	taught	taught
wear	wore	worn
write	wrote	written

G2-b Distinguish among the forms of *lie* and *lay*.

Writers and speakers frequently confuse the various forms of *lie* (meaning "to recline or rest on a surface") and *lay* (meaning "to put or place something"). *Lie* is an intransitive verb; it does not take a direct object: *The tax forms lie on the table.* The verb *lay* is transitive; it takes a direct object: *Please lay the tax forms on the table.* (See B2-b.)

		PAST	PRESENT
BASE FORM	PAST TENSE	PARTICIPLE	PARTICIPLE
lie (recline)	lay	lain	lying
lay (put)	laid	laid	laying

▶ Sue was so exhausted that she ~~laid~~ down for a nap.

(lay — inserted above "laid")

The past-tense form of *lie* (to recline) is *lay*.

▶ The patient had ~~laid~~ in an uncomfortable position all night.

(lain — inserted above "laid")

The past-participle form of *lie* (to recline) is *lain*. If the correct English seems too stilted, recast the sentence: *The patient had been lying in an uncomfortable position all night.*

▶ The customer gently ~~lay~~ the iPad on the help desk counter.

(laid — inserted above "lay")

The past-tense form of *lay* (to place) is *laid*.

▶ Letters dating from 1915 were ~~laying~~ in a corner of the chest.

(lying — inserted above "laying")

The present participle of *lie* (to rest on a surface) is *lying*.

G2-c Use -s (or -es) endings on present-tense verbs that have third-person singular subjects.

All singular nouns (*child*, *tree*) and the pronouns *he*, *she*, and *it* are third-person singular; indefinite pronouns such as *everyone* and *neither* are also third-person singular. When the subject of a sentence is third-person singular, its verb takes an *-s* or *-es* ending in the present tense. (See also G1.)

	SINGULAR		PLURAL	
FIRST PERSON	I	know	we	know
SECOND PERSON	you	know	you	know
THIRD PERSON	he/she/it	knows	they	know
	child	knows	parents	know
	everyone	knows		

▶ My neighbor ~~drive~~ to Marco Island every weekend.

(drives — inserted above "drive")

▶ Sulfur dioxide ~~turn~~ leaves yellow, ~~dissolve~~ marble, and ~~eat~~ away iron and steel.

(turns — inserted above "turn"; dissolves — inserted above "dissolve"; eats — inserted above "eat")

The subjects *neighbor* and *sulfur dioxide* are third-person singular, so the verbs must end in *-s*.

NOTE: Do not add the -s ending to the verb if the subject is not third-person singular. The writers of the following sentences added -s endings where they don't belong.

▶ I prepare~~s~~ system specifications for every installation.

  The pronoun *I* is first-person singular, so its verb does not require the -*s*.

▶ The wood floors require~~s~~ continual sweeping.

  The -*s* form is used only on present-tense verbs with third-person *singular* subjects.

G2-d Do not omit -*ed* endings on verbs.

Speakers who do not fully pronounce -*ed* endings in informal speech some-times omit them unintentionally in writing. For example, the -*ed* ending is not always fully pronounced in frequently used words and phrases such as *asked, fixed, pronounced, supposed to,* and *used to.*

Past tense

Use the ending -*ed* or -*d* to express the past tense of regular verbs. The past tense is used when the action occurred entirely in the past.

▶ In 1998, journalist Barbara Ehrenreich ~~decide~~ decided to try to live on

  minimum wage.

▶ Last summer, my counselor ~~advise~~ advised me to ask my graphic arts

  instructor for a recommendation.

Past participles

Past participles are used in three ways: (1) following *have, has,* or *had* to form one of the perfect tenses; (2) following *be, am, is, are, was, were, being,* or *been* to form the passive voice; and (3) as adjectives modifying nouns or pronouns. The perfect tenses are listed in G2-f, and the passive voice is discussed in W3-a. For a discussion of participles as adjectives, see B3-b.

▶ Robin has ~~ask~~ ^{asked} the Office of Student Affairs for more housing staff

for next year.

Has asked is present perfect tense (*have* or *has* followed by a past participle).

▶ Though it is not a new phenomenon, domestic violence is now
~~publicize~~ ^{publicized} more than ever.

Is publicized is a verb in the passive voice (a form of *be* followed by a past participle).

G2-e Do not omit needed verbs.

Linking verbs, used to link subjects to subject complements, are frequently a form of *be*: *be, am, is, are, was, were, being, been.* (See B2-b.) Some of these forms may be contracted (*I'm, she's, we're, you're, they're*), but they should not be omitted altogether.

▶ When we ^{are} quiet in the evening, we can hear the crickets.

▶ Sherman Alexie ^{is} a Native American author whose stories have been

made into a film.

Helping verbs, used with main verbs, include forms of *be, do,* and *have* and the modal verbs *can, will, shall, could, would, should, may, might,* and *must.* (See B1-c.) Some helping verbs may be contracted (*he's leaving, we'll celebrate, they've been told*), but they should not be omitted altogether.

▶ ~~We~~ ^{We've} been in Chicago since last Thursday.

> **For Multilingual Writers**   Some languages do not require a linking verb between a subject and its complement. English, however, requires a verb in every sentence. See M3-a.
>
> • Every night, I read to my daughter. When I ^{am} too busy, her older
>
> brother reads to her.

G2-f Choose the appropriate verb tense.

Tenses indicate the time of an action in relation to the time of the speaking or writing about that action. Tenses are classified as present, past, and future, with simple, perfect, and progressive forms for each tense.

The most common problem with tenses — confusing shifts from one tense to another — is discussed in section S4. Other problems with tenses are detailed in this section, after the following survey of tenses.

Survey of tenses

SIMPLE TENSES (base form or -s form)   *For general facts, states of being, and habitual actions.*

SIMPLE PRESENT

SINGULAR

		PLURAL	
I	walk, ride, am	we	walk, ride, are
you	walk, ride, are	you	walk, ride, are
he/she/it	walks, rides, is	they	walk, ride, are

SIMPLE PAST

SINGULAR

		PLURAL	
I	walked, rode, was	we	walked, rode, were
you	walked, rode, were	you	walked, rode, were
he/she/it	walked, rode, was	they	walked, rode, were

SIMPLE FUTURE

I, you, he/she/it, we, they   will walk, ride, be

PERFECT TENSES (a form of *have* plus past participle)   *For an action that was or will be completed at the time of another action*

PRESENT PERFECT

I, you, we, they   have walked, ridden, been
he/she/it   has walked, ridden, been

PAST PERFECT

I, you, he/she/it, we, they   had walked, ridden, been

FUTURE PERFECT

I, you, he/she/it, we, they   will have walked, ridden, been

> **For Multilingual Writers** See M1-a for more specific examples of verb tenses that can be challenging for multilingual writers.

PROGRESSIVE FORM (a form of _have_ plus present participle)   _For actions in progress_

PRESENT PROGRESSIVE

I	am walking, riding, being
he/she/it	is walking, riding, being
you, we, they	are walking, riding, being

PAST PROGRESSIVE

I, he/she/it	was walking, riding, being
you, we, they	were walking, riding, being

FUTURE PROGRESSIVE

I, you, he/she/it, we, they	will be walking, riding, being

PRESENT PERFECT PROGRESSIVE

I, you, we, they	have been walking, riding, being
he/she/it	has been walking, riding, being

PAST PERFECT PROGRESSIVE

I, you, he/she/it, we, they	had been walking, riding, being

FUTURE PERFECT PROGRESSIVE

I, you, he/she/it, we, they	will have been walking, riding, being

NOTE: The progressive forms are not normally used with certain verbs, such as _believe, know,_ and _seem._

Special uses of the present tense

Use the present tense when expressing general truths, when writing about literature, and when quoting, summarizing, or paraphrasing an author's views.

General truths or scientific principles should appear in the present tense unless such principles have been disproved.

> ▶ Galileo taught that the earth ~~revolved~~ *revolves* around the sun.

Because Galileo's teaching has not been discredited, the verb should be in the present tense. The following sentence, however, is acceptable: *Ptolemy taught that the sun revolved around the earth.*

When writing about a work of literature, you may be tempted to use the past tense. The convention in the humanities, however, is to describe fictional events in the present tense.

> In Masuji Ibuse's *Black Rain*, a child ~~reached~~ ^{reaches} for a pomegranate
> in his mother's garden, and a moment later he ~~was~~ ^{is} dead, killed
> by the blast of the atomic bomb.

When you are quoting, summarizing, or paraphrasing the author of a nonliterary work, use present-tense verbs such as *writes, reports, asserts,* and so on to introduce the source. This convention is usually followed even when the author is dead (unless a date or the context specifies the time of writing).

> Dr. Jerome Groopman ~~argued~~ ^{argues} that doctors are "susceptible to the
> subtle and not so subtle efforts of the pharmaceutical industry to
> sculpt our thinking" (9).

In MLA style, signal phrases are written in the present tense, not the past tense. (See also MLA-3c.)

APA NOTE: When you are documenting a paper with the APA (American Psychological Association) style of in-text citations, use past-tense verbs such as *reported* or *demonstrated* or present perfect verbs such as *has reported* or *has demonstrated* to introduce the source. (See APA-3c.)

The past perfect tense

The past perfect tense (*had* plus past participle) is used for an action already completed by the time of another past action or for an action already completed at some specific past time.

Everyone *had spoken* by the time I arrived.

I pleaded my case, but Paula *had made up* her mind.

Writers sometimes use the simple past tense when they should use the past perfect.

> By the time dinner was served, the guest of honor ^{had} left.

The past perfect tense is needed because the action of leaving was already completed at a specific past time (when dinner was served).

Some writers tend to overuse the past perfect tense. Do not use the past perfect if two past actions occurred at the same time.

> wrote
> ▶ When Ernest Hemingway lived in Cuba, he ~~had written~~ *For Whom*
> ^
> *the Bell Tolls.*

Sequence of tenses with infinitives and participles

An infinitive is the base form of a verb preceded by *to*. (See B3-b.) Use the present infinitive to show action at the same time as or later than the action of the verb in the sentence.

> pay
> ▶ Barb had hoped to ~~have paid~~ the bill by May 1.
> ^

The action expressed in the infinitive (*to pay*) occurred later than the action of the sentence's verb (*had hoped*).

Use the perfect form of an infinitive (*to have* followed by the past participle) for an action occurring earlier than that of the verb in the sentence.

> have joined
> ▶ Dan would like to ~~join~~ the navy, but he could not swim.
> ^

The liking occurs in the present; the joining would have occurred in the past.

Like the tense of an infinitive, the tense of a participle is governed by the tense of the sentence's verb. Use the present participle (ending in *-ing*) for an action occurring at the same time as that of the sentence's verb.

Hiking the Appalachian Trail, we spotted many wildflowers.

Use the past participle (such as *given* or *helped*) or the present perfect participle (*having* plus the past participle) for an action occurring before that of the verb.

Discovered off the coast of Florida, the Spanish galleon yielded many treasures.

Having worked her way through college, Lee graduated debt-free.

G2-g Use the subjunctive mood in the few contexts that require it.

There are three moods in English: the *indicative*, used for facts, opinions, and questions; the *imperative*, used for orders or advice; and the *subjunctive*, used in certain contexts to express wishes, requests, or conditions contrary to fact. For many writers, the subjunctive causes the most problems.

Forms of the subjunctive

In the subjunctive mood, present-tense verbs do not change form to indicate the number and person of the subject (see G1). Instead, the subjunctive uses the base form of the verb (*be, drive, employ*) with all subjects. Also, in the subjunctive mood, there is only one past-tense form of *be*: *were* (never *was*).

It is important that you *be* [not *are*] prepared for the interview.

We asked that she *drive* [not *drives*] more slowly.

If I *were* [not *was*] you, I'd try a new strategy.

Uses of the subjunctive

The subjunctive mood appears only in a few contexts: in contrary-to-fact clauses beginning with *if* or expressing a wish; in *that* clauses following verbs such as *ask, insist, recommend, request*, and *suggest*; and in certain set expressions.

IN CONTRARY-TO-FACT CLAUSES BEGINNING WITH *IF* When a subordinate clause beginning with *if* expresses a condition contrary to fact, use the subjunctive *were* in place of *was*.

▶ If I ~~was~~ a member of Congress, I would vote for that bill.
    were

▶ The astronomers would be able to see the moons of Jupiter

▶ tonight if the weather ~~was~~ clearer.
    were

The writer is not a member of Congress, and the weather is not clear.

Do not use the subjunctive mood in *if* clauses expressing conditions that exist or may exist.

If Dana *wins* the contest, she will leave for Barcelona in June.

IN CONTRARY-TO-FACT CLAUSES EXPRESSING A WISH In formal English, use the subjunctive *were* in clauses expressing a wish or desire.

INFORMAL   I wish that Dr. Vaughn *was* my professor.

FORMAL   I wish that Dr. Vaughn *were* my professor.

IN *THAT* CLAUSES FOLLOWING VERBS SUCH AS *ASK, INSIST, REQUEST*, AND SUGGEST Because requests have not yet become reality, they are expressed in the subjunctive mood.

▶ Professor Moore insists that her students ~~are~~ on time.
    be

▶ We recommend that Lambert ~~files~~ form 1050 soon.
    file

IN CERTAIN SET EXPRESSIONS   The subjunctive mood, once more widely used, remains in certain set expressions: *be that as it may, as it were, far be it from me*, and so on.

G3 Pronouns

Pronouns are words that substitute for nouns (see B1-b). Pronoun errors are typically related to the four topics discussed in this section:

    a. pronoun-antecedent agreement (singular vs. plural)
    b. pronoun reference (clarity)
    c. pronoun case (personal pronouns such as *I* vs. *me, she* vs. *her*)
    d. pronoun case (*who* vs. *whom*)

For more help with pronouns, consult the glossary of usage (W1).

G3-a Make pronouns and antecedents agree.

Many pronouns have antecedents, nouns or pronouns to which they refer. A pronoun and its antecedent agree when they are both singular or both plural.

SINGULAR   *Dr. Ava Berto* finished *her* rounds.

PLURAL   The hospital *interns* finished *their* rounds.

Indefinite pronouns

Indefinite pronouns refer to nonspecific persons or things.

anybody	each	everyone	nobody	somebody
anyone	either	everything	no one	someone
anything	everybody	neither	nothing	something

For Multilingual Writers   The pronouns *he, his, she, her, it*, and *its* must agree in gender (masculine, feminine, or neuter) with their antecedents, not with the words they modify.

    Steve visited *his* [not *her*] sister in Seattle.

Traditionally, indefinite pronouns have been treated as singular in formal English. However, using a singular pronoun usually results in a sentence that is sexist, and the traditional alternative (*he or she*) is now often considered noninclusive.

SEXIST	*Everyone* performs at *his* own fitness level.
SEXIST	*Everyone* performs at *her* own fitness level.
NONINCLUSIVE	*Everyone* performs at *his or her* own fitness level.

Since using *he/his* or *she/her* to refer generically to any person is considered sexist, and using *he or she* or *his or her* is wordy and doesn't include people who prefer not to refer to themselves as *he* or *she,* it is becoming increasingly acceptable in many contexts to use the nonbinary plural pronoun *they* to refer to an indefinite pronoun: *everyone performs at their own fitness level.*

The following are usually your best options for revision.

1. Make the antecedent plural.
2. Rewrite the sentence so that no problem of agreement exists.
3. Use the plural pronoun *they* to refer to the singular antecedent ("singular *they*").

▶ When ~~someone travels~~ people travel outside the United States for the first time, ~~he needs~~ they need to apply for a passport.

▶ ~~When someone travels outside the United States for the first~~ Anyone who travels outside the United States for the first time ~~time, he~~ needs to apply for a passport.

▶ When someone travels outside the United States for the first time, ~~he needs~~ they need to apply for a passport.

If you change a pronoun from singular to plural (or vice versa), check to be sure that the verb agrees with the new pronoun (see G1-e).

See W4-e for more on avoiding sexist and noninclusive language.

NOTE: When using pronouns to refer to people, choose the pronouns that they would use to refer to themselves. Doing so shows respect and communicates your audience awareness. Some transgender and gender-fluid individuals refer to themselves by new pronouns (*ze/hir*, for example), but if you are unfamiliar with such preferences, *they* and *them* are acceptable gender-neutral options.

Generic nouns

A generic noun represents a typical member of a group, such as a typical student, or any member of a group, such as a lawyer. Although generic nouns may seem to have plural meanings, they traditionally have been considered singular. However, you should avoid using *he* to refer to generic nouns, as in *A runner must train if he wants to excel.* As with indefinite pronouns, the singular use of *they* is becoming increasingly acceptable with generic nouns.

When you have trouble with generic nouns, you will usually have the same revision options as mentioned earlier in this section for indefinite pronouns.

> ▶ ~~A medical student~~ must study hard if ~~he wants~~ to succeed.
>   Medical students   they want

> ▶ A medical student must study hard ~~if he wants~~ to succeed.

> ▶ A medical student must study hard if ~~he wants~~ to succeed.
>   they want

Collective nouns

Collective nouns such as *jury, committee, audience, crowd, class, troop, family, team,* and *couple* name a group. Ordinarily the group functions as a unit, so the noun should be treated as singular; if the members of the group function as individuals, however, the noun should be treated as plural. (See also G1-f.)

AS A UNIT   The *committee* granted *its* permission to build.

AS INDIVIDUALS   The *committee* put *their* signatures on the document.

When treating a collective noun as plural, many writers prefer to add a clearly plural antecedent such as *members* to the sentence: *The members of the committee put their signatures on the document.*

> ▶ After only an hour of deliberation, the jury returned ~~their~~ verdict.
>   its

There is no reason to draw attention to the individual members of the jury, so *jury* should be treated as singular.

Compound antecedents

> *President Obama and Chinese president Xi* held a meeting at which *they*
>
> formally signed the 2016 Paris climate agreement.

With compound antecedents joined with *or* or *nor* (or with *either . . . or* or *neither . . . nor*), make the pronoun agree with the nearer antecedent.

Either *Bruce* or *Tom* should receive first prize for *his* poem.

Neither the *mouse* nor the *rats* could find *their* way through the maze.

NOTE: If one of the antecedents is singular and the other plural, as in the second example, put the plural one last to avoid awkwardness.

EXCEPTION: If one antecedent is male and the other female, do not follow the traditional rule. The sentence *Either Bruce or Elizabeth should receive first prize for her short story* makes no sense. The best solution is to recast the sentence: *The prize for best short story should go to either Bruce or Elizabeth.*

G3-b Make pronoun references clear.

In the sentence *When Andrew returned home, he took a nap*, the noun *Andrew* is the antecedent of the pronoun *he*. A pronoun should refer clearly to its antecedent.

Ambiguous reference

Ambiguous pronoun reference occurs when a pronoun could refer to two possible antecedents.

▶ ~~When Gloria set the pitcher~~ on the glass-topped table~~. it broke.~~
The pitcher broke when Gloria set it

▶ Tom told James, ~~that he had~~ won the lottery.
"You have "

What broke — the pitcher or the table? Who won the lottery — Tom or James? The revisions eliminate the ambiguity.

Implied reference

A pronoun should refer to a specific antecedent, not to a word that is implied but not present in the sentence.

▶ After braiding Ann's hair, Sue decorated ~~them~~ with ribbons.
the braids

The pronoun *them* referred to Ann's braids (implied by the term *braiding*), but the word *braids* did not appear in the sentence.

Modifiers, such as possessives, cannot serve as antecedents. A modifier may strongly imply the noun that a pronoun might logically refer to, but it is not itself that noun. See the following example.

> In ~~Jamaica Kincaid's~~ "Girl," ~~she~~ portrays a mother-daughter
>
> relationship laced with tension.

Jamaica Kincaid

Using the possessive form of an author's name to introduce a source leads to a problem later in this sentence: The pronoun *she* cannot refer logically to a possessive modifier (*Jamaica Kincaid's*). The revision substitutes the noun *Jamaica Kincaid* for the pronoun *she*, thereby eliminating the problem.

Broad reference of this, that, which, *and* it

For clarity, the pronouns *this, that, which,* and *it* should ordinarily refer to specific antecedents rather than to whole ideas or sentences. When a pronoun's reference is needlessly broad, either replace the pronoun with a noun or supply an antecedent to which the pronoun clearly refers.

> By advertising on TV, pharmaceutical companies gain exposure for
>
> their prescription drugs. Patients respond to ~~this~~ by requesting drugs
>
> they might not need.

the ads

The writer substituted the noun *ads* for the pronoun *this*, which referred broadly to the idea expressed in the preceding sentence.

> Romeo and Juliet were both too young to have acquired much
>
> wisdom, ~~and~~ that accounts for their rash actions.

a fact

The writer added an antecedent (*fact*) that the pronoun *that* clearly refers to.

Indefinite use of they, it, *and* you

Do not use the pronoun *they* to refer indefinitely to persons who have not been specifically mentioned. *They* should always refer to a specific antecedent.

> In June, ~~they~~ voted to charge a fee for students to participate in sports
>
> and music programs.

the school board

The word *it* should not be used indefinitely in constructions such as *It is said on television* . . . or *In the book, it says that* . . .

> ~~In the~~ article ~~it~~ states that male moths can smell female moths from
>
> several miles away.

The

The pronoun *you* is appropriate only when the writer is addressing the reader directly: *Once you have kneaded the dough, let it rise in a warm place.* Except in informal contexts, however, *you* should not be used to mean "anyone in general." Use a noun instead.

> Ms. Pickersgill's *Guide to Etiquette* stipulates that ~~you~~ should not
>
>   *a guest*
>
> arrive at a party too early or leave too late.

G3-c Distinguish between pronouns such as *I* and *me*.

The personal pronouns in the following chart change what is known as *case form* according to their grammatical function in a sentence. Pronouns functioning as subjects or subject complements appear in the *subjective* case; those functioning as objects appear in the *objective* case; and those showing ownership appear in the *possessive* case.

	SUBJECTIVE CASE	OBJECTIVE CASE	POSSESSIVE CASE
SINGULAR	I	me	my
	you	you	your
	he/she/it	him/her/it	his/her/its
PLURAL	we	us	our
	you	you	your
	they	them	their

Pronouns in the subjective and objective cases are frequently confused. Most of the rules in this section specify when to use one or the other of these cases (*I* or *me*, *he* or *him*, and so on). See the end of this section for a special use of pronouns and nouns in the possessive case.

Subjective case (*I, you, he, she, it, we, they*)

When a pronoun is used as a subject complement (a word following a linking verb), your ear may mislead you, since the incorrect form is frequently heard in casual speech. (See B2-b on subject complements.)

> During the Lindbergh trial, Bruno Hauptmann repeatedly
>
> denied that the kidnapper was ~~him.~~
>
>   *he.*
>
> If *kidnapper was he* seems too stilted, rewrite the sentence: *During the Lindbergh trial, Bruno Hauptmann repeatedly denied that he was the kidnapper.*

Objective case (me, you, him, her, it, us, them)

When a personal pronoun is used as a direct object, an indirect object, or the object of a preposition, it must be in the objective case.

DIRECT OBJECT	Bruce found Tony and brought *him* home.
INDIRECT OBJECT	Alice gave *me* a surprise party.
OBJECT OF A PREPOSITION	Jessica wondered if the call was for *her*.

Compound word groups

When a subject or an object appears as part of a compound structure, you may occasionally become confused. To test for the correct pronoun, mentally strip away all of the compound word group except the pronoun in question.

▶ Janice was indignant when she realized that the salesclerk was
  insulting her mother and ~~she.~~
  _{her.}
  ^

Her mother and her is the direct object of the verb *was insulting*. Strip away the words *her mother and* to hear the correct pronoun: *was insulting her* (not *was insulting she*).

When a pronoun functions as a subject or a subject complement, it must be in the subjective case.

SUBJECT	Sylvia and *he* shared the award.
SUBJECT COMPLEMENT	Greg announced that the winners were Sylvia and *he*.

▶ The most traumatic experience for her father and ~~I~~ occurred long
  me
  ^
  after her operation.

Her father and me is the object of the preposition *for*. Strip away the words *her father and* to test for the correct pronoun: *for me* (not *for I*).

When in doubt about the correct pronoun, some writers try to avoid making the choice by using a reflexive pronoun such as *myself*. Using a reflexive pronoun in such situations is incorrect in U.S. English.

▶ Nidra gave my cousin and ~~myself~~ some good tips on traveling in New
  me
  ^
  Delhi.

My cousin and me is the indirect object of the verb *gave*. For correct uses of *myself*, see the glossary of usage (W1).

Appositives

Appositives are noun phrases that rename nouns or pronouns. A pronoun used as an appositive has the same function (usually subject or object) as the word(s) it renames.

▶ The managers, Dr. Bell and ~~me,~~ **I,** could not agree on a plan.

> The appositive *Dr. Bell and I* renames the subject, *managers*. Test: *I could not agree* (not *Me could not agree*).

▶ The reporter found only two witnesses, the bicyclist and ~~I.~~ **me.**

> The appositive *the bicyclist and me* renames the direct object, *witnesses*. Test: *found me* (not *found I*).

Comparisons with *than* or *as*

When a comparison begins with *than* or *as*, your choice of a pronoun will depend on your intended meaning. To test for the correct pronoun, mentally complete the sentence: *My roommate likes football more than I* [*do*].

▶ In our report on nationalized health care in the United States, we argued that Canadians are better off than ~~us.~~ **we.**

> *We* is the subject of the verb *are*, which is understood: *Canadians are better off than we* [*are*]. If the correct English seems too formal, you can always add the verb.

▶ We respected no other candidate as much as ~~she.~~ **her.**

> This sentence means that we respected no other candidate as much as *we respected her*. *Her* is the direct object of the understood verb *respected*.

We *or* us *before a noun*

When deciding whether *we* or *us* should precede a noun, choose the pronoun that would be appropriate if the noun were omitted.

▶ ~~Us~~ **We** tenants would rather fight than move.

> Test: *We would rather fight* (not *Us would rather fight*).

Subjects and objects of infinitives

An infinitive is the word *to* followed by the base form of a verb. (See B3-b.) Subjects of infinitives are an exception to the rule that subjects must be in the subjective case. Whenever an infinitive has a subject, it must be in the objective case. Objects of infinitives also are in the objective case.

<blockquote>

                     me   *her*

▶ Sue asked John and ~~I~~ to drive the mayor and ~~she~~ to the airport.
</blockquote>

John and me is the subject of the infinitive *to drive; mayor and her* is the direct object of the infinitive.

Possessive case to modify a gerund

A pronoun that modifies a gerund or a gerund phrase should be in the possessive case (*my, our, your, his, her, its, their*). A gerund is a verb form ending in *-ing* that functions as a noun. Gerunds frequently appear in phrases; when they do, the whole gerund phrase functions as a noun. (See B3-b.)

<blockquote>

                    your

▶ The chances of ~~you~~ being hit by lightning are slim.
</blockquote>

Your modifies the gerund phrase *being hit by lightning.*

Nouns as well as pronouns may modify gerunds. To form the possessive case of a noun, use an apostrophe and an *-s* (*victim's*) or just an apostrophe (*victims'*). (See P4-a.)

<blockquote>

                                         aristocracy's

▶ The old order in France paid a high price for the ~~aristocracy~~

exploiting the lower classes.
</blockquote>

The possessive noun *aristocracy's* modifies the gerund phrase *exploiting the lower classes.*

G3-d Distinguish between *who* and *whom.*

The choice between *who* and *whom* (or *whoever* and *whomever*) occurs primarily in subordinate clauses and in questions. *Who* and *whoever,* subjective-case pronouns, are used for subjects and subject complements. *Whom* and *whomever,* objective-case pronouns, are used for objects.

In subordinate clauses

When *who* and *whom* (or *whoever* and *whomever*) introduce subordinate clauses, their case is determined by their function *within the clause they introduce.*

In the following two examples, the pronouns *who* and *whoever* function as the subjects of the clauses they introduce.

▶ First prize goes to the runner ~~whom~~ *who* earns the most points.
  ^

The subordinate clause is *who earns the most points.* The verb of the clause is *earns,* and its subject is *who.*

▶ Maya Angelou's *I Know Why the Caged Bird Sings* should be read by *whoever* ~~whomever~~ is interested in the effects of racism on children.
  ^

The writer selected the pronoun *whomever,* thinking that it was the object of the preposition *by.* However, the object of the preposition is the entire subordinate clause *whoever is interested in the effects of racial prejudice on children.* The verb of the clause is *is,* and the subject of the verb is *whoever.*

In questions

When *who* and *whom* (or *whoever* and *whomever*) are used to open questions, their case is determined by their function within the question.

▶ *Who* ~~Whom~~ was responsible for creating that computer virus?
  ^

Who is the subject of the verb *was.*

When *whom* functions as the object of a verb or the object of a preposition in a question, it appears out of normal order. To choose the correct pronoun, mentally restructure the question.

▶ *Whom* ~~Who~~ did the Democratic Party nominate in 2004?
  ^

Whom is the direct object of the verb *did nominate.* This becomes clear if you restructure the question: *The Democratic Party did nominate whom in 2004?*

For subjects or objects of infinitives

An infinitive is the word *to* followed by the base form of a verb. (See B3-b.) Subjects of infinitives are an exception to the rule that subjects must be in the subjective case. The subject of an infinitive must be in the objective case. Objects of infinitives also are in the objective case.

▶ When it comes to money, I know *whom* ~~who~~ to believe.
  ^

The infinitive phrase *whom to believe* is the direct object of the verb *know,* and *whom* is the subject of the infinitive *to believe.*

G4 Adjectives and adverbs

Adjectives modify nouns or pronouns. They usually come before the word they modify; occasionally they function as complements following the word they modify. Adverbs modify verbs, adjectives, or other adverbs. (See B1-d and B1-e.)

Many adverbs are formed by adding *-ly* to adjectives (*normal, normally; smooth, smoothly*). But don't assume that all words ending in *-ly* are adverbs or that all adverbs end in *-ly*. Some adjectives end in *-ly* (*lovely, friendly*), and some adverbs don't (*always, here, there*). When in doubt, consult a dictionary.

> **For Multilingual Writers**   Placement of adjectives and adverbs can be a tricky matter for multilingual writers. See M3-f and M4-b.

G4-a Use adjectives to modify nouns.

Adjectives ordinarily precede the nouns they modify (*tall building*). But they can also function as subject complements or object complements, following the nouns they modify.

Subject complements

A subject complement follows a linking verb and completes the meaning of the subject. (See B2-b.) When an adjective functions as a subject complement, it describes the subject.

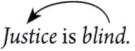
Justice is *blind.*

Verbs such as *smell, taste, look,* and *feel* may be linking verbs. If the word following one of these verbs describes the subject, use an adjective; if the word following the verb modifies the verb, use an adverb.

ADJECTIVE	The detective looked *cautious.*
ADVERB	The detective looked *cautiously* for fingerprints.

The adjective *cautious* describes the detective; the adverb *cautiously* modifies the verb *looked.*

Linking verbs suggest states of being, not actions. Notice, for example, the different meanings of *looked* in the preceding examples. To look cautious suggests the state of being cautious; to look cautiously is to perform an action in a cautious way.

> **For Multilingual Writers**   In English, adjectives are not made plural to agree with the words they modify: *The red* [not *reds*] *roses were a surprise.*

▶ The lilacs in our yard smell especially ~~sweetly~~ this year.
  ^{sweet}

The verb *smell* suggests a state of being, not an action. Therefore, it should be followed by an adjective, not an adverb.

▶ The drawings looked ~~well~~ after the architect made changes.
  ^{good}

The verb *looked* is a linking verb suggesting a state of being, not an action. The adjective *good* is appropriate following the linking verb to describe *drawings*. (See also G4-c.)

Object complements

An object complement follows a direct object and completes its meaning. (See B2-b.) When an adjective functions as an object complement, it describes the direct object.

Sorrow makes *us wise.*

Object complements occur with verbs such as *call, consider, create, find, keep,* and *make.* When a modifier follows the direct object of one of these verbs, use an adjective to describe the direct object; use an adverb to modify the verb.

| ADJECTIVE | The referee called the plays *perfect.* |
| ADVERB | The referee called the plays *perfectly.* |

The first sentence means that the referee considered the plays to be perfect; the second means that the referee did an excellent job of calling the plays.

G4-b Use adverbs to modify verbs, adjectives, and other adverbs.

When adverbs modify verbs (or verbals), they nearly always answer the question When? Where? How? Why? Under what conditions? How often? or To what degree? When adverbs modify adjectives or other adverbs, they usually qualify or intensify the meaning of the word they modify. (See B1-e.)

Adjectives are often used incorrectly in place of adverbs in casual speech.

▶ The travel arrangement worked out ~~perfect~~ for everyone.
                           perfectly

▶ The manager must see that the office runs ~~smooth~~ and ~~efficient.~~
                                     smoothly   *efficiently.*

The adverb *perfectly* modifies the verb *worked out*; the adverbs *smoothly* and *efficiently* modify the verb *runs*.

▶ The chance of recovering lost property looks ~~real~~ slim.
                                     really

Only adverbs can modify adjectives or other adverbs. *Really* intensifies the meaning of the adjective *slim*.

G4-c Distinguish between *good* and *well*, *bad* and *badly*.

Good is an adjective (*good performance*). *Well* is an adverb when it modifies a verb (*speak well*). The use of the adjective *good* in place of the adverb *well* to modify a verb is common in casual speech.

▶ We were glad that Sanya had done ~~good~~ on the CPA exam.
                            well

The adverb *well* modifies the verb *had done*.

Confusion can arise because *well* is an adjective when it modifies a noun or pronoun and means "healthy" or "satisfactory" (*The babies were well and warm*).

▶ Adrienne did not feel ~~well,~~ but she performed anyway.

As an adjective following the linking verb *did feel*, *well* describes Adrienne's health.

Bad is always an adjective and should be used to describe a noun; *badly* is always an adverb and should be used to modify a verb. The adverb *badly* is often used inappropriately to describe a noun, especially following a linking verb.

▶ The sisters felt ~~badly~~ when they realized they had left their brother

out of the planning.

The adjective *bad* is used after the linking verb *felt* to describe the noun *sisters*.

G4-d Use comparatives and superlatives with care.

Most adjectives and adverbs have three forms: the positive, the comparative, and the superlative.

POSITIVE	COMPARATIVE	SUPERLATIVE
fast	faster	fastest
friendly	friendlier	friendliest
carefully	more carefully	most carefully
bad	worse	worst
good	better	best

Comparative versus superlative

Use the comparative to compare two things, the superlative to compare three or more.

▶ Which of these two protein shakes is ~~best?~~ better?

▶ Zhao is the ~~more~~ most qualified of the three candidates running for state senator.

Forming comparatives and superlatives

To form comparatives and superlatives of most one- and two-syllable adjectives, use the endings -er and -est: smooth, smoother, smoothest; easy, easier, easiest. With longer adjectives, use more and most (or less and least for downward comparisons): exciting, more exciting, most exciting; helpful, less helpful, least helpful.

Some one-syllable adverbs take the endings -er and -est (fast, faster, fastest), but longer adverbs and all of those ending in -ly form the comparative and superlative with more and most (or less and least).

The comparative and superlative forms of some adjectives and adverbs are irregular: good, better, best; well, better, best; bad, worse, worst; badly, worse, worst.

▶ The Kirov is the ~~talentedest~~ most talented ballet company we have seen.

▶ According to our projections, sales at local businesses will be ~~worser~~ worse than those at the chain stores this winter.

Double comparatives or superlatives

Do not use double comparatives or superlatives. When you have added
-er or *-est* to an adjective or adverb, do not also use *more* or *most* (or *less* or
least).

▶ Of all her family, Julia is the ~~most~~ happiest about the move.

likely
▶ All the polls indicated that Gore was more ~~likelier~~ to win than Bush.

Absolute concepts

Avoid expressions such as *more straight, less perfect, very round,* and *most
unique.* Either something is unique or it isn't. It is illogical to suggest that absolute concepts come in degrees.

unusual
▶ That is the most ~~unique~~ wedding gown I have ever seen.

valuable
▶ The painting is more ~~priceless~~ because it is signed.

G4-e Avoid double negatives.

English uses two negatives only if a positive meaning is intended: *The orchestra was not unhappy with its performance* (meaning that the orchestra was
happy). Using a double negative to emphasize a negative meaning creates an
illogical sentence.

Negative modifiers such as *never, no,* and *not* should not be paired with
other negative modifiers or with negative words such as *neither, none, no one,
nobody,* and *nothing.*

anything
▶ The city is not doing ~~nothing~~ to see that the trash is collected during

the strike.

Not doing nothing suggests the opposite of the writer's intended meaning.

The modifiers *hardly, barely,* and *scarcely* are considered negatives in
English, so they should not be used with negatives such as *not, no one,* and
never.

can
▶ Maxine is so weak that she ~~can't~~ hardly climb stairs.

G5 Sentence fragments

A sentence fragment is a word group that pretends to be a sentence. Sentence fragments are easy to recognize when they appear out of context, like these:

> When the cat leaped onto the table.

> Running for the bus.

When fragments appear next to related sentences, however, they are harder to spot.

> We had just sat down to dinner. When the cat leaped onto the table.

> I tripped and twisted my ankle. Running for the bus.

Recognizing sentence fragments

To be a sentence, a word group must consist of at least one full independent clause. An independent clause includes a subject and a verb, and it either stands alone or could stand alone.

To test whether a word group is a complete sentence or a fragment, use the flowchart in this chapter. By using the flowchart, you can see exactly why *When the cat leaped onto the table* is a fragment: It has a subject (*cat*) and a verb (*leaped*), but it begins with a subordinating word (*When*). *Running for the bus* is a fragment because it lacks a subject and a verb (*Running* is a verbal, not a verb). (See also B3-b and B3-e.)

Repairing sentence fragments

You can repair most fragments in one of two ways:

- Pull the fragment into a nearby sentence.
- Rewrite the fragment as a complete sentence.

▶ We had just sat down to dinner./~~When~~ ^when^ the cat leaped onto the table.

▶ ^Running for the bus,^ I tripped and twisted my ankle. ~~Running for the bus.~~

> **For Multilingual Writers**   Unlike some other languages, English requires a subject and a verb in every sentence (except in commands, where the subject *you* is understood but not present: *Sit down*). See M3-a and M3-b.
>
> ▶ Students usually ^are^ very busy at the end of the semester.

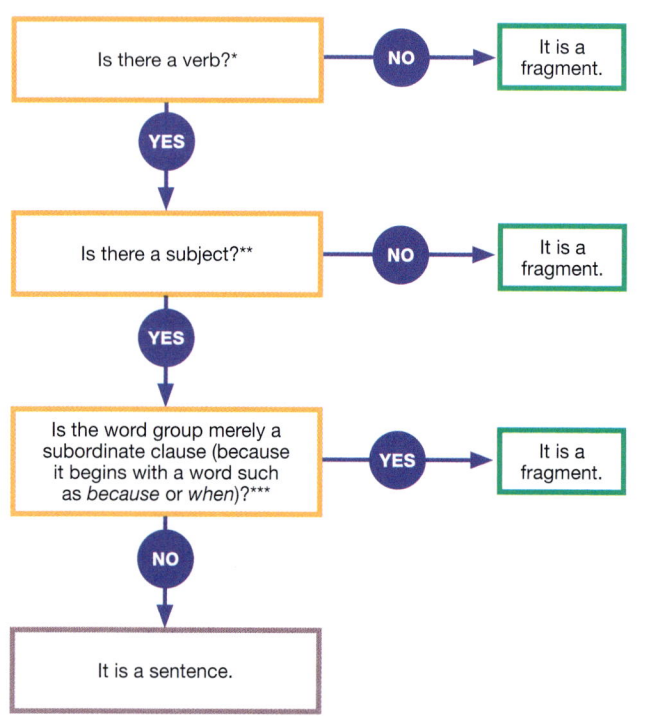

Test for fragments

*Do not mistake verbals for verbs. A verbal is a verb form (such as *walking* or *to act*) that does not function as the verb of a clause. (See B3-b.)

**The subject of a sentence may be *you*, understood but not present in the sentence. (See B2-a.)

***A sentence may open with a subordinate clause, but the sentence must also include an independent clause. (See G5-a and B4-a.)

If you find any fragments, try one of these methods of revision (see G5-a to G5-c):

1. Attach the fragment to a nearby sentence.

2. Rewrite the fragment as a complete sentence.

G5-a Attach fragmented subordinate clauses or turn them into sentences.

A subordinate clause is patterned like a sentence, with both a subject and a verb, but it begins with a word that marks it as subordinate. The following words commonly introduce subordinate clauses.

after	if	when
although	since	where
as	so that	whether
because	than	which
before	that	while
even though	unless	who
how	until	why

Subordinate clauses function within sentences as adjectives, as adverbs, or as nouns. They cannot stand alone. (See B3-e.)

Most fragmented clauses can be pulled into a sentence nearby.

>   *because*
> ▶ **Americans have come to fear the Zika virus/~~Because~~ it is transmitted**
>   ^
>
> **by the common mosquito.**

Because introduces a subordinate clause, so it cannot stand alone. (For punctuation of subordinate clauses appearing at the end of a sentence, see P2-f.)

> ▶ **Although psychiatrist Peter Kramer expresses concerns about**
>   *many*
> **Prozac/, ~~Many~~ other doctors believe that the benefits of**
>   ^
>
> **antidepressants outweigh the risks.**

Although introduces a subordinate clause, so it cannot stand alone. (For punctuation of subordinate clauses at the beginning of a sentence, see P1-b.)

If a fragmented clause cannot be attached to a nearby sentence or if you feel that attaching it would be awkward, try turning the clause into a sentence. The simplest way to do this is to delete the opening word or words that mark it as subordinate.

> ▶ **Uncontrolled development is taking a toll on the environment.**
>   *Across*
> **~~So that across~~ the globe, fragile ecosystems are collapsing.**
>   ^

G5-b Attach fragmented phrases or turn them into sentences.

Like subordinate clauses, phrases function within sentences as adjectives, as adverbs, or as nouns. They cannot stand alone. Fragmented phrases are often prepositional or verbal phrases; sometimes they are appositives, words or word groups that rename nouns or pronouns. (See B3-a, B3-b, and B3-c.)

Often a fragmented phrase may simply be pulled into a nearby sentence.

▶ The archaeologists worked slowly/, ~~Examining~~ and labeling every
  examining

  pottery shard they uncovered.

The word group beginning with *Examining* is a verbal phrase.

▶ The patient displayed symptoms of ALS/, ~~A~~ neurodegenerative
  a

  disease.

A neurodegenerative disease is an appositive renaming the noun *ALS*. (For punctuation of appositives, see P1-e.)

If a fragmented phrase cannot be pulled into a nearby sentence effectively, turn the phrase into a sentence. You may need to add a subject, a verb, or both.

▶ Jamie explained how to access our new database. ~~Also~~ how to
  She also taught us

  submit expense reports and request vendor payments.

The revision turns the fragmented phrase into a sentence by adding a subject and a verb.

G5-c Attach other fragmented word groups or turn them into sentences.

Other word groups that are commonly fragmented include parts of compound predicates, lists, and examples introduced by *for example, in addition,* or similar expressions.

Parts of compound predicates

A predicate consists of a verb and its objects, complements, and modifiers (see B2-b). A compound predicate includes two or more predicates joined with a coordinating conjunction such as *and, but,* or *or.* Because the parts of a compound predicate have the same subject, they should appear in the same sentence.

▶ The woodpecker finch of the Galápagos Islands carefully selects a
                               and
twig of a certain size and shape/~~And~~ then uses this tool to pry out
                               ^
grubs from trees.

The subject is *finch*, and the compound predicate is *selects . . . and . . . uses*. (For
punctuation of compound predicates, see P2-a.)

Lists

To correct a fragmented list, often you can attach it to a nearby sentence with a
colon or a dash. (See P3-d and P6-b.)

▶ It has been said that there are only three indigenous American art
               musical
forms/: ~~Musical~~ comedy, jazz, and soap opera.
      ^

Sometimes terms such as *especially*, *namely*, *like*, and *such as* introduce
fragmented lists. Such fragments can usually be attached to the preceding
sentence.

▶ In the twentieth century, the South produced some great American
                such
writers/, ~~Such~~ as Flannery O'Connor, William Faulkner, Alice
      ^
Walker, and Tennessee Williams.

Examples introduced by *for example*, *in addition*, or similar expressions

Other expressions that introduce examples or explanations can lead to unintentional fragments. Although you may begin a sentence with some of the following words or phrases, make sure that what follows has a subject and a verb.

also	for example	mainly
and	for instance	or
but	in addition	that is

Often the easiest solution is to turn the fragment into a sentence.

▶ In his memoir, Primo Levi describes the horrors of living in a
                          he worked
concentration camp. For example, ~~working~~ without food and
suffered
~~suffering~~ emotional abuse.
^

The writer corrected this fragment by adding a subject — *he* — and substituting
verbs for the verbals *working* and *suffering*.

G5-d Exception: A fragment may be used for effect.

Writers occasionally use sentence fragments for special purposes.

FOR EMPHASIS	Following the dramatic Americanization of their children, even my parents grew more publicly confident. *Especially my mother.*
	— Richard Rodriguez
TO ANSWER A QUESTION	Are these new drug tests 100 percent reliable? *Not in the opinion of most experts.*
TRANSITIONS	*And now the opposing arguments.*
EXCLAMATIONS	*Not again!*
IN ADVERTISING	*Fewer carbs. Improved taste.*

Although fragments are sometimes appropriate, writers and readers do not always agree on when they are appropriate. For most college writing, you will find it safer to write in complete sentences.

G6 Run-on sentences

Run-on sentences are independent clauses that have not been joined correctly. An independent clause is a word group that can stand alone as a sentence. (See B4-a.) When two independent clauses appear in one sentence, they must be joined in one of these ways:

- with a comma and a coordinating conjunction (*and, but, or, nor, for, so, yet*)
- with a semicolon (or occasionally with a colon or a dash)

Recognizing run-on sentences

There are two types of run-on sentences. When a writer puts no mark of punctuation and no coordinating conjunction between independent clauses, the result is called a *fused sentence.*

┌────── INDEPENDENT CLAUSE ──────┐ ┌──────

FUSED   Air pollution poses risks to all humans it can be

──── INDEPENDENT CLAUSE ───┐
deadly for people with asthma.

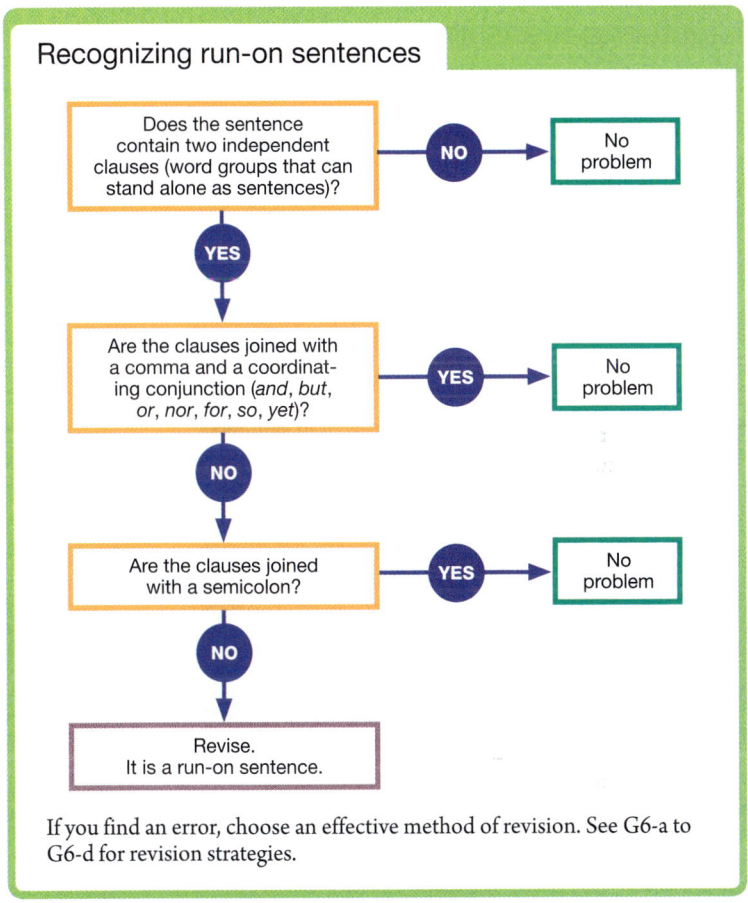

Recognizing run-on sentences

Does the sentence contain two independent clauses (word groups that can stand alone as sentences)? — **NO** → No problem

YES

Are the clauses joined with a comma and a coordinating conjunction (*and, but, or, nor, for, so, yet*)? — **YES** → No problem

NO

Are the clauses joined with a semicolon? — **YES** → No problem

NO

Revise. It is a run-on sentence.

If you find an error, choose an effective method of revision. See G6-a to G6-d for revision strategies.

A far more common type of run-on sentence is the *comma splice* — two or more independent clauses joined with a comma but without a coordinating conjunction. In some comma splices, the comma appears alone.

COMMA SPLICE	Air pollution poses risks to all humans, it can be deadly for people with asthma.

In other comma splices, the comma is accompanied by a joining word that is *not* a coordinating conjunction. There are only seven coordinating conjunctions in English: *and, but, or, nor, for, so,* and *yet.*

COMMA SPLICE	Air pollution poses risks to all humans, however, it can be deadly for people with asthma.

However is a transitional expression, not a coordinating conjunction, and cannot be used with only a comma to join two independent clauses (see G6-b).

Writer's Choice
Clustering ideas in meaningful ways

When you draft, you may rush to write down your ideas before you forget them. Writers at all levels of experience do this. When you're generating ideas, you may not worry too much about grammar and punctuation, so you may end up with some run-on sentences. In later drafts you will need to revise so that your **audience** understands your meaning.

RUN-ON SENTENCE Students can succeed in college by attending classes and keeping up with homework, visiting instructors during office hours can also be important, participating in campus events and clubs can help students succeed, too.

Several ideas compete for attention in this draft sentence:

- Students can succeed in college.
- Attending classes is important.
- Doing homework is important.
- Visiting instructors during office hours is important.
- Participating in campus events can help students succeed.
- Participating in campus clubs can help students succeed.

As a writer, ask yourself: How can I cluster the ideas in a way that best communicates my meaning?

POSSIBLE REVISION Students can succeed in college by attending classes and keeping up with homework, by visiting instructors during office hours, and by participating in campus events and clubs.

POSSIBLE REVISION In addition to attending class and keeping up with homework, students can succeed in college by visiting instructors during office hours. Participating in campus events and clubs is another way to foster success.

In each revision, the ideas are clustered, making the passage easier to read. The first revision places equal emphasis on all the different actions students can take to succeed in college. The second revision focuses on the importance of communicating with instructors.

Identifying, separating, and grouping ideas — all with your **purpose** and **audience** in mind — can help you revise run-on sentences.

Revise a run-on sentence

To revise a run-on sentence, you have four choices.

1 Use a comma and a coordinating conjunction (*and, but, or, nor, for, so, yet*).

▶ Air pollution poses risks to all humans, ^*but* it can be deadly for people with asthma.

2 Use a semicolon (or, if appropriate, a colon or a dash). A semicolon may be used alone; it can also be accompanied by a transitional expression.

▶ Air pollution poses risks to all humans/; ^ it can be deadly for people with asthma.

▶ Air pollution poses risks to all humans/; ^*however,* it can be deadly for people with asthma.

3 Make the clauses into separate sentences.

▶ Air pollution poses risks to all humans/. ~~it~~ ^*It* can be deadly for people with asthma.

4 Restructure the sentence; try subordinating a clause.

▶ *Although air* ^ ~~Air~~ pollution poses risks to all humans, it can be deadly for people with asthma.

One of these revision techniques usually works better than the others for a particular sentence. The fourth technique, the one requiring the most extensive revision, is often the most effective.

G6-a Consider separating the clauses with a comma and a coordinating conjunction.

There are seven coordinating conjunctions in English: *and, but, or, nor, for, so,* and *yet.* When a coordinating conjunction joins independent clauses, it is usually preceded by a comma. (See P1-a.)

▶ Some lesson plans include exercises, **but** completing them should not be the focus of all class periods.

▶ Many law enforcement officials admit that the polygraph is unreliable, ~~however,~~ **yet** they still use it as an assessment tool.

However is a transitional expression, not a coordinating conjunction, so it cannot be used with only a comma to join independent clauses. (See also G6-b.)

G6-b Consider separating the clauses with a semicolon, a colon, or a dash.

When the independent clauses are closely related and their relation is clear without a coordinating conjunction, a semicolon is one acceptable method of revision. (See P3-a.)

▶ Tragedy depicts the individual confronted with the fact of death**/;** comedy depicts the adaptability of human nature.

A semicolon is required between independent clauses that have been linked with a transitional expression such as *however, therefore, moreover, in fact,* or *for example.* (For a longer list, see P3-a.)

▶ In her film adaptation, the director changed key details of the plot**/;** in fact, she added whole scenes that do not appear in the story.

A colon or a dash may be more appropriate if the first independent clause introduces the second or if the second clause summarizes or explains the first. (See P3-d and P6-b.) In formal writing, the colon is usually preferred to the dash.

▶ Nuclear waste is hazardous: ~~this~~ **This** is an indisputable fact.

▶ The female black widow spider is often a widow of her own

making/she has been known to eat her partner after mating.

A colon is an appropriate method of revision if the first independent clause introduces a quoted sentence.

▶ Nobel Peace Prize winner Al Gore had this to say about climate

change/: "The truth is that our circumstances are not only new; they

are completely different than they have ever been in all of human

history."

G6-c Consider making the clauses into separate sentences.

▶ Why should we spend money on space exploration/? ~~we~~ **We** have

enough underfunded programs here on Earth.

A question and a statement should be separate sentences.

▶ Some studies have suggested that sexual relationships set

bonobos apart from common chimpanzees/. ~~according~~ **According** to

some scientists, these differences have been exaggerated.

Using a comma alone to join two independent clauses creates a comma splice.

NOTE: When two quoted independent clauses are divided by explanatory words, make each clause its own sentence.

▶ "It's always smart to learn from your mistakes," my supervisor

declared/. "~~it's~~ **"It's** even smarter to learn from the mistakes of

others."

G6-d Consider restructuring the sentence, perhaps by subordinating one of the clauses.

If one of the independent clauses is less important than the other, turn the less important clause into a subordinate clause or phrase. (For more about subordination, see S6.)

▶ One of the most famous advertising slogans is Wheaties cereal's
"Breakfast of Champions," ~~it~~ associated the cereal with famous
    ^which
athletes.

▶ Mary McLeod Bethune, ~~was~~ the seventeenth child of former slaves,
~~she~~ founded the National Council of Negro Women.

Minor ideas in these sentences are now expressed in subordinate clauses or phrases.

M

Multilingual Writers and ESL Topics

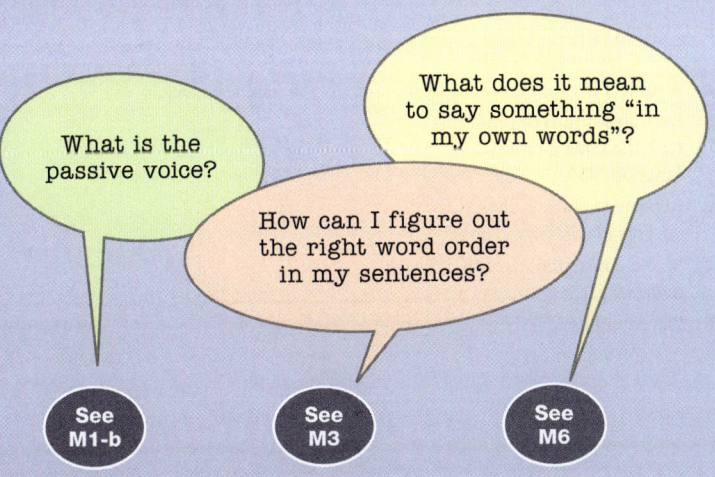

What is the passive voice?

See M1-b

How can I figure out the right word order in my sentences?

See M3

What does it mean to say something "in my own words"?

See M6

M Multilingual Writers and ESL Topics

This section of *A Writer's Reference* is primarily for multilingual writers. You may find this section helpful if you learned English as a second language (ESL) or if you speak a language other than English or a variety of English your friends and family.

M1 Verbs

Both native and nonnative speakers of English encounter challenges with verbs. Section M1 focuses on specific challenges that multilingual writers sometimes face. You can find more help with verbs in other sections in the book:

> making subjects and verbs agree (G1)
> using irregular verb forms (G2-a, G2-b)
> using correct verb endings (G2-c, G2-d)
> choosing the correct verb tense (G2-f)
> avoiding inappropriate uses of the passive voice (W3-a)

M1-a Use the appropriate verb form and tense.

This section offers a brief review of English verb forms and tenses. For additional help, see G2-f and B1-c.

Basic verb forms

Every main verb in English has five forms, which are used to create all of the verb tenses in English. The Basic verb forms chart shows these forms for the regular verb *help* and the irregular verbs *give* and *be*. See G2-a for a list of common irregular verbs.

Basic verb forms

	Regular verb *help*	Irregular verb *give*	Irregular verb *be**
BASE FORM	help	give	be
PAST TENSE	helped	gave	was, were
PAST PARTICIPLE	helped	given	been
PRESENT PARTICIPLE	helping	giving	being
-S FORM	helps	gives	is

*Be also has the forms *am* and *are*, which are used in the present tense.

Verb tenses

Section G2-f describes all the verb tenses in English, showing the forms of a regular verb (*walk*), an irregular verb (*ride*), and the verb *be* in each tense. The chart in M1-a provides more details about the tenses commonly used in the active voice in writing; the chart in M1-b gives details about tenses commonly used in the passive voice.

Verb tenses commonly used in the active voice

For descriptions and examples of all verb tenses, see G2-f. For verb tenses commonly used in the passive voice, see the chart in M1-b.

Simple tenses

For general facts, states of being, habitual actions

Simple present	Base form or *-s* form
● general facts	College students often *study* late at night.
● states of being	Water *becomes* steam at 100 degrees centigrade.
● habitual, repetitive actions	We *donate* to a different charity each year.
● scheduled future events	The train *arrives* tomorrow at 6:30 p.m.

NOTE: For other uses of the present tense, see G1.

Simple past	Base form + *-ed* or *-d* or irregular form
● actions completed at a specific time in the past	The storm *destroyed* their property. She *drove* to Montana three years ago.
● facts or states of being in the past	When I *was* young, I usually *walked* to school with my sister.

Simple future	*will* + base form
● future actions, promises, or predictions	I *will exercise* tomorrow. The snowfall *will begin* around midnight.

Simple progressive forms

For continuing actions

Present progressive	*am, is, are* + present participle
● actions in progress at the present time, not continuing indefinitely	The students *are taking* an exam in Room 105. The valet *is parking* the car.
● future actions (with *leave, go, come, move*, etc.)	I *am leaving* tomorrow morning.

Verb tenses commonly used in the active voice, *continued*

Past progressive — ***was, were* + present participle**

- actions in progress at a specific time in the past — They *were swimming* when the storm struck.

- *was going to, were going to* for past plans that did not happen — We *were going to* drive to Florida for spring break, but the car broke down.

NOTE: Some verbs are not normally used in the progressive: *appear, believe, belong, contain, have, hear, know, like, need, see, seem, taste, understand,* and *want.*

>   want
> ▶ I ~~am wanting~~ to see August Wilson's *Radio Golf.*
>   ^

Perfect tenses

For actions that happened before another present or past time

Present perfect — ***has, have* + past participle**

- repetitive or constant actions that began in the past and continue to the present — I *have loved* cats since I was a child. Amy *has worked* in Kenya for ten years.

- actions that happened at an unknown or unspecific time in the past — Ola *has visited* Aleppo three times.

Past perfect — ***had* + past participle**

- actions that began or occurred before another time in the past — She *had* just *crossed* the street when the runaway car crashed into the building.

NOTE: For more on the past perfect, see G2-f. For uses of the past perfect in conditional sentences, see M1-e.

Perfect progressive forms

For continuous past actions before another present or past time

Present perfect progressive — ***has, have* + *been* + present participle**

- continuous actions that began in the past and continue to the present — Yolanda *has been trying* to get a job in Boston for five years.

Past perfect progressive — ***had* + *been* + present participle**

- actions that began and continued in the past until another past action — By the time I moved to Georgia, I *had been supporting* myself for five years.

M1-b To write a verb in the passive voice, use a form of *be* with the past participle.

When a sentence is written in the passive voice, the subject receives the action instead of doing it. (See W3-a.)

> The solution *was measured* by the lab assistant.

> The picnic *has been rescheduled* twice because of rain.

To form the passive voice, use a form of *be* — *am, is, are, was, were, being, be,* or *been* — followed by the past participle of the main verb: *was chosen, are remembered.* (Sometimes a form of *be* follows another helping verb: *will be considered, could have been broken.*)

▶ *Dreaming in Cuban* was ~~writing~~ by Cristina García.
                 written

In the passive voice, the past participle *written,* not the present participle *writing,* must follow *was* (the past tense of *be*).

▶ The child is being ~~test.~~
                tested.

The past participle *tested,* not the base form *test,* must be used with *is being* to form the passive voice.

For details on forming the passive voice in various tenses, consult the following chart. (The active voice is generally stronger and more direct than the passive. The passive voice does have appropriate uses; see W3-a.)

Verb tenses commonly used in the passive voice

For details about commonly used verb tenses in the active voice, see the chart in M1-a.

Simple tenses (passive voice)

Simple present
- general facts
- habitual, repetitive actions

am, is, are + past participle
Breakfast *is served* daily.
The receipts *are counted* every night.

Simple past
- completed past actions

was, were + past participle
He *was punished* for being late.

Verb tenses commonly used in the passive voice, *continued*

Simple future

will be + past participle

- future actions, promises, or predictions

The decision *will be made* by the committee next week.

Simple progressive forms (passive voice)

Present progressive

am, is, are + being + past participle

- actions in progress at the present time

The new stadium *is being built* with private money.

- future actions (with *leave, go, come, move,* etc.)

Jo *is being moved* to a new class next month.

Past progressive

was, were + being + past participle

- actions in progress at a specific time in the past

We thought we *were being followed.*

Perfect tenses (passive voice)

Present perfect

has, have + been + past participle

- actions that began in the past and continue to the present

The flight *has been delayed* because of storms in the Midwest.

- actions that happened at an unknown or unspecific time in the past

Wars *have been fought* throughout history.

Past perfect

had + been + past participle

- actions that began or occurred before another time in the past

He *had been given* all the hints he needed to complete the puzzle.

NOTE: Future progressive, future perfect, and perfect progressive forms are not used in the passive voice.

M1-c Use the base form of the verb after a modal.

The modal verbs are *can, could, may, might, must, shall, should, will,* and *would.* (*Ought to* is also considered a modal verb.) The modals are used with the base form of a verb to show ability, certainty, necessity, permission, obligation, or possibility.

Modals and the verbs that follow them do not change form to indicate tense. For a summary of modals and their meanings, see the chart in this section. (See also G2-e.)

▶ The art museum will <u>launch</u>es its fundraising campaign next month.
                          ^

The modal *will* must be followed by the base form *launch*, not the present-tense form *launches*.

▶ The translator could <u>speak</u>e many languages, so the ambassador
                         ^

hired her for the European tour.

The modal *could* must be followed by the base form *speak*, not the past-tense form *spoke*.

TIP: Do not use *to* before a main verb that follows a modal.

▶ Gina can ~~to~~ drive us home if we miss the last train.

For the use of modals in conditional sentences, see M1-e.

Modals and their meanings

can

- general ability (present)   Ants *can survive* anywhere, even in space. Jorge *can run* a marathon faster than his brother.
- informal requests or permission   *Can* you *tell* me where the light is? Sandy *can borrow* my calculator.

could

- general ability (past)   Lea *could read* when she was only three years old.
- polite, informal requests or permission   *Could* you *give* me that pen?

may

- formal requests or permission   *May* I *see* the report? Students *may park* only in the yellow zone.
- possibility   I *may try* to finish my homework tonight, or I *may wake up* early and *finish* it tomorrow.

might

- possibility   Funding for the language lab *might double* by 2021.

NOTE: *Might* usually expresses a stronger possibility than *may*.

Modals and their meanings, *continued*

must

- necessity (present or future)

  To be effective, welfare-to-work programs *must provide* access to job training.

- strong probability

  Amy *must be* nervous. [She is probably nervous.]

- near certainty (present or past)

  I *must have left* my wallet at home. [I almost certainly left my wallet at home.]

should

- suggestions or advice

  Diabetics *should drink* plenty of water every day.

- obligations or duties

  The government *should protect* citizens' rights.

- expectations

  The books *should arrive* soon. [We expect the books to arrive soon.]

will

- certainty

  If you don't leave now, you *will be* late for your rehearsal.

- requests

  Will you *help* me study for my psychology exam?

- promises and offers

  Jonah *will arrange* the carpool.

would

- polite requests

  Would you *help* me carry these books? I *would like* some coffee. [*Would like* is more polite than *want*.]

- habitual or repeated actions (in the past)

  Whenever Elena needed help with sewing, she *would call* her aunt.

M1-d To make negative verb forms, add *not* in the appropriate place.

If the verb is the simple present or past tense of *be* (*am, is, are, was, were*), add *not* after the verb to form a negative statement.

George is *not* a member of the club.

For simple present-tense verbs other than *be*, use *do* or *does* plus *not* before the base form of the verb. (For the correct forms of *do* and *does*, see the Subject-verb agreement at a glance chart in G1-a.)

▶ Mariko ~~not~~ want more dessert.
  does ^

▶ Mariko does not want~~s~~ more dessert.

For simple past-tense verbs other than *be*, use *did* plus *not* before the base form of the verb.

▶ They did not ~~planted~~ corn this year.
  plant ^

In a verb phrase consisting of one or more helping verbs and a present or past participle (*is watching, were living, has played, could have been driven*), use the word *not* after the first helping verb.

▶ Inna should have ~~not~~ gone dancing last night.
  not ^

▶ Bonnie is ~~no~~ singing this weekend.
  not ^

NOTE: English allows only one negative in an independent clause to express a negative idea; using more than one is an error known as a *double negative* (see G4-e).

▶ We could not find ~~no~~ books about the history of our school.
  any ^

M1-e In a conditional sentence, choose verb tenses according to the type of condition expressed in the sentence.

Conditional sentences contain two clauses: a subordinate clause (usually starting with *if, when,* or *unless*) and an independent clause. The subordinate clause (sometimes called the *if* or *unless* clause) states the condition or cause; the independent clause states the result or effect. In each example in this section, the subordinate clause (*if* clause) is marked SUB, and the independent clause is marked IND. (See B3-e, on subordinate clauses.)

Factual

Factual conditional sentences express relationships based on facts. If the relationship is a scientific truth, use the present tense in both clauses.

┌──────── SUB ────────┐ ┌─ IND ─┐
If water *cools* to 32 degrees Fahrenheit, it *freezes.*

If the sentence describes a condition that is (or was) habitually true, use the same tense in both clauses.

┌───── SUB ─────┐ ┌───── IND ─────┐
When Sue *jogs* along the canal, her dog *runs* ahead of her.

┌───── SUB ─────┐ ┌─── IND ───┐
Whenever the coach *asked* for help, I *volunteered*.

Predictive

Predictive conditional sentences are used to predict the future or to express future plans or possibilities. To form a predictive sentence, use a present-tense verb in the subordinate clause; in the independent clause, use the modal *will*, *can*, *may*, *should*, or *might* plus the base form of the verb.

┌───── SUB ─────┐ ┌───── IND ─────┐
If you *practice* regularly, your tennis game *should improve*.

┌───── SUB ─────┐ ┌──── IND ────┐
We *will lose* our remaining wetlands unless we *act* now.

TIP: In all types of conditional sentences (factual, predictive, and speculative), *if* or *unless* clauses do not use the modal verb *will*.

▶ If Liv ~~will pass~~ her history test, she will graduate this year.
   passes
   ^

Speculative

Speculative conditional sentences express unlikely, contrary-to-fact, or impossible conditions. English uses the past or past perfect tense in the *if* clause, even for conditions in the present or the future.

Unlikely possibilities If the condition is possible but unlikely in the present or the future, use the past tense in the subordinate clause; in the independent clause, use *would*, *could*, or *might* plus the base form of the verb.

┌──── SUB ────┐ ┌──── IND ────┐
If I *won* the lottery, I *would travel* to Egypt.

The writer does not expect to win the lottery. Because this is a possible but unlikely present or future situation, the past tense is used in the subordinate clause.

Conditions contrary to fact In conditions that are currently unreal or contrary to fact, use the past-tense verb *were* (not *was*) in the *if* clause for all subjects. (See also G2-g, on the subjunctive mood.)

> were
▶ If I ~~was~~ president, I would make student loan debt a priority.
  ^

The writer is not president, so *were* is correct in the *if* clause.

Events that did not happen In a conditional sentence that speculates about an event that did not happen or was impossible in the past, use the past perfect tense in the *if* clause; in the independent clause, use *would have, could have,* or *might have* with the past participle. (See also past perfect tense, p. 411.)

```
         ┌──────── SUB ────────┐ ┌──────────── IND ────────────┐
         If I had saved more money, I would have visited Laos last year.
```

The writer did not save more money and did not travel to Laos. This sentence shows a possibility that did not happen.

M1-f Become familiar with verbs that may be followed by gerunds or infinitives.

A gerund is a verb form that ends in *-ing* and is used as a noun: *sleeping, dreaming.* An infinitive is the word *to* plus the base form of the verb: *to sleep, to dream.* The word *to* is an infinitive marker, not a preposition, in this use. (See B3-b.)

A few verbs may be followed by either a gerund or an infinitive; others may be followed by a gerund but not by an infinitive; still others may be followed by an infinitive but not by a gerund.

Verb + gerund or infinitive (no change in meaning)

The following commonly used verbs may be followed by a gerund or an infinitive, with little or no difference in meaning:

begin	hate	love
continue	like	start

I love *skiing*. I love *to ski*.

Verb + gerund or infinitive (change in meaning)

With a few verbs, the choice of a gerund or an infinitive changes the meaning dramatically:

forget	stop
remember	try

She stopped *speaking* to Lucia. [She no longer spoke to Lucia.]

She stopped *to speak* to Lucia. [She paused so that she could speak to Lucia.]

Verb + gerund

These verbs may be followed by a gerund but not by an infinitive:

admit	discuss	imagine	put off	risk
appreciate	enjoy	miss	quit	suggest
avoid	escape	postpone	recall	tolerate
deny	finish	practice	resist	

Bill enjoys *playing* [not *to play*] the piano.

Jamie quit *smoking*.

Verb + infinitive

These verbs may be followed by an infinitive but not by a gerund:

agree	decide	manage	plan	wait
ask	expect	mean	pretend	want
beg	help	need	promise	wish
claim	hope	offer	refuse	would like

Jill has offered *to water* [not *watering*] the plants while we are away.

Joe finally managed *to find* a parking space.

A few of these verbs may be followed either by an infinitive directly or by a noun or pronoun plus an infinitive:

ask	help	promise	would like
expect	need	want	

We asked *to speak* to the congregation.

We asked *Rabbi Abrams to speak* to our congregation.

Verb + noun or pronoun + infinitive

With certain verbs in the active voice, a noun or pronoun must come between the verb and the infinitive that follows it. The noun or pronoun usually names a person who is affected by the action of the verb.

advise	encourage	remind
allow	have ("own")	require
cause	instruct	tell
command	order	warn
convince	persuade	

The class encouraged Luis to tell the story of his escape.

The counselor *advised Haley to take* four courses instead of five.

Verb + noun or pronoun + unmarked infinitive

An unmarked infinitive is an infinitive without *to*. A few verbs (often called *causative verbs*) may be followed by a noun or pronoun and an unmarked infinitive.

> have ("cause")
> help
> let ("allow")
> make ("force")

▶ Rose had the attendant ~~to~~ wash the windshield.

▶ Frank made me ~~to~~ carry his book for him.

▶ Administrators will not let students ~~to~~ return to campus until the governor has lifted the state of emergency.

Help can be followed by a noun or pronoun and either an unmarked or a marked infinitive.

Emma *helped Brian wash* the dishes.

Emma *helped Brian to wash* the dishes.

NOTE: The infinitive is used in some typical constructions with *too* and *enough*.

TOO + ADJECTIVE + INFINITIVE
The gift is *too large to wrap*.

ENOUGH + NOUN + INFINITIVE
Our emergency pack has *enough bottled water to last* a week.

ADJECTIVE + *ENOUGH* + INFINITIVE
Some of the hikers felt *strong enough to climb* another thousand feet.

M2 Articles

Articles (*a, an, the*) are part of a category of words known as *noun markers* or *determiners*.

M2-a Be familiar with articles and other noun markers.

English uses noun markers to help identify the nouns that follow. In addition to articles (*a, an,* and *the*), noun markers include the following, which are covered in other sections of this book:

- possessive nouns, such as *Elena's* (P4-a)
- possessive pronoun/adjectives: *my, your, his, her, its, our, their* (B1-b)
- demonstrative pronoun/adjectives: *this, that, these, those* (B1-b)
- quantifiers: *all, any, each, either, every, few, many, more, most, much, neither, several, some,* and so on (M2-d)
- numbers: *one, twenty-three,* and so on

Using articles and other noun markers

Articles and other noun markers always appear before nouns; sometimes other modifiers, such as adjectives and adverbs, come between a noun marker and a noun.

> ART N
> Felix is reading a book about mythology.

> ART ADJ   N
> We took an exciting trip to Alaska last summer.

> NOUN
> MARKER ADV   ADJ   N
> That very delicious meal was expensive.

In most cases, do not use an article with another noun marker.

▶ ~~The~~ Natalie's older brother lives in Wisconsin.

Expressions like *a few, the most,* and *all the* are exceptions: *a few potatoes, all the rain.* See also M2-d.

Types of articles and types of nouns

To choose an appropriate article for a noun, first determine whether the noun is *common* or *proper*, *count* or *noncount*, *singular* or *plural*, and *specific* or *general*. The chart in M2-a describes the types of nouns.

Articles are classified as *indefinite* and *definite*. The indefinite articles, *a* and *an*, are used with general nouns. The definite article, *the*, is used with specific nouns. (The last section of the Types of nouns chart explains general and specific nouns.)

A and *an* both mean "one" or "one among many." Use *a* before a consonant sound: *a banana, a vacation, a happy child, a united family*. Use *an* before a vowel sound: *an eggplant, an uncle, an honorable person*.

The shows that a noun is specific; use *the* with one or more than one specific thing: *the newspaper, the soldiers*.

M2-b Use *the* with most specific common nouns.

The definite article, *the*, is used with most nouns — both count and noncount — that the reader can identify specifically. Usually the identity will be clear to the reader for one of the following reasons.

1. The noun has been previously mentioned.

▶ A truck cut in front of our van. When *the* truck skidded a few seconds

   later, we almost crashed into it.

   > The article *A* is used before *truck* when the noun is first mentioned. When the noun is mentioned again, it needs the article *the* because readers can now identify which truck skidded — the one that cut in front of the van.

2. A phrase or clause following the noun restricts its identity.

▶ Bryce warned me that *the* GPS in his car was not working.

   > The phrase *in his car* identifies the specific GPS.

NOTE: Descriptive adjectives do not necessarily make a noun specific. A specific noun is one that readers can identify within a group of nouns of the same type.

▶ If I win the lottery, I will buy ~~the~~ *a* brand-new bright red sports car.

   > The reader cannot identify which specific brand-new bright red sports car the writer will buy. Even though *car* has many adjectives in front of it, it is a general noun in this sentence.

3.   A superlative adjective such as *best* or *most intelligent* makes the noun's identity specific. (See also G4-d.)

                   the
▶ **Our petite daughter dated tallest boy in her class.**
                              ^

The superlative *tallest* makes the noun *boy* specific. Although there might be several tall boys, only one boy can be the tallest.

4.   The noun describes a unique person, place, or thing.

                                      the
▶ **During an eclipse, one should not look directly at sun.**
                                             ^

There is only one sun in our solar system, so its identity is clear.

5.   The context or situation makes the noun's identity clear.

                 the
▶ **Please don't slam door when you leave.**
                     ^

Both the speaker and the listener know which door is meant.

6.   The noun is singular and refers to a scientific class or category of items (most often animals, musical instruments, and inventions).

                The tin
▶ ~~Tin~~ **whistle is common in traditional Irish music.**
       ^

The writer is referring to the tin whistle as a class of musical instruments.

Types of nouns

Common or proper

Common nouns
- name general persons, places, things, or ideas
- begin with lowercase

Examples

religion	beauty
knowledge	student
rain	country

Proper nouns
- name specific persons, places, things, or ideas
- begin with capital letter

Examples

Hinduism	President Adams
Philip	Washington Monument
New Jersey	Supreme Court
Vietnam	Renaissance

➡

Types of nouns, *continued*

Count or noncount (common nouns only)

Count nouns
- name persons, places, things, or ideas that can be counted
- have plural forms

Examples
girl, girls
city, cities
goose, geese
philosophy, philosophies

Noncount nouns
- name things or abstract ideas that cannot be counted
- cannot be made plural

Examples
water   patience
silver   knowledge
furniture   air

NOTE: See M2-c for lists of commonly used noncount nouns.

Singular or plural (both common and proper)

Singular nouns (count and noncount)
- represent one person, place, thing, or idea

Examples
backpack   rain
country   beauty
woman   Nile River
achievement   Block Island

Plural nouns (count only)
- represent more than one person, place, thing, or idea
- must be count nouns

Examples
backpacks   Ural Mountains
countries   Falkland Islands
women   achievements

Specific (definite) or general (indefinite) (count and noncount)

Specific nouns
- name persons, places, things, or ideas that can be identified within a group of the same type

Examples
The students in Professor Martin's *class* should study.

The airplane carrying *the senator* was late.

The furniture in *the truck* was damaged.

General nouns
- name categories of persons, places, things, or ideas (often plural)

Examples
Students should study.

Books bridge *gaps* between *cultures*.

The airplane has made commuting between *cities* easy.

M2-c Use *a* (or *an*) with common singular count nouns that refer to "one" or "any."

If a count noun refers to one unspecific item (not a whole category), use the indefinite article, *a* or *an*. *A* and *an* usually mean "one among many" but can also mean "any one."

▶ My English professor asked me to bring ^*a*^ dictionary to class.

> The noun *dictionary* refers to "one unspecific dictionary" or "any dictionary."

▶ We want to rent ^*an*^ apartment close to the lake.

> The noun *apartment* refers to "any apartment close to the lake," not a specific apartment.

Choosing articles for common nouns

Use *the*

- if the reader has enough information to identify the noun specifically

  COUNT: Please turn on *the lights.* We're going to *the zoo* tomorrow.

  NONCOUNT: *The food* throughout Italy is excellent.

Use *a* or *an*

- if the noun refers to one item *and* if the item is singular but not specific

  COUNT: Bring *a pencil* to class. Charles wrote *an essay* about his first job.

NOTE: Do not use *a* or *an* with plural or noncount nouns.

Use a quantifier (*enough, many, some,* etc.)

- if the noun represents an unspecified amount of something
- if the amount is more than one but not all items in a category

  COUNT (PLURAL): Amir showed us *some photos* of India. *Many turtles* return to the same nesting site each year.

  NONCOUNT: We didn't get *enough rain* this summer.

NOTE: Sometimes no article conveys an unspecified amount: *Amir showed us photos of India.*

Choosing articles for common nouns, *continued*

Use no article

- if the noun represents all items in a category
- if the noun represents a category in general

COUNT (PLURAL): *Students* can attend the show for free.

NONCOUNT: *Coal* is a natural resource.

NOTE: *The* is occasionally used when a singular count noun refers to all items in a class or a specific category: *The bald eagle is no longer endangered in the United States.*

M2-d Use a quantifier such as *some* or *more*, not *a* or *an*, with a noncount noun to express an approximate amount.

Do not use *a* or *an* with noncount nouns. Also do not use numbers or words such as *several* or *many*; they must be used with plural nouns, and noncount nouns do not have plural forms. (See the Commonly used noncount nouns chart for lists of commonly used noncount nouns.)

▶ Dr. Snyder gave us ~~an~~ information about the Peace Corps.

▶ Do you have ~~many~~ money with you?

You can use quantifiers such as *enough, less,* and *some* to suggest approximate amounts or nonspecific quantities of noncount nouns: *a little salt, any homework, enough wood, less information, much pollution.*

M2-e Do not use articles with nouns that refer to all of something or to something in general.

When a noncount noun refers to all of its type or to a concept in general, it is not marked with an article.

▶ ~~The~~ kindness is a virtue.
  Kindness

The noun represents kindness in general; it does not represent a specific type of kindness, such as *the kindness he showed me after my mother's death.*

Commonly used noncount nouns

Food and drink

beef, bread, butter, candy, cereal, cheese, cream, meat, milk, pasta, rice, salt, sugar, water, wine

Nonfood substances

air, cement, coal, dirt, gasoline, gold, paper, petroleum, plastic, rain, silver, snow, soap, steel, wood, wool

Abstract nouns

advice, anger, beauty, confidence, courage, employment, fun, happiness, health, honesty, information, intelligence, knowledge, love, poverty, satisfaction, wealth

Other

biology (and other areas of study), clothing, equipment, furniture, homework, jewelry, luggage, machinery, mail, money, news, poetry, pollution, research, scenery, traffic, transportation, violence, weather, work

NOTE: A few noncount nouns (such as *love*) can also be used as count nouns: *He had two loves: music and archery.*

▶ In some places, ~~the~~ rice is preferred to all other grains.

> The noun *rice* represents rice in general. To refer to a specific type or serving of rice, the definite article is appropriate: *The rice my husband served last night is the best I've ever tasted.*

In most cases, when you use a count noun to represent a general category, make the noun plural. Do not use unmarked singular count nouns to represent whole categories.

▶ ~~Fountain is~~ an expensive element of landscape design.
     Fountains are

> *Fountains* is a count noun that represents fountains in general.

EXCEPTION: In some cases, *the* can be used with singular count nouns to represent a class or specific category: *The Chinese alligator is smaller than the American alligator.* See also number 6 in M2-b.

M2-f Do not use articles with most singular proper nouns. Use *the* with most plural proper nouns.

Since singular proper nouns are already specific, they typically do not need an article: *Prime Minister Trudeau, Jamaica, Lake Huron, Mount Etna.*

There are, however, many exceptions. In most cases, if the proper noun consists of a common noun with modifiers (adjectives or an *of* phrase), use *the* with the proper noun.

> ▶ We visited ^the^ Great Wall of China last year.

> ▶ Rob wants to be a translator for ^the^ Central Intelligence Agency.

The is used with most plural proper nouns: *the McGregors, the Bahamas, the Finger Lakes, the United States.*

Using *the* with geographic nouns

When to omit *the*

streets, squares, parks	Ivy Street, Union Square, Denali National Park
cities, states, counties	Miami, New Mexico, Bee County
most countries, continents	Italy, China, South America, Africa
bays, single lakes	Tampa Bay, Lake Geneva
single mountains, islands	Mount Everest, Crete

When to use *the*

country names with *of* phrase	the United States (of America), the People's Republic of China
large regions, deserts	the East Coast, the Sahara
peninsulas	the Baja Peninsula, the Sinai Peninsula
oceans, seas, gulfs	the Pacific Ocean, the Dead Sea, the Persian Gulf
canals and rivers	the Panama Canal, the Amazon
mountain ranges	the Rocky Mountains, the Alps
groups of islands	the Solomon Islands

Geographic names create problems because there are so many exceptions to the rules. When in doubt, consult the Using *the* with geographic nouns chart, check a dictionary, or ask a native speaker.

M3 Sentence structure

Although their structure can vary widely, sentences in English generally flow from subject to verb to object or complement: *Bears eat fish.* This section focuses on the major challenges that multilingual students face when writing sentences in English. For more details on the parts of speech and the elements of sentences, consult sections B1–B4.

M3-a Use a linking verb between a subject and its complement.

Some languages, such as Russian and Turkish, do not use linking verbs (*is, are, was, were*) between subjects and complements (nouns or adjectives that rename or describe the subject). Every English sentence, however, must include a verb. For more on linking verbs, see G2-e.

>   is
> ▶ Jim intelligent.
>   ^

>   are
> ▶ Many streets in San Francisco very steep.
>   ^

M3-b Include a subject in every sentence.

Some languages, such as Spanish and Japanese, do not require a subject in every sentence. Every English sentence, however, needs a subject.

>   She seems
> ▶ Your aunt is very energetic. ~~Seems~~ young for her age.
>   ^

Commands are an exception: The subject *you* is understood but not present in the sentence.

> [You] Give me the book.

The word *it* is used as the subject of a sentence describing the weather or temperature, stating the time, indicating distance, or suggesting an environmental fact.

>   It is
> ▶ ~~Is~~ raining in the valley and snowing in the mountains.
>   ^

>   It is
> ▶ ~~Is~~ 9:15 a.m.
>   ^

In most English sentences, the subject appears before the verb. Some sentences, however, are inverted: The subject comes after the verb. In these sentences, a placeholder called an *expletive* (*there* or *it*) often comes before the verb.

> EXP　V　⌐——— S ———⌐
> There are many people here today.
>
> ⌐——— S ———⌐　V
> (Many people are here today.)

▶ ~~Is~~ *There is* an apple pie in the refrigerator.

▶ As you know, *there are* many religious sects in India.

Notice that the verb agrees with the subject that follows it: *apple pie is, sects are.* (See G1-g.)

Sometimes an inverted sentence has an infinitive (*to work*) or a noun clause (*that she is intelligent*) as the subject. In such sentences, the placeholder *it* is needed before the verb. (See also B3-b and B3-e.)

> EXP V　　　⌐— S —⌐
> It is important to study daily.
>
> ⌐— S —⌐　　V
> (To study daily is important.)

▶ Because the road is flooded, *it* is necessary to change our route.

TIP: The words *here* and *there* can be used as placeholders, but they cannot be used as subjects. When they mean "in this place" (*here*) or "in that place" (*there*), they are adverbs, which are never subjects.

▶ I just returned from Japan. ~~There~~ *It* is very beautiful/ *there.*

▶ ~~Here~~ *This school* offers a master's degree in physical therapy; ~~there~~ *that school* has only a bachelor's program.

M3-c Do not use both a noun and a pronoun to perform the same grammatical function in a sentence.

English does not allow a subject to be repeated in its own clause.

▶ The doctor ~~she~~ advised me to cut down on salt.

The pronoun *she* cannot repeat the subject, *doctor.*

Do not add a pronoun even when a word group comes between the subject and the verb.

▶ The watch that I lost on vacation ~~it~~ was in my backpack.

The pronoun *it* cannot repeat the subject, *watch*.

Some languages allow "topic fronting," placing a word or phrase (a "topic") at the beginning of a sentence and following it with an independent clause that explains something about the topic. This form is not allowed in English because the sentence seems to start with one subject but then introduces a new subject in an independent clause.

┌─ TOPIC ─┐ ┌──── IND CLAUSE ────┐
INCORRECT   The seeds I planted them last fall.

The sentence can be corrected by bringing the topic (*seeds*) into the independent clause.

> *the seeds*
▶ ~~The seeds~~ I planted ~~them~~ last fall.
> ^

M3-d Do not repeat a subject, an object, or an adverb in an adjective clause.

Adjective clauses begin with relative pronouns (*who, whom, whose, which, that*) or relative adverbs (*when, where*). Relative pronouns usually serve as subjects or objects in the clauses they introduce; another word in the clause cannot serve the same function. Relative adverbs should not be repeated by other adverbs later in the clause.

┌────── ADJ CLAUSE ──────┐
The cat ran under the car that was parked on the street.

▶ The cat ran under the car that ~~it~~ was parked on the street.

The relative pronoun *that* is the subject of the adjective clause, so the pronoun *it* cannot be added as a subject.

▶ Myrna enjoyed the investment seminars that she attended ~~them~~ last week.

The relative pronoun *that* is the object of the verb *attended*. The pronoun *them* cannot also serve as an object.

Sometimes the relative pronoun is understood but not present in the sentence. In such cases, do not add another word with the same function as the omitted pronoun.

▶ Myrna enjoyed the investment seminars she attended ~~them~~ last week.

The relative pronoun *that* is understood after *seminars* even though it is not present in the sentence.

If the clause begins with a relative adverb, do not use another adverb with the same meaning later in the clause.

▶ The office where I work ~~there~~ is one hour from the city.

The adverb *there* cannot repeat the relative adverb *where*.

M3-e Avoid mixed constructions beginning with *although* or *because*.

A word group that begins with *although* cannot be linked to a word group that begins with *but* or *however*. The result is an error called a *mixed construction* (see also S5-a). Similarly, a word group that begins with *because* cannot be linked to a word group that begins with *so* or *therefore*.

If you want to keep *although* or *because*, drop the other linking word.

▶ Although Nikki Giovanni is best known for her poetry for adults,

~~but~~ she has written several books for children.

▶ Because German and Dutch are related languages, ~~therefore~~

tourists from Berlin can usually read a few signs in Amsterdam.

If you want to keep the other linking word, omit *although* or *because*.

▶ ~~Although~~ Nikki Giovanni is best known for her poetry for adults,

but she has written several books for children.

▶ ~~Because~~ German and Dutch are related languages/; therefore,

tourists from Berlin can usually read a few signs in Amsterdam.

For advice about using commas and semicolons with linking words, see P1-a and P3-a.

M3-f Do not place an adverb between a verb and its direct object.

Adverbs modifying verbs can appear in various positions: at the beginning or end of a sentence, before or after a verb, or between a helping verb and its main verb.

> *Slowly*, we drove along the rain-slick road.

> Mia handled the teapot *very carefully*.

> Martin *always* wins our tennis matches.

> Christina is *rarely* late for our lunch dates.

> My daughter has *often* spoken of you.

> The election results were being *closely* followed by analysts.

However, an adverb cannot appear between a verb and its direct object.

> carefully
> ▶ Mother wrapped ~~carefully~~ the gift.
>   ^

The adverb *carefully* cannot appear between the verb, *wrapped*, and its direct object, *the gift*.

M4 Using adjectives

M4-a Distinguish between present participles and past participles used as adjectives.

Both present and past participles may be used as adjectives. The present participle always ends in *-ing*. Past participles usually end in *-ed, -d, -en, -n,* or *-t.* (See G2-a.)

PRESENT PARTICIPLES	confusing, speaking, boring
PAST PARTICIPLES	confused, spoken, bored

Like all other adjectives, participles can come before nouns; they also can follow linking verbs, in which case they describe the subject of the sentence. (See B2-b.)

Use a present participle to describe a person or thing *causing or stimulating an experience.*

> The *boring lecture* put us to sleep. [The lecture caused boredom.]

Use a past participle to describe a person or thing *undergoing an experience.*

The *audience* was *bored.* [The audience experienced boredom.]

Participles that describe emotions or mental states often cause the most confusion.

annoying/annoyed	exhausting/exhausted
boring/bored	fascinating/fascinated
confusing/confused	frightening/frightened
depressing/depressed	satisfying/satisfied
exciting/excited	surprising/surprised

M4-b Place cumulative adjectives in an appropriate order.

Adjectives usually come before the nouns they modify and may also come after linking verbs. (See B1-d and B2-b.)

ADJ   N   V   ADJ
Janine wore a new necklace. Janine's necklace was new.

Order of cumulative adjectives

FIRST   **ARTICLE OR OTHER NOUN MARKER**   a, an, the, her, Joe's, two, many, some

         EVALUATIVE WORD   attractive, dedicated, delicious, ugly, disgusting

         SIZE   large, enormous, small, little

         LENGTH OR SHAPE   long, short, round, square

         AGE   new, old, young, antique

         COLOR   yellow, blue, crimson

         NATIONALITY   French, Peruvian, Vietnamese

         RELIGION   Catholic, Protestant, Jewish, Muslim

         MATERIAL   silver, walnut, wool, marble

LAST   **NOUN/ADJECTIVE**   tree (as in *tree* house), kitchen (as in *kitchen* table)

         THE NOUN MODIFIED   house, coat, bicycle, bread, woman, coin

         My large blue wool **coat** *is in the attic.*

Cumulative adjectives are adjectives that build on one another, cannot be joined by the word *and*, and are not separated by commas (P2-d). These adjectives must be listed in a particular order. If you use cumulative adjectives before a noun, see the Order of cumulative adjectives chart. The chart is only a guide; don't be surprised if you encounter exceptions.

▶ My dorm room has only a desk and a ~~plastic red stained~~ chair.
(correction above: stained red plastic)

M5 Prepositions and idiomatic expressions

M5-a Become familiar with prepositions that show time and place.

The most frequently used prepositions in English are *at, by, for, from, in, of, on, to,* and *with*. Prepositions can be difficult to master because the differences among them are subtle and idiomatic. The chart in this section is limited to three troublesome prepositions that show time and place: *at, on,* and *in*.

Not every possible use is listed in the chart, so don't be surprised when you encounter exceptions and idiomatic uses that you must learn one at a time. For example, in English a person rides *in* a car but *on* a bus, plane, train, or subway.

▶ My first class starts ~~on~~ 8:00 a.m.
(correction above: at)

▶ The farmers go to market ~~in~~ Wednesday.
(correction above: on)

M5-b Use nouns (including *-ing* forms) after prepositions.

In a prepositional phrase, use a noun (not a verb) after the preposition. Sometimes the noun will be a gerund, the *-ing* verb form that functions as a noun (see B3-b).

▶ Our student government is good at ~~save~~ money.
(correction above: saving)

Distinguish between the preposition *to* and the infinitive marker *to*. If *to* is a preposition, it should be followed by a noun or a gerund.

▶ We are dedicated to ~~help~~ the poor.
(correction above: helping)

At, *on*, and *in* to show time and place

Showing time

AT   *at* a specific time: *at* 7:20, *at* dawn, *at* dinner

ON   *on* a specific day or date: *on* Tuesday, *on* June 4

IN   *in* a part of a 24-hour period: *in* the afternoon, *in* the daytime [but *at* night]

   in a year or month: *in* 2008, *in* July

   in a period of time: finished *in* three hours

Showing place

AT   *at* a meeting place or location: *at* home, *at* the club

   at the edge of something: sitting *at* the desk

   at the corner of something: turning *at* the intersection

   at a target: throwing the snowball *at* Lucy

ON   *on* a surface: placed *on* the table, hanging *on* the wall

   on a street: the house *on* Spring Street

   on an electronic medium: *on* television, *on* the Internet

IN   *in* an enclosed space: *in* the garage, *in* an envelope

   in a geographic location: *in* San Diego, *in* Texas

   in a print medium: *in* a book, *in* a magazine

If *to* is an infinitive marker, it should be followed by the base form of the verb.

                    help
▶ We want to ~~helping~~ the poor.
                    ^

To test whether *to* is a preposition or an infinitive marker, insert a word that you know is a noun after the word *to*. If the noun makes sense in that position, *to* is a preposition. If the noun does not make sense after *to*, then *to* is an infinitive marker.

Zoe is addicted *to* _____.

They are planning *to* _____.

In the first sentence, a noun (such as *magazines*) makes sense after *to*, so *to* is a preposition and should be followed by a noun or a gerund: Zoe is addicted *to magazines*. Zoe is addicted *to running*.

In the second sentence, a noun (such as *magazines*) does not make sense after *to*, so *to* is an infinitive marker and must be followed by the base form of the verb: They are planning *to build* a new school.

M5-c Become familiar with common adjective + preposition combinations.

Some adjectives appear only with certain prepositions. These expressions are idiomatic and may be different from the combinations used in your native language.

▶ Paula is married ~~with~~ Jon.
                to

Check an ESL dictionary for combinations that are not listed in the chart in this section.

M5-d Become familiar with common verb + preposition combinations.

Many verbs and prepositions appear together in idiomatic phrases. Pay special attention to the combinations that are different from the combinations used in your native language.

▶ Your success depends ~~of~~ your effort.
                      on

Adjective + preposition combinations

accustomed to	connected to	guilty of	preferable to
addicted to	covered with	interested in	proud of
afraid of	dedicated to	involved in	responsible
angry with	devoted to	involved with	for
ashamed of	different from	known as	satisfied with
aware of	engaged in	known for	scared of
committed to	engaged to	made of (*or*	similar to
concerned	excited about	made from)	tired of
about	familiar with	married to	worried about
concerned with	full of	opposed to	

Check an ESL dictionary for combinations that are not listed in the chart in this section.

Verb + preposition combinations

agree with	compare with	forget about	speak to (*or*
apply to	concentrate on	happen to	speak with)
approve of	consist of	hope for	stare at
arrive at	count on	insist on	succeed at
arrive in	decide on	listen to	succeed in
ask for	depend on	participate in	take advantage of
believe in	differ from	rely on	take care of
belong to	disagree with	reply to	think about
care about	dream about	respond to	think of
care for	dream of	result in	wait for
compare to	feel like	search for	wait on

M6 Paraphrasing sources effectively

Effective paraphrasing is an important skill for writing in college. You will frequently paraphrase information from your textbooks to answer homework and exam questions, and you will especially need this skill when you are writing essays that incorporate information from other writers. However, learning how to paraphrase can be challenging because often the topics and the vocabulary are new and unfamiliar to multilingual writers.

The purpose of paraphrasing is to restate an author's ideas in your own words. Most writers find the following process for paraphrasing useful:

1. Read and understand the text.
2. Put the text aside.
3. Express the information in your own words.
4. Compare your paraphrase to the original text to check that you have used different words and different sentence structures but have kept the author's meaning.

This process provides an effective way to paraphrase; it requires that the writer have a large vocabulary and well-developed sentence-writing abilities.

Sometimes it's hard to find the right words to paraphrase a sentence or to know whether a paraphrase has the same meaning as the original source.

The following sections provide rules of thumb that can help you develop skill with paraphrasing. For more on how to paraphrase effectively, see R2-c and MLA-3a.

M6-a   Avoid replacing a source's words with synonyms.

Learning to paraphrase will help you communicate the ideas of authors effectively and avoid plagiarism — using another person's ideas or words without giving credit to that person. However, even if you tell your reader that information comes from another author, you can still commit plagiarism if you change only the words but do not make the *presentation* of the information your own.

Some writers misinterpret the instructions to "use your own words"; they simply replace words in the source with synonyms, words that have similar meanings. Such word-by-word paraphrases frequently result in awkward sentence structures and inaccuracy. Meaning in English often comes from phrases and sentences rather than from individual words. Also, synonyms have similar meanings, but they rarely have *identical* meanings. Sometimes a synonym requires a different sentence structure than the original word does.

The following examples illustrate some of the problems that can arise with word-by-word paraphrasing.

Here is a short passage from Rebecca Webber's article "Make Your Own Luck."

ORIGINAL SOURCE

People who spot and seize opportunity are different. They are more open to life's forking paths, so they see possibilities others miss. And if things don't work out the way they'd hoped, they brush off disappointment and launch themselves headlong toward the next fortunate circumstance. As a result, they're happier and more likely to achieve their goals.

— Rebecca Webber, "Make Your Own Luck," p. 64

The following is a word-by-word paraphrase of the sentences highlighted in yellow.

UNACCEPTABLE PARAPHRASE: MEANING CHANGED

Persons who see and grab chances are diverse. They are further exposed to life's dividing trails, and they view prospects others ignore.

The first problem with this paraphrase is that the student who wrote it used the same sentence structure as in the original passage. Because she did not use her own sentence structure, this paraphrase is plagiarized. Second, the words that the student substituted are not exact synonyms, so the paraphrase has lost some of the meaning of the original passage.

- The word *grab* is an informal synonym of the word *seize* and may not be acceptable in a formal paper.
- *Diverse* and *different* have similar, but not identical, meanings. The word *different* in the original passage implies that people who are open to opportunities are different from people who are not open to opportunities. Using *diverse* in this context implies that people who welcome opportunity are different from one another. Using *diverse* distorts the meaning of the sentence.
- Using *exposed* instead of *open* changes the meaning in a significant way. *Exposed* implies that something negative has happened to these people, while *open* is a positive character trait.

As you paraphrase, keep in mind that simply substituting synonyms into the original passage does not guarantee an accurate paraphrase.

The following paraphrase of the sentence highlighted in blue demonstrates another potential problem with word-by-word paraphrases. Using synonyms often requires changing the surrounding sentence structure because in English the same word can be more than one part of speech. For example, *work* can be either a noun or a verb; in the following paraphrase, the student has substituted the noun *effort* for the verb *work*, but it is not an appropriate substitution.

UNACCEPTABLE PARAPHRASE: AWKWARD RESULT

And if everything don't effort out the manner they'd wanted, they rebuff disappointment and throw themselves impulsive toward the next lucky situation.

- When the student changed *things* to *everything*, she also needed to change the verb from the plural form (*don't*) to the singular form (*doesn't*).
- Using *effort* in place of *work* is inappropriate. *Effort* is a synonym for the noun *work* but not a synonym for the verb *work*. The part of speech of a word is an important consideration when choosing a synonym.
- When the student substituted *manner* for *way*, she should have used a different structure: *in the manner*.
- Although *headlong* has a similar meaning to *impulsive*, in the original passage *headlong* is an adverb modifying the verb *launch*; *impulsive* is an adjective. An adjective cannot replace an adverb in a sentence.

M6-b Determine the meaning of the original source.

Rather than trying to paraphrase word for word within each sentence, a better approach is to look at an entire passage and try to understand its meaning as well as how the information is organized before you try to present it in your own words. Look at the meaning of each phrase or clause rather than just the meaning of each word.

ORIGINAL SOURCE

People who spot and seize opportunity are different. They are more open to life's forking paths, so they see possibilities others miss. And if things don't work out the way they'd hoped, they brush off disappointment and launch themselves headlong toward the next fortunate circumstance. As a result, they're happier and more likely to achieve their goals.

The topic sentence of a paragraph is important. The topic sentence here (the first sentence in the paragraph) tells you about a particular group of people; from the title of the article, you can tell that Webber is talking about people who create their own luck. Lucky people, according to the author, have different characteristics from people who are not lucky. The rest of the paragraph then describes how lucky people are different.

Here is the original passage as the student writer annotated it. She worked through the original passage, repeatedly asking herself, "What is the author's point here?"

ORIGINAL SOURCE WITH STUDENT ANNOTATIONS

↗— Lucky people?

People who spot and seize opportunity are different. They are

↗— More willing to take risks?

more open to life's forking paths, so they see possibilities others

miss. And if things don't work out the way they'd hoped, they

↗— Don't get discouraged/upset   keep looking? ↘

brush off disappointment and launch themselves headlong

toward the next fortunate circumstance. As a result, they're

↗— More positive personalities overall

happier and more likely to achieve their goals.

M6-c Present the author's meaning in your own words.

If you analyze a paragraph in its entirety rather than look at each word individually, you should be able to organize your information differently from the way the original author did and write a better paraphrase. As you analyze a source, you may still need to figure out the meaning of certain words, but do not focus on word-for-word substitutions. Here is one student's paraphrase of Rebecca Webber's work using her annotations of the text (see M6-b).

ACCEPTABLE PARAPHRASE

Individuals notice and respond to life's chances in different ways. Some people notice opportunities that other people might not notice, they are more willing to take risks, and they do not get discouraged if their decisions do not work out. Because they do not get discouraged easily, they are able to stay positive and content and to continue to search enthusiastically for the next opportunity (Webber 64).

This paraphrase presents the student's understanding of the author's meaning — without using words or sentence structure from the original. Notice that the paraphrase includes a citation. The idea is still Webber's idea, so a citation is needed, but the student uses her own words to communicate the information from Webber's article.

P

Punctuation and Mechanics

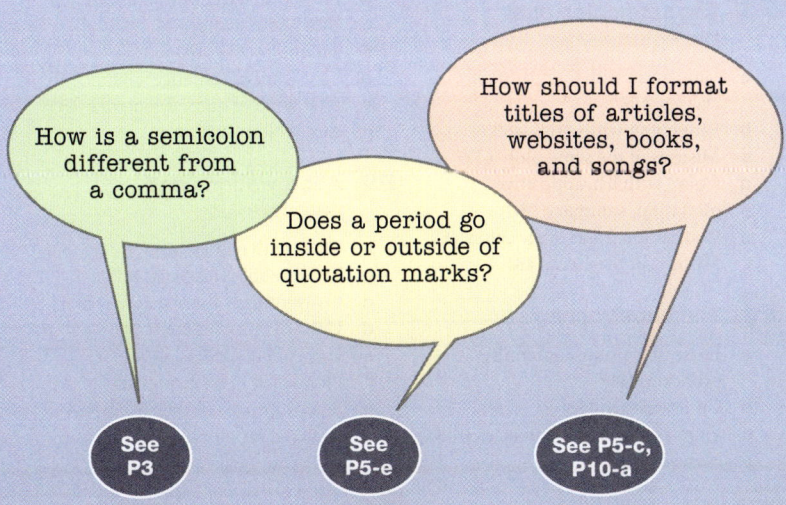

How is a semicolon different from a comma?

See P3

Does a period go inside or outside of quotation marks?

See P5-e

How should I format titles of articles, websites, books, and songs?

See P5-c, P10-a

P Punctuation and Mechanics

P1 The comma

The comma was invented to help readers. Without it, sentence parts can collide into one another unexpectedly, causing misreadings.

| CONFUSING | If you cook Elmer will do the dishes. |
| CONFUSING | While we were eating a rattlesnake approached our campsite. |

Add commas in the logical places (after *cook* and *eating*), and suddenly all is clear. No longer is Elmer being cooked and the rattlesnake being eaten.

Various rules have evolved to prevent such misreadings and to speed readers along through complex grammatical structures. Those rules are detailed in this section. (Section P2 explains when not to use commas.)

P1-a Use a comma before a coordinating conjunction joining independent clauses.

When a coordinating conjunction connects two or more independent clauses — word groups that could stand alone as separate sentences — a comma must precede the conjunction. There are seven coordinating conjunctions in English: *and, but, or, nor, for, so,* and *yet.*

A comma tells readers that one independent clause has come to a close and that another is about to begin.

▶ **The department sponsored a seminar on college survival skills,**

and it also hosted a barbecue for new students.

EXCEPTION: If the two independent clauses are short and there is no danger of misreading, the comma may be omitted.

The plane took off and we were on our way.

TIP: As a rule, do *not* use a comma with a coordinating conjunction that joins only two words, phrases, or subordinate clauses. (See P2-a. See also P1-c for commas with coordinating conjunctions joining three or more elements.)

▶ **A good money manager controls expenses/and invests surplus**

dollars to meet future needs.

The word group following *and* is not an independent clause; it is the second half of a compound predicate (*controls . . . and invests*).

P1-b Use a comma after an introductory clause or phrase.

The most common introductory word groups are clauses and phrases functioning as adverbs. Such word groups usually tell when, where, how, why, or under what conditions the main action of the sentence occurred. (See B3-a, B3-b, and B3-e.)

A comma tells readers that the introductory clause or phrase has come to a close and that the main part of the sentence is about to begin.

▶ **When Irwin was ready to iron, his cat tripped on the cord.**
                                  ^

Without the comma, readers may think that Irwin is ironing his cat. The comma signals that *his cat* is the subject of a new clause, not part of the introductory one.

EXCEPTION: The comma may be left out after a short adverb clause or phrase if there is no danger of misreading. *In no time we were at 2,800 feet.*

Sentences also frequently begin with participial phrases that function as adjectives, describing the noun or pronoun immediately following them. The comma tells readers that they are about to learn the identity of the person or thing described; therefore, the comma is usually required even when the phrase is short. (See B3-b.)

▶ **Buried under layers of younger rocks, the earth's oldest rocks**
                                         ^
   contain no fossils.

NOTE: Other introductory word groups include transitional expressions and absolute phrases (see P1-f).

P1-c Use a comma between all items in a series.

When three or more items are presented in a series, those items should be separated from one another with commas. Items in a series may be single words, phrases, or clauses.

▶ **Langston Hughes's poetry is concerned with racial pride, social**

   justice, and the diversity of the African American experience.
        ^

Although some writers view the last comma in a series as optional, most experts advise using the comma because its omission can result in ambiguity or misreading.

▶ **My uncle willed me all of his property, houses, and boats.**
                                                    ^

Did the uncle will his property *and* houses *and* boats — or simply his property, consisting of houses and boats? If the former meaning is intended, a comma is necessary to prevent ambiguity.

P1-d Use a comma between coordinate adjectives not joined with *and*. Do not use a comma between cumulative adjectives.

When two or more adjectives each modify a noun separately, they are coordinate.

Roberto is a *warm, gentle, affectionate* father.

If the adjectives can be joined with *and*, the adjectives are coordinate, so you should use commas: *warm* and *gentle* and *affectionate* (*warm, gentle, affectionate*). Adjectives that do not modify the noun separately are cumulative.

Three large gray shapes moved slowly toward us.

Beginning with the adjective closest to the noun *shapes*, these modifiers lean on one another, piggyback style, with each modifying a larger word group. *Gray* modifies *shapes*, *large* modifies *gray shapes*, and *three* modifies *large gray shapes*. Cumulative adjectives cannot be joined with *and* (not *three* and *large* and *gray shapes*).

COORDINATE ADJECTIVES

▶ **Should patients with severe, irreversible brain damage be put on life**
                                   ^

support systems?

Adjectives are coordinate if they can be connected with *and*: *severe* and *irreversible*.

CUMULATIVE ADJECTIVES

▶ **Ira ordered a rich/chocolate/layer cake.**

Ira didn't order a cake that was rich and chocolate and layer. He ordered a *layer cake* that was *chocolate*, a *chocolate layer cake* that was *rich*.

P1-e Use commas to set off nonrestrictive (nonessential) elements. Do not use commas to set off restrictive (essential) elements.

Certain word groups that modify nouns or pronouns can be restrictive or nonrestrictive — that is, essential or not essential to the meaning of a sentence. These word groups are usually adjective clauses, adjective phrases, or appositives.

Restrictive elements

A restrictive element defines or limits the meaning of the word it modifies; it is therefore essential to the meaning of the sentence and is not set off with commas. If you remove a restrictive modifier from a sentence, the meaning changes significantly, becoming more general than you intended.

> **RESTRICTIVE (NO COMMAS)**
>
> The campers need clothes *that are durable.*
>
> Scientists *who study the earth's structure* are called geologists.

The first sentence does not mean that the campers need clothes in general. The intended meaning is more limited: The campers need durable clothes. The second sentence does not mean that scientists in general are called geologists; only those scientists who specifically study the earth's structure are called geologists. The italicized word groups are essential and are therefore not set off with commas.

Nonrestrictive elements

A nonrestrictive modifier describes a noun or pronoun whose meaning has already been clearly defined or limited. Because the modifier contains nonessential or parenthetical information, it is set off with commas. If you remove a nonrestrictive element from a sentence, the meaning does not change dramatically. Some meaning may be lost, but the defining characteristics of the person or thing described remain the same.

> **NONRESTRICTIVE (WITH COMMAS)**
>
> The campers need sturdy shoes, *which are expensive.*
>
> The scientists, *who represented eight different universities,* met to review applications for the prestigious Belker Award.

In the first sentence, the campers need sturdy shoes, and the shoes happen to be expensive. In the second sentence, the scientists met to review applications for the award; that they represented eight different universities is informative but not critical to the meaning of the sentence. The nonessential information in both sentences is set off with commas.

NOTE: Often it is difficult to tell whether a word group is restrictive or nonrestrictive without seeing it in context and considering the writer's meaning. Both of the following sentences are grammatically correct, but their meaning is slightly different.

> The dessert made with fresh raspberries was delicious.
>
> The dessert, made with fresh raspberries, was delicious.

In the first example, the phrase *made with fresh raspberries* tells which of two or more desserts the writer is referring to. In the example with commas, the phrase merely adds information about one dessert.

Adjective clauses

Adjective clauses are patterned like sentences, containing subjects and verbs, but they function within sentences as modifiers of nouns or pronouns. They always follow the word they modify, usually immediately. Adjective clauses begin with a relative pronoun (*who, whom, whose, which, that*) or with a relative adverb (*where, when, why*). (See also B3-e.)

Nonrestrictive adjective clauses are set off with commas; restrictive adjective clauses are not.

NONRESTRICTIVE CLAUSE (WITH COMMAS)

▶ Ed's house, which is located on thirteen acres, was completely
furnished with bats in the rafters and mice in the kitchen.

The adjective clause *which is located on thirteen acres* does not restrict the meaning of *Ed's house*; the information is nonessential and is therefore set off with commas.

RESTRICTIVE CLAUSE (NO COMMAS)

▶ The giant panda/that was born at the San Diego Zoo in 2003/
was sent to China in 2007.

Because the adjective clause *that was born at the San Diego Zoo in 2003* identifies one particular panda out of many, the information is essential and is therefore not set off with commas.

NOTE: Use *that* only with restrictive (essential) clauses. Many writers prefer to use *which* only with nonrestrictive (nonessential) clauses, but usage varies.

Adjective phrases

Prepositional or verbal phrases functioning as adjectives may be restrictive or nonrestrictive. Nonrestrictive phrases are set off with commas; restrictive phrases are not.

NONRESTRICTIVE PHRASE (WITH COMMAS)

▶ The helicopter, with its million-candlepower spotlight
illuminating the area, circled above.

The *with* phrase is nonessential because its purpose is not to specify which of two or more helicopters is being discussed. The phrase is not required for readers to understand the meaning of the sentence.

RESTRICTIVE PHRASE (NO COMMAS)

▶ One corner of the attic was filled with newspapers/dating from

the early 1900s.

Dating from the early 1900s restricts the meaning of *newspapers,* so the comma should be omitted.

Appositives

An appositive is a noun or noun phrase that renames a nearby noun. Nonrestrictive appositives are set off with commas; restrictive appositives are not.

NONRESTRICTIVE APPOSITIVE (WITH COMMAS)

▶ Darwin's most important book, *On the Origin of Species,* was the
result of many years of research.

Most important restricts the meaning to one book, so the appositive *On the Origin of Species* is nonrestrictive and should be set off with commas.

RESTRICTIVE APPOSITIVE (NO COMMAS)

▶ The song/"Viva la Vida/" was blasted out of huge amplifiers at the

concert.

Once they've read *song,* readers still don't know precisely which song the writer means. The appositive following *song* restricts its meaning, so the appositive should not be set off with commas.

P1-f Use commas to set off transitional and parenthetical expressions, absolute phrases, and word groups expressing contrast.

Transitional expressions

Transitional expressions serve as bridges between sentences or parts of sentences. They include conjunctive adverbs such as *however, therefore,* and *moreover* and transitional phrases such as *for example, as a matter of fact,* and *in other words.* (For complete lists of these expressions, see P3-a.)

When a transitional expression appears between independent clauses in a compound sentence, it is preceded by a semicolon and is usually followed by a comma. (See P3-a.)

▶ Minh did not understand our language; moreover, he was

unfamiliar with our customs.

When a transitional expression appears at the beginning of a sentence or in the middle of an independent clause, it is usually set off with commas.

▶ **Natural foods are not always salt-free; celery, for example, contains**
　　∧　　　　　　∧
　more sodium than most people think.

EXCEPTION: If a transitional expression blends smoothly with the rest of the sentence, calling for little or no pause in reading, it does not need to be set off with a comma. Expressions such as *also, at least, certainly, consequently, indeed, of course, moreover, no doubt, perhaps, then,* and *therefore* do not always call for a pause.

Alice's bicycle is broken; *therefore* you will need to borrow Sue's.

Parenthetical expressions

Expressions that are distinctly parenthetical, providing only supplemental information, should be set off with commas. They interrupt the flow of a sentence or appear at the end as afterthoughts.

▶ **Evolution, as far as we know, doesn't work this way.**
　　　∧　　　　　　　∧

Absolute phrases

An absolute phrase, which modifies the whole sentence, usually consists of a noun followed by a participle or participial phrase. (See B3-d.) Absolute phrases may appear at the beginning or at the end of a sentence and should be set off with commas.

```
┌──────── ABSOLUTE PHRASE ────────┐
│   N  PARTICIPLE                 │
```
The sun appearing for the first time in a week, we were at last able to begin the archaeological dig.

▶ **Elvis Presley made music industry history in the 1950s, his**
　　　　　　　　　　　　　　　　　　　　　　　∧
　records having sold more than ten million copies.

NOTE: Do not insert a comma between the noun and the participle in an absolute construction.

▶ **The next contestant/being five years old, the host adjusted the**
　height of the microphone.

Word groups expressing contrast

Sharp contrasts beginning with words such as *not, never,* and *unlike* are set off with commas.

▶ Unlike Robert, Celia loves using Instagram.
      ^

P1-g Use commas to set off nouns of direct address, the words *yes* and *no*, interrogative tags, and mild interjections.

▶ Forgive me, Angela, for forgetting your birthday.
          ^   ^

▶ The film was faithful to the book, wasn't it?
                              ^

P1-h Use commas with expressions such as *he said* to set off direct quotations.

▶ In his "Letter from Birmingham Jail," Martin Luther King Jr.

   wrote, "We know through painful experience that freedom is never
        ^

   voluntarily given by the oppressor; it must be demanded by the

   oppressed" (225).

See P5 on the use of quotation marks and pages 167–68 on citing literary sources in MLA style.

P1-i Use commas with dates, addresses, titles, and numbers.

Dates

In dates, set off the year with a pair of commas.

▶ On December 12, 1890, orders were sent out for the arrest of
                 ^   ^
   Sitting Bull.

EXCEPTIONS: Commas are not needed if the date is inverted or if only the month and year are given: 15 April 2009; January 2018.

Addresses

The elements of an address or a place name are separated with commas. A zip code, however, is not preceded by a comma.

▶ **Please send the package to Greg Tarvin at 708 Spring Street,**
   ˄
Washington, IL 61571.
   ˄

Titles

If a title follows a name, set off the title with a pair of commas.

▶ **Ann Hall, MD, has been appointed to the board of trustees.**
   ˄   ˄

Numbers

In numbers more than four digits long, use commas to separate the numbers into groups of three, starting from the right. In numbers four digits long, a comma is optional.

3,500 [*or* 3500]   100,000   5,000,000

EXCEPTIONS: Do not use commas in street numbers, zip codes, telephone numbers, or years with four or fewer digits.

P2 Unnecessary commas

Many common misuses of the comma result from a misunderstanding of the major comma rules presented in P1.

P2-a Do not use a comma with a coordinating conjunction that joins only two words, phrases, or subordinate clauses.

Though a comma should be used before a coordinating conjunction joining independent clauses (see P1-a) or with a series of three or more elements (see P1-c), these rules should not be extended to other compound word groups.

▶ **Ron discovered a leak/and came back to fix it.**

The coordinating conjunction *and* links two verbs in a compound predicate: *discovered* and *came.*

▶ We knew that she had won**/** but that the election was close.

The coordinating conjunction *but* links two subordinate clauses, each beginning with *that*.

P2-b Do not use a comma to separate a verb from its subject or object.

A sentence should flow from subject to verb to object without unnecessary pauses. Commas may appear between these major sentence elements only when a specific rule calls for them.

▶ Zoos large enough to give the animals freedom to roam**/** are

becoming more popular.

The comma should not separate the subject, *Zoos*, from the verb, *are becoming*.

P2-c Do not use a comma before the first or after the last item in a series.

Though commas are required between items in a series (P1-c), do not place them either before or after the whole series.

▶ Other causes of asthmatic attacks are**/** stress, change in temperature,

and cold air.

▶ Even novels that focus on horror, evil, and alienation**/** often have

themes of spiritual renewal and redemption.

P2-d Do not use a comma between cumulative adjectives, between an adjective and a noun, or between an adverb and an adjective.

Commas are required between coordinate adjectives (those that can be joined with *and*), but they do not belong between cumulative adjectives (those that cannot be joined with *and*). (For a full discussion, see P1-d.)

▶ In the corner of the closet, we found an old**/** maroon hatbox.

A comma should never be used between an adjective and the noun that follows it.

▶ **It was a senseless, dangerous/mission.**

Nor should a comma be used between an adverb and an adjective that follows it.

▶ **Rehabilitation often helps severely/injured patients.**

P2-e Do not use commas to set off restrictive elements.

Restrictive elements are modifiers or appositives that restrict the meaning of the nouns they follow. Because they are essential to the meaning of the sentence, they are not set off with commas. (For a full discussion of restrictive and nonrestrictive elements, see P1-e.)

▶ **Drivers/who think they own the road/make cycling a dangerous sport.**

The modifier *who think they own the road* restricts the meaning of *Drivers* and is essential to the meaning of the sentence. Putting commas around the *who* clause falsely suggests that all drivers think they own the road.

▶ **Margaret Mead's book/*Coming of Age in Samoa*/stirred up**

considerable controversy when it was published in 1928.

Since Mead wrote more than one book, the appositive contains information essential to the meaning of the sentence.

P2-f Do not use a comma to set off a concluding adverb clause that is essential for meaning.

When adverb clauses introduce a sentence, they are nearly always followed by a comma (see P1-b). When they conclude a sentence, however, they are not set off by a comma if their content is essential to the meaning of the earlier part of the sentence. Adverb clauses beginning with *after, as soon as, because, before, if, since, unless, until,* and *when* are usually essential.

▶ **Don't visit Paris at the height of the tourist season/unless you**

have booked hotel reservations.

Without the *unless* clause, the meaning of the sentence might at first seem broader than the writer intended.

When a concluding adverb clause is nonessential, it should be preceded by a comma. Clauses beginning with *although, even though, though,* and *whereas* are usually nonessential.

▶ **The lecture seemed to last only a short time, although it had**
   ^
actually gone on for more than an hour.

P2-g Do not use a comma after a phrase that begins an inverted sentence.

Though a comma belongs after most introductory phrases (see P1-b), it does not belong after phrases that begin an inverted sentence. In an inverted sentence, the subject follows the verb, and a phrase that ordinarily would follow the verb is moved to the beginning.

▶ **At the bottom of the hill/sat the stubborn mule.**

P2-h Avoid other common misuses of the comma.

Do not use a comma in the following situations.

AFTER A COORDINATING CONJUNCTION (*AND, BUT, OR, NOR, FOR, SO, YET*)

▶ **Occasionally TV talk shows are performed live, but/more**
often they are recorded.

AFTER *SUCH AS* OR *LIKE*

▶ **Shade-loving plants such as/begonias, impatiens, and coleus**
can add color to a shady garden.

AFTER *ALTHOUGH*

▶ **Although/the air was balmy, the water was cold.**

BEFORE A PARENTHESIS

▶ **Sylvia knew that her score was low/(only 22), but she felt confident**
about her admissions essay.

TO SET OFF AN INDIRECT (REPORTED) QUOTATION

▶ Samuel Goldwyn once said/that a verbal contract isn't worth the paper it's written on.

WITH A QUESTION MARK OR AN EXCLAMATION POINT

▶ "Why don't you try it?/" she coaxed. "You can't do any worse than the rest of us."

P3 The semicolon and the colon

The semicolon is used to connect major sentence elements of equal grammatical rank. The colon is used primarily to call attention to the words that follow it.

P3-a Use a semicolon between closely related independent clauses.

Between independent clauses with no coordinating conjunction

When two independent clauses appear in one sentence, they are usually linked with a comma and a coordinating conjunction (*and, but, or, nor, for, so, yet*). If the clauses are closely related and the relation is clear without a conjunction, they may be linked with a semicolon instead.

> In film, a low-angle shot makes the subject look powerful; a high-angle shot does just the opposite.

A semicolon must be used whenever a coordinating conjunction has been omitted between independent clauses. To use merely a comma creates a type of run-on sentence known as a *comma splice*. (See G6.)

▶ In 1800, a traveler needed six weeks to get from New York to Chicago/; in 1860, the trip by train took only two days.

Between independent clauses linked with a transitional expression

Transitional expressions include conjunctive adverbs and transitional phrases.

CONJUNCTIVE ADVERBS

accordingly	however	now
also	incidentally	otherwise
anyway	indeed	similarly
besides	instead	specifically
certainly	likewise	still
consequently	meanwhile	subsequently
conversely	moreover	then
finally	nevertheless	therefore
furthermore	next	thus
hence	nonetheless	

TRANSITIONAL PHRASES

after all	even so	in fact
as a matter of fact	for example	in other words
as a result	for instance	in the first place
at any rate	in addition	on the contrary
at the same time	in conclusion	on the other hand

When a transitional expression appears between independent clauses, it is preceded by a semicolon and usually followed by a comma.

▶ **Many corals grow very gradually/; in fact, the creation of a coral reef can take centuries.**

When a transitional expression appears in the middle or at the end of the second independent clause, the semicolon goes *between the clauses.*

▶ **Biologists have observed laughter in primates other than humans/; chimpanzees, however, sound more like they are panting than laughing.**

Transitional expressions should not be confused with the coordinating conjunctions *and, but, or, nor, for, so,* and *yet,* which are preceded by a comma when they link independent clauses. (See P1-a.)

P3-b Use a semicolon between items in a series containing internal punctuation.

▶ Researchers point to key benefits of positive thinking: It leads to high self-esteem, especially in people who focus on their achievements**/;** it helps make social interactions, such as those with co-workers, more enjoyable**/;** and, most important, it results in better sleep and overall health.

Without the semicolons, the reader would have to sort out the major groupings, distinguishing between important and less important pauses according to the logic of the sentence. By inserting semicolons at the major breaks, the writer does this work for the reader.

P3-c Avoid common misuses of the semicolon.

Do not use a semicolon in the following situations.

BETWEEN A SUBORDINATE CLAUSE AND THE REST OF THE SENTENCE

▶ Although children's literature was added to the National Book Awards in 1969**/,** it has had its own award, the Newbery Medal, since 1922.

BETWEEN AN APPOSITIVE AND THE WORD IT REFERS TO

▶ The scientists were fascinated by the species *Argyroneta aquatica***/,** a spider that lives underwater.

TO INTRODUCE A LIST

▶ Some of my favorite celebrities have their own blogs**/:** Katy Perry, Beyoncé, and Zooey Deschanel.

BETWEEN INDEPENDENT CLAUSES JOINED BY *AND, BUT, OR, NOR, FOR, SO,* **OR** *YET*

▶ Five of the applicants had worked with spreadsheets**/,** but only one was familiar with database management.

EXCEPTION: If one or both of the independent clauses contain a comma, you may use a semicolon with a coordinating conjunction between the clauses.

P3-d Use a colon after an independent clause to direct attention to a list, an appositive, a quotation, or a summary or an explanation.

A LIST

The daily exercise routine should include at least the following: ten minutes of stretching, forty abdominal crunches, and a twenty-minute run.

AN APPOSITIVE

My roommate seems to live on two things: sushi and social media.

A QUOTATION

Consider the words of Benjamin Franklin: "There never was a good war or a bad peace."

A SUMMARY OR AN EXPLANATION

Faith is like love: It (or it) cannot be forced.

The novel is clearly autobiographical: The (or the) author even gives his own name to the main character.

NOTE: For other ways of introducing quotations, see "Introducing quoted material" in P5-e. When an independent clause follows a colon, begin with a capital letter. Some disciplines use a lowercase letter instead. See MLA-5a, APA-5a, and CMS-5a for variations.

P3-e Use a colon according to convention.

SALUTATION IN A LETTER Dear Editor:

HOURS AND MINUTES 5:30 p.m.

PROPORTIONS The ratio of women to men was 2:1.

TITLE AND SUBTITLE *The Glory of Hera: Greek Mythology and the Greek Family*

CHAPTER AND VERSE IN SACRED TEXT Luke 2:14, Qur'an 67:3

P3-f Avoid common misuses of the colon.

A colon must be preceded by a full independent clause. Therefore, avoid using a colon in the following situations.

BETWEEN A VERB AND ITS OBJECT OR COMPLEMENT

▶ Some important vitamins found in vegetables are**/** vitamin A, thiamine, niacin, and vitamin C.

BETWEEN A PREPOSITION AND ITS OBJECT

▶ The heart's two pumps each consist of**/** an upper chamber, or atrium, and a lower chamber, or ventricle.

AFTER *SUCH AS*, *INCLUDING*, OR *FOR EXAMPLE*

▶ The NCAA regulates college athletic sports, including**/** basketball, baseball, softball, and football.

P4 The apostrophe

P4-a Use an apostrophe to indicate that a noun is possessive.

Possessive nouns usually indicate ownership, as in *Tim's hat* or *the lawyer's desk*. Frequently, however, ownership is only loosely implied: *the tree's roots, a day's work*. If you are not sure whether a noun is possessive, try turning it into an *of* phrase: *the roots of the tree, the work of a day*. (Pronouns also have possessive forms. See P4-d.)

When to add -'s

1. If the noun does not end in *-s*, add -'s.

   Luck often propels a rock musician's career.

   The Children's Defense Fund is a nonprofit organization that supports programs for poor and minority children.

2. If the noun is singular and ends in -s or an *s* sound, add -'*s* to show possession.

>   Lois's sister spent last year in India.

>   Her article presents an overview of Marx's teachings.

NOTE: To avoid potentially awkward pronunciation, some writers use only the apostrophe with a singular noun ending in -s: *Sophocles'*.

When to add only an apostrophe

If the noun is plural and ends in -s, add only an apostrophe.

>   Both diplomats' briefcases were searched by guards.

Joint possession

To show joint possession, use -'*s* or (-*s*') with the last noun only; to show individual possession, make all nouns possessive.

>   Have you seen Joyce and Greg's new camper?

>   John's and Marie's expectations of marriage couldn't have been more different.

Joyce and Greg jointly own one camper. John and Marie individually have different expectations.

Compound nouns

If a noun is compound, use -'*s* (or -*s*') with the last element.

>   My father-in-law's memoir about his childhood in Sri Lanka was published in October.

Indefinite pronouns

Indefinite pronouns refer to no specific person or thing: *everyone, someone, no one, something*. (See B1-b.)

>   Someone's raincoat has been left behind.

P4-b Use an apostrophe to mark omissions in contractions and numbers.

In a contraction, the apostrophe takes the place of one or more missing letters. *It's* stands for *it is*, *can't* for *cannot*.

>   It's a shame that Frank can't go on the tour.

The apostrophe is also used to mark the omission of the first two digits of a year or years.

The reunion for the class of '12 is tonight.

I am studying the music of the '60s.

P4-c Do not use an apostrophe in certain situations.

An apostrophe typically is not used to pluralize numbers, letters, abbreviations, and words mentioned as words. Note the few exceptions and be consistent throughout your paper.

Plural of numbers

Do not use an apostrophe in the plural of any numbers.

Oksana skated nearly perfect figure 8s.

The 1920s are known as the Jazz Age.

Plural of letters

Italicize the letter and use roman (regular) font style for the -s ending. (Do not italicize academic grades.)

Two large *P*s were painted on the door.

He received two Ds for the first time in his life.

EXCEPTIONS: To avoid misreading, use an apostrophe to form the plural of lowercase letters and the capital letters *A* and *I*.

Beginning readers often confuse *b*'s and *d*'s.

Students with straight A's earn high honors.

MLA NOTE: MLA recommends using an apostrophe for the plural of single capital and lowercase letters: *H*'s, *p*'s.

Plural of abbreviations

Do not use an apostrophe to pluralize an abbreviation.

Harriet has thirty DVDs on her desk.

Marco earned two PhDs before his thirtieth birthday.

Plural of words mentioned as words

Generally, omit the apostrophe to form the plural of words mentioned as words. If the word is italicized, the *-s* ending appears in roman (regular) type.

> We've heard enough *maybe*s.

Words mentioned as words may also appear in quotation marks. When you choose this option, use the apostrophe.

> We've heard enough "maybe's."

P4-d Avoid common misuses of the apostrophe.

Do not use an apostrophe with nouns that are not possessive or with the possessive pronouns *its, whose, his, hers, ours, yours,* and *theirs.*

> ▶ Some ~~outpatient's~~ have special parking permits.
>   outpatients

> ▶ Each area has ~~it's~~ own conference room.
>   its

It's means "it is." The possessive pronoun *its* contains no apostrophe despite the fact that it is possessive.

> ▶ We attended a reading by Junot Díaz, ~~who's~~ work focuses on the
>   whose
>
>   Dominican immigration experience.

Who's means "who is." The possessive pronoun is *whose.*

P5   Quotation marks

Writers use quotation marks primarily to enclose direct quotations of another person's spoken or written words. You will also find these other uses and exceptions:

- for quotations within quotations (single quotation marks: P5-b)
- for titles of short works (P5-c)
- for words used as words (P5-d)
- with other marks of punctuation (P5-e)
- no quotation marks for indirect quotations, paraphrases, and summaries (P5-a)
- no quotation marks for long quotations (P5-a)

P5-a Use quotation marks to enclose direct quotations.

Direct quotations of a person's words, whether spoken or written, must be in quotation marks.

> "Twitter," according to social media researcher Jameson Brown, "is the best social network for brand to customer engagement."

In dialogue, begin a new paragraph to mark a change in speaker.

> "Mom, his name is Willie, not William. A thousand times I've told you, it's *Willie.*"
> "Willie is a derivative of William, Lester. Surely his birth certificate doesn't have Willie on it, and I like calling people by their proper names."
> "Yes, it does, ma'am. My mother named me Willie K. Mason."
>
> — Gloria Naylor

If a single speaker utters more than one paragraph, introduce each paragraph with a quotation mark, but do not use a closing quotation mark until the end of the speech.

Exception: indirect quotations

Do not use quotation marks around indirect quotations. An indirect quotation reports someone's ideas without using that person's exact words. In academic writing, indirect quotation is called *paraphrase* or *summary.* (See R2-c.)

> Social media researcher Jameson Brown finds Twitter the best social media tool for companies that want to reach their consumers.

Exception: long quotations

Long quotations of prose or poetry are generally set off from the text by indenting. Quotation marks are not used because the indented format tells readers that the quotation is taken word for word from the source.

> After making an exhaustive study of the historical record, James Horan evaluates Billy the Kid like this:
>
> > The portrait that emerges of [the Kid] from the thousands of pages of affidavits, reports, trial transcripts, his letters, and his testimony is neither the mythical Robin Hood nor the stereotyped adenoidal moron and pathological killer. Rather Billy appears as a disturbed, lonely young man, honest, loyal to his friends, dedicated to his beliefs, and betrayed by our institutions and the corrupt, ambitious, and compromising politicians of his time. (158)

The number in parentheses is a citation handled according to MLA style (see MLA-3b).

MLA, APA, and CMS have specific guidelines for what constitutes a long quotation and how it should be indented (see MLA-3b, APA-3b, and CMS-3a, respectively).

P5-b Use single quotation marks to enclose a quotation within a quotation.

Megan Marshall notes that Elizabeth Peabody's school focused on "not merely 'teaching' but 'educating children morally and spiritually as well as intellectually from the first' " (107).

P5-c Use quotation marks around the titles of short works.

Short works include newspaper and magazine articles, poems, short stories, songs, episodes of television and radio programs, and chapters or subdivisions of books.

James Baldwin's story "Sonny's Blues" tells the story of two brothers who come to understand each other's suffering.

NOTE: Titles of long works such as books, plays, television and radio programs, films, magazines, and so on are put in italics. (See P10-a.)

P5-d Quotation marks may be used to set off words used as words.

Although words used as words are ordinarily italicized (see P10-b), quotation marks are also acceptable. Be consistent throughout your paper.

The terms "migrant" and "refugee" are frequently confused.

The terms *migrant* and *refugee* are frequently confused.

P5-e Use punctuation with quotation marks according to convention.

This section describes the conventions American publishers use in placing various marks of punctuation inside or outside quotation marks. It also explains how to punctuate when introducing quoted material. (For the use of quotation marks in MLA, APA, and CMS styles, see MLA-3b, APA-3b, and CMS-3a, respectively. The examples in this section show MLA style.)

Periods and commas

Place periods and commas inside quotation marks.

> "I'm here as part of my service-learning project," I told the classroom teacher. "I'm hoping to become a reading specialist."

This rule applies to single quotation marks as well as double quotation marks. (See P5-b.) It also applies to all uses of quotation marks: for quoted material, for titles of works, and for words used as words.

EXCEPTION: In the MLA and APA styles of parenthetical in-text citations, the period follows the citation in parentheses.

> James M. McPherson comments, approvingly, that the Whigs "were not averse to extending the blessings of American liberty, even to Mexicans and Indians" (48).

Colons and semicolons

Put colons and semicolons outside quotation marks.

> Harold wrote, "I regret that I am unable to attend the fundraiser for diabetes research"; his letter, however, came with a substantial contribution.

Question marks and exclamation points

Put question marks and exclamation points inside quotation marks unless they apply to the whole sentence.

> Dr. Abram's first question on the first day of class was "What three goals do you have for the course?"

> Have you heard the old proverb "Do not climb the hill until you reach it"?

In the first sentence, the question mark applies only to the quoted question. In the second sentence, the question mark applies to the whole sentence.

NOTE: In MLA and APA styles for a quotation that ends with a question mark or an exclamation point, the parenthetical citation and a period should follow the entire quotation.

> Rosie Thomas asks, "Is nothing in life ever straight and clear, the way children see it?" (77).

Introducing quoted material

After a word group introducing a quotation, choose a colon, a comma, or no punctuation at all, whichever is appropriate in context.

Formal introduction   If a quotation is formally introduced, a colon is appropriate. A formal introduction is a full independent clause, not just an expression such as *he writes* or *she explained.*

> Thomas Friedman provides a challenging yet optimistic view of the future: "We need to get back to work on our country and on our planet. The hour is late, the stakes couldn't be higher, the project couldn't be harder, the payoff couldn't be greater" (25).

Expression such as *he writes*   If a quotation is introduced with an expression such as *he writes* or *she explained* — or if it is followed by such an expression — a comma is needed.

> "With regard to air travel," Stephen Ambrose notes, "Jefferson was a full century ahead of the curve" (53).

> "Unless another war is prevented it is likely to bring destruction on a scale never before held possible and even now hardly conceived," Albert Einstein wrote in the aftermath of the atomic bomb (29).

Blended quotation   When a quotation is blended into the writer's own sentence, either a comma or no punctuation is appropriate, depending on the way in which the quotation fits into the sentence structure.

> The future champion could, as he put it, "float like a butterfly and sting like a bee."

> Virginia Woolf wrote in 1928 that "a woman must have money and a room of her own if she is to write fiction" (4).

Beginning of sentence   If a quotation appears at the beginning of a sentence, use a comma after it unless the quotation ends with a question mark or an exclamation point.

> "I've always thought of myself as a reporter," American poet Gwendolyn Brooks has stated (162).

> "What is it?" she asked, bracing herself.

Interrupted quotation   If a quoted sentence is interrupted by explanatory words, use commas to set off the explanatory words. If two successive quoted sentences from the same source are interrupted by explanatory words, use a comma before the explanatory words and a period after them.

> "Everyone agrees journalists must tell the truth," Bill Kovach and Tom Rosenstiel write. "Yet people are befuddled about what 'the truth' means" (37).

P5-f Avoid common misuses of quotation marks.

Do not use quotation marks to draw attention to familiar slang, to disown trite expressions, or to justify an attempt at humor.

▶ The economist noted that his prediction for a 5 percent decline

was only a ⫽ ballpark figure.⫽

Do not use quotation marks around the title of your own essay.

P6 Other punctuation marks

P6-a End punctuation

The period

Use a period to end all sentences except direct questions or genuine exclamations. Also use periods in abbreviations according to convention.

To end sentences   Most sentences should end with a period. A sentence that reports a question instead of asking it directly (an indirect question) should end with a period, not a question mark.

▶ The professor asked whether talk therapy was more beneficial

than antidepressants⫽.
              ^

If a sentence is not a genuine exclamation, it should end with a period, not an exclamation point.

▶ After years of research, Dr. Low finally solved the equation⫽.
                                                        ^

In abbreviations A period is conventionally used in abbreviations of titles and Latin words or phrases, including the time designations for morning and afternoon.

Mr.	i.e.	a.m. (or AM)
Ms.	e.g.	p.m. (or PM)
Dr.	etc.	

NOTE: If a sentence ends with a period marking an abbreviation, do not add a second period.

Do not use a period with postal abbreviations for states: MD, TX, CA.

Current usage is to omit the period in abbreviations of organization names, academic degrees, and designations for eras.

NATO	NIH
IRS	BS
UNESCO	PhD
AFL-CIO	BC
UCLA	BCE

The question mark

A direct question should be followed by a question mark.

What is the horsepower of a 777 engine?

Do not use a question mark after an indirect question, one that is reported rather than asked directly. Use a period instead.

▶ He asked me who was teaching the math course this year~~?~~.
                                                        ^

The exclamation point

Use an exclamation point after a word group or sentence to express exceptional feeling or to provide special emphasis. The exclamation point is rarely appropriate in academic writing.

When Mischa entered the room, I switched on the lights, and we all yelled, "Surprise!"

TIP: Do not overuse the exclamation point.

▶ In the fisherman's memory, the fish lives on, increasing in length and

weight with each passing year, until at last it is big enough to shade a

fishing boat~~!~~.
          ^

This sentence doesn't need to be pumped up with an exclamation point. It is emphatic enough without it.

P6-b The dash, parentheses, and brackets

The dash

When typing, use two hyphens to form a dash (--). Do not put a space before or after the dash. If your word processing program has what is known as an "em-dash" (—), you may use it instead, with no space before or after it.

Use a dash to set off parenthetical material that deserves emphasis.

> One of music's rising trends — lyrics that promote the use of synthetic drugs — is leading some artists to speak out against their peers.

Use a dash to set off appositives that contain commas. An appositive is a noun or noun phrase that renames a nearby noun. Ordinarily most appositives are set off with commas (P1-e), but when the appositive itself contains commas, a pair of dashes helps readers see the relative importance of all the pauses.

> In my hometown, people's basic needs — food, clothing, and shelter — are less costly than in a big city like Los Angeles.

A dash can also be used to introduce a list, a restatement, an amplification, or a dramatic shift in tone or thought.

> Along the wall are the bulk liquids — sesame seed oil, honey, safflower oil, and that half-liquid "peanuts only" peanut butter.

> In his last semester, Peter tried to pay more attention to his priorities — applying to graduate school and getting financial aid.

> Everywhere we looked there were little kids — a bag of Skittles in one hand and a parent's sleeve in the other.

> Kiere took a few steps back, came running full speed, kicked with all his might — and missed the ball.

In the first two examples, the writer could also use a colon. (See P3-d.) The colon is more formal than the dash and not quite as dramatic.

TIP: Unless there is a specific reason for using the dash, avoid it. Unnecessary dashes create a choppy effect.

Parentheses

Use parentheses to enclose supplemental material, minor digressions, and afterthoughts.

> Nurses record patients' vital signs (temperature, pulse, and blood pressure) several times a day.

Use parentheses to enclose letters or numbers labeling items in a series.

> Regulations stipulated that only the following equipment could be used on the survival mission: (1) a knife, (2) thirty feet of parachute line, (3) a book of matches, (4) two ponchos, (5) an E tool, and (6) a signal flare.

TIP: Rough drafts are likely to contain unnecessary parentheses. As writers head into a sentence, they often think of additional details, using parentheses to work them in as best they can. Such sentences usually can be revised to add the details without parentheses.

> *from*   *to*
> ▶ **Researchers have said that seventeen million (estimates run**
>   ^   ^
> **as high as twenty-three million) Americans have diabetes.**

Brackets

Use brackets to enclose any words or phrases that you have inserted into an otherwise word-for-word quotation.

> *Audubon* reports that "if there are not enough young to balance deaths, the end of the species [California condor] is inevitable" (4).

The sentence quoted from the *Audubon* article did not contain the words *California condor* (since the context of the full article made clear what species was meant), so the writer needed to add the name in brackets.

The Latin word "sic" in brackets indicates that an error in a quoted sentence appears in the original source.

> According to the review, Adele's performance was brilliant, "exceding [sic] the expectations of even her most loyal fans."

Do not overuse "sic," however, since calling attention to others' mistakes can appear snobbish. The preceding quotation, for example, might have been paraphrased instead: *According to the review, even Adele's most loyal fans were surprised by the brilliance of her performance.*

NOTE: For advice on using "sic" in MLA, APA, and CMS styles, see MLA-3b, APA-3b, and CMS-3a, respectively.

P6-c The ellipsis mark

The ellipsis mark consists of three spaced periods. Use an ellipsis mark to indicate that you have deleted words from an otherwise word-for-word quotation.

> Shute acknowledges that treatment for autism can be expensive: "Sensory integration therapy . . . can cost up to $200 an hour" (82).

If you delete a full sentence or more in the middle of a quoted passage, use a period before the three ellipsis dots.

> "If we don't properly train, teach, or treat our growing prison population," says Luis Rodríguez, "somebody else will. . . . This may well be the safety issue of the new century" (16).

TIP: Ordinarily, do not use the ellipsis mark at the beginning or at the end of a quotation. Readers will understand that the quoted material is taken from a longer passage. (If you have cut some words from the end of the final quoted sentence, however, MLA requires an ellipsis mark.)

In quoted poetry, use a full line of ellipsis dots to indicate that you have dropped a line or more from the poem, as in this example from "To His Coy Mistress" by Andrew Marvell:

> Had we but world enough, and time,
> This coyness, lady, were no crime.
> . . . .
> But at my back I always hear
> Time's wingèd chariot hurrying near; (1–2, 21–22)

P6-d The slash

Use the slash to separate two or three lines of poetry that have been run into your text. Add a space both before and after the slash.

> In the opening lines of "Jordan," George Herbert pokes gentle fun at popular poems of his time: "Who says that fictions only and false hair / Become a verse? Is there in truth no beauty?" (1–2).

Four or more lines of poetry should be handled as an indented quotation. (See pp. 465–66.)

The slash may occasionally be used to separate paired terms such as *pass/fail* and *producer/director*. Do not use a space before or after the slash. Be sparing in this use of the slash. In particular, avoid the use of *and/or*, *he/she*, and *his/her*. Instead of using *he/she* and *his/her* to solve sexist language problems, you can usually find more graceful and more inclusive alternatives. (See W4-e and G3-a.)

P7 Spelling and hyphenation

You learned to spell from repeated experience with words in both reading and writing. As you proofread, you can probably tell if a word doesn't look quite right. In such cases, the solution is simple: Look up the word in a dictionary.

P7-a Become familiar with the major spelling rules.

i *before* e *except after* c

In general, use i before e except after c and except when it sounds like *ay*, as in *neighbor* and *weigh*.

I BEFORE *E*	relieve, believe, sieve, niece, fierce, piece
E BEFORE *I*	receive, deceive, sleigh, freight, eight
EXCEPTIONS	seize, either, weird, height, foreign, leisure

Suffixes

Final silent -e   Generally, drop a final silent -*e* when adding a suffix that begins with a vowel. Keep the final -*e* if the suffix begins with a consonant.

combine, combination	achieve, achievement
desire, desiring	care, careful
prude, prudish	entire, entirety
remove, removable	gentle, gentleness

Words such as *changeable, judgment, argument,* and *truly* are exceptions.

Final –y   When adding -*s* or -*d* to words ending in -*y*, ordinarily change -*y* to -*ie* when the -*y* is preceded by a consonant but not when it is preceded by a vowel.

comedy, comedies	monkey, monkeys
dry, dried	play, played

With proper names ending in -*y*, however, do not change the -*y* to -*ie* even if it is preceded by a consonant: *the Doughertys.*

Final consonants   If a final consonant is preceded by a single vowel *and* the consonant ends a one-syllable word or a stressed syllable, double the consonant when adding a suffix beginning with a vowel.

bet, betting	occur, occurrence
commit, committed	

Plurals

-s *or* –es   Add -*s* to form the plural of most nouns; add -*es* to singular nouns ending in -*s*, -*sh*, -*ch*, and -*x*.

table, tables	church, churches
paper, papers	dish, dishes

For Multilingual Writers Spelling varies slightly among English-speaking countries. Variations can be confusing for some multilingual students in the United States. Following is a list of some common words with different American and British spellings. Consult a dictionary for others.

AMERICAN	BRITISH
canceled, traveled	cancelled, travelled
color, humor	colour, humour
judgment	judgement
realize, apologize	realise, apologise
defense	defence
anemia, anesthetic	anaemia, anaesthetic
theater, center	theatre, centre
connection, inflection	connexion, inflexion

Ordinarily add -s to nouns ending in -o when the -o is preceded by a vowel. Add -es when it is preceded by a consonant.

radio, radios   hero, heroes
video, videos   tomato, tomatoes

Other plurals To form the plural of a hyphenated compound word, add -s to the chief word even if it does not appear at the end.

mother-in-law, mothers-in-law

English words derived from other languages such as Latin, Greek, or French sometimes form the plural as they would in their original language.

medium, media   chateau, chateaux
criterion, criteria

P7-b Discriminate between words that sound alike but have different meanings.

Words that sound alike or nearly alike but have different meanings and spellings are called *homophones*. The following sets of words are commonly confused. A careful writer will double-check their every use. (See also the glossary of usage, W1.)

affect (verb: to exert an influence)
effect (verb: to accomplish; noun: result)

its (possessive pronoun: of or belonging to it)
it's (contraction of *it is* or *it has*)

loose (adjective: free, not securely attached)
lose (verb: to fail to keep, to be deprived of)

principal (adjective: most important; noun: head of a school)
principle (noun: a fundamental guideline or truth)

their (possessive pronoun: belonging to them)
they're (contraction of *they are*)
there (adverb: that place or position)

who's (contraction of *who is* or *who has*)
whose (possessive form of *who*)

your (possessive pronoun: belonging to you)
you're (contraction of *you are*)

P7-c Be alert to commonly misspelled words.

absence	conceivable	independence	publicly
accidentally	conscience	intelligence	quiet
accommodate	conscientious	irrelevant	quite
achievement	conscious	knowledge	receive
acknowledge	criticism	library	recognize
acquire	criticize	license	referred
address	decision	lightning	restaurant
all right	definitely	loneliness	rhythm
amateur	descendant	maintenance	roommate
analyze	desperate	necessary	schedule
apparently	different	noticeable	seize
appearance	embarrass	occasion	separate
arctic	emphasize	occurred	siege
argument	environment	pamphlet	sincerely
arrangement	especially	parallel	sophomore
ascend	exaggerated	particularly	strictly
athlete	exercise	permanent	subtly
attendance	existence	perseverance	succeed
basically	familiar	phenomenon	surprise
beautiful	fascinate	physically	thorough
beginning	February	practically	tomorrow
believe	foreign	precede	transferred
benefited	forty	preference	truly
business	fourth	preferred	unnecessarily
cemetery	friend	prejudice	usually
commitment	government	presence	weird
committed	harass	prevalent	whether
committee	height	privilege	writing
competitive	humorous	proceed	

P7-d Consult the dictionary to determine how to treat a compound word.

The dictionary indicates whether to treat a compound word as hyphenated (*water-repellent*), as one word (*waterproof*), or as two words (*water table*). If the compound word is not in the dictionary, treat it as two words.

▶ The prosecutor chose not to cross-examine any witnesses.

▶ All students are expected to record their data in a small

  note book.

▶ Alice walked through the looking glass into a backward world.

P7-e Hyphenate two or more words used together as an adjective before a noun.

▶ Today's teachers depend on both traditional textbook material

  and web-delivered content.

▶ Richa Gupta is not yet a well-known candidate.

  Generally, do not use a hyphen when such compounds follow the noun.

▶ After our television campaign, Richa Gupta will be well known.

  Do not use a hyphen to connect -*ly* adverbs to the words they modify.

▶ A slowly moving truck tied up traffic.

P7-f Hyphenate fractions and certain numbers when they are spelled out.

For numbers written as words, use a hyphen in all fractions (*two-thirds*) and in all forms of compound numbers from twenty-one to ninety-nine (*thirty-five, sixty-seventh*).

P7-g Use a hyphen with the prefixes *all-*, *ex-* (meaning "former"), and *self-* and with the suffix *-elect*.

▶ The private foundation is funneling more money into self-help projects.
^

▶ The Student Senate bylaws require the president-elect to attend all
^

senate meetings before the transfer of office.

P7-h Use a hyphen in certain words to avoid ambiguity.

Without the hyphen, there would be no way to distinguish between words such as *re-creation* and *recreation*.

Bicycling in the city has always been my favorite form of recreation.

The film was praised for its astonishing re-creation of nineteenth-century London.

Hyphens are sometimes used to separate awkward double or triple letters in compound words (*anti-intellectual, cross-stitch*).

P7-i Check for correct word breaks when words must be divided at the end of a line.

In academic writing, it's best to set your computer applications not to hyphen-ate automatically. This setting will ensure that only words already containing a hyphen (such as *long-distance* or *pre-Roman*) will be hyphenated at the ends of lines.

Email addresses, URLs, and DOIs need special attention when they occur at the end of a line of text or in bibliographic citations. You must make a decision about hyphenation in each case.

Do not insert a hyphen to divide online addresses. Instead, break an email address after the @ symbol or before a period. Rules related to how to break URLs and DOIs vary by discipline. For specific guidelines, see MLA-5, APA-5, and CMS-5.

P8 Capitalization

In addition to the rules in this section, a good dictionary can tell you when to use capital letters.

P8-a Capitalize proper nouns and words derived from them; do not capitalize common nouns.

Proper nouns are the names of specific persons, places, and things. All other nouns are common nouns. The following types of words are usually capitalized: names of deities, religions, religious followers, sacred books; words of family relationship used as names; particular places; nationalities and their languages, races, tribes; educational institutions, departments, particular courses; government departments, organizations, political parties; historical movements, periods, events, documents; and trade names.

PROPER NOUNS	COMMON NOUNS
God (used as a name)	a god
Book of Common Prayer	a sacred book
Uncle Pedro	my uncle
Father (used as a name)	my father
Lake Superior	a picturesque lake
the Capital Center	a center for advanced studies
the South	a southern state
Wrigley Field	a baseball stadium
University of Wisconsin	a state university
Geology 101	geology
the Democratic Party	a political party
the Enlightenment	the eighteenth century
Advil	a painkiller

Months, holidays, and days of the week are treated as proper nouns; the seasons and numbers of the days of the month are not.

> Our academic year begins on a Tuesday in early September, right after Labor Day.

> Graduation is in late spring, on the second of June.

EXCEPTION: Capitalize Fourth of July (or July Fourth) when referring to the holiday.

Names of school subjects are capitalized only if they are names of languages. Names of particular courses are capitalized.

> This semester Lee is taking math, physics, French, and English.

> Professor Obembe offers Modern American Fiction 501 to graduate students.

Do not capitalize common nouns to make them seem important.

P8-b Capitalize titles of persons when used as part of a proper name but usually not when used alone.

Professor Margaret Barnes; Dr. Eun Ju Kim; John Scott Williams Jr.

District Attorney Marshall was reprimanded for badgering the witness.

The district attorney was elected for a two-year term.

Usage varies when the title of an important public figure is used alone: *The president* [or *The President*] *vetoed the bill.*

P8-c Capitalize titles according to convention.

In both titles and subtitles of works mentioned in the text of a paper, major words such as nouns, pronouns, verbs, adjectives, and adverbs should be capitalized. Minor words such as articles, prepositions, and coordinating conjunctions are not capitalized unless they are the first or last word of a title or subtitle. (In APA style, also capitalize all words of four or more letters. See APA-5.)

Capitalize the second part of a hyphenated term in a title if it is a major word but not if it is a minor word. Capitalize chapter titles and the titles of other major divisions of a work following the same guidelines used for titles of complete works.

Seizing the Enigma: The Race to Break the German U-Boat Codes
A River Runs through It
"I Want to Hold Your Hand"

To see why some titles are italicized and others are put in quotation marks, see P10-a and P5-c.

Titles of works are handled differently in the APA reference list. See "Preparing the list of references" in APA-5a.

P8-d Capitalize the first word of a sentence.

The first word of a sentence should be capitalized. When a sentence appears within parentheses, capitalize its first word unless the parentheses appear within another sentence.

Early detection of breast cancer significantly increases survival rates. (See table 2.)

Early detection of breast cancer significantly increases survival rates (see table 2).

P8-e Capitalize the first word of a quoted sentence but not a quoted word or phrase.

> Loveless writes, "If failing schools are ever to be turned around, much more must be learned about how schools age as institutions" (25).

> Russell Baker has written that in this country, sports are "the opiate of the masses" (46).

If a quoted sentence is interrupted by explanatory words, do not capitalize the first word after the interruption. (See also P5-e.)

> "If you want to go out," he said, "tell me now."

When quoting poetry, copy the poet's capitalization exactly. Many poets capitalize the first word of every line of poetry; a few contemporary poets dismiss capitalization altogether.

> it was the week   that
> i felt the city's narrow breezes rush about
> me   — Don L. Lee

P8-f Know your options when the first word after a colon begins an independent clause.

When a group of words following a colon could stand on its own as a complete sentence, MLA recommends using lowercase for the first word except in certain situations (such as if the sentence following the colon is a question). APA calls for capitalizing it.

MLA

> Clinical trials called into question the safety profile of the drug: a high percentage of participants reported severe headaches.

APA

> Clinical trials called into question the safety profile of the drug: A high percentage of participants reported severe headaches.

Always use lowercase for a list or an appositive that follows a colon (see P3-d).

> Students were divided into two groups: residents and commuters.

P9 Abbreviations and numbers

P9-a Use common abbreviations for titles immediately before and after proper names.

TITLES BEFORE PROPER NAMES	TITLES AFTER PROPER NAMES
Mr. Rafael Zabala	William Albert Sr.
Ms. Nancy Linehan	Thomas Hines Jr.
Dr. Margaret Simmons	Robert Simkowski, MD
Rev. John Stone	Mia Chin, LLD

Do not abbreviate a title if it is not used with a proper name: *My history professor* [not *prof.*] *is an expert on race relations in South Africa.*

Avoid redundant titles such as *Dr. Amy Day, MD.* Choose one title or the other: *Dr. Amy Day* or *Amy Day, MD.*

P9-b Use abbreviations only when you are sure your readers will understand them.

Familiar abbreviations for the names of organizations, companies, countries, academic degrees, and common terms, written without periods, are generally acceptable.

CIA	MD
NBA	PhD
FBI	NAACP
CEO	DVD

Talk show host Conan O'Brien is a Harvard graduate with a BA in history.

When using an unfamiliar abbreviation (such as *NASW* for National Association of Social Workers) or a potentially ambiguous abbreviation (such as *AMA*, which can refer to either the American Medical Association or the American Management Association), write the full name followed by the abbreviation in parentheses at the first mention of the name. Then use just the abbreviation throughout the rest of the paper.

NOTE: An abbreviation that can be pronounced as a word is called an *acronym*: *NATO, AWOL, FOMO.*

P9-c Use *BC, AD, a.m., p.m., No.*, and *$* only with specific dates, times, numbers, and amounts.

The abbreviation *BC* ("before Christ") follows a date, and *AD* ("*anno Domini*") precedes a date. Acceptable alternatives are *BCE* ("before the common era") and *CE* ("common era"), both of which follow a date.

40 BC (or 40 BCE)	6:00 p.m. (or PM)
AD 44 (or 44 CE)	No. 12 (or no. 12)
4:00 a.m.	(or AM) $150

Avoid using *a.m., p.m., No.*, or *$* when not accompanied by a specific numeral: *in the morning* (not *in the a.m.*).

P9-d Units of measurement

The following are typical abbreviations for units of measurement. Most social sciences and related fields use metric units (*km, mg*), but in other fields and in everyday use, US standard units (*mi, lb*) are typical. Generally, use abbreviations for units when they appear with numerals; spell out the units when they are used alone or when they are used with spelled-out numbers (see also P9-h).

METRIC UNITS	US STANDARD UNITS
m, cm, mm	yd, ft, in.
km, kph	mi, mph
kg, g, mg	lb, oz

Results were measured in pounds.

Runners in the 5-km race had to contend with pouring rain.

Use no periods after abbreviations for units of measurement, except the abbreviation for "inch" (*in.*), to distinguish it from the preposition *in*.

P9-e Be sparing in your use of Latin abbreviations.

Latin abbreviations are acceptable in notes and bibliographies.

e.g. (Latin *exempli gratia*, "for example")

et al. (Latin *et alia*, "and others")

etc. (Latin *et cetera*, "and so forth")

i.e. (Latin *id est*, "that is")

N.B. (Latin *nota bene*, "note well")

In the text of a paper in most academic fields, use the appropriate English phrases.

P9-f Plural of abbreviations

To form the plural of most abbreviations, add *-s*, without an apostrophe: *PhDs*, *DVDs*. Do not add *-s* to indicate the plural of units of measurement: *mm* (not *mms*), *lb* (not *lbs*), *in.* (not *ins.*).

P9-g Avoid inappropriate abbreviations.

In academic writing, abbreviations for the following are not commonly accepted.

PERSONAL NAMES   Charles (not Chas.)

DAYS OF THE WEEK   Monday (not Mon.)

HOLIDAYS   Christmas (not Xmas)

MONTHS   January, February, March (not Jan., Feb., Mar.)

COURSES OF STUDY   political science (not poli. sci.)

DIVISIONS OF WRITTEN WORKS   chapter, page (not ch., p.)

STATES AND COUNTRIES   Massachusetts (not MA or Mass.)

PARTS OF A BUSINESS NAME   Adams Lighting Company (not Adams Lighting Co.); Zeiss and Brothers (not Zeiss and Bros.)

NOTE: Use abbreviations for units of measurement when they are preceded by numerals (*13 cm*). Do not abbreviate them when they are used alone. See P9-d.

EXCEPTION: Abbreviate states and provinces in complete addresses, and always abbreviate "District of Columbia" as *DC* when used with *Washington*.

P9-h Follow the conventions in your discipline for spelling out or using numerals to express numbers.

In the humanities, which generally follow Modern Language Association (MLA) style, use numerals only for specific numbers larger than one hundred: *353; 1,020*. Spell out numbers one hundred and below and large round numbers: *eleven, thirty-five, fifteen million*. Treat related numbers in a passage consistently: *The survey found that 9 of the 157 students had not taken a course on alcohol use.*

The social sciences and other disciplines that follow American Psychological Association (APA) style use numerals for all but the numbers one through nine. Spell out numbers from one to nine even when they are used with related numerals in a passage: *The survey found that nine of the 157 respondents had not taken a course on alcohol use.*

If a sentence begins with a number, spell out the number or rewrite the sentence.

> One hundred fifty
> ► ~~150~~ children in our program need expensive dental treatment.
>   ^

Rewriting the sentence may be less awkward if the number is long: *In our program, 150 children need expensive dental treatment.*

P9-i Use numerals according to convention in dates, addresses, and so on.

DATES   July 4, 1776; 56 BC; AD 30

ADDRESSES   77 Latches Lane, 519 West 42nd Street

PERCENTAGES   55 percent (or 55%)

FRACTIONS, DECIMALS $^{15}/_{16}$, 0.047

SCORES   7 to 3, 21–18

STATISTICS   average age 37, average weight 180

SURVEYS   4 out of 5

EXACT AMOUNTS OF MONEY $105.37; $106,000

DIVISIONS OF BOOKS   volume 3, chapter 4, page 189

DIVISIONS OF PLAYS   act 3, scene 3 (or act III, scene iii)

TIME OF DAY   4:00 p.m., 1:30 a.m.

NOTE: When not using *a.m.* or *p.m.*, write out the time in words (*two o'clock in the afternoon, twelve noon, seven in the morning*).

P10 Italics

This section describes conventional uses for italics. (If your instructor prefers underlining, simply substitute underlining for italics in the examples in this section.)

Some computer and online applications do not allow for italics. To indicate words that should be italicized, you can use underscore marks or asterisks before and after the words.

I am planning to write my senior thesis on _The Book Thief_.

NOTE: Excessive use of italics to emphasize words or ideas, especially in academic writing, is distracting and should be avoided.

P10-a Italicize the titles of works according to convention.

Titles of the following types of works should be italicized.

TITLES OF BOOKS   *The Color Purple, The Round House*

MAGAZINES   *Time, Scientific American, Slate*

NEWSPAPERS   *The Baltimore Sun, Orlando Sentinel*

PAMPHLETS   *Common Sense, Facts about Marijuana*

LONG POEMS   *The Waste Land, Paradise Lost*

PLAYS   *The Humans, Hamilton*

FILMS   *Casablanca, Argo*

TELEVISION OR STREAMING SERIES   *The Voice, Killing Eve*

RADIO PROGRAMS OR PODCASTS   *All Things Considered, Code Switch*

MUSICAL COMPOSITIONS   *Porgy and Bess*

WORKS OF VISUAL ART   *American Gothic*

VIDEO GAMES   *Everquest, Call of Duty*

DATABASES OR WEBSITES [MLA]   *JSTOR, Salon*

SOFTWARE OR APPS [MLA]   *Photoshop, Instagram*

The titles of other works — including short stories, essays, episodes of radio and television programs, songs, and short poems — are enclosed in quotation marks. (See P5-c.)

NOTE: Do not use italics when referring to the Bible, titles of books in the Bible (Genesis, not *Genesis*), or titles of legal documents (the Constitution, not the *Constitution*).

P10-b Italicize other terms according to convention.

Ships, spacecraft, and aircraft

Queen Mary 2, Endeavour, Wright Flyer

The success of the Soviets' *Sputnik* energized the US space program.

Non-English words

> Shakespeare's Falstaff is a comic character known for both his excessive drinking and his general *joie de vivre*.

EXCEPTION: Do not italicize foreign words that have become a standard part of the English language — "laissez-faire," "fait accompli," "modus operandi," and "per diem," for example.

Words mentioned as words, letters mentioned as letters, and numbers mentioned as numbers

> Tomás assured us that the chemicals could probably be safely mixed, but his *probably* stuck in our minds.

> Some toddlers have trouble pronouncing the letters *f* and *s*.

> A big *3* was painted on the stage door.

NOTE: Quotation marks may be used instead of italics to set off words mentioned as words. (See P5-d.)

B

Basic Grammar

Will I be a better writer if I know grammar basics?

See B1–B4

B Basic Grammar

B1 Parts of speech

Traditional grammar recognizes eight parts of speech: noun, pronoun, verb, adjective, adverb, preposition, conjunction, and interjection. Many words can function as more than one part of speech. For example, depending on its use in a sentence, the word *paint* can be a noun (*The paint is wet*) or a verb (*Please paint the ceiling next*).

B1-a Nouns

A noun is the name of a person, place, thing, or concept.

>   **N**   **N**   **N**
> The *lion* in the *cage* growled at the *zookeeper*.

Nouns sometimes function as adjectives modifying other nouns. Because of their dual roles, nouns used in this manner may be called *noun/adjectives*.

>   **N/ADJ**   **N/ADJ**
> The *leather* notebook was tucked in the *student's* backpack.

Nouns are classified in a variety of ways. *Proper* nouns are capitalized, but *common* nouns are not (see P8-a). For clarity, writers choose between *concrete* and *abstract* nouns (see W5-b). The distinction between *count* nouns and *noncount* nouns can be especially helpful to multilingual writers (see M2-a). Most nouns have singular and plural forms; *collective* nouns may be either singular or plural, depending on how they are used (see G1-f and G3-a). *Possessive* nouns require an apostrophe (see P4-a).

B1-b Pronouns

A pronoun is a word used in place of a noun. Usually the pronoun substitutes for a specific noun, known as its *antecedent*.

>   **ANT**   **PN**
> When the *battery* wears down, we recharge *it*.

Although most pronouns function as substitutes for nouns, some can function as adjectives modifying nouns. Such pronouns may be called *pronoun/adjectives*.

> **PN/ADJ**
> *That* bird was at the same window yesterday morning.

Pronouns are classified in the following ways.

Personal pronouns   Personal pronouns refer to specific persons or things. They always function as substitutes for nouns.

Singular: I, me, you, she, her, he, him, it, they (see G3-a)

Plural: we, us, you, they, them

Possessive pronouns   Possessive pronouns indicate ownership.

Singular: my, mine, your, yours, her, hers, his, its, their/theirs (see G3-a)

Plural: our, ours, your, yours, their, theirs

Some of these possessive pronouns function as adjectives modifying nouns: *my, your, her, his, its, our, their.*

Intensive and reflexive pronouns   Intensive pronouns emphasize a noun or another pronoun (The senator *herself* met us at the door). Reflexive pronouns name a receiver of an action identical with the doer of the action (Paula cut *herself*).

Singular: myself, yourself, himself, herself, itself, themselves (see G3-a)

Plural: ourselves, yourselves, themselves

Relative pronouns   Relative pronouns introduce subordinate clauses functioning as adjectives (The writer *who won the award* refused to accept it). The relative pronoun, in this case *who*, also points back to a noun or pronoun that the clause modifies (*writer*). (See B3-e.)

who, whom, whose, which, that

The pronouns *whichever, whoever, whomever, what,* and *whatever* are sometimes considered relative pronouns, but they introduce noun clauses and do not point back to a noun or pronoun. (See "Noun clauses" in B3-e.)

Interrogative pronouns   Interrogative pronouns introduce questions (*Who* is expected to win the election?).

who, whom, whose, which, what

Demonstrative pronouns   Demonstrative pronouns identify or point to nouns. Frequently they function as adjectives (*This* chair is my favorite), but they may also function as substitutes for nouns (*This* is my favorite chair).

this, that, these, those

Indefinite pronouns   Indefinite pronouns refer to nonspecific persons or things. Most are always singular (*everyone, each*); some are always plural (*both, many*); a few may be singular or plural (see G1-e). Most indefinite pronouns function as substitutes for nouns (*Something* is burning), but some can also function as adjectives (*All* campers must check in at the lodge).

all	anything	everyone	nobody	several
another	both	everything	none	some
any	each	few	no one	somebody
anybody	either	many	nothing	someone
anyone	everybody	neither	one	something

Reciprocal pronouns   Reciprocal pronouns refer to individual parts of a plural antecedent (By turns, the penguins fed *one another*).

each other, one another

NOTE: See also pronoun-antecedent agreement (G3-a), pronoun reference (G3-b), distinguishing between pronouns such as *I* and *me* (G3-c), and distinguishing between *who* and *whom* (G3-d).

B1-c Verbs

The verb of a sentence usually expresses action (*jump, think*) or being (*is, become*). It is composed of a main verb possibly preceded by one or more helping verbs.

MV
The horses *exercise* every day.

HV   MV
The task force report *was* not *completed* on schedule.

HV HV   MV
No one *has been defended* with more passion than our pastor.

Notice that words, usually adverbs, can intervene between the helping verb and the main verb (was *not* completed). (See B1-e.)

Helping verbs

There are twenty-three helping verbs in English: forms of *have, do,* and *be,* which may also function as main verbs; and nine modals, which function only as helping verbs. *Have, do,* and *be* change form to indicate tense; the nine modals do not.

FORMS OF *HAVE, DO,* AND *BE*

have, has, had

do, does, did

be, am, is, are, was, were, being, been

MODALS

can, could, may, might, must, shall, should, will, would

The verb phrase *ought to* is often classified as a modal as well.

Main verbs

The main verb of a sentence is always the kind of word that would change form if put into these test sentences:

BASE FORM	Usually I (*walk, ride*).
PAST TENSE	Yesterday I (*walked, rode*).
PAST PARTICIPLE	I have (*walked, ridden*) many times before.
PRESENT PARTICIPLE	I am (*walking, riding*) right now.
-S FORM	Usually he/she/it (*walks, rides*).

If a word doesn't change form when slipped into the test sentences, you can be certain that it is not a main verb. For example, the noun *revolution*, though it may seem to suggest an action, can never function as a main verb. Just try to make it behave like one (*Today I revolution . . . , Yesterday I revolutioned . . .*) and you'll see why.

When both the past-tense and the past-participle forms of a verb end in *-ed*, the verb is regular (*walked, walked*). Otherwise, the verb is irregular (*rode, ridden*). (See G2-a.)

The verb *be* is highly irregular, having eight forms instead of the usual five: the base form *be*; the present-tense forms *am, is,* and *are*; the past-tense forms *was* and *were*; the present participle *being*; and the past participle *been*.

Helping verbs combine with main verbs to create tenses. (See G2-f.)

NOTE: Some verbs are followed by words that look like prepositions but are so closely associated with the verb that they are a part of its meaning. These words are known as particles. Common verb-particle combinations include *bring up, drop off, give in, look up, run into,* and *take off*.

TIP: For more information about using verbs, see these sections of the handbook: active verbs (W3), subject-verb agreement (G1), English verb forms (G2-a to G2-d), verb tense and mood (G2-f and G2-g), and verbs for multilingual writers (M1).

B1-d Adjectives

An adjective is a word used to modify, or describe, a noun or pronoun. An adjective usually answers one of these questions: Which one? What kind of? How many?

ADJ
the *playful* dog [Which dog?]

ADJ
qualified applicants [What kind of applicants?]

ADJ
nine months [How many months?]

Adjectives usually precede the words they modify. They may also follow linking verbs, in which case they describe the subject. (See B2-b.)

        ADJ
The decision was *unpopular.*

The definite article *the* and the indefinite articles *a* and *an* are also classified as adjectives.

ART   **ART**   **ART**
A defendant should be judged on *the* evidence provided to *the* jury, not on hearsay.

Some possessive, demonstrative, and indefinite pronouns can function as adjectives: *their, its, this, all* (see B1-b). And nouns can function as adjectives when they modify other nouns: *apple pie* (the noun *apple* modifies the noun *pie*; see B1-a).

TIP: You can find more details about using adjectives in G4. If you are a multilingual writer, you may find help with articles and specific uses of adjectives in M2 and M4.

B1-e Adverbs

An adverb is a word used to modify, or qualify, a verb (or verbal), an adjective, or another adverb. It usually answers one of these questions: When? Where? How? Why? Under what conditions? To what degree?

Pull *firmly* on the emergency handle. [Pull how?]

Read the text *first* and *then* complete the exercises. [Read when? Complete when?]

Place the flowers *here.* [Place where?]

Adverbs modifying adjectives or other adverbs usually intensify or limit the intensity of the word they modify.

    ADV
Be *extremely* kind, and you will have many friends.

        ADV
We proceeded *very* cautiously in the dark house.

The words *not* and *never* are classified as adverbs.

> **For Multilingual Writers**   Multilingual writers can find more about the placement of adverbs in M3-f.

B1-f Prepositions

A preposition is a word placed before a noun or a pronoun to form a phrase that modifies another word in the sentence. The prepositional phrase functions as an adjective or an adverb.

> P   P   P
> The winding road *to* the summit travels *past* craters *from* an extinct volcano.

To the summit functions as an adjective modifying the noun *road*; *past craters* functions as an adverb modifying the verb *travels*; *from an extinct volcano* functions as an adjective modifying the noun *craters*. (For more on prepositional phrases, see B3-a.)

English has a limited number of prepositions. The most common are included in the following list.

about	below	inside	plus
above	beside	into	since
across	besides	like	through
after	between	near	throughout
against	beyond	next	to
along	by	of	under
among	despite	off	until
around	down	on	up
as	during	out	upon
at	for	outside	with
before	from	over	within
behind	in	past	without

Some prepositions are more than one word long. *Along with, as well as, in addition to, next to,* and *rather than* are examples.

TIP: Prepositions are used in idioms such as *capable of* and *dig up* (see W5-d). For specific issues for multilingual writers, see M5.

B1-g Conjunctions

Conjunctions join words, phrases, or clauses, and they indicate the relation between the elements joined.

Coordinating conjunctions   A coordinating conjunction is used to connect grammatically equal elements. (See S1-b and S6.) The coordinating conjunctions are *and, but, or, nor, for, so,* and *yet.*

> The sociologist interviewed children *but* not their parents.

> Write clearly, *and* your readers will appreciate your efforts.

In the first sentence, *but* connects two noun phrases; in the second, *and* connects two independent clauses.

Correlative conjunctions   Correlative conjunctions come in pairs; they connect grammatically equal elements.

> either . . . or
> neither . . . nor
> not only . . . but also
> whether . . . or
> both . . . and

> *Either* the painting was brilliant *or* it was a forgery.

Subordinating conjunctions   A subordinating conjunction introduces a subordinate clause and indicates the relation of the clause to the rest of the sentence. (See B3-e.) The most common subordinating conjunctions are *after, although, as, as if, because, before, if, in order that, once, since, so that, than, that, though, unless, until, when, where, whether,* and *while.* (For a complete list, see the chart in B3-e.)

> *When* the fundraiser ends, we expect to have raised more than half a million dollars.

Conjunctive adverbs   Conjunctive adverbs connect independent clauses and indicate the relation between the clauses. They can be used with a semicolon to join two independent clauses in one sentence, or they can be used alone with an independent clause. The most common conjunctive adverbs are *finally, furthermore, however, moreover, nevertheless, similarly, then, therefore,* and *thus.* (For a complete list, see P3-a.)

> The photographer failed to take a light reading; *therefore,* all the pictures were underexposed.

> During the day, the kitten sleeps peacefully. *However,* when night falls, the kitten is wide awake and ready to play.

Conjunctive adverbs can appear at the beginning or in the middle of a clause.

> When night falls, *however,* the kitten is wide awake and ready to play.

TIP: The ability to distinguish between conjunctive adverbs and coordinating conjunctions will help you avoid run-on sentences and make punctuation decisions (see G6, P1-a, and P1-f). The ability to recognize subordinating conjunctions will help you avoid sentence fragments (see G5).

B1-h Interjections

An interjection is a word used to express surprise or emotion (*Oh! Hey! Wow!*).

B2 Sentence patterns

The vast majority of English sentences conform to one of these five patterns:

> subject/verb/subject complement
> subject/verb/direct object
> subject/verb/indirect object/direct object
> subject/verb/direct object/object complement
> subject/verb

Adverbial modifiers (single words, phrases, or clauses) may be added to any of these patterns, and they may appear nearly anywhere — at the beginning, in the middle, or at the end.

Predicate is the grammatical term given to the verb plus its objects, complements, and adverbial modifiers.

B2-a Subjects

The subject of a sentence names whom or what the sentence is about. The simple subject is always a noun or pronoun; the complete subject consists of the simple subject and any words or word groups modifying the simple subject.

The complete subject

To find the complete subject, ask Who? or What?, insert the verb, and finish the question. The answer is the complete subject.

┌─── COMPLETE SUBJECT ───┐
The devastating effects of famine can last for many years.

Who or what can last for many years? *The devastating effects of famine.*

┌─────────── COMPLETE SUBJECT ───────────┐
Adventure novels that contain multiple subplots are often made into successful movies.

Who or what are often made into movies? *Adventure novels that contain multiple subplots.*

COMPLETE
┌── SUBJECT ──┐
In our program, student teachers work full-time for ten months.

Who or what works full-time for ten months? *Student teachers.* Notice that *In our program, student teachers* is not a sensible answer to the question. (It is not wise to assume that the subject must always appear first in a sentence.)

The simple subject

To find the simple subject, strip away all modifiers in the complete subject. This includes single-word modifiers such as *the* and *devastating*, phrases such as *of famine*, and subordinate clauses such as *that contain multiple subplots*.

┌─SS─┐
The devastating effects of famine can last for many years.

┌─SS─┐
Adventure novels that contain multiple subplots are often made into successful movies.

A sentence may have a compound subject containing two or more simple subjects joined with a coordinating conjunction such as *and, but,* or *or.*

┌──── SS ────┐ ┌─SS─┐
Great commitment and a little luck make a successful actor.

Understood subjects

In imperative sentences, which give advice or issue commands, the subject is understood but not actually present in the sentence. The subject of an imperative sentence is understood to be *you.*

[*You*] Put your hands on the steering wheel.

Subject after the verb

Although the subject ordinarily comes before the verb (*The planes took off*), occasionally it does not. When a sentence begins with *There is* or *There are* (or *There was* or *There were*), the subject follows the verb. In such inverted constructions, the word *There* is an expletive, an empty word serving merely to get the sentence started.

┌─SS─┐
There are *eight planes waiting to take off.*

Occasionally a writer will invert a sentence for effect.

┌─SS─┐
Joyful is *the child whose school closes for snow.*

Joyful is an adjective, so it cannot be the subject. Turn this sentence around and its structure becomes obvious.

The *child* whose school closes for snow is joyful.

In questions, the subject frequently appears between the helping verb and the main verb.

HV ┌── SS ──┐ MV
Do *Kenyan marathoners* train year-round?

TIP: The ability to recognize the subject of a sentence will help you edit for fragments (G5), subject-verb agreement (G1), pronouns such as *I* and *me* (G3-c), missing subjects (M3-b), and repeated subjects (M3-c).

B2-b Verbs, objects, and complements

Section B1-c explains how to find the verb of a sentence. A sentence's verb is classified as linking, transitive, or intransitive, depending on the kinds of objects or complements the verb can (or cannot) take.

Linking verbs and subject complements

Linking verbs connect the subject to a subject complement, a word or word group that completes the meaning of the subject by renaming or describing it.

If the subject complement renames the subject, it is a noun or noun equivalent (sometimes called a *predicate noun*).

┌────────────── S ──────────────┐ ┌─V─┐ ┌─SC─┐
An e-mail message requesting personal information may be a scam.

If the subject complement describes the subject, it is an adjective or adjective equivalent (sometimes called a *predicate adjective*).

┌──── S ────┐ V SC
Last month's temperatures were mild.

Whenever they appear as main verbs (rather than helping verbs), the forms of *be* — *be, am, is, are, was, were, being, been* — usually function as linking verbs. In the preceding examples, for instance, the main verbs are *be* and *were*.

Verbs such as *appear, become, feel, grow, look, make, seem, smell, sound,* and *taste* are linking when they are followed by a word or word group that renames or describes the subject.

```
        ┌──S──┐┌─V─┐    SC
As it thickens, the sauce will look unappealing.
```

Transitive verbs and direct objects

A transitive verb takes a direct object, a word or word group that names a receiver of the action.

```
┌────S────┐  S  ┌────DO────┐
The hungry cat clawed the bag of dry food.
```

The simple direct object is always a noun or pronoun, in this case *bag*. To find it, simply strip away all modifiers.

Transitive verbs usually appear in the active voice, with the subject doing the action and a direct object receiving the action. Active-voice sentences can be transformed into passive, with the subject receiving the action.

Transitive verbs, indirect objects, and direct objects

The direct object of a transitive verb is sometimes preceded by an indirect object, a noun or pronoun telling to whom or for whom the action of the sentence is done.

```
S   V  IO ┌─ DO ┐    S ┌─ V ┐ IO ┌ DO ┐
You give her some yarn, and she will knit you a scarf.
```

The simple indirect object is always a noun or pronoun. To test for an indirect object, insert the word *to* or *for* before the word or word group in question. If the sentence makes sense, the word or word group is an indirect object.

You give [to] *her* some yarn, and she will knit [for] *you* a scarf.

Transitive verbs, direct objects, and object complements

The direct object of a transitive verb is sometimes followed by an object complement, a word or word group that renames or describes the object.

```
S        V    DO  ┌────OC────┐
People often consider chivalry a thing of the past.
```

```
┌─S─┐  V  DO  ┌──OC──┐
The kiln makes clay firm and strong.
```

When the object complement renames the direct object, it is a noun or pronoun (such as *thing*). When it describes the direct object, it is an adjective (such as *firm* and *strong*).

Intransitive verbs

Intransitive verbs take no objects or complements.

┌────s────┐   v
The audience laughed.

┌───s───┐   v
The driver accelerated in the straightaway.

Nothing receives the actions of laughing and accelerating in these sentences, so the verbs are intransitive. Notice that such verbs may or may not be followed by adverbial modifiers. In the second sentence, *in the straightaway* is an adverbial prepositional phrase modifying *accelerated*. See B3-a.

NOTE: The dictionary will tell you whether a verb is transitive or intransitive. Some verbs can be both transitive and intransitive.

> **TRANSITIVE**   Sandra *flew* her small plane over the canyon.
>
> **INTRANSITIVE**   A flock of migrating geese *flew* overhead.

In the first example, *flew* has a direct object that receives the action: *her small plane*. In the second example, the verb is followed by an adverb (*overhead*), not by a direct object.

B3 Subordinate word groups

Subordinate word groups include phrases and clauses. Phrases are subordinate because they lack a subject and a verb; they are classified as prepositional, verbal, appositive, or absolute (see B3-a to B3-d). Subordinate clauses have a subject and a verb, but they begin with a word (such as *although*, *that*, or *when*) that marks them as subordinate (see B3-e).

B3-a Prepositional phrases

A prepositional phrase begins with a preposition such as *at, by, for, from, in, of, on, to,* or *with* (see B1-f) and usually ends with a noun or noun equivalent: *on the table, for him, by sleeping late*. The noun or noun equivalent is known as the object of the preposition.

Prepositional phrases function as adjectives or as adverbs. As an adjective, a prepositional phrase nearly always appears immediately following the noun or pronoun it modifies.

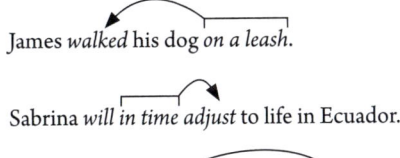

The hut had *walls of mud.*

Adjective phrases usually answer one or both of the questions Which one? and What kind of? If we ask Which walls? or What kind of walls? we get a sensible answer: *walls of mud.*

Adverbial prepositional phrases usually modify the verb, but they can also modify adjectives or other adverbs. When a prepositional phrase modifies the verb, it can appear nearly anywhere in a sentence.

James *walked* his dog *on a leash.*

Sabrina *will in time adjust* to life in Ecuador.

During a mudslide, the terrain *can change* drastically.

If a prepositional phrase is movable, you can be certain that it is adverbial.

In the cave, the explorers found well-preserved prehistoric drawings.

The explorers found well-preserved prehistoric drawings *in the cave.*

Adverbial word groups usually answer one of these questions: When? Where? How? Why? Under what conditions? To what degree?

James walked his dog *how? On a leash.*

Sabrina will adjust to life in Ecuador *when? In time.*

The terrain can change drastically *under what conditions? During a mudslide.*

In questions and subordinate clauses, a preposition may appear after its object.

What are you afraid *of* ?

We avoided the bike trail *that* John had warned us *about.*

B3-b Verbal phrases

A verbal is a verb form that does not function as the verb of a clause. Verbals include infinitives (the word *to* plus the base form of the verb), present participles (the -*ing* form of the verb), and past participles (the verb form usually ending in -*d*, -*ed*, -*n*, -*en*, or -*t*). (See G2-a and B1-c.)

INFINITIVE	PRESENT PARTICIPLE	PAST PARTICIPLE
to dream	dreaming	dreamed
to choose	choosing	chosen
to build	building	built

Instead of functioning as the verb of a clause, a verbal functions as an adjective, a noun, or an adverb.

ADJECTIVE	*Broken* promises cannot be fixed.
NOUN	Constant *complaining* becomes wearisome.
ADVERB	Can you wait *to celebrate*?

Verbals with objects, complements, or modifiers form verbal phrases.

In my family, *singing loudly* is more appreciated than *singing well*.

Like verbals, verbal phrases function as adjectives, nouns, or adverbs. Verbal phrases are ordinarily classified as participial, gerund, or infinitive.

Participial phrases

Participial phrases always function as adjectives. Their verbals are either present participles (such as *dreaming, asking*) or past participles (such as *stolen, reached*).

Participial phrases frequently appear immediately following the noun or pronoun they modify.

Congress shall make no *law abridging the freedom of speech or of the press.*

Participial phrases are often movable. They can precede the word they modify.

Being a weight-bearing joint, the *knee* is among the most frequently injured.

They may also appear at some distance from the word they modify.

Last night we saw a *play* that affected us deeply, *written with profound insight into the lives of immigrants.*

Gerund phrases

Gerund phrases are built around present participles (verb forms that end in *-ing*), and they always function as nouns: usually as subjects, subject complements, direct objects, or objects of a preposition.

— S —
Rationalizing a fear can eliminate it.

— SC —
The key to good sauce is browning the mushrooms.

— DO —
Lizards usually enjoy sunning themselves.

The American Heart Association has documented the benefits of diet
— OBJ OF PREP —
and exercise in reducing the risk of heart attack.

Infinitive phrases

Infinitive phrases, usually constructed around *to* plus the base form of the verb (*to call*, *to drink*), can function as nouns, as adjectives, or as adverbs. When functioning as a noun, an infinitive phrase may appear in almost any noun slot in a sentence, usually as a subject, subject complement, or direct object.

— S —
To live without health insurance is risky.

Infinitive phrases functioning as adjectives usually appear immediately following the noun or pronoun they modify.

The Nineteenth Amendment gave women the *right to vote*.

The infinitive phrase modifies the noun *right*. Which right? The *right to vote*.
Adverbial infinitive phrases usually qualify the meaning of the verb, telling when, where, how, why, under what conditions, or to what degree an action occurred.

Volunteers *rolled up* their pants *to wade through the floodwaters*.

NOTE: In some constructions, the infinitive is unmarked; that is, the *to* does not appear. (See M1-f.)

Graphs and charts can help researchers [*to*] *present complex data*.

B3-c Appositive phrases

Appositive phrases describe nouns or pronouns. Instead of modifying nouns or pronouns, however, appositive phrases rename them. In form they are nouns or noun equivalents. In the following example, the appositive *conversationalists at heart* renames the noun *Bloggers*.

> Bloggers, *conversationalists at heart*, are the online equivalent of radio talk show hosts.

B3-d Absolute phrases

An absolute phrase modifies a whole clause or sentence, not just one word. It consists of a noun or noun equivalent usually followed by a participial phrase.

> *Her words reverberating in the hushed arena*, the senator urged the crowd to support her former opponent.

B3-e Subordinate clauses

Subordinate clauses are patterned like sentences, having subjects and verbs and sometimes objects or complements. But they function within sentences as adjectives, adverbs, or nouns. They cannot stand alone as complete sentences.

A subordinate clause usually begins with a subordinating conjunction or a relative pronoun. The chart on page 508 classifies these words according to the kinds of clauses (adjective, adverb, or noun) they introduce.

Adjective clauses

Adjective clauses modify nouns or pronouns, usually answering the question Which one? or What kind of ? Most adjective clauses begin with a relative pronoun (*who*, *whom*, *whose*, *which*, or *that*). In addition to introducing the clause, the relative pronoun points back to the noun that the clause modifies.

> The coach chose *players who would benefit from intense drills*.

> A *book that goes unread* is a writer's worst nightmare.

Writer's Choice
Building credibility with appositives

Appositives rename a noun or pronoun. Writers often use them to help an **audience** better understand a person or thing or to give that person or thing fuller context. Consider the following pair of sentences.

> Helene Aumais surprised everyone by winning the Crescent City 10k road race.

> Helene Aumais, ==a woman who had never run more than a mile before last month==, surprised everyone by winning the Crescent City 10k road race.

In the second example, the writer uses an appositive to give more information about Helene Aumais, the subject of the sentence, and to suggest to readers why the win was so surprising.

As a college research writer, you will often use appositives to build your credibility as you cite sources within your own text. To come across as a knowledgeable researcher who draws on relevant and reliable sources of information, you can give the credentials for a source in an appositive phrase.

CITATION WITH NO CREDENTIALS	According to John Dunlosky, regular use of practice tests "can substantially boost student learning" (14).
CITATION WITH CREDENTIALS	According to John Dunlosky, ==a researcher and professor of psychology at Kent State University==, regular use of practice tests "can substantially boost student learning" (14).

The first sentence, while not incorrect, may prompt your readers to question who John Dunlosky is and, further, why anyone should care. The second sentence adds language that suggests Dunlosky's authority on the subject and that positions you as a credible researcher.

As a research writer, you use sources to help you fulfill your purpose — to inform or to persuade — and to help you meet the needs of your audience. Choosing to use appositives to introduce sources builds your credibility as a researcher.

Words that introduce subordinate clauses

Words introducing adjective clauses

RELATIVE PRONOUNS: that, which, who, whom, whose
RELATIVE ADVERBS: when, where, why

Words introducing adverb clauses

SUBORDINATING CONJUNCTIONS: after, although, as, as if, because, before, even though, if, in order that, once, since, so that, than, that, though, unless, until, when, where, whether, while

Words introducing noun clauses

RELATIVE PRONOUNS: which, who, whom, whose
OTHER PRONOUNS: what, whatever, whichever, whoever, whomever
OTHER SUBORDINATING WORDS: how, if, that, when, whenever, where, wherever, whether, why

Relative pronouns are sometimes "understood."

The things [*that*] *we cherish most* are the things [*that*] *we might lose.*

Occasionally an adjective clause is introduced by a relative adverb, usually *when, where,* or *why.*

The aging actor returned to the *stage where he had made his debut as Hamlet half a century earlier.*

The parts of an adjective clause are often arranged as in sentences (subject/verb/object or complement).

                                       S   V   DO
Sometimes it is our closest friends who disappoint us.

Frequently, however, the object or complement appears first, out of the normal order of subject/verb/object.

                             DO   S   V
They can be the very friends whom we disappoint.

TIP: For punctuation of adjective clauses, see P1-e and P2-e. For advice about avoiding repeated words in adjective clauses, see M3-d.

Adverb clauses

Adverb clauses modify verbs, adjectives, or other adverbs, usually answering one of these questions: When? Where? Why? How? Under what conditions? To what degree? They always begin with a subordinating conjunction (such as *after, although, because, that, though, unless,* or *when*). (For a complete list, see the chart earlier in this section.)

When the sun went down, the hikers *prepared* their camp.

Kate *would have made* the team *if she hadn't broken her ankle.*

Noun clauses

A noun clause functions just like a single-word noun, usually as a subject, a subject complement, a direct object, or an object of a preposition. It usually begins with one of the following words: *how, if, that, what, whatever, when, where, whether, which, who, whoever, whom, whomever, whose, why.* (For a complete list, see the chart earlier in this section.)

$\overline{\hspace{1cm}S\hspace{1cm}}$
Whoever leaves the house last must double-lock the door.

$\overline{\hspace{2cm}DO\hspace{2cm}}$
Copernicus argued that the sun is the center of the universe.

The subordinating word introducing the clause may or may not play a significant role in the clause. In the preceding examples, *Whoever* is the subject of its clause, but *that* does not perform a function in its clause.

As with adjective clauses, the parts of a noun clause may appear in normal order (subject/verb/object or complement) or out of their normal order.

      S   V   ─DO─
Loyalty is what keeps a friendship strong.

        DO S ──V──
A rooftop garden is what I have imagined.

B4 Sentence types

Sentences are classified in two ways: according to their structure (simple, compound, complex, or compound-complex) and according to their purpose (declarative, imperative, interrogative, or exclamatory).

B4-a Sentence structures

Depending on the number and the types of clauses they contain, sentences are classified as simple, compound, complex, or compound-complex.

Clauses come in two varieties: independent and subordinate. An independent clause contains a subject and a predicate, and it either stands alone or could stand alone as a sentence. A subordinate clause also contains a subject and a predicate, but it functions within a sentence as an adjective, an adverb, or a noun; it cannot stand alone. (See B3-e.)

Simple sentences

A simple sentence is one independent clause with no subordinate clauses.

┌─────────── INDEPENDENT CLAUSE ───────────┐
Without a passport, Eva could not visit her aunt in Peru.

A simple sentence may contain compound elements — a compound subject, verb, or object, for example — but it does not contain more than one full sentence pattern. The following sentence is simple because its two verbs (*comes in* and *goes out*) share a subject (*Spring*).

┌─────────── INDEPENDENT CLAUSE ───────────┐
Spring comes in like a lion and goes out like a lamb.

Compound sentences

A compound sentence is composed of two or more independent clauses with no subordinate clauses. The independent clauses are usually joined with a comma and a coordinating conjunction (*and, but, or, nor, for, so, yet*) or with a semicolon. (See P1-a and P3-a.)

┌── INDEPENDENT ──┐   ┌──── INDEPENDENT ────┐
│   CLAUSE   │   │   CLAUSE   │
The car broke down, but a rescue van arrived within minutes.

┌──── INDEPENDENT CLAUSE ────┐ ┌── INDEPENDENT ──┐
│   │ │   CLAUSE   │
A shark was spotted near shore; people left immediately.

Complex sentences

A complex sentence is composed of one independent clause with one or more subordinate clauses. (See B3-e.)

ADJECTIVE

SUBORDINATE
┌─── CLAUSE ───┐
The pitcher who won the game is a rookie.

ADVERB

SUBORDINATE
┌── CLAUSE ──┐
If you leave late, take a cab home.

NOUN

SUBORDINATE
┌──── CLAUSE ────┐
What matters most to us is a quick commute.

Compound-complex sentences

A compound-complex sentence contains at least two independent clauses and at least one subordinate clause. The following sentence contains two independent clauses, each of which contains a subordinate clause.

┌──── INDEPENDENT CLAUSE ────┐   ┌─ INDEPENDENT CLAUSE ─
                ┌──SUB CL──┐   ┌─SUB CL─
Tell the nurse practitioner how you feel, and she will decide whether you

┌────────┐
can go home.

B4-b Sentence purposes

Writers use declarative sentences to make statements, imperative sentences to issue requests or commands, interrogative sentences to ask questions, and exclamatory sentences to make exclamations.

DECLARATIVE	The echo sounded in our ears.
IMPERATIVE	Love your neighbor.
INTERROGATIVE	Did the better team win tonight?
EXCLAMATORY	We're here to save you!

Acknowledgments

Adler, Jonathan H., excerpt from "Little Green Lies: The Environmental Miseducation of America's Children," from *Policy Review*, Summer 1992. Copyright © 1992. Reprinted by permission of the Heritage Foundation.

Alsever, Jennifer, "What Is Crowdsourcing?," from *MoneyWatch*, May 1, 2008. Copyright © 2007 CBS Interactive Inc. All Rights Reserved. Used with permission.

Berger, Michelle, excerpt from "Volunteer Army," from *Audubon Magazine*, November–December 2010. Copyright © 2010 by the National Audubon Society. Reprinted by permission.

Bianchi, S. M., "The More They Change, the More They Stay the Same?: Understanding Family Change in the Twenty-First Century," from *Contemporary Sociology*, vol. 42, no. 3, pp. 324–331. Reprinted by permission of Sage Publications, Inc.; permission conveyed through Copyright Clearance Center, Inc.

Kabir, Nasreen Munni, "Playback Time: A Brief History of Bollywood 'Film Songs,'" from *Film Comment*, May–June 2002, pp. 41–43. Reprinted with permission from Film at Lincoln Center and *Film Comment*.

Klemm, W. R., "Neural Representations of the Sense of Self," from *Advances in Cognitive Psychology*, vol. 7, no. 1, March 2011, pp. 16–30. Copyright © 2010 University of Finance and Management in Warsaw. doi:10.2478/v10053-008-0084-2.

Pew Charitable Trusts, excerpt from "Collateral Costs: Incarceration's Effect on Economic Mobility." Copyright © 2017 The Pew Charitable Trusts. All Rights Reserved. Reproduced with permission. Any use without the express written consent of The Pew Charitable Trusts is prohibited.

Rothman, Joshua, "What Amazon's Purchase of Whole Foods Really Means," from *New Yorker*, June 24, 2017. Copyright © 2017 Condé Nast. Reprinted by permission.

Rudloe, Jack and Anne Rudloe, "Electric Warfare: The Fish That Kill with Thunderbolts," from *Smithsonian*, vol. 24, no. 5, August 1993, p. 94. Copyright © 1993 by Jack and Anne Rudloe. Reproduced with permission of the authors.

Swafford, Jan, excerpt from "Ludwig van Beethoven (1770–1827), Symphony No. 9 in D Minor, Opus 125." Boston Symphony Orchestra, May 3, 2012. Courtesy of Jan Swafford.

Taylor, Betsy, excerpt from "Big Box Stores Are Bad for Main Street," from David Masci, "The Consumer Culture," *CQ Researcher*, vol. 9, no. 44, November 19, 1999. Copyright © 1999 by CQ Press Researcher. Reprinted by permission of CQ Press Researcher, an imprint of Sage Publications, Inc.; permission conveyed through Copyright Clearance Center, Inc.

Index

Index

In addition to giving you page numbers, this index shows you which tabbed section to flip to. For example, the entry "*a* vs. *an*" directs you to section **M** (Multilingual Writers and ESL Topics), pages 422–23 and 425–26. Just flip to the appropriate tabbed section and then track down the exact pages you need.

Index Index-3
Multilingual/ESL menu
Revision symbols
Detailed menu

Z

Multilingual/ESL Menu

A complete section for multilingual writers:

"For Multilingual Writers" notes in other sections:

Revision Symbols

Letter-number codes refer to sections of this book.

abbr	faulty abbreviation **P9**		p	error in punctuation
adj	misuse of adjective **G4**		⌢	comma **P1**
add	add needed word **S2**		no ,	no comma **P2**
adv	misuse of adverb **G4**		;	semicolon **P3**
agr	faulty agreement **G1**, **G3-a**		:	colon **P3**
appr	inappropriate language **W4**		⌢	apostrophe **P4**
art	article **M2**		" "	quotation marks **P5**
awk	awkward		. ?	period, question mark **P6**
cap	capital letter **P8**		!	exclamation point **P6**
case	error in case **G3-c**, **G3-d**		— ( )	dash, parentheses **P6**
cliché	cliché **W5-e**		[ ] ...	brackets, ellipsis mark **P6**
coh	coherence **C3-c**		/	slash **P6**
coord	faulty coordination **S6-c**		pass	ineffective passive **W3**
cs	comma splice **G6**		pn agr	pronoun agreement **G3-a**
dev	inadequate development **C3-b**		proof	proofreading problem **C4-d**
dm	dangling modifier **S3-e**		ref	error in pronoun reference **G3-b**
-ed	error in -ed ending **G2-d**		run-on	run-on sentence **G6**
emph	emphasis **S6**		-s	error in -s ending **G2-c**
ESL	ESL grammar **M1**, **M2**, **M3**, **M4**, **M5**		sexist	sexist language **W4-e**
			shift	distracting shift **S4**
exact	inexact language **W5**		sl	slang **W4-c**
frag	sentence fragment **G5**		sp	misspelled word **P7**
fs	fused sentence **G6**		sub	faulty subordination **S6-d**
gl/us	see glossary of usage **W1**		sv agr	subject-verb agreement **G1**, **G2-c**
hyph	error in use of hyphen **P7**			
idiom	idiom **W5-d**		t	error in verb tense **G2-f**
inc	incomplete construction **S2**		trans	transition needed **C3-c**
irreg	error in irregular verb **G2-a**		usage	see glossary of usage **W1**
ital	italics **P10**		v	voice **W3**
jarg	jargon **W4-a**		var	sentence variety **S6-b**, **S6-c**, **S7**
lc	lowercase letter **P8**			
mix	mixed construction **S5**		vb	verb error **G2**
mm	misplaced modifier **S3-b**		w	wordy **W2**
mood	error in mood **G2-g**		//	faulty parallelism **S1**
nonst	nonstandard usage **W4-c**		^	insert
num	error in use of number **P9**		x	obvious error
om	omitted word **S2**		#	insert space
¶	new paragraph **C3**		⌒	close up space

Detailed Menu